Praise for *The Conscious Bride's Wedding Planner*

"Don't even think of getting married without this book. The wisdom and practical advice in these pages can save your sanity and shore up your relationships with your fiancé, family, and friends during this crucial rite of passage."

—Christiane Northrup, MD, author of *Women's Bodies, Women's Wisdom*

φ

"*The Conscious Bride's Wedding Planner* is an important guide through one of life's most vulnerable and exciting times. The author casts new light on an old subject, making it clear that the natural wisdom in a woman's own heart is the best bridal consultant she could possibly have."

—Marianne Williamson, author of *A Return to Love*

φ

"Finally, a wedding planner that puts the real needs of the bride first! No other guide helps the bride navigate the emotional adjustments of this transition while also leading her through the monthly wedding tasks. This book will be my gift to each newly engaged bride!"

—Christine Humston, professional wedding planner, Washington, DC

φ

Praise for *The Conscious Bride*

"*The Conscious Bride* offers engaged women the information they need to approach their wedding day with serenity and begin their marriage on a healthy foundation. If there is one book that will help women with a smooth wedding transition, this is it."

> —John Gray, Ph.D., author of *Men Are from Mars,*
> *Women Are from Venus*

"*The Conscious Bride* captures the true meaning of marriage as initiation. It deals with every detail of the rite of passage of the wedding, honoring the holding of the tension between conflicting emotions. Splendid!"

> —Marion Woodman, leading Jungian analyst and
> best-selling author of *Addiction to Perfection:*
> *The Still Unravished Bride*

"*The Conscious Bride* is a wonderful book to help women prepare themselves for their wedding, not just on the outside, but on the inside! The stories are inspiring, comforting, and beautifully presented. Every bride should read this book."

> —Barbara De Angelis, author of *Secrets About Life*
> *Every Woman Should Know*

THE Conscious Bride's *Wedding Planner*

How to Prepare Emotionally,
Practically, and Spiritually for a
Meaningful and Joyous Wedding

SHERYL PAUL

NEW HARBINGER PUBLICATIONS, INC.

Publisher's Note

This publication is designed to provide accurate and authoritative information in regard to the subject matter covered. It is sold with the understanding that the publisher is not engaged in rendering psychological, financial, legal, or other professional services. If expert assistance or counseling is needed, the services of a competent professional should be sought.

Distributed in the U.S.A. by Publishers Group West; in Canada by Raincoast Books; in Great Britain by Hi Marketing, Ltd.; in South Africa by Real Books, Ltd.; in Australia by Boobook; and in New Zealand by Tandem Press.

Copyright © 2003 by Sheryl Paul

New Harbinger Publications, Inc.
5674 Shattuck Avenue
Oakland, CA 94609

Cover design by Amy Shoup
Cover image by Wendell Webber/Getty Images
Interior photographs by Stockbyte and Digital Vision
Edited by Carole Honeychurch
Text design by Michele Waters & Amy Shoup

ISBN 1-57224-345-7 Paperback

All Rights Reserved

Printed in the United States of America

New Harbinger Publications' Web site address: www.newharbinger.com

05 04 03

10 9 8 7 6 5 4 3 2 1

First printing

Contents

Acknowledgments

If the only prayer you ever say in your entire life is "thank you," it will be enough.

—Meister Eckhart

I extend my deepest gratitude to

My grandparents, Isidore and Charlotte Brustein, whose unconditional love has given me wings to fly.

My parents, Jordan and Margaret Paul, who initiated my passion for rites of passage through the meaningful ceremony and celebration they created when I turned thirteen.

Jessica Williams and Carrie Dinow, women I could not live without.

Dr. Bruce Gregory, my teacher and guide, whose words and work have greatly influenced this book and my life.

My family, Eric and Karol Paul, Josh Paul, and the Paul clan in Missouri, for their consistently loving support.

Max Strom at Sacred Movement Yoga, for teaching me how to breathe.

My Conscious Weddings clients for their courage and willingness to tell their stories.

The folks at New Harbinger Publications for their creative vision.

Oprah Winfrey, Marion Woodman, and Dr. Christiane Northrup: extraordinary women who have supported my work and served as models for the kind of woman I strive to be.

My cat, Spunky, who's been my constant soul companion for seventeen years.

And Daev Finn, my inspiration.

A Conscious Wedding Planner

$\mathcal{Y}$our wedding can be one of the most beautiful and meaningful events of your life. When you take this step, you leave behind a phase of life called "singlehood" and cross over a great divide that lands you in the phase of life called "marriage." A wedding is traditionally comprised of two parts: the ceremony, which is a symbol of deepened commitment, and the reception, which is a time to celebrate and receive support from your community for the journey that is about to begin. The entire day is an acknowledgment of the decision to share the rest of your life with your chosen partner. Regardless of the specifics of a partnership—your sexual orientation, religion, class, race, culture, age, or previous marital status—a wedding is a worldwide rite of passage recognizing that one phase of life is ending so that a new phase can begin.

Yet the wedding is much more than a single day. In order for this rite of passage to be complete—to move through the engagement without losing your mind, arrive at your wedding day feeling serene and joyful, and enter your marriage on a healthy foundation—you not only need to take care of all the practical planning to create the event, but it's also necessary to complete a series of emotional tasks during the engagement. And though there's a lot of information and assistance out there for the important practical work we must do to create our wedding day, we live in a culture that does not prepare us for the emotional tasks, or even inform us that they exist. From the time we are young, we are inundated with images of the "perfect" wedding, and when the time arrives to plan the big day we find ourselves bombarded with endless details that are supposed to aid us in manifesting this perfection. Yet somewhere we know that perfection is an impossible ideal. And somewhere we know that there are other matters that need to be addressed. While the planning elements can be a special part of your day, they only make sense if they are aligned with your reasons for marrying and the values that you hope to incorporate into your marriage.

For many women, the planning comes to a halt when they encounter an emotional issue. For example, every time Kaitlyn started to plan her guest list, she would freeze. She couldn't move past this first planning task because to do so solidified the fact that she was actually getting married—and, deep down, she was terrified to get married. It took her some time to realize it, but encoded in the guest list were her fears and beliefs about marriage and commitment. As she said:

> *Like most of us, my most immediate role model of marriage is my parents. While on the outside it looks like they have a great marriage, I know the reality. The truth is that most of the time they make each other miserable. They have very different values around ways of spending time and that has caused a lot of conflict. Mostly, they seem dissatisfied and bored. Is that what marriage is? Frustration and boredom?*

Kaitlyn speaks for many women when she expresses her fears about marriage. To get married these days can be a leap of faith, and it takes courage to work through our fears so that we can move forward. As soon as Kaitlyn realized how paralyzing her fear was, she got the help she needed to learn how to let it pass through her body. Only when the fear was significantly diminished could she proceed with her planning and actually enjoy it.

Back then, if Kaitlyn had gone to a bookstore in search of information that would help her make sense of her emotional experience, she would have come up empty-handed. The majority of books that line the shelves of the wedding section have one goal: to help you plan a perfect wedding. They are not interested in how you're feeling because they assume that you are feeling pure, nonstop bliss. They are not interested in addressing your fears and expectations about marriage because their sole concern is the wedding day itself. They may include a side note or peripheral discussion on difficulties that could arise around blended families or future in-laws, but they generally stick to the nitty-gritty details of practical planning.

The Conscious Bride's Wedding Planner is designed to compassionately guide you through both the practical aspects and the emotional preparation for one of the most important transitions of your life. When I conceived of the book, I was driven by a hunch that women needed help not only with traditional wedding planning—buying a dress, designing the ceremony, and so on—but with their emotional "planning" as well. Brides know they're often scared, but what does this fear mean? Does all fear mean that they're not

supposed to marry? And why are they scared to begin with? The hundreds of clients I have counseled through their engagement and first years of marriage inspired me to create a series of concrete, hands-on tools that help women and their partners work through the various feelings, thoughts, and issues that inevitably arise during this time. Information is validating, but it is the exercises that transform the difficult feelings into positive experiences.

When women diligently worked through the assigned exercises, they noticed that they felt lighter, calmer, and more excited about their wedding. Sometimes it takes time for the joy to be released, but I've yet to work with a woman who did not enter her wedding day feeling the deepest sense of rightness and serenity about her union. The direct result of looking at and working through the uncomfortable feelings around the wedding is an opening to joy. Psychology understands that pain and joy live in the same box; if you stifle your pain

and fear, you will also cut off access to joy. Conversely, allowing the "darker" feelings room to exist allows them to breathe and move through and out of your body, inviting joy to enter.

Clearing some of your emotional barriers also makes it easier to do the practical planning for your wedding, and this planner is designed to help you plan your wedding both practically and emotionally. I will address each of the practical elements involved in creating a wedding—suggestions on your dress, how to find a florist, ways to handle the photography, and so forth—but I will also encourage you to explore the fears, grief, confusion, doubts, anxiety, and expectations embedded in each task. You may be surprised (or comforted) to read such words as "fear" and "grief" in a wedding planner. Yet the fact that you picked up this book reveals that you are aware that there is another side to the wedding process, one that directly contradicts the images of unblemished beauty and ecstasy that we are conditioned to believe should surround this time.

φ

A Rite of Passage: Acknowledging the Wedding's Shadow

Our culture presents a unilateral view of weddings. The pages of bridal magazines are adorned with brides who are "blessed" with flawless skin, buoyant hair, and glorious gowns (most of which cost over $10,000). The weddings we see in film and television are also encased in a fairy-tale air of ethereal beauty. Rationally, we may realize that the media is a master at presenting an impossible ideal and that these images are airbrushed, shaped, and molded until "perfection" is achieved, but it's difficult to escape the unconscious expectations that these images instill.

The real danger, however, is not the image of physical perfection that our culture propagates; it's the message that from the moment you get engaged until your one-year anniversary you should be riding on the white horse of joy. You should awaken each day feeling delighted at the prospect of getting married. You should lovingly gaze at your partner, thoroughly thrilled at the thought of spending the rest of your lives together. Your handsome father will walk you down the aisle; your proud mother will help you dress in the bridal suite. Your friends will encircle you with their support and joy.

Cut! Those are nice images, but who actually lives them? I don't know anyone who has, and I've spoken with thousands of engaged women and newlyweds over the years. When women contact me, they sound very similar to Delia, who called me in a panic:

I'm getting married in seven months and I'm so anxious. I'm terrified that I might have a panic attack on my wedding day. I love my partner, but I'm even having doubts about him. I've never felt this way before. What's wrong with me? Am I the only one? I'm having dreams about my ex-boyfriends. I don't want to be with them, but then why do I keep dreaming about them? I feel like a part of me is dying. And the worst part is that I feel like I have no one to talk to about it. I feel so alone.

In the context of how our culture views a wedding—as the pinnacle of joy in a woman's life—these feelings make no sense. But in the context of a rite of passage, where there is a letting go of a way of life and an entire identity, these feelings make perfect sense. Parts of Delia were dying, as with all partners on the precipice of marriage. These parts included her singlehood and illusions and fantasies of childhood. The woman she had been needed to make room for the woman she would become. The anxiety, the doubts, and the dreams about the ex-boyfriends were a normal and necessary part of the rite of passage. The tender sprout of her burgeoning new life could not take root until the old plants of singlehood had been weeded and the ground tilled. After many months of consistent emotional work, Delia arrived at her wedding day with a serenity she could not have imagined when she initially contacted me. She still speaks of it as one of the most joyful and magical days of her life.

And, just to be clear, I don't believe it's at all disempowering to recognize the change of identity. A woman is losing her singlehood, not her individuality and strength as a woman. And, for the record, men are in an equally profound process of loss and transition, where they are required to surrender their bachelor, "single-guy" ways and prepare to become a husband. It's not a loss of power that's the challenge here, but the transition to a new role and identity.

So, what is a rite of passage anyway? All rites of passage consist of three phases: an ending, referred to as a "rite of separation," an in-between zone, or "liminality," and a new beginning, or a "rite of incorporation." The Dutch anthropologist Arnold van Gennep introduced the term "rite of passage" to our culture in 1960. After spending years studying the ways of indigenous people, he learned that these three phases apply to any time when we are leaving one identity or way or life and moving to a new identity or way of life. In our culture these include adolescence, the onset of menstruation, graduating from high school, losing your virginity, graduating from college, a first job, getting fired, moving, getting married, buying a home, having a baby, divorce, abortion, empty nest, midlife, old age, and death.

With regard to the wedding, these three phases correspond to the engagement, wedding, and first year of marriage. For it is during the engagement that we are saying good-bye to an identity, the wedding that we are in an in-between zone (no longer single and not quite married), and the first year of marriage that we begin the new life and embrace the new level of commitment as a husband and wife. In indigenous cultures and many other cultures throughout the world, the bride and groom are carefully guided through these three phases by the elders of the society. Through a series of ancient and meaningful rituals, the members are then able to transition smoothly into their next phase of development. These cultures understand that one cannot endure these passages alone.

Not only do we often feel lost and alone during life's transitions, we barely recognize the wedding as a rite of passage. With a culture that emphasizes the beauty and the gain of this event, the element of loss is ignored. And just as there can be no rebirth of spring without the death of winter, so there can be no thorough passage into marriage without the loss of singlehood. The uncomfortable feelings—the grief, fear, loss, confusion—are only manageable in the context of a rite of passage.

Context brings understanding, which brings comfort. When we understand that the engagement, besides a time to plan your wedding, is also a time of letting go, we can allow the appropriate feelings to surface. For example, saying to Delia, "Grief is a normal response to loss," gave her permission to allow the sadness to exist. As soon as she felt normal and validated—as opposed to the "look on the bright side" message she received from the rest of her world—she stopped fighting her feelings and trying to make them go away.

The wedding's shadow is also evident in Delia's comment about feeling "so alone," a feeling that is shared unanimously by the women I counsel. Why is it that people don't want to hear about what's really going on with brides? We live in a "chin up" culture. When we graduate from high school and are about the enter the adult world, it's natural to feel not only pride and relief but also sadness, fear, confusion, and loneliness. But when we express these feelings we hear, "Look on the bright side! You're going away to college! You're out of the house now! You're free!" Yes, those statements are true, but they can only be fully embraced after the old life is grieved. As a culture, we seem to be terrified of grief. We shun what we view as "negative" emotions. But we do ourselves and our loved ones a great disservice when we don't allow these emotions to surface and work themselves out.

The Conscious Bride's Wedding Planner encourages you to be a conscious bride, which means that you embrace the full range of your emotional experience. You welcome in the joy and excitement and you accept the uncomfortable feelings as well. These may include the grief of letting go of singlehood, the fear of the depth of this commitment, the loss from loosening ties to your family of origin and transferring your primary allegiance to your husband, the disorientation of being in the in-between zone when you are no longer single and not quite married, the anxiety about the wedding day, and the confusion about what it means to be wife. Remember, all of these feelings are a normal and healthy part of the wedding process. And when they receive the attention they need, you can be more open to embrace the joy and excitement of this time.

A Rite of Courage

A rite of passage means change, and we live in a culture that fiercely resists change. There is a good reason for this: change is scary. Change is new; change is traveling into the unknown; change is letting go of the familiar and stepping into uncharted territory. As human beings, we generally resist and fear that which we do not know. And marriage is something you cannot possibly know until you have entered into it. When we are undergoing change, we often feel out of control. The sense of being out of control is one of the sensations that characterizes transitions and is the reason why moving is rated as the number-one stressor for humans (above loss of a loved one and divorce). When we move, we are leaving behind that which we know and moving into the new and unfamiliar. A rite of passage is no different, except that the move is internal.

My clients often ask me things like, "Why is this so scary? I've known this person for a long time, we've lived together, so what's actually going to change?" My response to them is, "I almost cannot put into words what makes this transition so terrifying. But when you're making one of the biggest commitments you will ever make, it's natural to feel scared." Again, this simple validation of their experience inevitably leads to a sigh of relief.

Setting the date often precipitates the anxiety and sense of feeling out of control that will accompany you intermittently throughout your engagement. Until that point, the wedding is more of a fantasy, the ring just a beautiful stone resting on your finger. But once you set the date, the wedding machinery is set into motion. The wheels start turning, the plans start moving, and all of a sudden you find yourself strapped in on the wedding train, headed straight to the thing called "marriage." It all becomes very real. If you take the time to slow down just for a moment, the mist that surrounds your fairy-tale fantasy will dissolve and you'll be left with the reality of the commitment you are entering. That's a good thing. It means you are ready to do the real work of the engagement.

φ

Getting Organized: Inside and Out

The traditional planner is nothing but a collection of checklists and worksheets that are supposed to help you plan your wedding. I don't know about you, but when I open one of those planners I immediately feel overwhelmed. If you were to plan a wedding according to the culturally imposed standards—which, let me remind you, are an impossible ideal of perfection—you would drive yourself crazy. And that's exactly what most women do.

The primary intention of this planner is to help you organize your inner and outer experience so that you can enjoy as much of this process as possible. I hope to help you feel less stressed and more peaceful, less confused and more clear. The less cluttered you are with confusing emotional experiences and overwhelming outer tasks, the more space you'll have to move through this rite of passage with grace. Like the traditional planner, this planner includes many checklists and worksheets, but at least half of them are intended to help you organize your inner world.

What does it mean to organize your emotional experience? It means taking the time to identify which areas of the transition are most affecting you, then doing the exercises that will help you work through these areas. So let's get started.

There are generally nine areas where women feel the transition. I will be going into detail on each of these areas in the chapter indicated, but this will serve as a rough road map as you get started on your inner journey. Check the issues that resonate for you:

○ Separating from friends and family (chapter 2)

○ Becoming an adult (chapter 3)

○ Grief from old losses and unfinished transitions (chapter 3)

○ Letting go of attachment to singlehood—identity and lifestyle (chapter 4)

○ Fears about marriage and commitment (chapter 5)

○ What is a wife? (chapter 5)

○ Experiences regarding fiancé: irritation, doubt, loneliness (chapter 7)

○ Limbo feelings (chapter 8)

○ Wedding-day issues (chapter 8)

It's important to identify which areas are affecting you the most so that you can start to process the emotions that are connected to that specific issue. The reasons why women often feel overwhelmed during the engagement have less to do with planning matters and more to do with feeling flooded by muddled thoughts and emotions. Once you identify your key areas, it's important to focus on one piece at a time. This will help you stay grounded and will help with the sense of being overwhelmed that tends to arise. When you sort your inner experience by first identifying and then addressing each sector, you can approach your external tasks with greater serenity.

Regardless of how prepared you may feel emotionally, you still need to plan your wedding! Our culture makes a very big deal about planning a wedding, and if you read a traditional planner you will find hundreds of pages of do's and don'ts about each detail of the affair. I have found that attempting to adhere to these tables of etiquette and achieve their ideal of perfection only overwhelms and creates insanity for an engaged couple. They make wedding planning sound as complex as planning a mission to Mars!

The simple, demystified truth is that there are, at most, about twelve basic planning areas that you will need to attend to: the location; the guest list, including the invitations; the dress; the ceremony, including who will marry you; the wedding rings; the reception; music; food; flowers; cake; photography; and the wedding night. And that's it. That's your wedding. This isn't to say that each of these areas doesn't require some time and focus, but, as with the emotional issues, if you approach one area at a time, the planning becomes entirely manageable.

In the back of this book you will find a basic timetable that will help guide you through the practical aspects of your journey. This checklist is intended to relieve anxiety, not create it. In other words, if you know that you're attending to the external details in a timely fashion, you will have more internal space to attend to the emotional process. The last thing you need is to realize a week before your wedding that you forgot to purchase your marriage license! Take some time to read through this checklist so that you have a basic overview of what you need to accomplish. Organization is one of the keys to a calm mind.

Dr. Bruce Gregory, a successful psychotherapist based in Los Angeles, uses a very simple method to help his clients organize their experience. He has them draw a circle and divide it into pieces of a pie, then fill in the pieces with each area of that topic. For example, if the client is dealing with grief, she will write "Grief" at the top of the pie. Then she will fill in the sectors with the disparate aspects of her grief: relationship with father; breakup last year; losing her cat; letting go of childhood, and so on. As Dr. Gregory states, "This is a way to organize nonlinear experience and contain the feeling of being overwhelmed. Using the circles helps to create space and supports addressing one piece at a time so you don't become flooded."

If you're not clear about how filling in these circles will help you, take a leap of faith and try it anyway! You will be amazed at how a simple external organizational task can help you organize your internal world. The mind seeks to create order out of chaos. Right now, it is quite likely that your inner world disintegrates into a jumble of chaos when you think about your wedding. The act of writing your current emotional and practical issues into the separate slices of the pie will satiate the mind's craving for order and offer you a new perspective.

One final suggestion: Right now, just start with simple words that articulate your emotional state ("sad," "scared," "excited," "confused") and the basic practical areas of your wedding as delineated above. As you move through this process and approach your wedding day, you can expand on the words or create new circles altogether to reflect your changing internal and external realities.

Make several photocopies of each pie. To print out copies of blank pies, see the Conscious Weddings Web site a www.consciousweddings.com.

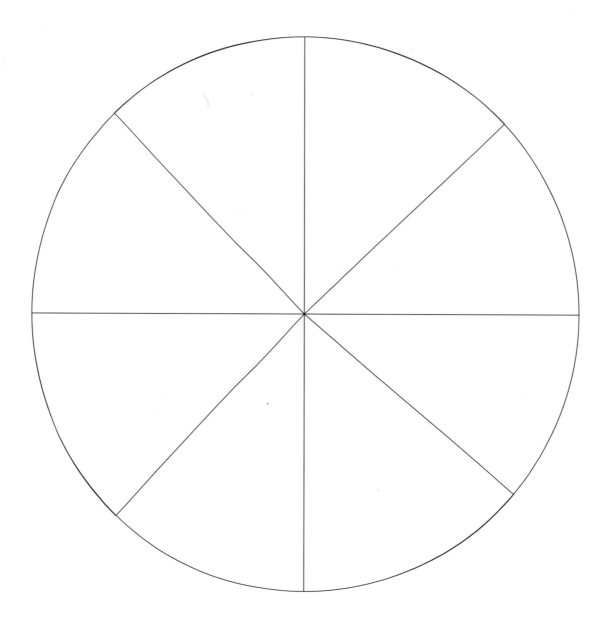

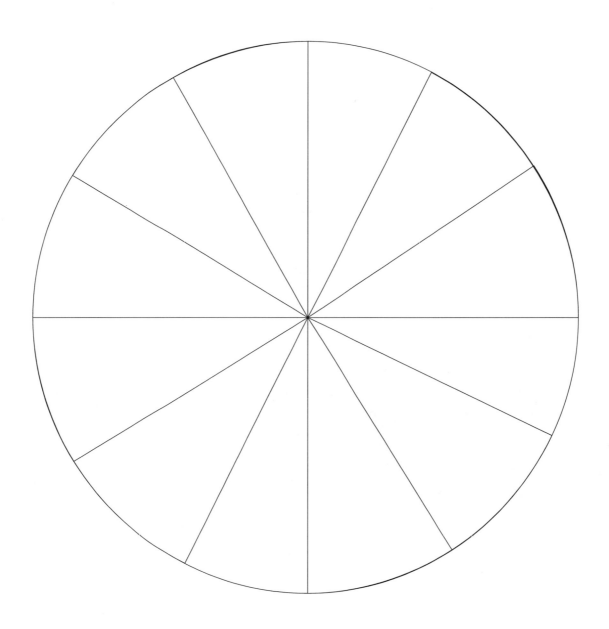

Common Distractions

There are many ways we can easily distract ourselves from experiencing the uncomfortable feelings that arise during the engagement, wedding, and first months of marriage. Instead of feeling the fear, grief, anger, confusion, disorientation, and numbness that characterize transition, we displace these feelings onto external objects, people, or experiences.

Why focus on your grief that your father will not see you marry because he passed away five years ago when you can call another florist or try on dresses at just one more bridal salon? The answer is that the grief will not go away, and if it's not addressed consciously, it will come out indirectly. You may find yourself arguing with your fiancé instead of feeling the grief. You may be lashing out at your mother and her new husband. You may find yourself gripped by a profound anxiety that prevents you from moving forward with the planning. The vast majority of wedding arguments occur because everyone—brides, grooms, mothers, fathers, friends—is involved in their own process of letting go. Instead of feeling the grief and talking about the fear, we argue about pink or mauve napkins and whether to serve chicken or fish at the reception. This overfocus on minute, inconsequential details provides the perfect distraction from the real, emotionally uncomfortable issues.

Check the ways that you find yourself externalizing your feelings as a way to distract yourself from feeling them.

○ *The general planning.* Going over lists in your mind, waking up with planning details running through your head, talking incessantly to friends and family about caterers, the dress, the flowers, placecards, invitations, and so on. Every free moment is filled with some aspect of the wedding, which assumes monumental importance as the day nears.

○ *One aspect of the planning.* "I've bought the dress but I still stop at bridal shops to look at all of the other dresses. I can't stop thinking about the dresses that I haven't chosen, and that this is the one dress that I will wear on my wedding day. What if it's not the exact perfect one?"

○ *Your fiancé.* Becoming irritated to the point of serious questioning about aspects of your fiancé that never bothered you before the engagement. "About six months into our engagement I became disgusted by the way he chewed. I never noticed it before, and suddenly I wanted to strangle him every time we ate together. Some mornings I would wake up and wonder if I was making a mistake." It's easier to focus on the things you don't like about him than it is to let yourself feel the natural, yet unavoidable, fear of getting married—this is the one person you will be with for the rest of your life and forever is a long time!

○ *In-laws and stepparents.* "Where will I place my stepmother at the reception? Do I give her a corsage? How will I handle the photographs?" (These are valid concerns, but when they dominate your thoughts to the point where you have no room to think about or feel anything else, this would be considered a distraction.)

What other ways do you distract yourself?

. . . .

. . . .

. . . .

. . . .

Once you identify the ways that you distract yourself, set your intention to notice how often the tendency arises. Soon you will become adept at asking yourself, "Do I really need to meet with one more photographer, or is there an uncomfortable feeling that I'm avoiding?"

φ

How to Use This Planner

This planner is your guide, and I encourage you to use it as actively as possible. Write in it, carry it with you, earmark the pages that are particularly helpful, underline, highlight … you get the point. When you have successfully arrived at the other side of your wedding, you will look back at this book and appreciate all the hard work you did.

As you work through the checklists and exercises, fill in as much or as little as you need. Remember, this process is intended to help you feel less overwhelmed, not more. I don't want to flood you with "work," but I also want to remind you that the more time and attention you give to sorting through your inner world, the more serenity you will have. Sometimes you may need to write and sometimes the exercise will spark a different activity or a conversation with a friend on a certain topic. This is your wedding; this is your journey. Nobody can tell you what you may need to do to attend to the mountains and valleys that appear on your inner landscape. You are the driver of this car.

How will the exercises help you? Actively doing these exercises provides a place for you to process your internal experience. While the traditional planner includes worksheets where you fill in the names and addresses of your caterer and florist, this planner also offers worksheets that will ask you to explore your emotional world (as well as the names and addresses of your caterer and florist!).

The backbone of this planner is the premise that, through active organization and expression of internal experience, you will find release and a sense of serenity, and open the doors for excitement and joy to enter. Sometimes it is enough to simply name your experience in your head: "I'm feeling scared of the commitment of marriage." Other times, you'll need to write about this fear, explore its roots, examine the legacy of your parents' relationship as your first role model of marriage, and work through old feelings from past boyfriends before the fear you carry about marriage can begin to be dislodged from its seat of power in your mind, allowing you to walk toward the altar with confidence. This planner will guide you through the process.

Each piece of your experience needs a resting place. For example, in chapter 8 I have provided space for you to record any dreams about your wedding that arise. Nearly every bride I have counseled shared a series of compelling and informative wedding dreams. Some of these dreams find their way to our sessions, but most are lost shortly after the dreamer wakes up. Yet, if the dreamer had had a convenient place in which to record the

dream, she may have done so, gained useful information, and been able to look back on it in months to come. The same is true for the grief, fear, and confusion that appear like road-blocks on your journey. There is a space for them in this book. They belong here.

This planner will be there for each step of your journey. When you're done with it, you will have created a unique document that chronicles one of the momentous rites of passages of your life. By doing so you will be sending a direct message to your psyche that says, "Your feelings are welcome here." For example, now that you know that chapter eight has a dream log, you will probably have a dream about your wedding in the next couple of weeks!

I will also walk you through each phase of the external planning. After all, this is your wedding, and of course you want it to be beautiful and meaningful, which means creatively thinking about things like the dress, the flowers, the photographer. I have provided worksheets on each of these items that will help you find a florist, interview photographers, and delegate your bridesmaids' duties. There is also a section in the back of the book where you can write down your final information so you can easily find the areas that you will be referencing again and again until your wedding day. You may also choose to print the sheets directly from the Conscious Weddings Web site.

Furthermore I will be reminding you at each step along the way to check in with yourself emotionally. It's frightfully easy to allow yourself to get sucked into a planning vortex until you find that the "wedding-devil" has possessed you. Consider this scenario: You are happily and consciously planning your wedding, completing the external tasks while paying attention to your inner world, when suddenly you become obsessed with a $4,000 dress. You had budgeted $1,500 for your dress, so it's way out of range. Yet you can't stop thinking about it. You absolutely must have it. Your wedding will be terrible unless you are wearing this dress.

It's at this point that I encourage you to stop. Stop the planning. Stop flipping through the magazines. Stop the doing. Set aside some time each day to drop out of your head and slow back down to the natural rhythm of your body. Your wedding isn't going anywhere, but your sanity is, and unless you take the time to attend to your inner world and explore where this obsession is coming from, you will most likely find yourself spinning down a very scary road.

As I said earlier, it's also important that you focus on one task and one issue at a time. If you're working on finding a location, stay with that task until you find a location. And when you are working on your fears about marriage and commitment, stay with those exercises until they feel complete. This doesn't mean that you ignore your grief from old losses while you are addressing your fears; rather, I encourage you to focus on the area that feels strongest, then move to another issue. Focusing on one issue at a time will help you avoid emotional flooding.

It is unlikely that you will relate to every section in this book. You may feel that you have completely separated from your family of origin, but the thought of giving up your singlehood sends you into a tailspin. Or you may not be ready to address each issue the first time you read the book, but as your wedding nears, the section on lashing out at your fiancé suddenly seems more applicable. Trust your own timetable. Trust your rhythm. Trust your body. Only you know which areas need your attention. The more emotional work you can do during the engagement, the more naturally you will adjust to marriage.

Also, while the language in this book implies that I'm writing for heterosexual couples, the information is by no means exclusive to that audience. Marriage is a worldwide experience, and entering into the archetype of marriage elicits the same thoughts, feelings, and expectations regardless of the specifics of a relationship. So, if you are entering into a same-sex marriage, know that this book was written for you as well, and please change the language where necessary to fit your relationship.

Similarly, this book is primarily geared toward first-time brides. The wedding and marriage archetypes are strongest the first time around, as the groove called "marriage" has not yet been etched into the psyche. In other words, if you have been married before, you have already relinquished your singlehood, created appropriate boundaries around family of origin, and confronted many of your fears about marriage. Marriage is no longer the mysterious unknown that it is for first-time brides. Still, your beliefs around commitment may be shaky, and I suggest you pay particular attention to the section in chapter 4 called "Letting Go of Old Loves," as it is highly likely that your thoughts and feelings about your ex will surface in waking and dream life. I also encourage you to work through the exercise in chapter 1 on setting your intention and take a thorough inventory of your reasons for marrying. This will provide comfort and guidance when the doubts of "why am I doing this again?" threaten to unground you.

Lastly, while this book is written for women, I realize that many men are an active part of the wedding process. This is one of the beautiful changes that reflects the growing equality between the sexes over the last thirty years. Men are getting married, too, and they deserve to be as involved as possible. This can present some challenges because you will have to consider the opinions and visions of another person! But planning a wedding that reflects the love and principles that you share is well worth the challenge of negotiation and compromise.

What matters most, what you can remind each other of in times of stress overload when the thought of eloping seems increasingly appealing, is why you're doing this. In the next chapter you will clarify your intentions for marrying, the vision you have of your wedding, and the principles of your marriage. But my guess is that your reasons for marrying have something to do with this: you love each other, you want to create a lifelong partnership, you feel guided to take sacred vows that honor this commitment, and you wish to celebrate and receive the support of your family and friends. At its core, this wedding is not about the dress, the flowers, the invitations, or the photographer; it's about your love and commitment to each other. It's about having the courage and grace to take this momentous step in your lives, and it's about looking into each other's eyes and saying, "I do," then learning what it means to live in the daily and ever-evolving commitment of marriage.

Congratulations, and many blessings on the journey.

CHAPTER 1

Laying the Groundwork

Emotional Tasks

Setting Your Intention φ *Creating Your Vision* φ
Defining Your Principles

Practical Task

Choosing Your Locations

Why Marry?

*M*arriage is a worldwide phenomenon. People across all spans of geography and time have created ceremonies to symbolize and celebrate the creation of a committed union between two people. While the traditions vary, the wedding generally follows a basic template: two families are brought together, sacred words are exchanged, the ritual is witnessed by the community, and a celebration occurs. After the event, the newly married couple retreats to their home and begins a new phase of their life as husband and wife. Yet while the format is constant, the reasons for initiating this event have dramatically evolved over time.

For the majority of history, people have married for economic, social, and religious reasons. Marriage has traditionally been a business agreement that said, "You go out and make the money; I'll stay home and care for the house and children." Socially, it was deemed improper to remain single past one's early twenties. In the eyes of the church, marriage preserved the sanctity of the family.

We are indebted to the courage and wisdom of the women's movement not only for breaking the chains that imprisoned both sexes, but also for encouraging our culture to examine institutions such as marriage. What does marriage mean today? If it's not a business agreement, then what is it? Women are no longer financially dependent on men. Men are recognizing that they are fully capable of doing their own cooking, cleaning, and laundry. It's more and more socially acceptable to have children outside of marriage. And many people have loosened the power that religion has held over dictating what is right and wrong in terms of the parameters of partnerships. So, if the old reasons don't necessarily apply, why do we still marry?

Why Do We Do It?

Here are some reasons why people generally marry in our culture. As you read down the list, notice which points resonate for you:

- We've been together long enough. It seems like the next thing to do.

- I feel pressure from my family.

- I feel pressure from my partner.

- I've been dreaming about my wedding day since I was a little girl and I can't wait to start planning.

- I'm thirty-five, and I should be married by now.

- I want to be taken care of (emotionally and/or financially).

- All my friends are married; I should be, too.

- I'm afraid I won't find anyone who loves me the way he does.

- It just feels right—I can't explain it.

- I am madly in love with him, and I just can't imagine life without him.

- He proposed, so I said yes. We had talked about it before, but I certainly wasn't expecting it now.

- We feel spiritually guided to take this next step in our relationship.

- I want to create a structure in which to raise children and I think marriage is stronger that just living together.

- I want to make a public statement that honors the love and commitment we share for one another.

- Not only can you choose your friends, you can also choose some of your relatives. By getting married, we are choosing to become a family (whether or not we have children).

- We are aligned in our values and principles, and I think we will make good life partners.

- I view marriage as a spiritual partnership. I take the vows as seriously as I would if I were entering a convent or a monastery. Relationship, for me, is a path for spiritual growth, and entering into marriage is the most sacred and profound level of my commitment.

The reasons for marrying are intimately connected to one's intention for embarking on this journey. And your intention is one of the core building blocks of your wedding and, more importantly, your marriage.

φ

Setting Your Intention: Bride and Groom

It is important that both of you are able to state with clarity and confidence why you are choosing to get married. All too often, we move toward the wedding blindly, pushed by an instinct that propels us through the planning until we wake up one morning in the day-to-day reality of a marriage. Your intention is your reason for marrying. It is the fuel that combines with the vision of your wedding to birth the action of marriage. Visually, we can represent it as

Intention + Vision = Action

As you can see from the list you just read, there are a myriad of reasons why people marry. Take a moment to ask yourself why you are getting married and write down the first thoughts that come to mind. Try not to censor or edit—just allow the words to flow as you witness what arises.

. . . .

. . . .

. . . .

. . . .

. . . .

. . . .

. . . .

. . . .

. . . .

. . . .

. . . .

. . . .

. . . .

. . . .

As you honestly examine your intentions, ask yourself, Are the majority of your reasons externally or internally based? Are you getting married to please others—family, friends, culture, partner—or because it feels genuinely right for you? Are you getting married because you're afraid of being alone or not finding anyone "better"? If your impetus is primarily derived from external sources or from fear, I strongly encourage you to take some time to evaluate your decision. Aside from having a child, marriage is the biggest commitment you will ever make. If you are entering into it to please others or to stave off your anxiety about being single, you will most likely find yourself running scared in the first months or years of marriage.

I also encourage you to ask your partner to think about his reasons for marrying. Ask him to read over the bulleted list above and tell you which reasons apply for him.

Now I invite you—or the two of you together—to take some time to formulate a clear and cohesive intention statement, a few sentences stating your reasons for getting married. It's important to get your intention sorted out now, because it will serve as a grounding point for every aspect of your planning. It is the rudder that will keep you on course. With each decision I encourage you to ask yourselves, "Which decision will truly support our intention? Is there alignment between our intention and our vision?" More specifically, you might ask questions like, "Does spending $3,000 on a dress really support our intention?" In order to create an authentic and meaningful wedding, each element in the outer realm must reflect your inner experience. The dress, rings, food, ceremony, and the like only make sense if they support your intention. What matters is creating a wedding that is in alignment with your reason for marrying. Everything else is secondary.

Your intention is your North Star. It will keep you on track when the fears become overwhelming and you want to say, "Wait, why am I getting married?" It will also ground you in the first years of your marriage—or even ten years into the game—when you are struggling and you forget why you married. We spend a lot of time thinking about the vows that we will hold to once we marry. But we are not guided to think about our reasons for entering into this commitment. This is your opportunity to do just that.

This intention has power, as words always do. Take your time as you craft the sentences. Your true intention already exists within you. It is simply a matter of reaching inside and finding the words that accurately express it.

My Intention: Bride

I, ... ,

am choosing to marry

. . . . , because

. . . .

. . . .

. . . .

. . . .

. . . .

. . . .

. . . .

. . . .

. . . .

. . . .

. . . .

. . . .

. . . .

. . . .

. . . . φ

. . . .

MY INTENTION: GROOM

I, ... ,

am choosing to marry

. . . . , because

. . . .

. . . .

. . . .

. . . .

. . . .

. . . .

. . . .

. . . .

. . . .

. . . .

. . . .

. . . .

. . . .

. . . .

. . . . φ

Envisioning Your Wedding

*N*ow that you have clarified your intention, the next question becomes, what kind of wedding do you want? Just as we have broken the centuries-old mold for our reasons for marrying, so we have risen above any single idea of what a "real" wedding looks like. Although our culture does present a predominantly traditional model, it also allows for wide variations on the theme. And just as there is no "right" reason for marrying, so there is no one way to have a wedding. What matters, once again, is that your wedding reflects your intention and is in alignment with the values and principles that the two of you hold.

The following worksheet will help you discover what type of wedding is right for you and your partner. If you're having trouble envisioning your wedding, see the "Envisioning Your Wedding Meditation" at www.consciousweddings.com.

WORKSHEET: ENVISIONING YOUR WEDDING

1. **WHAT ARE YOUR CHILDHOOD IMAGES AND FANTASIES OF YOUR WEDDING?** Include as many details as you can about the setting, your dress, how you imagined feeling, who would be there, and so on.

2. **WHAT ARE THE COLLECTIVE IMAGES THAT YOU HOLD?** What celebrity weddings, film and television weddings, and photographs from advertising emerged when you meditated on the collective wedding?

3. ARE THERE WEDDINGS THAT YOU RECENTLY ATTENDED THAT YOU REGARD AS THE QUINTESSENTIAL WEDDING? What did you like about them?

. . . .

. . . .

. . . .

. . . .

. . . .

4. WHAT IS THE WEDDING THAT YOU THINK YOUR FAMILY AND/OR YOUR RELIGIOUS INSTITUTION EXPECTS YOU TO HAVE?

. . . .

. . . .

. . . .

. . . .

. . . .

5. DESCRIBE THE VISION OF YOUR WEDDING.

. . . .

. . . .

. . . .

. . . .

. . . .

. . . .

. . . .

Choosing Your Locations

Your first practical step in terms of planning your wedding—after picking a date—will be to decide the location of your ceremony and reception. Deciding the location is a key first step of your wedding. Not only does it largely affect who will be invited and what style of wedding you will have, but many popular locations book a year in advance. If your "perfect" location is already taken, consider changing the date. Also, keep the word "perfect" in quotation marks and trust that another site will emerge that will equally suit your needs. The places to marry are as infinite as your imagination. Recall the vision that arose during your meditation, talk with your fiancé about his vision, and spend a few Sundays exploring different options. When you are following your vision, this first step of your journey can be exciting and fun.

If you are having trouble deciding where you want to marry, you can find site listings in the following locations:

- Personal references
- Internet
- Local wedding magazines
- Chamber of commerce

- Yellow pages
- Wedding consultants
- Regional bridal magazines

Reading through these possibilities may also spark your imagination.

Natural and Spiritual

- Retreat center
- Orchard
- Public beach
- Private garden
- Your favorite spot in nature
- Beach resort
- Synagogue

- Spiritual community
- Public park
- Public garden
- Your favorite hiking spot
- Mountain resort
- Church

Artistic

- Art gallery
- Movie studio lot
- Civic theater
- Lobby or courtyard of an old building (train stations, banks, etc.)

- Museum
- Concert hall
- Private theater

Down-to-Earth

- Your home or backyard
- Restaurant
- Community center
- Bed-and-breakfast

- A friend's home or backyard
- Hotel
- University facilities

Unusual

- Aquarium
- Amusement park
- Fairground
- Observatory

- Zoo
- Lighthouse
- Racetrack

Elegant

- Winery
- Castle
- Yacht

- Historic mansion
- Private estate
- Private club

Once you've narrowed down your search, make appointments at a few sites. Take the following worksheet with you to each site you visit. Make as many photocopies as you need.

SITE PLANNING WORKSHEET

General:

1. Can this site be used for both ceremony and reception? . . . .

2. Is there a designated area for the guests to wait for our arrival? . . . .

. . . .

3. If it's an outdoor facility, is there an alternative hall in case of bad weather?

. . . .

4. If outside, are there lights and heaters? . . . .

. . . .

5. If outside, is there an indoor space for grandparents and elderly to rest? . . . . . .

. . . .

6. Are there special rooms for the bride, groom, and attendants to change in?

. . . .

7. Are there adequate restrooms? . . . .

8. Is it wheelchair accessible? . . . .

9. Is there adequate parking? . . . .

FEES:

1. What is the fee? . . . .

2. What does this fee include? . . . .

. . . .

3. How many hours does this fee include? . . . .

4. Are there overtime fees? . . . .

5. Do you provide tables, chairs, linens, plates, and silverware? . . . .

. . . .

6. Are there discounts on certain days of the week, times, or seasons? . . . . . .

. . . .

7. Do you require a security deposit? If so, how much? When is it refunded?

. . . .

8. Does the rental fee include cleanup? . . . .

9. Is there an additional fee for parking? . . . .

10. Is liability insurance included in the rental fee? . . . .

FOOD AND DRINK:

1. Can we use our own caterer or do we have to use an in-house caterer?

. . . .

2. In there an adequate kitchen? . . . .

3. What is your policy regarding alcohol? Any restrictions? . . . .

   . . . .

4. Can we provide our own alcohol? . . . .

5. Is there a corkage fee with wine or champagne? . . . .

   If so, how much? . . . .

6. Is liquor liability insurance included in the rental fee? . . . .

   . . . .

MUSIC AND DANCE:

1. Is there a dance floor? . . . .

2. Is there a piano or other instrument on site? Extra fee to use them? . . . .

   . . . .

3. Is there a microphone? . . . .

4. Are there any music restrictions—style and how long it's played? . . . .

   . . . .

5. Do neighbors need to be notified if music is played loudly? . . . .

PHOTOGRAPHY:

1. Are there any regulations regarding photography or videography? . . . .

   . . . .

As you search for your location, make sure that it is in alignment with your vision and your principles. I cannot say it often enough: the practical details are meaningless unless they reflect who the two of you are as a couple and the values with which you wish to imbue your marriage. While your location is the foundation of your wedding, your principles are the foundation of your marriage. As you read through the next section, consider how your location and principles are connected.

Is There a Match?

As you begin to envision your wedding, ask yourself, does this imagined wedding reflect your values around love, money, beauty, spirituality, and connection? Does the outer vision of your wedding reflect the inner intention about why you are choosing to marry? At each stage of the planning, when your culture, your religion, or your family attempts to sway you in a direction that doesn't feel right to you, check in with your intention and revisit the images from your meditation. You may, for financial or familial reasons, need to relinquish some aspects of your ideal day. If you have chosen to allow your family to contribute or pay for your wedding, they may have strong opinions about certain aspects of the day. We will explore money matters in the next chapter, but what matters is that you don't conform to others' expectations at the expense of your integrity. Your intention and vision are the gauge that can keep you on track.

It's Not Just about Romance

A good marriage cannot thrive on love alone. As romantic as it sounds and as conditioned as we are to believe its veracity, marriage requires much more than a physical attraction and sexual chemistry to survive. It's true that it is often these elements that draw two people together. We are biologically wired to sniff out a combination of pheromones and physique that delight our senses, and if these qualities are completely lacking, it may put a strain on the union. But the truth—the unromantic, un-Hollywood, realistic truth—is that hair thins, bellies pooch, and breasts sag, and if the initial romantic spark that ignited your union is not balanced by shared principles and values, the bond will likely begin to break apart.

The myth of romantic love is very much alive in our culture. This means that we are conditioned to equate love with chemistry and a good partnership with physical attraction. In many ways, we have done a 180-degree turnaround from the values upon which the ancient Greeks based their decision to marry. But the pursuit of romantic love, which burst into our collective psyches with the courtly love of the Arthurian age, has superseded the methodical approach that guided the actions of our ancestors. We are no longer fueled by a levelheaded search to find a good, solid life partner. Rather, encouraged by the romanticism of our culture, we are seeking a soul mate, a heavenly union, "the one," a person who was divinely sent to match our fantasies and meet our every need.

Our unshakable belief in romantic love often fuels the doubt that arises between couples as the wedding nears. Countless women have contacted me to confess, in hushed tones, a variation on Amanda's concern:

I love my fiancé, but sometimes I have doubts about him. He's not everything I've always thought I should marry. I never had a sense of "this is the one." I don't even know if I believe that there is only one person I could have a good marriage with. We get along well and we make good partners, but sometimes I wonder if there's enough passion. Isn't it supposed to feel differently? This is certainly not how it's portrayed in the movies, where engaged couples seem madly in love all the time.

Amanda is courageously expressing one of our culture's great taboos. If there is one thing that women are terrified to admit, it's that they question if they are "in love" enough with their partner. A woman can have cold feet. She can be a little jittery or a little queasy on the morning of her wedding. But to admit that her sense of feeling in love wavers is unacceptable and leads her and those she confides in to question whether or not she should marry. In some cases, as I will explore in the next section, severe doubt could be an indication that there are red-flag issues in the relationship that need to be addressed before moving forward with a marriage commitment. But for the vast majority of the women I've worked with, the doubts are a normal and healthy part of the process and are usually connected to our cultural misunderstanding of the true meaning of love.

If you speak to couples who have been married for many years, they will tell you that the feeling of love—the stomach-fluttering, starry-eyed enchantment that is so prevalent in the first months of a relationship—ebbs and flows throughout the many years of marriage. Just as we cannot expect to feel happy every day of our lives, so we cannot expect to feel in love every day. The doubts that engaged women experience are often predicated on the notion that when the in-love feeling wanes, there is something wrong with their relationship. This would be true if real love was dependent on the feeling of love. But as those who have walked the long journey of marriage know, love is much more than a feeling—it is an action.

The reality of a mature, committed relationship is that you are going to be challenged to extend yourself beyond your comfort zone. Your partner is going to drive you crazy. He's going to irritate the heck out of you. He's going to look like a beautiful and sexy prince one moment and the next he might look like an ugly frog. You are going to vacillate between feeling in love and feeling out of love. This is the arc of a shared, intimate life with another human being. This is the arc of a marriage.

φ

The Importance of Principles

So, if marriage is not based on the feeling of love, what is it based on? One of the foundations of a good marriage is shared principles. "Principle" is a somewhat elusive word. *New Webster's Dictionary* (1975) defines a principle as "A basic doctrine or tenet; a law on which others are founded." The ancient philosophers believed that earth, water, fire, and air are the principles of life, and our country was founded upon the principles of democracy. How does all of this translate to human relationships?

Our principles comprise the basis of our values. They are the qualities that will stand forever and that are intrinsically woven into the fabric of who we are. They may derive from your cultural and familial upbringing, but you may have diverged from your conditioning to establish those principles that are meaningful for you and your partner. Principles promote life and well-being. They are the foundation of our actions in the world.

Just as it is crucial to clarify your intention for marrying, so it is important to have a clear sense of what principles the two of you intend to incorporate into your marriage. It's not enough to say, "We love each other. We are committed to each other." What do you love? What, exactly, are you committed to? Are your values in alignment or do you prioritize differently?

We expect a lot from our marriages. Think about it: we ask that a spouse be a best friend, a financial associate, a coparent, a roommate, a housecleaner, a provider, and, at the end of the day, a sexual partner. In order to increase the chances of success in at least some of these areas, it's important to take the time to clarify your principles. The principles are the building blocks of your marriage. Without them, the day-to-day challenges of life could easily take over and threaten to topple the structure of your relationship. But if you plant your marriage in healthy soil and work to create a solid foundation, the chances of creating and sustaining a good marriage increase.

Some examples of principles are:

- Clear and loving communication
- Commitment to your own and your partner's spiritual growth
- Honesty
- Intellectual curiosity
- Physical health
- Creativity
- Sexuality
- Family
- Financial abundance
- Laughter and play
- Appreciation
- Tolerance
- Courage
- Psychological growth
- Emotional healing
- Balance of separateness and togetherness, of work and play
- Safety and protection

Your principles are the strands of straw that you weave together to create the basket of your marriage. Take some time to meditate on the principles, or qualities, that you will use to weave this container. I encourage you to ask your partner to clarify his principles as well, and together create a list below of what you intend to incorporate into your marriage. As with your intention and your wedding vision, allow for this to emerge from the deeper layers within you, beyond the first layer of what you think you "should" include.

THE PRINCIPLES OF OUR MARRIAGE

We, ... and . . . . ,

intend to incorporate the following principles into our marriage:

* . . . .

* . . . .

* . . . .

* . . . .

* . . . .

Obstacles and Red Flags

For some women, the moment they hear they words "Will you marry me?" they are off and running at a mad pace to plan their wedding. There is no stopping their single-minded focus to plan the wedding they have been dreaming about since they were six years old. For others, there is some aspect of the planning that stops them dead in their tracks, and the fears may be so strong that they prevent even a vision of their wedding from materializing. As I mentioned in the introduction, encoded in the outer layers of a wedding are the deep-seated thoughts, feelings, and expectations that are embedded into this transition. Once the underlying emotion is exposed, the vision opens up and you can continue moving forward.

There are several reasons why you may have trouble envisioning your wedding:

1. You are allowing your family's expectations to cloud your true desires.

2. Your fears about marriage and commitment are preventing you from seeing the wedding day.

3. Your perfectionism is running the show and won't allow you to take a step in any direction—including envisioning your wedding—without criticizing you.

4. Imagining the people surrounding you at your wedding would mean facing the grief around the people who are no longer in your life.

5. You are plagued by doubts that you are not in love enough with your partner.

6. You feel you are too young to get married.

7. You are scared that you are marrying the wrong man.

When women contact me for help, one of the first questions they ask is, "How do I know that these negative feelings are not a sign that I shouldn't be getting married?" My answer to them is really two points:

1. Of the women who contact me, 95 percent are experiencing the normal and natural transition feelings that they would be feeling no matter who they were marrying.

2. As you begin to address the different sectors of your wedding transition pie, it will become clear to you which feelings are connected to your internal process, separate from your partner, and which are specific to your relationship.

So how do you know if you're making the right decision? Nobody can give you the answer, but if you take the time to address your feelings and summon the courage to ask yourself, very honestly, whether or not this decision is right for you at this time in your life, you will most likely receive a clear response. Your body holds your truth. Your dreams hold your wisdom. Your connection to your higher power, or the deepest part of yourself, holds your answers. If you ask women who later divorced if they knew that they were making a mistake before they married, most will say yes. They knew months before their wedding day that something was wrong and that they shouldn't go through with it. Some were unable to trust themselves; others lacked the courage to cancel. But the knowing, the truth, was there.

Every relationship has its problems. Unlike the versions of courtship we see in the media where conflicts are neatly resolved in twenty minutes, real-world partnerships are full of real challenges. Struggle is not a sign, in and of itself, that you shouldn't be getting married. The question to ask yourself is this: Do you have a sense of rightness about this decision? Within your body, not far from the surface of your skin, there is a place that can clearly distinguish between a yes response and a no response. For some women, this place of knowing is in their heart; for others it's in their solar plexus or their "gut" (as in, "I just have a gut feeling about it"). This place recognizes the fear that you have about rela-

tionships and marriage, but is also connected to something deeper and more profound. Have you checked into that place of knowing?

Of the hundreds of women I have counseled, approximately 5 percent chose to postpone or cancel their wedding. Fortunately, they realized before the wedding that, while they were experiencing some of their own fears about marriage and grief about letting go of singlehood, there were also serious red-flag relationship issues that had nothing to do with the transition. These issues can be roughly divided into three categories:

1. Their partner was struggling with an addiction: alcohol, drugs, pornography, work, or spending. It is highly unadvisable to move forward into marriage until the addict is in recovery.

2. The couple was out of alignment with their values and principles. For example, I recently counseled a young, independent career woman whose fiancé expected her to stop working and get pregnant immediately after the wedding. He was very clear that he wanted a housewife and stay-at-home mom and she was very clear that she would rather dig her own grave and lie down in it than assume those roles.

3. The woman clearly felt, "It doesn't feel right." Do not underestimate the power of instinct. If your body is screaming to you in the form of graphic dreams or extreme physical symptoms, trust that it is trying to communicate an important message. On the surface, your relationship may appear healthy, but the body and the unconscious often hold wisdom long before the conscious mind becomes aware. If this is the case, a skilled therapist or trusted friend can help you align with your truth.

Nobody is perfect. There isn't a man on this planet who is going to meet all of your needs and desires. In a culture that expects perfection, it can be a challenge to admit that your partner is not perfect, but that he's very, very good. If you sense that you will make compatible life partners, he's loving, you enjoy each other's company, and, most importantly, you have checked in with the deepest place in yourself that signals a sense of rightness about your union, then most likely you're making a good choice. Staying connected to the sense of rightness will help allay the doubts as they arise and will allow you to move forward with your planning.

A Creative Act: Planning from the Inside Out

Planning your wedding can be an intensely creative process. One of the keys to minimizing the stress is to continually remind yourself that you are in the midst of a creative act, as alive and exciting as working on a play or writing a book. You are an artist crafting one of the most significant rites of passages in your life. Together with your partner, and perhaps your mother or a close friend, you are weaving the container inside which your marriage will be born. The more you allow the images to emerge organically and on their own timetable, the more creative the process will be.

Like any artist, you must be willing to throw away the first ideas and start again. For as well as being in a creative time, you are also in a process of self-trust. As you may have discovered through the Envisioning Your Wedding worksheet, the creativity and the self-trust can arise only after you sift through what you've been fed about what a wedding "should" look like. Sometimes the first images are the cliché elements that you feel obligated to include: "I should get married in a big, white dress"; "We should be married by a priest or rabbi". Once again, there is no "should," no right way, when it comes to creating your day. There is only what feels authentic for the two of you.

CHAPTER 2

Money: The Uninvited Guest

Emotional Tasks
Addressing the Perfectionist φ *Separating from Friends and Family*

Practical Tasks
Planning Your Honeymoon φ *Setting the Budget*

The wedding industry is a fifty-billion-dollar business. As you enter into the world of weddings, it's important to recognize that you are being targeted by top marketers and advertisers to spend, spend, spend. You are not surrounded by a culture that wants to guide you through this rite of passage in a meaningful way, ensuring that you enter your marriage on a healthy foundation. Rather, your culture views you primarily as a consumer.

One of the wedding industry's primary marketing tools is to encourage the pursuit of perfection. This is a dangerous pursuit, for not only is perfection an impossible goal, but the obsession with it often leads to reckless spending and heavy debt loads that greet a newlywed couple on the other side of the honeymoon. With money as one of the top three stressors in a marriage, why would an engaged couple choose to begin their married life together in debt? If she were thinking rationally, a bride-to-be would most likely pass on the fringes and over-the-top extras that cause her to exceed her wedding budget. But when it comes to a wedding, the rational part of our brains is often superseded by the longing to replicate the images of wedding-day perfection that have been brewing and steeping in our subconscious for many years.

φ

The Quest for Perfection

When the time comes to plan your wedding, every image that you have consciously and subliminally absorbed throughout your life—from television coverage of celebrity weddings to $20,000 airbrushed photographs on the cover of *Bride's Magazine*—will rise to the surface and attempt to grab the reins of your planning. Unless you take the time to name the fantasy and repeatedly remind yourself that the images we see are illusory, you are liable to find yourself turning into the aptly-named and much-feared "Bridezilla."

Bridezilla is the nightmare bride who is obsessed with a single-minded goal during her engagement: to plan a perfect wedding. She has successfully been indoctrinated into a wedding culture that tells her that if she only spends enough money—purchasing this dress, these flowers, and those hand-engraved invitations—she will have a beautiful wedding *and thus, a beautiful marriage.* The correlation is indirect, but just as advertising tells men that if they buy a certain brand of beer they will also attract a certain brand of woman, this same industry tells women that if they create a wedding to match the media images, they will live happily ever after. Bridezilla is a product of our culture. The wedding and advertising industries have been priming her from the time she was a little girl, brilliantly training her so that from the moment she hears, "Will you marry me?" and slips the diamond ring onto her finger, she gallops out of the starting gate with credit card in hand, off to plan the wedding of her dreams.

There are several problems with a woman allowing Bridezilla to inhabit her body and control her engagement. The first and most painful is that she alienates her partner and loved ones. While she's riding around in a wild, maniacal frenzy, she has completely forgotten about why she's getting married and so has left her fiancé and everyone close to her standing in the dust. She is possessed by an energy that has nothing to do with a meaningful wedding or a successful marriage, and the longer she rides alone the more she alienates the people she loves. Many partners sadly report that they would have rather eloped than witness the strange possession that occurred during their engagement. Instead of feeling included in a planning process that should have equally involved them, the partner feels polarized and lonely. They have deep regrets that their marriage started on such shaky ground.

Another consequence of Bridezilla possession is that a manic high cannot last forever; inevitably she crashes after the wedding or honeymoon. Women often feel a profound sense of regret and self-betrayal in the aftermath of a wedding. In many cases, a woman will have spent a year of her life planning for a single day, and when the day comes and goes and life continues on as life does, she realizes that her "perfect" wedding, the wedding she went into severe debt for, the wedding she put the rest of her life on hold for, failed to solve her problems. Her partner is still an imperfect human being: he still leaves his socks on the floor; he still leaves his dirty dishes in the sink. In short, the newlyweds did not go riding off into the sunset on a white horse to live in a beautiful castle above the clouds, far away from the messiness of life. Real life followed her into a real marriage and, due to the possession, she spent no time during her engagement cultivating skills that would help her create a successful marriage.

If you find yourself consumed by the desire to create a "perfect" wedding, take some time to ask yourself the following questions.

PERFECTIONISM WORKSHEET

1. **WHO IS THIS WEDDING FOR?** Are you worrying about impressing others or are you focusing on creating an authentically meaningful day?

. . . .

. . . .

. . . .

. . . .

2. **ARE YOU ENJOYING THE PROCESS OF PLANNING YOUR WEDDING?** If so, what is enjoyable about it? If not, can you identify what is inhibiting the joy?

. . . .

. . . .

. . . .

. . . .

3. **WHAT DO YOU BELIEVE WILL HAPPEN IF YOU CREATE A "PERFECT" DAY?** In other words, do you believe a perfect wedding will create a perfect marriage? Said another way, do you believe that an "imperfect" wedding means you will not have a good marriage?

. . . .

. . . .

. . . .

. . . .

4. **IN YOUR EYES, WHAT IS A PERFECT WEDDING?** Describe it in detail.

. . . .

. . . .

. . . .

. . . .

5. **IN YOUR EYES, WHAT IS AN IMPERFECT WEDDING?** Describe it.

. . . .

. . . .

. . . .

. . . .

6. **What feelings of loss and separation might lie beneath the drive to perfection?**

. . . .

. . . .

. . . .

. . . .

Separating from Friends and Family

Perfectionism is fostered by our culture, but it also serves a psychological function: it is the perfect defense against feeling the loss, separation, and fear that often arise during the engagement. As Diana learned, perfection can be an expensive and, ultimately, unsatisfying goal to pursue:

> I was spending money hand over fist to make everything look so perfect. I just depended on what I had learned from my mother and the life I had grown up in because I knew that it was societally correct and would impress everybody; you know, the engraved invitations and everything in silk and taffeta, the handwritten menus, the right band, the right champagne. It wasn't me. After the wedding, I felt an immense sense of self-betrayal because the wedding was not an expression of us but an empty event where everything looked perfect.
>
> I wouldn't surrender anything. I wouldn't let go of control. I wouldn't face my fears. I wouldn't let people love me. I wouldn't feel anything. I wouldn't feel that my father wasn't there and that my family was broken up. I wouldn't feel all the loss and sacrifice I had been experiencing. I was unwilling to notice any loss or death prior to the event, even though this denial was sucking everything out of me. Once the event passed, all of that came back on me. Every time I opened my eyes I felt like I was dying. I spent my first months of marriage in a deep depression because of everything I refused to feel before the wedding.

For Diana, perfectionism shielded her from experiencing the distance with her mother and her father's absence. As long as she was consumed with planning a perfect wedding, her grief was kept at bay. For other women, like Frances, while perfection made an appearance, it was the arguments about money that served as a protection. She was so afraid of feeling the grief of the separation with her old life that she hid behind rancor around money, stirring up conflict that actually threatened to destroy her wedding experience. Several years after her wedding, she and her husband, Tom, still had sour feelings about the arguments that occurred between them and her father. None of them understood that they were in a process of separation, with Tom stepping in to "replace" the role that Frances's father had occupied. Instead of acknowledging these sad and uncomfortable feelings, they argued about the limousine and the reception costs.

Money is one of the main sources of arguments around a wedding. We normally view the fights about money as just that—spats about how and where to spend. Yet encoded in these arguments are important challenges that may require you to cut ties and set boundaries around parents and future in-laws, thereby taking the first steps toward creating your new family. For, in order to begin your marriage on a healthy foundation, you must first separate from your family of origin. This means taking a leap into a new phase of adulthood, one that establishes you as a very separate individual from your family and asserts your independence.

One of the purposes of a wedding is to launch a marriage, which is, in essence, a new family. The new family cannot be birthed until the old one is relinquished. This certainly doesn't mean that you permanently sever ties. Rather, the strong ties that bind you to parents and siblings must be loosened so that you can "tie the knot" with your partner.

The engagement marks the beginning of your moving away from your identity as a single woman and your primary allegiance to your family of origin and moving toward the identity of a wife and the new union with your husband. Ultimately, to solidify this bond with your groom, you must begin to loosen ties with those who helped form and mold your identity as a young woman. The engagement, besides a time to plan the wedding, is also a time when you are separating psychologically from your mother, father, and girlfriends, as well as from your current identity as a single woman. The engagement may also bring into focus the difficulties in your relationships. You may feel sadness that you do not have closer relationships with your mother, father, or friends, and this pain needs to be acknowledged. Instead of obsessing about perfection or arguing about money matters, check in with yourself to see where you are feeling this separation. The following checklist can help.

CHECKLIST: SEPARATION FROM FRIENDS & FAMILY

Check the boxes that apply:

SEPARATING FROM MY FRIENDS AND SIBLINGS

○ My [sisters, brothers, friends] have been number one in my life. As the wedding approaches, I can feel this allegiance changing.

○ My friends represent my singlehood and the part of my life that I'm leaving.

○ I feel closer to my friends than ever.

○ I feel more separate from my friends than ever.

○ I have had some arguments with my friends about the planning. I wonder if that's a distraction against feeling the impending break or change in our friendship.

○ All I want to do is spend time with my friends.

○ I feel alone, and as close as I feel to my friends, they can't go through this with me.

SEPARATING FROM MY MOTHER:

○ I feel like I'm leaving the nest.

○ I've had the urge to go home and spend time with my mom.

○ My mom is single, and it breaks my heart that I am "leaving" her.

○ I can feel my mother's pain about this separation. I think she's using the planning as a way to distract from feeling this loss.

○ This wedding has initiated a process of separating from my mother. I am finding who I am apart from who my mother thinks I am.

○ I miss my mother.

SEPARATING FROM MY FATHER

○ After my wedding, I will no longer be "Daddy's little girl."

○ When I take my husband's last name, I will be leaving my father's lineage.

○ I feel like I'm losing my father.

○ My dad has always been number one in my life. Now I am transferring this allegiance to my husband and this change feels [painful, exciting, strange].

○ My dad and I are not very close.

○ I feel like my dad is paying for this wedding to try to make up for how absent he has been in my life. Nothing could make up for that, and the wedding illuminates this pain.

Now that you have identified the areas of loss, you may want to further the awareness by journaling through your thoughts and feelings. Remember, the more you can express your feelings, the less you will use the planning as a way to distract youself. And the more you can share your feelings and bring this consciousness to those around you, the less you will argue about inconsequential details and money matters. Use the space below to write about your mother, father, siblings, and girlfriends. How do you feel you are separating from them? Have you felt closer lately or more distant?

A very effective way to communicate how you are feeling to those around you is to write letters. The more you let your loved ones know the truth and depth of your feelings—your sense of loss, your excitement, your fear—the more you give them permission to express the same. When the true feelings are acknowledged, the arguments about money and planning should disappear. You may also use the space below to begin to draft letters. You will have another opportunity to write more extensive letters to loved ones in chapter 7 because your feelings will likely transform and intensify as the wedding nears.

φ

Do You Want a Wedding or a Marriage?

It's very easy to become caught in the fantasy of planning this one perfect day at the expense, literally, of everything else. Many women are willing to spend all of their savings, which would prevent them from buying a house and saving for their children's future. Others recognize that they can either have a wedding or a marriage. Unfortunately, many women who choose the wedding, far exceeding their budget and going into debt in an attempt to create perfection, often feel betrayed by the empty promise that a perfect wedding would lead to "happily ever after."

One of the keys to a successful marriage is the ability of both partners to negotiate and compromise. For many couples, planning a wedding is the first time they are sharing money. Given that money is one of the most common topics that married couples argue about, we can realistically assume that conflict will arise for engaged couples as well. Far from being a reason to sound the alarms, money conflicts provide an opportunity to begin to develop communication tools around this potentially volatile area. Why wait until you have already tied the knot to discover that your partner is a spender while you are a saver? Our beliefs and behaviors around money often stem from our upbringing. Unless the two of you were raised in a very similar environment, it's unlikely that you will approach money from the same angle. And besides, opposites attract, so the chance that one of you is saver while the other is a spender is quite high!

Use the following worksheet to explore your relationship to money. I suggest you make a photocopy so that you can each fill one out. Money can be a difficult topic to discuss. If you are working with a rabbi, minister, or premarital counselor, you may choose to bring these documents to him or her and discuss them with a third person in the room. If you choose to discuss them alone, remember that money is often a metaphor for comfort, security, and safety. You may think you're discussing money, but if you can replace the trigger "money" with these kinder words, you will be able to keep the conversation in perspective. And if it turns combative, just remember that it's better to have this conversation now than after you are already married.

This questionnaire is written in general and somewhat black-and-white terms. Choose the answer that most closely reflects your view, even if it isn't an exact fit.

1. I am primarily a

   a. spender.

   b. saver.

2. Growing up, my family's attitude about money was

   a. relaxed and easy.

   b. full of anxiety about having enough, no matter how much we had.

   c. I have never thought about it and I have no idea. Money was kept under wraps.

3. My philosophy about credit cards is

   a. I have no credit card debt, and I feel very strongly about paying the full balance on my credit card(s) each month.

   b. I have credit card debt, and I don't have a problem with it. My family always had credit card debt, so it seems normal to me.

   c. I have credit card debt, but I'm not comfortable with it. I intend to do everything I can to pay it off as quickly as possible.

4. If I were to make a big purchase, such as a car or an expensive piece of furniture, I would

   a. wait until I had enough cash to buy it outright.

   b. have no problem buying it on credit.

5. With regard to food, I prefer to

   a. cook and eat at home most nights.

   b. dine out . . . . nights a week.

6. When I go out to eat, I like to

   a. dine at fine restaurants and enjoy top-quality food.

   b. eat good food, but the best isn't important to me—especially if it's outside my budget.

7. Having nice personal belongings—car, furniture, food, clothes—is

   a. very important to me. I like to buy the best, even if it's out of my price range.

   b. not very important to me. I like nice things, but I prefer a simple life.

8. I make $. . . . . per year. This amount is

   a. satisfactory.

   b. unsatisfactory. I would like to be making $. . . . . per year.

9. My partner makes $. . . . . per year. This amount is

   a. satisfactory.

   b. unsatisfactory. I wish he/she would make $. . . . . per year.

10. After we have children, I want to (or want my spouse to)

   a. take some time off, but then go back to work. We will continue to earn money as we do now.

   b. stop working for an indefinite amount of time. My spouse will become the primary wage earner.

11. When it comes to handling our money

   a. I will pay the bills and keep track of our accounts and investments.

   b. my partner will pay the bills and keep track of our money.

   c. we will do it together, or we will take turns.

12. [If you have not already joined money] After we marry, we will

   a. keep separate accounts.

   b. merge our money.

   c. start one joint account and each have separate accounts.

Remember, marriage is about negotiation and compromise. Don't panic if you are out of alignment in some of the ways you approach money. What matters is that you learn how to handle finances so that it works for both of you. This may take time and require outside help, but the sooner you begin to address this issue, the better.

φ

Ways to Save

If you're on a limited budget, which most of us are, you will have to make important decisions about where to spend your money. While I can offer practical ways to save, the most effective technique is to stay aligned with your intention and true to your vision. Most women find that if they maintain a clear focus about their reason for marrying, the external aspects fall easily into place. Still, money is money, and there are some practical and creative ways to save.

Prioritize

Decide what aspect of the wedding is most important to you. For some women, the dress is the centerpiece of the day; for others, a live band is a must. Hopefully, this area will reflect one of your values. If music is important, you most likely love to dance and want to have fun dancing at your reception. If flowers are important, I would guess that you place a high value on beauty and nature. Take some time to think about where you want to splurge and put your energy into one item of quality. And don't forget to check in with your fiancé!

Which external aspect of your wedding is most important to you and why?

. . . .

. . . .

. . . .

. . . .

. . . .

Make It Small

Consider shrinking your guest list. Many of the women I counsel express that they would have been just as happy, if not happier, with 75 guests instead of 120. Every guest carries a dollar amount, so make sure that the people you invite are the people you truly want to witness and celebrate the event. (See chapter 3.)

Keep It Casual

Many women regret the excessive spending that Bridezilla, or Bridezilla's mother, encouraged. As Jade shares,

I didn't have the wedding I wanted to have. I wanted to have a very low-key, backyard, bring-your-favorite-dish wedding, and what I got was this over $10,000 extravaganza. I appreciated the effort and money my mother put into it, but I felt disappointed as well. My mother planned my wedding. It started with me, but out of sheer frustration I gave it over to her. Of course she was also paying for it, which made it seem like what I wanted didn't

Call On Your Talents

One of my clients is getting married on her family's flower farm in Oregon. Needless to say, she and her sisters are growing the flowers for her wedding. Another client is an artist and is designing and addressing her own invitations. Still another loves to bake, so she's gathering her friends together and figuring out how to make the wedding cake! If you remember that the wedding is a creative event, you will be able to access your own resources.

Ask for Help

Ask your creative friends and family to contribute to an aspect of the planning, instead of giving a wedding gift. For example, Lena's friends wanted to take care of the flowers, so she gave them a budget and they created the bouquets and centerpieces. Aaron's grandmother and great aunt did all the cooking for his wedding. Do you know a seamstress, a baker, a chef, or a photographer? Don't be shy about asking for what you need. People are usually honored to help and offer their true gifts to you and your partner.

φ

Planning Your Honeymoon

Before you set your wedding budget and decide how much you will spend in each area, you'll need to begin thinking about your honeymoon. The reason for this early planning is twofold: one, if you have $10,000 to spend and your honeymoon will cost $3,000, this will give you a clear sense of how much you have left for your wedding; and two, many popular honeymoon destinations, like Hawaii and the Caribbean, book up a year in advance. The sooner you decide where you want to go, the more choices you'll have for accommodations and the better deal you'll find on airfares.

What kind of honeymoon do you want? As I mention in chapter 9, there is a reason most people choose a tropical location for their honeymoon. After spending several months planning your wedding, then undergoing a spiritually transformative experience, you and your new spouse will need time to rest and rejuvenate. But if you are more rugged types and have always envisioned going on a safari in Africa for your honeymoon, begin to explore this option now. Finding the right place takes time, so begin your search early. And when you get stressed out by wedding demands—both emotional and practical—your honeymoon will rise in your mind like a peaceful or exciting gift at the end of your long journey.

Use the following space to make notes on where the two of you see yourselves on your honeymoon.

. . . .

. . . .

. . . .

. . . .

. . . .

. . . .

. . . .

. . . .

. . . .

To help you decide where to go, search online for vacation sites, or make an appointment with a travel agent who can show you package deals and popular honeymoon destinations.

Once you have solidified your travel arrangements, make note of them in the back section of this planner.

PRACTICAL TIPS

- The price of your honeymoon can vary considerably depending on where you go and how long you stay. To save money, plan a domestic trip at a location you can drive to.

- Make all reservations using your maiden name. Unless you are traveling several months after your wedding, you won't have time to legally change your last name until you return from your honeymoon. Any discrepancy in your documents could cause problems at airports and in customs.

- If you're traveling abroad, find out several months ahead of time what immunizations you will need.

Your Wedding Budget

Now that you have sifted through and addressed the emotional tasks that often interfere with the ability to think clearly about money, you are ready to set a realistic budget for your wedding and honeymoon.

I have one piece of advice around your budget: DON'T GO INTO DEBT. I assure you that of the hundreds of women I have spoken with about their wedding, not a single one felt good about going into debt. The bottom line is that the wedding is one day of your life, and it's not worth spending your entire savings on it. No matter how perfect you want it to be or how much money you spend, it's not the wedding that's going to lead to "happily ever after."

I encourage you to be as honest and realistic as possible when you fill out this worksheet. Your budget and breakdown are the parameters that will keep you in check. Once you make the commitment to stick to your figures, then you know exactly what you have to work with. The rest is smooth sailing (and perhaps an occasional lesson in disappointment).

The following budget worksheet gives a general breakdown of the major wedding categories. Use this worksheet as a draft to figure out your estimated spending and the final budget worksheet in the back section to record your actual spending.

WORKSHEET: A PRELIMINARY BUDGET BREAKDOWN

YOUR CONTRIBUTION	$ . . . .
YOUR PARTNER'S CONTRIBUTION	$ . . . .
YOUR FAMILY'S CONTRIBUTION (IF APPLICABLE)	$ . . . .
YOUR PARTNER'S FAMILY'S CONTRIBUTION (IF APPLICABLE)	$ . . . .
TOTAL BUDGET:	$ . . . .

WEDDING ITEM	AMOUNT BUDGETED
COUNSELING	$ . . . .
INVITATIONS	$ . . . .
BRIDE'S WEDDING CLOTHES	$ . . . .
ACCESSORIES	$ . . . .
HAIR AND BEAUTY	$ . . . .

GROOM'S WEDDING CLOTHES	$ . . . .
CEREMONY (SITE FEE, OFFICIANT'S FEE)	$ . . . .
RINGS	$ . . . .
RECEPTION (SITE FEE, FOOD, BEVERAGES, CAKE)	$ . . . .
RENTALS	$ . . . .
FLOWERS	$ . . . .
MUSIC	$ . . . .
PHOTOGRAPHY/VIDEO	$ . . . .
OTHER MEALS	$ . . . .
TRANSPORTATION/WEDDING-NIGHT	$ . . . .
HONEYMOON	$ . . . .
ESTIMATED TOTAL:	$ . . . .

Inspiration: A Simple Wedding

Over the many years that I have been involved in the world of conscious weddings, I have encountered several couples who seem to embody the essence of a good, loving marriage. Given my field of interest, I always ask about their wedding day. While some tell the story of the unacknowledged emotions that led to engagement arguments and wedding disasters, others happily reminisce about their joyful day. One woman's story has always stayed with me, as it shows that a simple, inexpensive wedding can, indeed, lead to many years of good marriage.

> *Dennis and I were married on June 29, 1969, in the Stream Picnic Area of Tilden Park in Berkeley, California. A bouquet of ladybugs floated above our grassy spot and friends arrived wearing beads around their necks, flowers in their hair, and carrying incense sticks as their offering to us. We listened to the improvised music of bongo drums, flutes, and guitars and ate artichoke soufflé and a homemade carrot cake that had two little wooden figures from Cost Plus perched on its soft top. We drank champagne from plastic cups under a wise old redwood tree with tie-dyed decorations flapping and blowing in the breezes.*
>
> *Now we wink and chuckle at the astounding hippiness of the occasion, but our lives were blessed by the sensuous grace of that day. For all these years the ladybugs have floated through our dreams; the jolly artichoke soufflé has brought nourishment and spicy adventures;*

the voluptuous and spongy carrot cake has cushioned us through all the wild rides of our lives; the beads, the flowers, the incense, and the tie-dyed decorations have kept the free-moving, freethinking light and energy always present in our consciousnesses; and the redwood tree and its shade have sheltered us and given us moments of unexpected wisdom. We've heard the drums and the music, known when we were off-key or out of step, argued, got angry, reached for each other, laughed, cried, kissed, touched the most tender spots in each other's hearts, and picked up the rhythm and the melody to step, leap, and spin again as true partners in the most elegant and complicated dance of all.

Not only does this story exemplify the beauty of an inexpensive wedding, it also expresses the importance of feeling connected to the community of family and friends that show up to celebrate your union. Whether you're inviting 10 guests or 200 guests, chapter 3 will help you make sure that you feel good about the guest list you create and the invitations you send out.

φ

The Guest List

Emotional Tasks

Becoming an Adult φ *Grieving Old Losses*

Practical Tasks

Creating the Guest List φ *Designing the Invitations*

To someone who is not engaged in the process of planning a wedding, creating a guest list could seem like a simple task. What could possibly be difficult about deciding who you want to invite to your wedding? For some engaged couples the task may indeed be that simple. But for most, drafting a guest list illuminates several core issues. What may begin as a simple putting of a pen to paper quickly devolves into a challenging task. Women are often surprised by the energy encoded in a guest list.

With this one outer task of deciding who you want to witness and celebrate your wedding, several inner tasks are required. First, planning a wedding asks that you stand firmly and clearly in the shoes of adulthood. You are no longer a child playing at love, but a full-grown woman engaged in one of the most important life transitions and preparing for one of the deepest commitments of your life. Secondly, if you struggle with the need to please, you will be challenged to confront this part of yourself in the service of maintaining the integrity of your day. By utilizing a primary tool of adulthood, the sword of discrimination, you will be saying yes to some and no to many, and thus you will have to be willing to displease and disappoint. Along these lines, as you step into this new phase of adulthood, you may find yourself letting go of aspects of your childhood. You are no longer the person you have been, and the old identity, the old way of life, needs to be acknowledged and grieved. And finally, as you think about who will attend your wedding, thoughts of the people who are absent from your life—from either death or estrangement—become painfully present. Unless this pain is consciously addressed, it will make itself known in far more unpleasant ways.

To avoid the sense of self-betrayal that women often talk about, a bride-to-be must be willing to take these steps so can she create a guest list that reflects her intention and remains true to her vision of who will witness her wedding.

Full-Fledged Adulthood

These days, it's not uncommon to enter adulthood kicking and screaming. We often stumble through our twenties delaying maturity as long as possible. In our parents' and grandparents' generations, young members of society were expected to become fully matured adults by the time they were eighteen: men were expected to begin college or enter the workforce and women were expected to begin preparing for marriage and motherhood. Our generation has the luxury (or curse?) of keeping these responsibilities at arm's length. But with an impending marriage, we can no longer avoid the fact that mature adulthood, real adult responsibility, is staring us in the face. We are no longer playing at romance and love but are about to make the biggest commitment of our lives. It is important that we take the time to recognize the fears and thoughts that accompany this aspect of the transition so that we can make the leap as gracefully as possible.

Use the following checklist to help you identify the thoughts and feelings that are connected to this aspect of your experience. Remember that these feelings apply irrespective of your age; with each successive transition in life (adolescence, graduating from high school, first job, marriage, parenthood, etc.), we move further into our identity as an adult.

CHECKLIST: EMBRACING ADULTHOOD

Check the boxes that resonate:

◯ This wedding is making me feel like I'm being pushed into adulthood.

◯ I'm not playing at love and romance anymore. There is another human being who is directly affected by my actions.

◯ I feel like I am saying good-bye to the innocence of childhood.

◯ I wonder if I'm ready to assume the responsibilities of marriage and adulthood. There was no class in school that prepared me for this endeavor.

◯ Even though I'm (twenty-five, thirty-five, forty-five, fifty-five), I'm not old enough to get married and be a wife!

◯ I've never planned a party for this many people before. It feels so *adult*.

◯ Is this the beginning of planning big dinner parties and hosting the family holiday dinners?

Once you have begun to identify the specific phrases that express your experience, you can more readily name the feeling when it arises. The more specifically you can identify the various aspects of your fear, the more easily it will pass through your body. So instead of saying, "I'm scared," you can now say, "I'm scared of the responsibility of marriage," or the statement that best applies to you.

Most people resist some aspect of becoming an adult. Of course, you always have the option of balking at the responsibility and continuing on in your identity as a single person, but this will not bode well for your marriage. Real marriage requires real commitment. It requires you to step into an archetypal and ancient union that says, "I am committed to my partner. I am accountable to my partner. We are beginning a family together." This is no small task, and it will most likely elicit some uncomfortable feelings. Take some time to write further on any of the issues you checked above. What are your fears about taking on these responsibilities? What does it mean to you?

. . . .

. . . .

. . . .

. . . .

. . . .

φ

The Need to Please

Real adulthood requires many skills. One key skill is the ability to access your true voice and act on it, even if it means disappointing or hurting others. This means that when it comes time to decide on your guest list, you take the time to allow your true desires to emerge, and then you do what it takes to act on them. When you honor your feelings and assume the hard task of discrimination, your wedding becomes an authentic expression of your commitment, not a display for others. When you stay true to yourself and your vision, your wedding is *your* wedding, not your parents' or in-laws'. The adult is able to say yes when they truly feel that way and set a boundary when the answer is no. This means that when your parents insist on inviting Mrs. Greenspot, your mother's fourth cousin whom she hasn't seen since second grade, you are able to stand for yourself, set a firm and loving boundary, and thus preserve the integrity of your day.

For many women, this is easier said than done. We have been raised in a culture that encourages us to say yes even when we mean no. We are taught to push our own values and needs aside in order to please others. We shudder at the thought of disappointing someone. We want everyone to be happy.

Take Elizabeth, for example. She called me a year after her wedding, still harboring regrets and resentments about her day. In our first session, she poured out her wedding story, going into detail not only about her resentment toward her mother and sister for "bulldozing" her opinions, but also at herself for not speaking up.

By her third session with me, Elizabeth had begun to recognize that she had been a victim not only of her mother and sister but of the people-pleasing part of herself. As she worked through the assigned exercises and wrote letters to her mother, her sister, and herself, the resentment and regret began to diminish. But she could not alter the fact that she didn't have the wedding she wanted. The best she could do was accept that her wedding illuminated a powerful aspect of her personality that needed attention. Hopefully, around her next life transition, she will be able to access her true voice and stand up to her mother, sister, and anyone else who attempts to insert their opinions into her life.

Are you aware of the people-pleasing part of yourself? Are you concerned that this part might sway your decisions regarding who to invite to your wedding? Use the following worksheet to explore this aspect of yourself and use the cheat sheet to develop a script of how to diplomatically say, "No! You cannot come to my wedding!"

PEOPLE PLEASER WORKSHEET & CHEAT SHEET

1. **WHEN IN YOUR LIFE HAVE YOU ALLOWED OTHERS' OPINIONS TO DETERMINE YOUR DECISIONS?** In other words, when have you said yes when you really meant no? Think about friendships, past relationships, teachers, culture, and family. Let the memories emerge—don't edit, just brainstorm.

. . . .

. . . .

. . . .

. . . .

2. **WHO ARE YOU TRYING TO PLEASE AS YOU THINK ABOUT DESIGNING YOUR GUEST LIST?** Why is it important to please this person, these people, your culture, or your religion?

. . . .

. . . .

. . . .

. . . .

3. **WHAT DO YOU THINK WILL HAPPEN IF YOU DISPLEASE THOSE MENTIONED ABOVE OR DON'T INVITE CERTAIN PEOPLE TO YOUR WEDDING?**

. . . .

. . . .

. . . .

. . . .

Your landlord is going to assume she's invited; your neighborhood grocer will inquire about the date with a look of longing in his eye. Your mother is going to insist on inviting Mrs. What's-her-face and Mr. So-and-so. What do you do or say when these people insinuate their desires and insert their opinions?

1. *For the acquaintance:* practice the aikido of communication.

    Neighbor: Oh, I *love* weddings! Sooo, when are you getting married?
    You: On July 20th.

    And that's it! You resist the urge to fill in the empty space or silence. You simply answer the question, then step aside and let your "friend" sit in her own awkwardness. Her feelings are not your problem.

2. *For the family member or friend:* practice the art of sensitively saying no.

    Friend: So, I heard you're getting married . . .
    You: Yes. We haven't decided yet how big a wedding we are having, but it's possible that it will be quite small.

You always have the option of ignoring the hint and changing the subject. Just because someone hints, that doesn't mean you have to respond. I recommend that you have a number of subjects on hand that you can rely on to deflect the situation. It may even be asking the person for advice about something. People love to be asked advice and will usually drop whatever they were saying and throw themselves into sharing their opinions. They feel important when asked for advice and may never even notice that the issue of them coming to the wedding wasn't addressed. If it's someone who has been married, asking them about their wedding can deflect the invitation question.

Here are four things to remember about people pleasing:

1. There is an crucial distinction between pleasing and compromising, and an important skill of adulthood is to learn to distinguish between the two. Pleasing takes away from you and is done with the intention of protecting another's feelings. It is, ultimately, a dishonest act and leads to resentment and regret. Compromising, on the other hand, is a generous action. While there is a sacrifice, it's done with the intention of arriving at a decision that works for all parties involved. It leads to positive feelings and continues the creative flow of the wedding process.

2. If you are a people pleaser, you have spent a lifetime cultivating this behavior. Filling out a worksheet and reading a few pages in a book will not solve the problem. It can, however, begin to attune your radar to this aspect of yourself. The first step in consciousness is to bring a shadow part into the light and name it. Once you name it, you have already weakened its power.

3. The issues that appear during your engagement foreshadow the issues that will appear in your marriage. It's highly likely that if you encounter your people pleaser at any point in this planning process, she will also make herself known in future interactions with your husband and other significant people in your life. Now is the time to begin to notice the power she wields over your life. The more you notice and the more you can actively work with her and challenge her, the less power she will have. Every appearance she makes is an opportunity for growth. The process begins now.

4. Of course, the guest list is not the only area where you will be challenged to set boundaries and speak your truth. Florists will impose their opinions; photographers will sideline your requests. But if you can hold your ground with your immediate community—saying yes when you mean yes and a sensitive no to those who will not attend—you will not only create an authentically inspired guest list but you will be practicing a key skill that will serve the rest of your planning process and your adult life.

Letting Go of Childhood

Becoming an adult means, by definition, letting go of childhood. While you can and should incorporate aspects of your child self into your adult identity, you cannot simultaneously be an adult and a child. Paradoxically, adulthood does not happen overnight. Since adolescence, you have been letting go of aspects of childhood and slowly incorporating aspects of adulthood. The process has been in motion for many years and will continue for many years to come. What began with the realization that your parents weren't perfect continued with moving away from home, the development of financial independence, and the awareness of the ways in which you have inherited your parents' behavior. External tasks dovetail with inner growth to create the adult that you are today.

You may feel you have long outgrown childhood. But in each new phase of growth, or transition, an opportunity arises to further the development of your adult identity. Transitions are intensified reality, a microcosm of life squeezed into a condensed time period. As such, they illuminate the aspects of your personality that need work and provide a container inside which the memories and emotions of your child self are released. What does this have to do with your guest list? The more you act from an adult, present-day perspective, the more your wedding will reflect the woman you are today. Inviting childhood memories to surface is a healthy part of any transition process. The more you allow the past to emerge, the more you will find yourself grounded in the present.

Notes on Childhood Memories

Use this page to write down the fragments and flashes from your childhood that surface. These may arrive when you are walking, eating, driving, doing yoga, or in any other meditative time. The memories live in quiet and still places and emerge when your mind slows down to meet the natural pace of your body. The flashes may be positive, painful, or neutral; they may bring a smile to your face or tears to your eyes. This is part of the process of transition. It's the process of letting go of an old phase of life so that you can open the internal space for the new phase to be born. Welcome the memories. Invite them to dance through your body and onto this page.

Feeling Your Old Losses

Whether your memories were delightful or painful, they probably included some people who are no longer in your life. Transitions, while offering opportunities for growth, also activate grief from old losses. By definition, a transition is a loss and a gain, a letting go and a moving forward, an ending and a new beginning. During this process of change, our psyche remembers other times in our lives when we experienced loss. Again, when we have the courage to meet this process consciously, we have the opportunity to grieve losses that we either didn't know we were supposed to grieve or didn't have the support or resources to deal with at the time. Grief, like all emotions, has a unique life span. When we interfere with, bypass, or amputate the grieving process in any way, we are left with the remnants of incomplete grief in our bodies. Now you have an opportunity to finish these processes.

Check the losses in your life that feel incomplete:

○ End of significant relationships: friendships, romantic loves, family ties (many women find themselves having dreams about ex-boyfriends)

○ Estranged relationships

○ Divorce: parents, siblings, friends (it is very common for an upcoming marriage to bring up grief from divorces you have witnessed)

○ Death of a loved one

○ Illness that created a permanent change in your body

○ Abortion

○ Giving a child up for adoption

○ Your own adoption

○ Loss of home through fire or moving

○ Other: . . . .

If you invite it in and make the space to deal with it (as opposed to blocking it through incessant planning), grief around these areas of loss may surface throughout your engagement and even into your first months of marriage. Remember that grieving is counterintuitive to what we think we should be feeling during this time. It takes courage to admit that grief has invited itself to your engagement, but if you remind yourself that in the context of a rite of passage, a necessary loss makes room for the gain, then it makes sense. Transitions provide opportunities for tremendous healing. During this intensified slice of life, the grief can either become more deeply entrenched through denial or it can move up and out of your body through consciously addressing and allowing for the pain.

As with the memories from childhood, I suggest that you actively invite the grief into your life and write down the thoughts and feelings that surface.

(Note: A thorough exploration of grief extends beyond the scope of this book. If you find yourself flooded with emotions from the past, I encourage you to seek support. There are excellent resources—from books to support groups—for working with grief.

Grief should not be endured alone, and extensive grief requires extensive support.)

As with every other area of the planning, if the grief is not consciously acknowledged, it can create arguments with others or stagnation within you. These losses—especially when they are centered around family or friends—often play out around the guest list. Take Rachel, for example. She began our work together feeling highly anxious about her guest list due to the strained relationship she had had with her father for several years. Every time she sat down to draft a guest list, she froze. Should she have a very small wedding with only her intimate friends, in which case she wouldn't have to deal with her father, or a larger event that would include her wider community—and her father?

She knew that the decision had implications beyond the guest list and her wedding. With her impending marriage catapulting her into the next phase of adulthood where motherhood was likely to follow, she couldn't conceive of depriving her children of their only surviving grandfather (her fiancé's father had passed away). Her life suddenly seemed shorter and time more precious. After several sessions, it became clear that she had two choices: she could accept her grief around the estranged relationship and choose not to invite him to her wedding, or she could begin the difficult adult task of accepting her father as he is. She chose the latter. Her wedding provided the opportunity to step further into adulthood by grieving the loss of her childhood expectations, accepting his imperfections, and beginning to mend their relationship.

This worksheet will help you process the grief and loss in your life. Take time with these questions and answers, as they may activate long-buried feelings that you thought had disappeared. Remember that the more you acknowledge the losses now, the more prepared you'll be to feel joy on your wedding day.

WORKSHEET: DEALING WITH LOSS

1. **WHICH MEMBERS OF YOUR POTENTIAL GUEST LIST ELICIT SADNESS WHEN YOU THINK ABOUT THEM** (friends, stepmother, future mother-in-law, sisters, future sister-in-law, mother, father, other family member)?

. . . .

. . . .

. . . .

2. **WHAT EVENTS LED TO THE CONFLICT OR RUPTURE IN THE RELATIONSHIP?**

. . . .

. . . .

. . . .

. . . .

3. **SOMETIMES SIMPLY ACKNOWLEDGING THE GRIEF AND BRINGING IT OUT OF THE SHADOWS IS ENOUGH TO CREATE SUFFICIENT ACCEPTANCE AROUND THIS PERSON TO ALLOW YOU TO INVITE THEM TO YOUR WEDDING.** In other cases, you may need to approach the grief or the person more actively. What steps will you take to work through the distance and accept the relationship as it is today? Suggestions: write a letter that you will never send; write a letter that you will send; talk to a close friend, your fiancé, or a counselor about the situation; talk to the person directly about your feelings.

. . . .

. . . .

. . . .

. . . .

. . . .

. . . .

Do you feel ready to draft your guest list? Recall your intention and use the pages in the back to create your first draft. Keep in mind that it takes most couples several attempts, including many cross outs and re-inclusions, to arrive at the final list.

φ

Designing Your Invitations

While you won't mail your invitations until six to eight weeks prior to your wedding, it's natural that with the guest list in motion you will start to think about how you wish to announce your special day. Creating your invitations is a three-step process: the wording, the artistic presentation, and the inserts.

Step One: The Wording

The following are samples of simple wording, depending on who is hosting the wedding.

Bride's Parents Host

> Mr. and Mrs. Robert Allister
> request the honor of your presence
> to witness and celebrate
> the marriage of their daughter
> Deborah Allister
> to
> William Randall
>
> Sunday, the second of June
> Two thousand and three
> At 5 o'clock in the evening
> Casa del Mar Hotel
> Santa Monica, California
>
> Reception immediately following

Bride's Parents Host: Single Parent or One Parent Is Deceased

Mrs. Cynthia Dupree and, in spirit, Tom Dupree
invite those closest to their hearts
to join them in celebrating the
marriage of their daughter
Helen Dupree
to
Jonathan Williams

Saturday, the twenty-first of June
at twelve o'clock
First Baptist Church
Baltimore, Maryland

Bride and Groom Host

We request the
honor of your presence
to witness and celebrate the
sacred marriage ceremony of
Rachel Miller and Brian Weiss
on
Sunday, September 20th, 2003
at 5:30 p.m.
under
The Great Oak Tree
at Sequoia Public Park
Three Rivers, California

Reception immediately following

Use the following worksheet to create a draft of the wording of your invitation. If your parents are hosting your wedding, remember to ask them if they have any preferences or requests.

Step Two: The Artistry and Design

Your invitation is the first tangible piece of your wedding that your loved ones will see. As such, you will want it to reflect the essence of the two of you and the style of your wedding. It is perfectly acceptable to choose a basic, formal wedding invitation that is simple and elegant, but if you want to include something unique, consider adding a visual motif or a symbol that you plan to incorporate into your wedding. For example, Rachel and Brian, the couple in the third wording sample, chose to include a tree motif in their invitations since they would be married under a tree. They found several ways of carrying this symbol into other aspects of their wedding, like using the same tree on the programs and on their *ketubah* (Jewish marriage contract). Other couples have used symbols such as two hands, two interlacing rings, or a favorite spiritual poem. Once you decide on the wording and a simple motif, the next step is to design it. You have several options:

- *Create it yourselves.* If one of you is artistically inclined—or computer literate—you may choose to design the invitations yourselves. This option not only saves money

but allows you the freedom to design it according to your unique vision. It also assures that no one will have a similar invitation, and allows the two of you to imbue the cards with your essence.

- *Go to a stationery store.* Any fine stationery store will be able to assist you in wording and designing your invitation. They have extensive notebooks that give samples to choose from. Look in your yellow pages to find one close to you. An upscale or independent stationery store will usually have creative staff on hand who can help you design a unique invitation.

- *Ask a friend.* Perhaps one of your friends has an artistic skill or is gifted on a computer graphics program. Go ahead and ask—helping you design and execute your invitations makes a wonderful wedding gift!

Use the following space to jot down your preliminary design ideas including any colors, themes, paper styles, or small poems that come to mind.

WORKSHEET: YOUR INVITATION

. . . .

. . . .

. . . .

. . . .

. . . .

. . . .

. . . .

Step Three: The Inserts

Nested in the invitation are several smaller components. These may include the following:

- *RSVP card and envelope.* A small card that indicates if your guest(s) will or will not attend. If you are offering several menu options, you may choose to include these options on the back and ask your guest(s) to select one. A self-addressed, stamped envelope completes this insert.

- *Reception card.* If your ceremony and reception are at different sites, enclose a small card which provides the name and address of the reception location. Consider including directions or a map on the back.

With a basic guest list and a general idea of your invitations in place, you can now focus your energy on one of the key elements of your wedding: the dress. Keep your fantasy mind in check and your authentic vision at the forefront as you make your foray into the bridal-gown world and prepare to purchase one of the primary symbols of your day.

CHAPTER 4

The Wedding Dress

Emotional Task
Letting Go of Singlehood

Practical Tasks
Asking for Help φ *Finding Your Dress*

The White Dress

When you envisioned your wedding as a little girl, it was probably the dress that glowed white and luminous in the forefront of the fantasy. When we envision our wedding now, it's the dress that often assumes a prominent position. The dress leads the processional of objects that comprise the wedding day, with flowers, photographs, and food stepping into line behind its stunning lead. The dress, like any object into which we pour vast amounts of time, money, and energy, is like an inanimate guest on your list. It's important that its presence at your wedding makes sense.

Many women today reveal that they felt almost ashamed of succumbing to the collective model and wanting to wear a traditional gown. They also reveal an inner conflict about the connotation of the color white as a symbol of virginity, given that most women are no longer virgins when they marry. As Kelsey states:

> *I've always been a feminist and balked at the thought of wearing a big, white wedding dress. But when I walked into the store and tried on my long-sleeved lace and silk gown, it just felt right. It was hard to reconcile the tradition with my feminism. How does this dress make sense in the context and meaning of my life?*

We cannot deny that the dress remains a primary symbol of the wedding, and the urge to wear the white gown is often insistent. In order to avoid feeling hypocritical, we must bring our understanding up to date.

For most of history, the wedding dress symbolized the end of a woman's life as an individual and the beginning of her role as a dependent wife. Today the dress no longer symbolizes the death of individuality, but of singlehood. When a woman crosses over the threshold into marriage, she's leaving behind her attachments to an identity that no longer fits. Wearing the white dress on her last day of being single is a profound and archetypal way of acknowledging and saying good-bye to this aspect of her life.

If we broaden the terms, we can still speak of the dress using the words "innocence," "maidenhood," and "virginity." As we leave behind the innocence of childhood, the white dress comes to represent the most innocent part of ourselves. As we let go of the symbolic maiden, she who is carefree and responsible to no one, the dress comes to represent the most unattached aspects of singlehood. And as we move into the maturity of full partnership, we are stepping into the full blossom and power of our womanhood. Far from being a misogynistic act, marriage today requires that we maximize our intelligence and strength as a woman. If we call on Marianne Williamson's definition of virgin, "a woman unto herself," then instead of becoming devirginized on our wedding day, we become revirginized (1993, p. 11)!

Marriage today is a spiritual journey toward wholeness. There is a sacrifice involved, but it's not the sacrifice of one's strength as a separate woman. In fact, a good marriage is dependent upon each partner's ability to bring a solid self into the partnership and to walk the wavering tightrope of togetherness and separateness. So if the surrendering is not of individuality, then what is it? It is a sacrifice of singlehood, and as you step more fully into your power as a woman during this next phase, you must relinquish the identity that has carried you to this moment in your life. The dress is the symbol of this identity.

φ

Letting Go of Singlehood

As the symbol of singlehood, the dress carries a high emotional charge, and while it is a main figure of the wedding, it's important to recognize the emotional undercurrents so that you can keep its value in perspective. Unless the grief about letting go of singlehood and the fears about marriage are brought to consciousness, the dress can easily become the magnet onto which the iron shards of difficult emotions are attracted. Of course, other aspects of planning also become ways to distract, but the dress, with its profound symbolism, tends to be a focal point of distraction. In fact, when my clients are running off course with obsessions about any planning detail, I bring them back to reality with the phrase, "It's not about the dress!" In other words, the physical objects are carrying the emotional charge, and as soon as the emotions are processed, sanity is restored and the planning can continue.

Letting go of attachments to the identity and lifestyle of being single is a very common area where women feel the fear and grief of this transition. Regardless of your age, how long you've been with your partner, or whether or not you've lived together, your identity is still "single." You check the "single" box at the doctor's office. You file as single on your income taxes. You may be more committed to your partner than to anything else in your life, but until you have taken your vows and exchanged your rings, you are still single. The wedding marks the transition from singlehood to wifehood. For the transition to be thorough, the thoughts and emotions connected to the end of an identity need recognition and attention. Otherwise you will enter marriage with your single identity still dangling behind you, impairing your ability to fully embrace your husband and incorporate your new level of commitment.

The following statements have come directly from my clients. Check the issues that resonate for you to help you specifically identify and articulate your feelings about letting go of this phase of your life.

CHECKLIST: LETTING GO OF SINGLEHOOD

- ○ I feel envious of young women in their early twenties. They seem so free and single.
- ○ I somehow equate marriage with a big ass and saggy boobs—I'm not ready for that!
- ○ I'm scared about not being able to go out to bars and flirt with men.
- ○ I still want to be attractive to men.
- ○ I wish I had the chance to experience some things again (college, dating, clubbing, traveling).
- ○ I'll miss going to clubs and flirting.
- ○ I'm good at being single. It's comfortable and familiar.
- ○ I don't want to give up my freedom.
- ○ It seems like everything exciting is equated with being single.
- ○ I long to be twenty-one again.
- ○ I'm scared I won't be able to take trips with my girlfriends.
- ○ I have to change the way I relate to half the people in the world—men!
- ○ My life is over.
- ○ I'm afraid I will lose my sexual fire.
- ○ You mean I can never have sex with anyone else . . . ever again?!
- ○ I feel like I'm losing my youth.
- ○ I can feel my childhood slipping away.
- ○ I have mixed feelings about taking on my husband's last name—it's an honor, but I feel the loss of the name I've had for . . . . . . years.
- ○ I am losing my independence.
- ○ When we move in together, will I ever have space and time to myself?
- ○ Is . . . . . . going to be the last person I ever sleep with?

○ I like my life now. I love living [alone, with my best friend, with my sister]. Why does this have to change?

○ I will never be able to travel alone.

○ Other: . . . .

Deciding What's True

It's important to distinguish between the true beliefs about giving up singlehood and the false beliefs. For example, it is true that as a married woman you will most likely be changing the way you relate to men. But is it really true that your life will be over and that you'll never have any fun again? No! And is it true that you will never be able to go away for the weekend with your girlfriends? Not unless you and your future husband make that agreement. In other words, a lot of the fears that women feel about letting go of singlehood are not based in reality, but they indicate a need to recognize that there is a change happening and to allow yourself to grieve this change.

When grieving the loss or change of an identity, the mind wants to grab onto tangible experiences because it's confusing to grieve something as amorphous as an identity. With most losses in life we can point to the thing that we are leaving or losing—a house, a city, a job, a person—but with a loss of identity, there is nothing to point to. The truth is that the loss is less about anything tangible, like the loss of your last name or your own apartment, and more about the general sense that you are leaving one life stage and moving into a new stage of life. When women say, "I cried all weekend—it was an unnamed grief," they are referring to this most difficult-to-name of losses. The most important step, after distinguishing the true and false beliefs and putting some of the unnecessary fears to rest, is to let the feelings in. You don't have to understand them. You only have to trust that they are a very important part of your transition, and the more you let yourself feel them, the better off you'll be.

Use the following worksheet to help you distinguish the false beliefs from the truth.

WORKSHEET: DISTILLING FALSE BELIEFS

1. WHICH OF THE BOXES THAT YOU CHECKED ARE FALSE BELIEFS?

. . . .

. . . .

. . . .

2. WHERE DO YOU THINK THESE FALSE BELIEFS CAME FROM?

. . . .

. . . .

. . . .

3. HOW CAN YOU FIND OUT THE TRUTH AROUND THESE FALSE BELIEFS? (Talk to your fiancé and share your fears; talk to other married women; get in touch with your truth about partnership as opposed to the messages and behaviors that have been modeled for you.)

. . . .

. . . .

. . . .

Once you have distilled the false beliefs, you are left with your true grief about saying goodbye to this identity. The next step is to concretize the feelings around this ending. One exercise that women have found effective is to create a collage of the images that represent your single life. Use personal photographs, magazine cutouts, old letters, drawings, and any other artifacts that symbolize singlehood to create a visual representation of the identity you are leaving. Another powerful way to honor the ending is to write a goodbye letter to your single self. Include what you have loved about being single, your fears about this phase of life ending, the important people who have helped shape your singlehood, and any other thoughts and emotions that will help you let go of attachments to this identity. Use the following page to write the letter.

Good-Bye Letter to Your Single Self

· ·

· ·

· ·

· ·

· ·

· ·

· ·

· ·

· ·

· ·

· ·

· ·

· ·

· ·

· ·

· ·

· φ

Letting Go of Old Loves

Memories, thoughts, and feelings about ex-boyfriends and lovers are inextricably linked to the singlehood identity. For some of us, the single past means a past with men: men we loved, men we loathed, men who adored us, men who enchanted us, men who broke our hearts, men we flirted with, men we left, men who "got away." Because our culture maintains that once you're engaged you must have eyes and thoughts only for your intended, to admit that exes pop into your mind may feel taboo. As Laura said, "I'm getting married. I've made my choice. I'm not allowed to think about those other men, those past relationships." But, just as stifling the grief around losses only fans the flames, so attempting to stifle feelings about exes magnifies their intensity.

Use the following worksheet to help sort through your thoughts and feelings about past loves. I also encourage you to record any dreams about ex-partners in your journal as they arise. Try not to feel embarrassed or ashamed about any of these memories. They are a natural part of your transition and do not mean that you're marrying the wrong man.

WORKSHEET: LETTING GO OF THE PAST

1. WHICH PAST PARTNERS HAVE BEEN FLOATING INTO YOUR CONSCIOUSNESS LATELY?

. . . .

. . . .

. . . .

. . . .

2. WHAT THOUGHTS AND MEMORIES ARE CONNECTED TO THESE PARTNERS?

. . . .

. . . .

. . . .

. . . .

3. HOW DO THESE THOUGHTS AND MEMORIES MAKE YOU FEEL?

. . . .

. . . .

. . . .

. . . .

4. DO YOU NEED TO TAKE ANY ACTIONS TO BRING CLOSURE TO THESE PAST RELA-
TIONSHIPS (make a phone call, write a letter that you may not send)?

. . . .

. . . .

. . . .

. . . .

Meaningful Bridal Shower Rituals

As you separate from your singlehood identity you may find yourself drawn to spend more time with your girlfriends. A wise part of you recognizes that your friends—married or not—represent a phase of life that you are leaving, and you feel guided to bask in their presence a little longer. While the intimacy in your friendships will continue to deepen after you marry, there is often a longing to be with your friends as your wedding nears. Meaningful ritual is a way to honor that you're leaving the life of girlhood as well as providing the container inside which your women friends can facilitate the transition. As I wrote in my first book, *The Conscious Bride* (2000, p. 42):

> It is important to acknowledge the transition away from the carefree nature of adolescence and singlehood. Our bridal showers and bachelorette parties attempt to celebrate one last time the woman's singlehood, but more often than not they fail to create a safe space for the bride to explore her emotional and psychological state. The traditional bridal shower where the woman receives lingerie and cookware does little to assist the bride with her transition. True to many aspects of

the wedding, it focuses on the external feminine needs to the exclusion of the inner world.

Women often ask about ways to create meaningful ceremonies at their bridal showers. If you and/or your friends are creating your shower and are at a loss for meaningful ritual ideas, refer them to www.consciousweddings.com.

φ

Asking for Help

Most people know that the bridesmaids, sisters, and mother usually plan the wedding shower. But what else are your key players traditionally responsible for? As this is an event that involves many people, some of whom have probably never planned a wedding before, it's important to clearly communicate to your loved ones how you would like them to help. Whether you are having a formal or informal wedding, you will need assistance with the planning tasks that arise. This is a new adventure for all of you, so if you ask your best friend to be your maid of honor, you will both want to know what this entails practically. Also, let your fiancé know what his friends and family typically assist with. Use the following lists as general suggestions when it comes to delegating tasks and assigning roles.

Bride's Attendants' Tasks (friends, sisters, mother)

- ○ Help the bride with prewedding tasks, including shopping for her gown, addressing invitations, and making wedding favors

- ○ Plan a bridal shower

- ○ Create a wedding-day emergency kit

- ○ Help organize bridesmaids on the wedding day

- ○ Help the bride get ready on the wedding day

- ○ Adjust the bride's train at the altar

- ○ Hold the bride's bouquet during vows

- ○ Sign the marriage license as witness

- ○ Decorate the wedding-night suite

- ○ Other: . . . .

Groom's Attendants' Tasks (friends, brothers, father)

○ Help the groom shop for wedding-day clothes

○ Offer assistance with planning details

○ Host a bachelor party

○ Organize groomsmen on the wedding day

○ Help the groom dress on the wedding day

○ Distribute ceremony programs

○ Seat the guests

○ Sign the marriage license as witness

○ Pay the officiant after the ceremony

○ Make the first toast to the couple

○ Announce key events (dancing, toasts, cake cutting)

○ Help direct vendors

○ Drive the couple to the wedding-night destination or airport

○ Decorate the getaway car

○ Other: . . . .

φ

Now You're Ready: Finding Your Dress

Now that you have extracted the emotional components from the tangible task, you are ready to find your dress. Finding your dress is a balancing act between honoring the natural desire to want to look beautiful on your wedding day and reminding yourself that it's just a dress! The truth is that if you are in alignment with your intention, true to your vision, and addressing your uncomfortable emotions, you will radiate beauty and joy. It's your wedding, you are consecrating and celebrating your love and commitment, and it's a day that acknowledges the most divine aspect in you and your beloved. By contrast, if you plough through the planning, allow Bridezilla to run the show, and forget all about the man you're marrying, no dress in the world is going to make you look beautiful. I have seen the most physically attractive women wearing gorgeous gowns who looked like ghosts on their wedding day. But those who shine really shine, and the dress is a lovely reflection of their inner peace and joy.

There are basically five options for purchasing your dress.

1. *New:* This is a dress that you find at a bridal salon, an outlet, or online. These dresses are usually formal and more expensive. The best way to find salons is to check your local phone book, search online, or ask friends who have married in your area.

2. *Custom-made:* If you want a one-of-a-kind dress and you have a creative flair, you may decide to design your gown with a dressmaker. If you are seeking a more casual dress, a friend or relative may make it. If you are looking for a traditional gown, I would suggest finding a reputable dressmaker in your area who specializes in wedding gowns.

3. *Partially custom-made:* If you want an original gown but don't have a clear vision of exactly what you want, consider working with a dressmaker who carries several original designs. Not only will you save money by avoiding the retail store markup, but you will work with a caring professional who will create a gown to fit you from the start. Search online for dressmakers who specialize in wedding gowns, some of whom can work with you even if you don't live in their city. Check out www.sanni.com for one such artist, Sanni Diesner, who has received national acclaim for her gorgeous gowns and has worked with women from around the country to help them create the dress of their dreams.

4. *Secondhand gowns:* Most people only wear their dress once and then either stick it in their closet for the next sixty years or sell it on consignment to a secondhand store. There are thousands of gorgeous gowns out there that you can buy for a fraction of what they originally cost. There are also consignment sites online and a significant selection on eBay. Some women feel attached to the idea of wearing something fresh and pure on their wedding day. I do understand this impulse, but if it comes to saving a thousand

---

WAYS TO SAVE

Hand-me-downs: Wear the gown that your mother, grandmother, sister, or friend wore.

Rent a gown: Check your yellow pages for stores that specialize in renting gorgeous gowns for a reasonable price.

Jilted dresses: Call bridal salons in your area to see if they have gowns that have not been picked up. You may be able to save up to 50 percent since the bride most likely has already paid for half the dress with a deposit.

Bridesmaid in white: Wedding boutiques jack up the prices of a gown simply because it's placed in the bride's section. You might find a beautiful, simple white gown in the bridesmaid section for a fraction of the price.

Buy your size: Order the dress that is closest to your largest measurement so that you can keep alterations to a minimum. This means that if you are between an eight and a ten, buy the ten (your ego may momentarily suffer, but your pocketbook will thank you).

dollars, a good dry cleaning and simple spiritual cleansing will make a once-worn gown feel like new!

5. *Reusable:* One of the main regrets for brides is that they will never wear their gown again. With the dress as the symbol of singlehood, it makes sense that it will only be worn once. However, for second-time brides and women who don't relate to this symbolism, a practical option is to buy a beautiful white dress at a non bridal store that you can wear again. For a beach or backyard summer wedding, a simple, elegant, and beautiful white dress is a sane and practical option.

As far as style, in my opinion there are no rules of etiquette. Some may say that the style is determined by the location of your wedding—for instance, a beach wedding calls for a simple dress—but if you feel beautiful and it makes sense to you, get it. My only suggestion is to stay internally aligned as opposed to externally motivated. In other words, if you select your dress based on the opinions of your mother, sister, religion, or fiancé, you will probably have regrets. Yes, take them with you to the bridal salons. Respect their opinions. But your ultimate gauge is your inner guide saying yes or no.

If you are planning a formal wedding I suggest that you begin your search early to avoid feeling pressured or stressed. Ideally, searching for your gown should be a fun experience, as if you are on a quest to find the one that speaks directly to you. This may take some time, so as soon as you decide on your location and date, start thinking about your dress. This will provide an opportunity to try on several gowns as well as stake out the sales if you have your eye on a particularly overpriced store. Still, if the first dress you try on sings out "yes!" that's probably the one for you. As with every other practical task, there are no rules of right and wrong. This is a matter of trusting your body, listening to your psyche, and remembering that there is no such thing as perfect. There is only what works for you.

φ

Finding Your Dress: Use Your Intuition

As you begin your journey to find your dress, certain words or flashes of phrases may pop into your mind that reflect the essence of the dress you envision yourself wearing. Pay attention to these words: they are signals from your unconscious, or the most creative and authentic part of yourself, that are signposts to point you in the right direction. Most likely these are words that speak to the essence of who you are, the highest and most sacred part that you intend to present to your partner on your wedding day.

CHECKLIST: RESONANT WORDS

Check any of the following words and phrases that resonate when you think about your dress:

○ elegant	○ antique	○ silk	○ woman
○ simple	○ flowers	○ lace	○ my whole self
○ luminous	○ vines	○ pearls	○ my essential nature
○ special	○ white	○ sequins	○ the purest part of myself
○ flowing	○ cream	○ princess	
○ renaissance	○ gold	○ queen	○ love

What other words and phrases come to mind when you think about your dress?

. . . .

. . . .

If you are visually oriented, you may have a mental picture of the dress that you would like to find. Use the following space to sketch the images that you see in your mind's eye.

You might keep in mind that women often share that the dress they envisioned for themselves was not the dress that looked best on them. As Kirsten said, "What I had in mind was short sleeves, on the shoulder, and what I walked out with was long sleeves, off the shoulder." The point here is to be flexible and keep an open mind when you make the leap from the page to reality. The goal is to feel beautiful, free, and comfortable in your dress, which may or may not mean you relinquish the vision you've carried since you were ten years old.

As you begin to search for your dress, you can make photocopies of the wedding dress contact sheet in the back and use it to take notes. You can find stores through your local phone book, asking friends, searching the Internet, and looking at ads in national and local wedding magazines and newspapers. When you find your gown, shoes, and accessories, use the final contact sheet in the back section to fill in your important information.

DRESSED FROM HEAD TO TOE:
YOUR HEADPIECE AND SHOES

In today's wedding culture, you have as many options for headpieces and shoes as you do for gowns. The following headpiece options accompany the veil as alternative possibilities:

- Wreaths
- Headbands
- Combs
- Loose flowers
- Tiaras
- Barrettes
- Hair gems

Your headpiece choice is determined by your dress style and your particular preferences. If you have always dreamed of wearing a tiara, follow that impulse. This is also a great area to borrow from family members or friends who have recently married. Someone may have worn just the beautiful floral hair clip that you're looking for.

Open-toed or closed? Simple or floral? High-heeled or ballet slippers? Whatever you choose for shoes, make sure that they are comfortable. You will be standing, dancing, and walking for most of your day, so find shoes that combine comfort with style and break them in during the weeks before your wedding. Consider buying shoes that you can dye another color so that you can wear them again.

Sometimes women encounter internal stumbling blocks when they are searching for their dress. They feel impeded by either parts of themselves or external voices from finding the dress that speaks to their essential nature. The following are some common psychological impediments. Check those that apply.

○ I don't feel worthy to wear such an expensive, gorgeous gown.

○ I'm scared of feeling so vulnerable and beautiful on my wedding day.

○ I'm scared of being the center of attention.

○ I don't feel entitled to spend so much money.

○ I'm scared about what my family will think. I can hear their voices in my head: "You spent how much on a dress you will only wear once?"

○ Other: . . . .

If you checked any of the above phrases, use it as a first line to expand on that feeling:

. . . .

. . . .

. . . .

. . . .

. . . .

. . . .

. . . .

. . . .

While I am typically against spending thousands and thousands of dollars on a wedding dress, I also encourage you to buy the dress that you absolutely love. For some women, they may find that dress for $300 at a used clothing store that specializes in wedding gowns. For others, particularly if they have a specific vision, they may need to have a dress made. It's important to stay within your budget, but be aware that when you are making your budget you may have old family voices dictating your final amounts. As you become aware of those unhealthy voices, you may decide to revise your budget so that it reflects your truth.

You deserve to shine like a queen on your wedding day. You deserve to meet your beloved at the altar with your whole self, adorned in a gown that reflects the highest part of your being and the deepest beauty in your nature. When we fall in love, we glow from the meeting of two essences. On the wedding day, these essences shine through again. It is a sacred day. It is a special day. It is when the goddesslike nature of you meets the godlike nature of him and you take vows that you intend to keep for your lifetime. It is important that you are dressed for the occasion.

φ

CHAPTER 5

The Ceremony

Emotional Task

Addressing Fears and Exploring Expectations about Marriage and Commitment φ Considering What It Means to Be a Wife

Practical Tasks

Choosing Your Officiant φ Creating the Ceremony φ Writing Your Vows

Symbols of the Ceremony

A spiritual consecration—a union that is "beautiful and enduring"—occurs through rituals and symbols. Each element of the ceremony has a tradition of symbolism, and understanding its significance can help you find meaning in the day. All too often in our culture, we blindly follow tradition, acting more on superstition or a sense of "that's the way it's done" than a real sense of meaningful connection. You know that you're supposed to wear "something old, something new, something borrowed, something blue," but did you know that this phrase comes from an Italian saying intended to bring good luck to the bride and increase the chances of a male heir? Every culture around the world has symbols, traditions, and rituals that are designed to acknowledge the separation from the old life, sanctify the union, welcome in good and ward off evil, and shower the couple with fertility. Whether you are following the template of your religious institution or crafting your own ceremony, the more you understand the symbols that are used, the more connected to your day you will feel.

An object's meaning is not fixed in time; rather, what determines an object's meaning is the meaning we ascribe to it. In this way, the meaning can change over time and depending on who interprets the object. As we saw in the last chapter, the white wedding gown as a symbol of virginity no longer makes sense for most women. When we widen our lens and redefine our vocabulary, the objects retain their power while our interpretation evolves. In fact, as the interpersonal and intrapersonal relations between men and women have evolved, so does our understanding of marriage and our understanding of the rituals and symbols that comprise the event that commences marriage. Just as the engagement is much more than a time to plan a wedding, so the icons that comprise the wedding day—the flowers, the dress, the rings—also hold more significance than we initially ascribe to them. Viewed on the backdrop of rites of passage, each element of the wedding assumes a radically different meaning from how it is commonly seen. The following interpretations are not set in stone but are offered as guideposts to help you find meaning in the elements of your day.

Bridesmaids and Groomsmen

Your attendants are pillars of support and symbols of the singlehood identity and way of life. Whether the members of the wedding party are single or married, this constellation of loved ones often carry the grief of saying good-bye to the fold of singlehood. In Lithuania, the bridesmaids enact a "wailing ritual" before the ceremony, in which they gather around the bride and dramatically wail to express and signify their grief around this separation and loss.

Bouquet

The bouquet is another symbol of singlehood. Like the dress, the flowers in the bouquet represent different aspects of a woman's essence, both the aspects that she's giving away and the aspects she will hold close to her heart during her marriage. The flowers stand for her beauty, her truth, her purity, and her essence as a woman. Each flower carries its own meaning. A rose, for example, symbolizes happy love; ivy symbolizes wedded love; and a calla lily represents both majestic beauty and death. (Some brides consciously choose to incorporate the calla lily into their bouquet as a way to acknowledge the aspect of themselves that is dying.) When the bride tosses her bouquet, she is ritually letting go of her identity as a single person in the world.

Veil

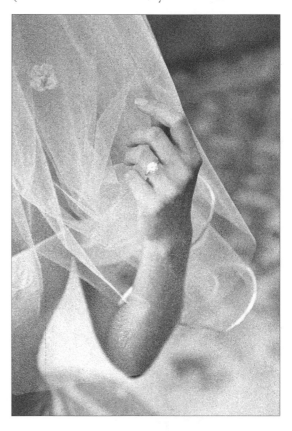

The veil can be seen as an amulet of protection. In the bride's vulnerable state, when she stands at the altar in the midst of a transformation, the veil is an object that offers a thin shield between her and the rest of the world. To be veiled provides the bride with an opportunity to turn her eyes inward and reflect on what she says. The veil is also a symbol that recognizes the holiness of this moment. Many people veil themselves during worship or prayer as a means of providing a separation between the world of spirit and the earthly realm. Some women shun the veil because they feel it is laced with connotations of female submission. But like the wedding dress, the veil can be interpreted anew as our understanding of the wedding and marriage evolves. If we choose to view it as such, it can be used as a gift during a profound moment of spiritual transformation.

Headdress, Hairstyle, and Makeup

These are all secular symbols of protection, stature, and femininity. In lieu of a veil, many women are currently choosing to wear an alternate headdress. What's interesting about this shift in practice is that it is in alignment with the rituals of nearly every other culture around the world. Cross-culturally, the headpiece and hairstyle carry great significance for the bride, and often the women of her community will spend hours constructing and setting the details of her headdress and hair. The following example is from a beautiful book by Tiziana and Gianni Baldizzone (2001), called *Wedding Ceremonies*.

For the Miaos of China the headdress is the central piece of a bride's wedding attire. The woman wears an elaborate silver and floral piece made by a highly skilled craftsman. Silver is a sign of wealth, as well as a protection against "the evil eye." Animal figures and designs are worked into the silver, rendering each element of this extraordinary piece a symbol for her union. The young woman proudly carries the symbols of strength, abundance, fertility, and the myths and legends of her people atop her head and into her new marriage.

Chuppah (Bridal Canopy)

The chuppah is a symbol of the couple's first home. Like the mikvah, the chuppah is a Jewish symbol that has been adopted by many non-Jews because of its beautiful and accessible meaning. Basically, it's a piece of cloth supported by four posts that the couple stands under during the ceremony. The cloth can be a prayer shawl, a special blanket, a quilt, or a family heirloom like a tablecloth. Many couples design and create their own

chuppah from materials and paints that are meaningful to them. It may be self-supporting or may be held by attendants who signify the couple's support system. The chuppah is open on all sides to show that the couple's home will be open to all.

Flowered Arch

A variation on the huppa with no religious connotations, the flowered arch represents the threshold to the couple's home. An arch, or threshold, is a universal symbol that represents leaving one way of life and moving into a new phase. In Joseph Campbell's words, the threshold symbolizes "a mystery of transfiguration—a rite, or moment, or spiritual passage, which, when complete, amounts to a dying and a birth" (1949, p. 51). The couple stands in front of the arch during the ceremony, then passes beneath it to ritually enact the transition from singlehood into marriage.

Witness

Your witness stands as a reminder that we are not alone, that a wedding takes place within the context of a community. Every wedding, no matter the size, the setting, or the style, requires at least one witness. It is a privilege and an honor to stand as witness to the great events of life. Witnesses are the mirrors that reflect the beauty and truth of the moment. With open hearts, they absorb the magnitude of the ceremony and remind the newlyweds that marriage does not exist within a vacuum. One witness can fulfill this role, but a congregation of many witnesses weaves a marriage basket that contains the bride and groom throughout the day and into their marriage. To witness is not merely to watch, but to open the pores of body and soul and hold the energy of this event forever in your heart.

Fire: Candles and Torches

Fire is a symbol of commencing a sacred ceremony and of protection. Lighting candles or torches (if you are outdoors) is a way to signal that the ceremony has begun. Fire imbues a sacred element and is often accompanied by a call to the spiritual realm to witness the ceremony and protect the newlyweds. Fire also has cleansing properties and is used to clear the space of "evil" or negativity.

Cup

This is a symbol of union. Sharing from a single cup and drinking together is the first action toward union that the bride and groom take. Eating and drinking together are worldwide rituals of communion. The unity begins with the couple during the ceremony and continues by including the community during the reception feast.

Vows

Your vows are the sacred words spoken to consecrate a commitment. A vow is a spiritual promise. When someone speaks vows during a sacred ceremony—whether it's a monk upon entering a monastery or the bride and groom at their wedding—they are publicly acknowledging that they will hold to these words and are calling upon the witnesses and Spirit to help them keep their promises. The vows are the climax of the ceremony as they express the deepest intentions of the bride and groom to remain committed to their principles and to honor the highest aspects of their partner. Vows are an expression of love in the deepest sense of the word, a recognition that marriage is a crucible that calls us to access our resources and seek support in times of need so that we may grow and remain true to ourselves and each other.

Rings

Rings are the symbol of the marriage vows. The roundness of the ring symbolizes the eternal nature of the love; the precious metal that is poured into the mold symbolizes the strength of the commitment. An excerpt from *Into the Garden: A Wedding Anthology*, edited by Robert Hass and Stephen Mitchell (1974, p. 142), says it well:

> Rings are an ancient symbol, blessed and simple. Round like the sun, like the eye, like arms that embrace. Circles, for love that is given comes back round again and again. Therefore, may these symbols remind you that your love, like the sun, illumines; that your love, like the eye, must see clearly; and that your love, like arms that embrace, is a grace upon this world.

As often as the wedded couple sees the rings upon their fingers, they are reminded of the vows that they pledged to each other during this high moment of their wedding day.

Jumping the Broom

A symbol of the new home and new life together, jumping the broom is an African-American tradition that originated during slavery and is incorporated into many modern weddings. As slaves were considered property and had no legal rights, they were not allowed to legally marry. Guided by an impulse toward ceremony that ran deep in their cultural heritage, they created rituals from the objects at hand. When a couple took vows in front of a witness then leapt over a broom handle, their union was recognized as a marriage.

The practice has been adopted by other cultures, predominantly by pagans. Handfasting.info, a Web site that describes the pagan wedding ceremony of handfasting, explains the significance of jumping the broom:

> The broom represents a threshold. The handfasted couple, although still individuals, begin a new life together. Jumping over the broom represents crossing this threshold into new territory, a life vitally connected to another's. The leap that the couple takes over the broom is also symbolic. Starting a new life with another person does require a "leap of faith." But by taking the leap, the individuals make a gesture of dedication to working together through the tough times ahead.

Breaking the Glass

This is traditionally a Jewish custom but has been adopted by many cultures and is a symbol of closure. Ritualwell.org offers the following explanations of the reasons for this custom:

- To ward off evil ghosts who are naturally attracted to joy because of their envy and might otherwise come and upset the wedding party.

- To remind the bride and groom that relationships, like glass, are fragile and that once broken, they cannot be easily put back together.

- To recall, even at this moment of great joy . . . that the world is not whole, and others suffer as we rejoice. We commit ourselves to repair the world.

- To be a final sound in the couple's ears, so that, even in moments of difficulty, they can recall this sound and this moment and realize that their wedding day is always close at hand.

- To be a great finale!

After the glass is broken, the couple usually kisses amidst shouts of "siman tov v'mazel tov" (congratulations)!

φ

Addressing Your Fears about Marriage and Commitment

Understanding the meanings of the symbols ignites your creative fires and begins the process of crafting your ceremony. As the outer pieces fall into place, you begin to envision you and your partner being wed. The joy of your commitment is supported by symbols that meaningfully reflect your love and the values of your shared life. The time of your wedding is near.

Yet, thinking about the ceremony can also activate beliefs and fears about marriage. As long as we're focused on the guest list or the dress, we can avoid the realization that at its core the wedding is about the commitment that is affirmed and ratified through the ceremony, which can bring up a lot of fear. After all, I think it's safe to say that we all have fears and beliefs about the nature of marriage and commitment today. Just as we must grieve the loss of singlehood so that we don't displace the emotions onto the planning, so we must recognize and address our fears around marriage so that they don't sabotage the beauty of the wedding day.

To marry these days is an act of faith. Most of us are acutely aware of the high divorce rate in this country, and many of us come from broken homes ourselves. We're aware that when we marry we surrender ourselves to love, and with this surrender comes the possibility of losing this love to divorce, deflation of the love, or death. We are also aware that with intimacy and a merged level of commitment comes the challenge of maintaining our identity as a separate individual within the marriage. Remember, conscious questioning and exploration of legitimate issues should not be equated with doubt. On the contrary, it's usually when women feel secure in their love and commitment that they can allow these fears sufficient room to breathe.

Identifying your fears is the first step toward healing them. Once they are made conscious, you have more freedom to write and talk about them, thereby diminishing their power and allowing you to move forward with joy toward your wedding day. The following checklist will help you identify your fears.

CHECKLIST: FEARS ABOUT MARRIAGE & COMMITMENT

Check the fears and beliefs that apply to you:

- ○ I'm scared our marriage won't last.

- ○ I'm scared that the passion will fade, and we won't feel excited by each other anymore.

- ○ Marriage consists of phases of constant bickering sandwiched between the monotony of everyday life.

- ○ We will get bored with each other.

- ○ We will take each other for granted.

- ○ I'm scared he'll cheat on me.

- ○ I'm scared I'll cheat on him.

- ○ I'm scared something terrible will happen to him—that he will die.

○ I'm scared our sex life will gradually dwindle and eventually the fire will die completely.

○ I'm scared that we'll grow apart.

○ I'm scared he won't be attracted to me when I'm older.

○ I'm scared I won't be attracted to him when he's older.

○ What is a good marriage? I don't have any role models of passionate, fulfilling, lifelong marriages.

○ I'm aware of the effect my parents' divorce has on my beliefs about marriage.

○ I am aware of the effect my fiancé's parents' divorce has on his beliefs about marriage.

○ I'm scared of losing myself in the marriage.

○ I'm scared of feeling suffocated by my partner.

○ I'm scared of not having my own space.

○ I'm scared my inner spark will become dimmer and dimmer as the marriage progresses.

○ Other: . . . .

If you have been married before, your fears will probably carry remnants from your previous marriage. Include the following boxes in your inventory:

○ I feel [terrified, thrilled, relieved, anxious, excited, calm] to be getting married again.

○ This feels [similar to, different from] the last time I was engaged.

○ I'm scared it won't work out ... again.

○ I'm scared that while my fiancé seems so wonderful now, eventually he'll turn into the same kind of man my ex-husband was.

○ I'm scared that I will eventually become as miserable as I felt in my last marriage.

○ I'm scared I'm going to repeat the same issues I struggled with last time.

○ I'm scared this one will also end in divorce.

○ I'm scared that no one and nothing is good enough for me.

○ I'm scared I'll see that many of my problems in my first marriage were me.

○ I'm scared to commit again.

O It took me a long time to regain my strength after my divorce. What if I lose it again?

O My belief in marriage is shaky. Can marriage ever really work?

O Other: . . . .

It takes courage to allow yourself to feel and identify your fears. Letting yourself feel your fear counteracts the guidance from our wedding culture, which is indirectly encouraging you to bypass these uncomfortable feelings by consuming yourself with the planning.

Remembering two truths will help support you through the process: one, the fear is a completely normal part of one of the biggest commitments of your life; and two, the more you acknowledge and work through your fears, the more presence and joy you'll experience as your wedding nears. A conscious journey is sometimes scarier than an unconscious one, but the rewards are well worth it.

φ

Fiancé Fear

Sometimes your fears are focused on the generalities of the commitment and a lack of trust in the union of marriage. Other times they are focused specifically on your fiancé. This is some of the scariest fear to manage, yet every bride that I've worked with experiences it at some point. If you know that having fears about your fiancé is normal, you will be able to ride the wave with more grace.

There will be times during your engagement (and throughout your marriage) when nearly everything about your partner—what he says, how he looks, how he dresses, his laugh, his mannerisms—drives you crazy. Left unattended and set against the ever-present backdrop of "forever," these normal irritations can easily grow into distorted monsters that say things like, "I can't do this. I want out!" Before taking any action, I encourage you to slow down and find that still place inside you that knows the rightness of your decision. Recall your intention. Settle into the vision of your wedding. Align with the clear "yes" that has led you to this moment.

When the mere presence of your fiancé overwhelms you, it's probably because he is serving as a mirror for your own fear. You may not even know what you are afraid of, but as you tumble through the waves of your engagement that land on the shore of your marriage, the barnacles of fear that are attached to the crevices of your psyche will make themselves known. This is the process of transition. Far from being a reason to run, the appearance of fear is a call to heal the deep-seated barriers to intimacy that we all carry. It's an opportunity to learn how to surrender, to trust, and to move closer toward love.

Working with Fear

Fear is a powerful and convincing force, and when it inhabits your body it can turn you into someone alien and unkind. There are several effective ways to combat fear, the most important being the recognition that it is present and in the driver's seat. After all, how can you combat something that you don't know exists or that you refuse to acknowledge? As with the grief and loss you've been working with, the more space you allow for the fear to move and breathe, the more quickly it will work itself through, leaving you to return to an openhearted place of love.

That said, fear appears in layers and deeper levels of intensity as we move into deeper levels of intimacy in our partnerships. Marriage, by definition, is a deepening of the commitment and love that you share, so the journey toward marriage will naturally engender fear. As you experiment with different ways of working with and battling fear, try to maintain a compassionate attitude toward yourself. Know that you are gripped by an unimaginably strong energy, and that sometimes it takes a long time to remove oneself from its grip. That is part of the journey of marriage: dismantling fear so that love can grow and blossom. In *The Unimaginable Life,* Julia Loggins (1997, pp. 145–146), expresses this concept beautifully:

> It's so easy to forget that we're in this together. What a paradox Big Love is! In giving our whole hearts and souls to each other, we trigger each other's deepest fears of love and rejection. In being loved, we feel our own inability and inexperience at receiving pure devotion. And in our discomfort we strike out at our Beloved, the person we've waited our whole lives for, as if he's some mugger in a back alley!

When fear arises, experiment with the following tools as ways to either give it room or refuse to allow it to control your words and actions:

- *Speak it aloud.* Naming the fear, saying "I'm feeling scared right now," diminishes its power. Fear likes to hide and rule from a secret place in your psyche. When you expose its game, it immediately begins to shrink and slink away.

- *Imagine space around the fear.* Once you recognize that you are afraid, see if you can identify where fear lives in your body. If, for example, you experience the fear in your throat, you may feel a tightness and constriction there. If you imagine widening the circle around the fear, you will be giving it room to breathe, which will soon weaken its hold on you. It's when we fight the fear that the constriction increases. Relaxing into it allows it to dissolve.

- *Say no when it arises.* Fear is like a petulant child, and sometimes it needs a good talking to and clear boundaries. Left to its own devices, fear can rule your life, much like an out-of-control child. But if you refuse to be a victim to its convictions and express a firm, clear no, it will begin to understand who is in control of your psyche.

- *Talk to it.* Ask it what it wants, and be willing to combat the answer with the truth. For example, fear might say, "I want you to call off the wedding," and you will need to be able to access your deeper truth that knows that canceling is not the right decision for you. These conversations may go on for several minutes, and you may need to have them over a series of days or weeks. But eventually, fear will get the picture that the truth is much stronger than a fear-based lie.

- *Challenge it.* Many of our fears come from the legacy of marriage that has been handed down for thousands of years. For example, you may resonate with the fear of losing yourself after you marry. This is an understandable fear, given that until very recently women have been expected to sacrifice themselves to their marriage. You probably saw your mother and grandmother giving up their needs to please or support their husband. But is this the reality of your relationship? If you're entering the marriage as equal partners, you will remain equal partners after the wedding. Take some time to deconstruct each of your fears. Challenge them and replace them with the truth.

- *Talk about it with a friend.* Being willing to talk about these feelings is immensely effective in reducing their power. As I mentioned before, fear thrives in the secret, dark places of your inner world. It does not want you to receive outside support because a close friend, someone who knows you and your partner well, will most likely say things that combat the convincing lines that fear is feeding you. Don't keep your fear hidden. At the same time, try to find someone who understands that fear is a normal part of the relationship process and is particularly acute during transition. Otherwise you might be met with the dreaded, "Maybe you're making a mistake."

- *Express your gratitude.* Accessing gratitude is one of the fastest ways to dissolve fear. It's nearly impossible to feel fear and gratitude simultaneously; it's as if they move through the same channel, and if one is in motion, the other must step aside. Not only does the expression of gratitude release you from your fear, but studies have shown that one of the keys to a successful marriage is the daily expression of appreciation. It's never too early to begin this proven marriage-strengthening habit.

If you like, you can go now to the worksheet in chapter 7 called "Appreciating Your Partner" to write down a list of everything you love about your partner. This will serve as a general list that you can refer to when fear creeps up and gets the best of you. I encourage you to make copies of this list and complete it as often as possible, including the small, daily details that you appreciate about your partner. These could be general ("I love how often you make me laugh") or specific ("I appreciate that you take the trash cans out to the curb every week"). No action is too small to go unnoticed. Appreciation is one of those basic human needs that we all require to thrive in our relationships. When you finish with the lists, share them with your partner.

φ

Explore Your Expectations

Not only do we enter marriage with fears, but we also carry with us a host of expectations and beliefs about the nature of this institution. It's important that these are made conscious and shared with your part-ner so you have an opportunity to address them before your wedding day. If you think it's scary to talk about these feelings and beliefs now, imagine the terror of realizing, two weeks into your marriage, that your new husband expects you to cook for him every night! Or perhaps you carry an expectation that after you marry he'll start taking care of you finan-cially (just like your dad did with your mom). You might think you know each other very well, but inside each of you lurks an unconscious blueprint for marriage handed down through the generations. Take some time to photocopy this worksheet, give it to your partner, and spend an evening bringing your expectations to consciousness and discussing the answers.

WORKSHEET: EXPLORING YOUR EXPECTATIONS OF MARRIAGE

1. **DESCRIBE YOUR GRANDPARENTS' AND PARENTS' MARRIAGES.** What were their agreements around the division of labor, financial responsibilities, caring for the children, and cleaning the house? How did these agreements work for them?

. . . .

. . . .

. . . .

. . . .

2. **WHAT DO YOU THINK WILL CHANGE BETWEEN YOU AND YOUR PARTNER AFTER YOU MARRY?**

. . . .

. . . .

. . . .

. . . .

3. **DO YOU HAVE ANY ROLE MODELS FOR A HEALTHY MARRIAGE?** If so, what is it about their relationship that you respect and admire?

. . . .

. . . .

. . . .

Fill in the blanks:

4. **MY MOST NEGATIVE THOUGHTS ABOUT MARRIAGE ARE**

. . . .

. . . .

. . . .

5. MY MOST POSITIVE THOUGHTS ABOUT MARRIAGE ARE

. . . .

. . . .

. . . .

6. THE MOST IMPORTANT QUALITIES FOR A SUCCESSFUL MARRIAGE ARE

. . . .

. . . .

. . . .

7. I HOPE AFTER WE GET MARRIED MY SPOUSE WILL STOP

. . . .

. . . .

. . . .

8. I HOPE AFTER WE MARRY MY SPOUSE WILL START TO

. . . .

. . . .

. . . .

. . . .

9. I'M AFRAID THAT AFTER WE MARRY MY SPOUSE WILL EXPECT ME TO

. . . .

. . . .

. . . .

. . . .

. . . .

For a second marriage:

10. MY EX-HUSBAND OR EX-WIFE WAS THE KIND OF PARTNER WHO EXPECTED ME TO

. . . .

. . . .

. . . .

. . . .

What Is a Wife?

After the initial postwedding letdown, the real questions begin. The first and biggest of these questions is: What does it mean to be a wife today? In the months immediately preceding and following the wedding, this question will probably be roaming through your mind. Coming to terms with what this new identity means to you is one of the primary adjustments you'll be making during the first year of marriage.

We live in a unique age. For most of modern history, the role of wife was clearly defined. Her place was in the home, where she would raise the children, do the cleaning, cook the meals, arrange the social calendar, and entertain her husband's work associates. While the definition was constricting and often anathema to a woman's freedom, she knew her place and followed the path that was laid out before her. Since women have gained their reproductive freedom and have made significant strides toward gender-role equality, we no longer need to adhere to this historically prescribed role. We are our own women, free to make choices that are in alignment with the wise and powerful beings that we are.

So, if a wife is not someone who cooks and cleans, who is she? What defines this role? What will be different about you once you are married? What, exactly, is a "wife"? There isn't one answer. The identity of wife is as individual as your marriage. But the question is an important one, and in order to step fully into this new identity, I encourage you to spend some time contemplating what the word and role mean to you.

Many women balk at the word itself. "Wife" is laden with a cultural history that subjugated women and viewed us as the chattel of men. Why would we have any positive associations with a word that almost reeks of weakness and dependency? Before you can think about what the identity means to you, you may need to wade through your associations. Then you can rinse the word of its negative implications and redefine it on your own terms, just as you may have had to do with the wedding dress or the rings. Where a wedding ring once symbolized the link that chained a wife to her husband, now it stands as a beautiful symbol of the mutual love and commitment between partners. And where the word "wife" may have been associated with weak and boring dependency, we can alter our associations to reflect the strong, independent, mature women that we are today.

Some women choose to remove the word "wife" from their thinking altogether. They define themselves in terms of the reality of the relationship with their husband, not in an abstract term that tells them what a wife or a marriage should be. Beth, married to Brian for twenty years, explains her views:

When we married, the expectation was that we were supposed to complete each other. The image of marriage that was given to me was that we were like a puzzle, and where you have pieces missing, the other person will fill in. Over several years of marriage, we realized that this image didn't work for us. We started to redefine our marriage and our roles. "Wife" to me now means being a partner to Brian. And somewhere in there I just took the word "marriage" out of my thinking. It

didn't make sense to me. What I understand is my commitment to loving Brian, and that is splendid. My commitment is to loving him individually, as a person. It's not an idea, it's not a theory, it's him and my commitment to love him more than anyone else. I only have so much time in a day, and as far as my priorities go and my capacity to love, he is the one whom I choose to love and be committed to. My energy is directed there first. I can't address "wife" or "marriage." I can only speak in terms of my love and commitment to Brian.

Use the following worksheet to help you identify both your negative and positive associations to the word "wife," then flesh out the images of the word that you were handed down by your mother and grandmother.

WHAT ARE YOUR NEGATIVE ASSOCIATIONS WITH THE WORD "WIFE"?

- ○ Boring
- ○ Dowdy
- ○ Homebound
- ○ Isolated
- ○ An appendage of her husband
- ○ Weak
- ○ Dependent
- ○ Nonsexual
- ○ Other: . . . .

WHAT ARE YOUR POSITIVE ASSOCIATIONS WITH THE WORD "WIFE"?

- ○ Alive
- ○ Powerful
- ○ Nurturing
- ○ Devoted
- ○ Sexually satisfied and satisfying
- ○ Committed to her partnership
- ○ Mature
- ○ Striving to maintain the balance between togetherness and separateness, intimacy and solitude
- ○ Other: . . . .

YOUR NEGATIVE EXPECTATIONS ABOUT WHAT IT MEANS TO BE A WIFE:

- ○ I will become a boring person who never has fun or does exciting things out in the world.
- ○ I will be attached to my husband.
- ○ I will lose my individuality, the spark that attracted him to me in the first place.

○ He will expect me to start cooking and cleaning, even though I haven't done those things so far.

○ I will never be able to travel alone.

○ Other: . . . .

YOUR POSITIVE EXPECTATIONS ABOUT WHAT IT MEANS TO BE A WIFE:

○ I am becoming an intimate half of an honest, respectful partnership.

○ I have taken the next step into adulthood, and as a wife I will be continuing my development as a mature woman.

○ I'm moving through the life phases, letting go of singlehood and becoming a wife, which paves the way to possibly becoming a mother.

○ Other: . . . .

Our associations to the word "wife" also derive from the role models of our mother and grandmothers. Articulating and teasing apart the blueprints you were handed down will help you decide which aspects of "wifehood" you wish to toss aside and which you wish to emulate.

1. DESCRIBE THE KIND OF WIFE YOUR MOTHER IS OR WAS:

. . . .

. . . .

. . . .

. . . .

2. DESCRIBE THE KIND OF WIFE YOUR GRANDMOTHERS ARE OR WERE:

. . . .

. . . .

. . . .

. . . .

3. **WHICH OF YOUR MOTHER'S AND GRANDMOTHERS' QUALITIES DO YOU INTEND NOT TO EMULATE?** For example, if your grandmother packed your grandfather's bags when they went on a trip, is this representative of a quality you'd rather not emulate in your marriage?

. . . .

. . . .

. . . .

. . . .

4. **WHICH OF YOUR MOTHER'S AND GRANDMOTHERS' QUALITIES AROUND WIFEHOOD DO YOU WISH TO EMULATE?**

. . . .

. . . .

. . . .

. . . .

5. **IS THERE ANYONE, ACTUAL OR FICTIONAL, FRIEND OR CELEBRITY, WHO EMBODIES THE KIND OF WIFE YOU'D LIKE TO BE?** If so, who, and what is it about them that you would like to emulate?

. . . .

. . . .

. . . .

. . . .

Clarifying with Interviews

Many of my clients feel bereft of the role models that will help them define what the wife identity means to them. They feel as if they are standing on the frontier without a road map or compass. While in some ways the self-definition of an identity can only come from within, it can also be helpful to find real people who represent the kind of wife that you'd like to be.

One way to crystallize your vision is to conduct spontaneous or planned interviews with married women whom you respect. Set your intention to encounter strong, independent women who are willing to talk about how they define themselves as wives and what the role means to them. Ask people you know (aunts, mothers, cousins, friends, teachers) or new acquaintances (professors, doctors, flight attendants, the person sitting next to you on the subway). Soon you will have a verbal collage to sustain you. Their words will help you develop a sense of who you want to be in your marriage and what the word "wife" means to you.

INTERVIEWS: WHAT IT MEANS TO BE A WIFE

Use the following space to transcribe the answers:

INTERVIEW 1

NAME: . . . . LENGTH OF MARRIAGE: . . . .

. . . .

. . . .

. . . .

INTERVIEW 2

NAME: . . . . LENGTH OF MARRIAGE: . . . .

. . . .

. . . .

. . . .

INTERVIEW 3

NAME: . . . . LENGTH OF MARRIAGE: . . . .

. . . .

. . . .

. . . .

Laying the Groundwork for Ceremony

If the wedding is the birthday of the marriage, then the engagement is the prenatal phase when the marriage is gestating. Just as a growing fetus requires proper nutrition to grow into a healthy baby, so a growing partnership requires proper care and attention to grow into a healthy marriage. The ceremony is the actual birth, and the more you prepare for it the more joy and presence you will experience on that day.

Preparing for a ceremony means initiating rituals that will create a strong structure of support and will facilitate the unfolding of the event. It means nurturing your growing relationship and acknowledging that the partnership itself (as well as the two of you as individuals) is in the midst of transition, which means that it needs to be nurtured by a special kind of focused attention. It means recognizing that a spiritual ceremony doesn't just fall from the sky. As Victoria, who had a glorious wedding day, thoughtfully reflects in *The Conscious Bride* (Paul Nissinen 2000, pp. 135–136):

> We had put a lot of time and thought into the spiritual side of our engagement and wedding and it paid off.... I think the reason why a lot of the magic happened is because we didn't wait until the last minute to try to get spiritual. That was my point when we first got engaged. I knew then that it was too much pressure to try to get as deep as you can be on that one day. You have to lay the groundwork. You have to prepare on all levels.

Spiritual beauty requires time and attention to blossom. Just as flowers must be grown for your bouquet and wheat must be pounded and sifted for your cake, so subtle and invisible actions must take place to create a strong ceremony. As we have seen, our culture focuses on the wedding elements that are seen and heard. It has become a day that expresses an elaborate, expensive, and external value for others. A true wedding has nothing to do with impressing others, and some of the actions you take will never be seen by anyone but you and your fiancé. But when you arrive at your wedding day with a serenity and joy that exudes far and wide, these actions will be felt.

The following ideas are simple actions that will facilitate a spiritual ceremony. These, and others that you create, are the building blocks of your wedding day.

- *Preceremony ceremony.* On the wedding date of each preceding month (if your wedding is on the fifth then the fifth of each month) create a simple ritual between you and your fiancé. This may be taking a hike in nature, lighting a candle at the top of the hill, and saying a prayer for the two of you. This may be going into your backyard, sitting across from each other, and expressing your fears and your excitements about the upcoming wedding and marriage. This may be simply turning off the phones and spending a focused hour in silence, each meditating on the wedding. What matters is that you set an intention on this day to focus your attention on the wedding. These thoughts will lay the spiritual groundwork for the day.

- *A chuppah of principles.* A similar idea comes from Victoria and Miles. Each half-Jewish, they decided to incorporate the chuppah into their ceremony. On the twentieth of each of the nine months preceding their wedding (their wedding was June 20), they went to a fabric store together and selected a twelve-by-twelve piece of fabric. Each of the nine fabric squares represented one of their marriage principles: love, family, physical union, protection, creativity, abundance, nature, home, and the divine. As Victoria explains, "The idea was to take the whole year while planning the wedding to think about our principles, as opposed to at the last minute while reviewing or writing our vows. Our principles were reflected in the fabric that we thought "looked" like that concept. We wanted to put energy and ceremony into that time of the month all year so we'd be geared for how that felt and we'd have a context for anticipation, ritual, and intention for that day."

- *Flowered arch and ribbons of blessings.* If you and your beloved are people who enjoy working with your hands and connecting with the earth, consider constructing the arch under which you will marry. Building and working on a project together is a symbolic and embodied way to solidify your partnership. (The next major project you may create together is a baby!) Whether you make or buy an arch, the next step is to weave flowers into it. Again, these can be homegrown or store-bought. Finally, include long, white ribbons in your invitations with a request that your guests inscribe them with a marriage blessing and return them with the RSVP card. Tying the ribbons onto the arch can be incorporated into the ceremony or the reception. And after the wedding, you can place the arch at the entrance to your home or in your backyard as a constant reminder of the threshold you crossed together.

- *Print a program.* A wedding program is traditionally a straightforward document that outlines the events of the day. A more meaningful program can include an explanation of the symbols used in the ceremony, a paragraph that expresses the intentions and principles that inspired your day, and the readings or blessings incorporated into your ceremony. Not only will this further include the congregation into the ceremony by demystifying the symbols, but it will give them something interesting to read while they're waiting!

Whether you build an arch or light a candle, choosing a ceremonial action will help guide you and your fiancé to feel prepared for the transformative experience of the ceremony.

φ

The Structure of a Ceremony

*I*f you're being married by a minister, rabbi, or priest, they will most likely use the standard ceremony they follow for every wedding they preside over. They may ask if you have a special reading or blessing that you would like to incorporate and if you wish to write your own vows. Other than that, all you're required to do is show up and receive the words and rituals of your cultural and religious heritage. On the other hand, if you're cocreating the ceremony with a layperson or alternative officiant, you may be asked to offer ideas and make suggestions on what you would like to include. Either way, understanding the elements of a ceremony will help you feel more connected to and present for the event.

Designing or cocreating your ceremony can be a daunting task, especially if you are not well-versed in the language and structure of ceremony (which most of us aren't). Following a template is helpful in that, once the outline is created, all you have to do is fill in the details. Most Western ceremonies are structured according to the following template:

1. Processional

The official march that begins the ceremony. After your guests are seated, your family members and wedding party walk down the aisle, preparing the way for the bride to enter. The traditional order of the processional is as follows: groom, best man, and officiant enter using a side door and stand facing the guests; grandparents; parents of the groom; mother of the bride; bridesmaids; maid of honor; ring bearer and flower girl; father of the bride escorts the bride. This is simply a blueprint; you will decide the order that makes the most sense for you.

2. Welcome

A brief statement that welcomes the congregation, acknowledges the role of the witness, and embraces the community into the fold of the ceremony.

3. Opening blessing

This statement or blessing expresses your intentions for marrying and communicates your vision of marriage.

4. Readings

Selected excerpts from literature, scriptures, and poetry are read to support the vision and offer inspiration and guidance on the journey of marriage.

5. Personal message from officiant to bride and groom

The officiant often shares their impressions on how they see the couple, and also reflects on the challenges and gifts that each bring to the marriage.

6. Vows

The vows are the climax of the ceremony. The exchange of vows accompanied by the ring ceremony are the threshold that separate two single individuals from a unified married couple.

7. Unity candle

Lighting a candle together is a ritual that seals the vows and symbolizes the beginning of a deepened shared life.

8. Ring ceremony

Rings are tangible symbols of the vows, and through a formal ritual the vows are embodied in the rings.

9. Closing reading or blessing

Further readings or final blessings that bring closure to the ceremony.

10. Pronouncement

The pronouncement is the final verbal seal and the words that lead to the physical exclamation point of the closing seal. Couples vary on how they want the pronouncement to be expressed, for instance, "I now present to you Mr. and Mrs. John Smith" or "It is my great pleasure to present for the first time Mary and John Smith." When the woman is retaining her last name you have to be a bit more creative with the pronouncement. Some couples choose to forgo this ritual altogether.

11. Closing seal

The closing seal is the exclamation point of the ceremony. It's the last physical act that brings closure and completion. It is usually a moment of great joy where the congregation breaks out into applause and shouts of congratulations. Examples include breaking the glass, jumping the broom, and the kiss.

12. Recessional

The final exit. The bride and groom leave first, followed by the reverse order of the processional.

Choosing Your Officiant

Selecting an officiant—or the person who marries you—is one of the most important parts of your ceremony. This person will not only be your grounding force during your ceremony, but they will also help you prepare for the ritual during the weeks leading up to your wedding. As previously mentioned, if you are marrying in your church or synagogue, the decision is made for you, and you probably have a special relationship with the minister, priest, or rabbi who will perform the ceremony. But if you are a member of the growing population of couples who marry outside of a religious institution, nearly anyone can preside over your wedding.

While you can always get married at city hall or by a variety of qualified people who can conduct weddings, I strongly encourage you to choose an officiant with whom you have a personal relationship. During the weeks leading up to your wedding and especially during the ceremony, it's likely that you will feel an unfamiliar combination of excitement and fear, which then creates the sensation of floating through a dream. Nothing exacerbates this unreal sensation more than being led through one of life's most sacred transitions by a virtual stranger. And nothing can bring you back to earth and into your body more than looking into the familiar and loving eyes of a trusted friend or relative.

> If your officiant has never conducted a wedding before, they will need to obtain the document that allows them to legally marry you. The process is simple, free, and can be done online at www.ulc.org.

Consider asking one of the following people to preside over your wedding:

- a close friend

- a family member

- a counselor or therapist

- a spiritual leader

Interview Questions for a Prospective Officiant

1. Have you ever presided over a wedding ceremony?

2. What is your religious or spiritual orientation and how much of this would you want to include in the ceremony?

3. Have you ever led a group ritual or ceremony?

4. Would you feel honored or burdened by the responsibility of marrying us?

5. How many times would you meet with us prior to the ceremony?

6. How much would you want us to participate in creating the ceremony?

7. If you haven't presided over a wedding ceremony, do you have anyone who could mentor you through this process?

8. What is your view of marriage?

As you interview prospective candidates, you'll want to take down their contact information and any points you'd like to remember. Remember to put the final contact information in the back section.

For Your Officiant

If this is one of the first weddings that your officiant has conducted, they may appreciate some tips along the way. No matter who marries you, the more information they have about you, the more personal and meaningful the ceremony will be. Answering the following potent questions and sharing them with your officiant will not only help them get to know you better but will also initiate important conversations between you and your partner. I suggest you photocopy these pages and answer the questions separately, sharing them first with each other, then offering them to your officiant.

WORKSHEET: CEREMONY PREPARATION

1. WHEN WAS THE MOMENT YOU KNEW THIS WAS THE PERSON YOU WANTED TO MARRY?

. . . .

. . . .

. . . .

2. WHAT DOES "MARRIAGE" MEAN TO YOU?

. . . .

. . . .

. . . .

3. HOW ARE YOU GOING TO WEATHER THE STORMS THAT MAY ARISE?

. . . .

. . . .

. . . .

4. IS DIVORCE AN OPTION FOR YOU IN THIS MARRIAGE AND IF SO, UNDER WHAT CIRCUMSTANCES?

. . . .

. . . .

. . . .

5. WHAT DOES BEING A WIFE OR HUSBAND MEAN TO YOU?

. . . .

. . . .

. . . .

6. WHY DO . . . . AND . . . . [YOUR NAMES] BELONG TOGETHER?

. . . .

. . . .

. . . .

. . . .

7. HOW DO CHILDREN FACTOR INTO YOUR MARRIAGE?

. . . .

. . . .

. . . .

. . . .

If one or both of you have been married before and divorced, the following questions will help clear the ground for this marriage.

8. **WHAT WAS THE BOTTOM-LINE REASON FOR DIVORCE IN YOUR PREVIOUS MARRIAGE?**

. . . .

. . . .

. . . .

. . . .

9. **IF DIVORCE IS NOT AN OPTION, WHAT WILL BE THE BOTTOM LINE THAT KEEPS YOU IN THIS MARRIAGE FOR LIFE?**

. . . .

. . . .

. . . .

. . . .

10. **HOW HAVE YOU CLEARED THE SPACE AROUND THE TERMS, CONCEPTS, AND EXPECTATIONS OF "MARRIAGE," "WIFE," AND "HUSBAND" FOR THIS MARRIAGE TO START ON FRESH GROUND?**

. . . .

. . . .

. . . .

. . . .

Now that you have examined the symbols of the ceremony, identified and communicated your fears and expectations about marriage, chosen a prewedding ritual, and deconstructed the basic template, you are ready to craft your ceremony! Use the following worksheet, as well as the sample readings at the end of this chapter, to break ground on the design of your day. Write down notes and general ideas that you will bring to your officiant. What would you like them to communicate in the opening blessing? How clearly can you state your marriage vision? How would you like your officiant to present you during the pronouncement? Be as clear as possible on the elements that matter to you. Also make note of members of your wedding party who will be participating in the ceremony, such as who will read the prayers, light the candle, or offer the rings.

There is space to jot down notes and phrases that you will include in your personal vows. Writing your vows can be a daunting exercise, and I will offer more complete guidance and suggestions in the next section.

WORKSHEET: CRAFTING YOUR CEREMONY

1. PROCESSIONAL

. . . .

. . . .

2. WELCOME

. . . .

. . . .

. . . .

. . . .

. . . .

3. OPENING BLESSING

. . . .

. . . .

. . . .

. . . .

. . . .

. . . .

4. READINGS

   1. . . . .

     . . . .

   2. . . . .

     . . . .

   3. . . . .

     . . . .

5. PERSONAL MESSAGE FROM OFFICIANT TO BRIDE AND GROOM

. . . .

. . . .

. . . .

. . . .

6. VOWS

. . . .

. . . .

. . . .

. . . .

. . . .

. . . .

7. UNITY CANDLE—OR OTHER SYMBOLIC ACT (SEVEN BLESSINGS, KETUBAH, ETC.)

. . . .

. . . .

. . . .

. . . .

8. RING CEREMONY

· ·

· ·

· ·

· ·

9. CLOSING READING OR BLESSING

· ·

· ·

· ·

· ·

10. PRONOUNCEMENT

· ·

· ·

· ·

· ·

11. CLOSING SEAL

· ·

· ·

· ·

· ·

12. RECESSIONAL

· ·

· ·

Crafting Your Vows

As mentioned earlier in the chapter, your vows are your spiritual promises. They are real and meaningful, and can sustain you during times when your marriage passes through a dark storm. When you begin to write your vows, think about the essence of what you're really promising. Just as the dress has evolved over time to mirror our modern views, so the vows have changed to reflect the equality of marriage. Few people are willing to make a vow that binds them "to love and obey" their partner. What are you willing to promise? What do you intend to uphold throughout your marriage?

Some couples choose to write their vows together to avoid any sense of competition on the wedding day ("his vows were more touching than hers!"). Another option is to briefly express why you love your partner, then move into the vows together. If you decide to cowrite your vows, consider writing them separately first, then sitting down with both sets in front of you as you creatively find a way to express your joint commitments.

Even if you choose to write your own vows, you may also wish to include aspects of the traditional or contemporary versions. For instance, here is an example of more traditional vows:

TRADITIONAL VOWS

I, ... take you, ...
to be my wedded wife/husband: to have
and to hold from this day forward; for better, for worse;
for richer, for poorer; in sickness and in health;
to love and to cherish so long as we both shall live.
This is my solemn vow.

More contemporary vows might sound like this:

CONTEMPORARY VOWS

I, ... take you, ...
to be my wife/husband from this day forward, to join with
you and to share all that is to come, to give and to receive,
to speak and to listen, to inspire and to respond, and to be
loyal to you throughout our life with all my being.

Spiritual Vows

Your personal, unique vows are an expression of the commitments you will make on your wedding day. As such, no one can tell you exactly what to say or how to say it. Like any creative inspiration, the vows may come to you when you're falling asleep or waking up, washing dishes or folding laundry, taking a shower or a walk. If you don't want your process to be influenced by another's words, I suggest you do not read the following list. But if you need some direction, you can use this list of "sample vows" as a springboard to activate the flow of the creative wellspring where your vows live. As you read through the list, notice which lines reverberate with a "yes!" inside your body. Also notice the different ways you can begin your vows: "I promise," "I will," "I intend," "I vow," "I pledge," "I acknowledge." Transfer these vows and other ideas to the space provided in the preceding section.

SAMPLE VOWS

- I acknowledge you as my spiritual partner, here to teach me about love.

- I promise to support you to become all you can be.

- I intend to learn about love every day—how to give and receive love and how to show my love through actions.

- I will tell the truth.

- I will share my heart, soul, and body with you, including fears and joys as they arise.

- I vow to celebrate your body in all its changing forms.

- I intend to continue learning about who I am, challenging myself in mind, body, and spirit, so that I may grow into the woman/man I'm meant to be.

- I promise to seek support in times of need.

- I intend to keep agreements.

- I vow to be faithful to my spiritual path and to support you in yours.

- I let go of all that holds me back from loving you.

- I pledge myself entirely to this path of marriage.

Selected Readings

There are a plethora of books that contain hundreds of wedding readings. On the Conscious Weddings Web site you will find several readings that articulate the poetics of marriage without glossing over the reality. Most of these selections honor marriage as a spiritual path, a crucible where we are called to challenge our deepest fears so that we may move into an ever-widening circle of love.

φ

Understanding the symbols of a wedding ritual and crafting your ceremony can be a creative and fulfilling experience. What matters most is the spirit of the ceremony, and remembering this will help ground and soothe you when the details feel overwhelming. Similarly, while the symbols of the reception can imbue more meaning into that aspect of your day, it's the intention that matters most. As you read the next chapter and begin to arrange the details of the reception, continually reminding yourself of your intention (to celebrate, to have fun) will keep you sane and centered throughout the process.

φ

The Reception

Emotional Tasks

Remembering to Breathe φ *Honoring the Loss*

Practical Task

Setting the Details: Finding the Food, Cake, Flowers, Music, Photographer, and Wedding-Night Accommodations

A Time to Receive

In the first moments following the ceremony, the witness circle of family and friends gather to embrace the couple and launch them into their new life. For the couple, their spiritual work is over, and the reception is the time to literally receive the love, support, and joy of the guests. Where the primary intention of the ceremony is to wed the bride and groom, the primary intention of the reception is to connect with the friends and family who have come to witness this momentous event. Too often in our culture we become so consumed with planning the perfect event that we lose sight of the true meaning of this portion of the day. If we allow ourselves to become seduced by a wedding industry that tells us that the success of this day is dependent upon finding the perfect cake, napkins, and party favors, we will forget what truly matters. What matters is that we experience the joy and love that overflows on a wedding day. What matters is that the newly married couple can join in the celebration of the birth of their new marriage.

As with the ceremony, the elements of the reception—the food, cake, flowers, music—exist for an express purpose: to facilitate celebration, offer blessings, and incorporate the witness circle into the first layers of the couple's marriage. The concept of incorporation is a key component of the reception. To review from the introduction, the three phases of a rite of passage are rites of separation, in which the woman is separating from her old identity and lifestyle; liminality, or the in-between zone when she is no longer single and not quite married; and rites of incorporation, in which the woman, now an intimate half of a married couple, completes the transition into her new identity and embraces this phase in her life. To incorporate literally means "to bring into the body," and rites of incorporation are the objects and rituals of the reception that bring the events of the ceremony into the physical and spiritual bodies of the bride and groom. When we return to what matters, we remember that the symbols and rituals of the reception are used to receive: receive blessings, receive protection, receive support, receive connection.

φ

Symbols of the Reception

Each facet of the reception is replete with meaning. In many cultures, the actions, foods, rituals, and words at a wedding contain a world of meaning intended to guide the couple and their family into this new union. On a recent plane flight, I sat next to man from a tribe in Cameroon who shared extensively about the wedding rituals and traditions of his culture. He told me about a ritual where the parents of the bride and groom walk down two separate paths that meet at the newlyweds' home. Each set of parents carries an exquisite pillow that they will offer to the couple and place in their new home. The ritual acknowledges that two families, coming from two separate paths, are joining together, and that the parents' role is to support the young people as they establish their life. As I listened to him I thought, "How beautiful, and how sad for our culture. For instead of offering pillows we tend to argue over limousine costs and seating arrangements."

On what basis have you chosen the food items on your menu? Do you know what the symbolism of the wedding cake is? Our culture glosses over the symbolic meaning of food and cake, instead encouraging brides and grooms to base their selections on convenience, cost, or taste preference. There is nothing wrong with these reasons, but they can bypass the possibility of creating a reception filled with meaning, which then enhances how connected the newly married couple feel to their celebration. Finding and creating meaningful connections requires a few dedicated moments of thoughtful consideration. Sometimes merely understanding the significance of a ritual that you were already planning on enacting—like the receiving line—can completely change how connected you feel to the act. Consider the origins and traditional meanings of reception rituals, below.

The Receiving Line

The receiving line makes physical the process of receiving. With a moment's thought, the symbolism of this ritual is clear, yet, sadly, many couples forgo the receiving line because it doesn't fit into the structure of their day. A reception can be a chaotic and energy-filled event, with guests from every corner of your life wanting to spend a moment with the crowned couple. Most women say that their one frustration on their wedding day was not being able to really connect with their guests. Sometimes the hours pass so quickly that there are some people that the bride never makes contact with! While the reception isn't a time for profound connection, the receiving line ensures a moment of one-on-one contact with each and every person at the wedding. A hug or handshake in these first precious moments after the ceremony physically incorporates the couple into the community fold.

> **CREATIVE IDEA:** Make or buy a rectangular fabric long enough to be held by all of the guests. After the ceremony, while the bride and groom are having a moment alone or making their way to the reception site, the maid of honor, mother, or wedding coordinator lines up the guests in two straight or circular rows and has them hold the fabric above their heads. When the couple arrives, they walk slowly through the tunnel, making contact with each person as they pass. The tunnel symbolizes the extended home of the community, as well as the passage into marriage, which the hands of all the loved ones present help to uphold.

Food

One of the most important functions of the food at a reception is to incorporate (to bring into the body) a sense of community among the guests. Partaking of a celebratory feast together is a worldwide ritual of inclusion. Specific foods represent different principles in various cultures. For example, in China the most important wedding foods are lobster, which represents a male dragon, and chicken, which represents a female phoenix. Together, these foods represent balance in the new marriage. In many ways, the wedding banquet in China is as important as the ceremony in terms of creating the new bond between the couple, the two families, and the guests. Each food in the banquet represents a specific quality, and when all present bring the foods into their bodies, they are symbolically holding that principle for the married couple. In general, food at a Chinese banquet symbolizes happiness, longevity, or fertility. The specific foods and their meaning are as follows:

> **CREATIVE IDEA:** Select your food based on its meaning and associations in your life, then write a word or phrase that encapsulates this meaning next to that food item on the buffet table or menu. For example, if you associate salad with health and vitality, write "Health & Vitality" on a small card and place it next to the salad bowl. When your guests are partaking of this food, they are metaphorically incorporating your associations into their bodies.

Shark's fin soup : wealth

Roast suckling pig : virginity

Peking duck : completeness; the red color symbolizes joy and celebration

Fowl : peace

Vegetable with sea cucumber : selflessness

Noodles : longevity

Desserts : sweet and long life

Tea : a sign of respect

Our culture does not have standard foods whose meaning is known by all. While this may leave us searching for a blueprint to follow, it also opens the possibility of finding your own foods that symbolize certain elements of your shared life. Think about the principles you listed in chapter 1. Then consider which foods could represent those principles and how you could incorporate them into your reception.

Cake

The cake is a symbol of fertility. The tradition of the wedding cake dates back to the ancient Greeks and Romans, who made an offering of fruits, nuts, and honey cake to the gods and asked for approval and blessings on the couple. Over thousands of years, the tradition has evolved from honey cake to fruit buns to the introduction of white icing by a French chef. Today we find brides and grooms in every country around the world following the custom of baking and eating a special cake.

When you are cutting the cake and passing out slices to your guests, remember that you are symbolically inviting each member of your party to bless you with fertility and happiness. You may decide to say a prayer or toast in honor of the blessings that your cake imparts when each guest takes a bite. If you don't plan to have children, think about "fertility" in the widest sense of the word to include blessings of creative abundance.

CREATIVE IDEA: Bring together your women friends, including your mother and grandmother, and bake your own wedding cake. Women uniting around the fire is an ancient way of connecting, and as you sift and infuse your stories, laughter, tears, memories, and prayers into the layers, you will be creating a cake of meaning and beauty. If you haven't read the book or seen the film *Like Water for Chocolate,* I highly recommend it to witness the profound way in which emotions are infused into baking and cooking.

Flowers

Generally, the meaning of flowers is simply that they are objects of beauty, though there are specific meanings for individual flowers. Flowers do not symbolize beauty, as they are beauty itself. The most common flowers and their meaning when used at a wedding are

Rose : love

Freesia : sweetness

Lily : summer and abundance

Baby's breath : happiness

Ivy : wedded love, fidelity, affection

Daisy : innocence, loyal love

CREATIVE IDEA: Grow your own! This idea comes from Holly, a client with a family of green thumbs who decided to begin planting the seeds for Holly's wedding, both literally and metaphorically, months before the day.

My sisters, mom, and I have always worked in the garden together. When I told them I was getting married, we immediately discussed the idea of growing our own flowers. I loved this idea, as I knew that not only would it guarantee time together in the months prior to my wedding, but they would also be infusing their effort and beauty into my bouquet and decorations. When I've told people we did this, they love the idea but don't think they could do it themselves. It's easier than you think; I would recommend it to anyone getting married. The flowers were gorgeous, inexpensive, and a direct labor of love.

Iris : faith and wisdom

Gladiolus : strength of character

As with food, there are no universal meanings for flowers. When choosing your flowers, it's best to rely on instinct and your unique sensibility. In other words, what speaks to you? Perhaps you have a special association to yellow roses. Or perhaps bunches of daisies remind you of those your fiancé brought you when you first began dating. Try to stay connected to the meanings and associations that resonate for the two of you.

Music and Dance

Music acts as an expression of joy and celebration, while dance symbolizes relationships. If music is an important part of your reception, most likely it's because you want to open up the floor and invite people to dance. Dance is one of the most frequently used metaphors for marriage (for instance, "marriage is like a dance") and dancing together brings the action of the ceremony and the celebration of the reception into the body. Like eating together, it's a worldwide ritual of incorporating the community into the first layers of a marriage. When the community dances together, not only are they having fun, but they're solidifying the strength of the circle that embraces the newlyweds. The couple usually begins the festivities with a "first dance."

CREATIVE IDEA: Learn the tango (or another dance). This creative idea comes from a client who balked at the tradition of a first dance. As she explains:

We decided several months before the wedding that we didn't like the idea of a "first dance," so we decided to come up with our own surprise for everyone. For months we practiced (with a dance teacher) how to do the tango. My husband and I are not dancers at all, so this would really surprise people. The night of the wedding, they introduced us after the ceremony and we went right into our first dance. We had the band play a super-cheesy song and just started to swing back and forth slowly. Suddenly, Aaron broke out and screamed at the band, "Stop! Stop! This isn't good! Come on—we need something better!" All the guests were astonished—everyone gasped! What was he doing? Aaron grabbed a rose and slowly walked around me, and we broke out into the best tango of our lives! When we completed the tango, we ended it with a final kiss—and then a high-five! It was at this moment that Aaron and I felt most connected.

Why did this make it meaningful? It was the only thing that went untouched by anyone else. (Only the vendors knew about it—not one guest.) It was our own little secret, and something that we built together from scratch. It defied the norm (and we liked that), it set the right pace for the party, and it was classy, not too crazy.

Cushioned between the ceremony's kiss and the "consummation" at the end of the evening, the first dance is included in the series of physical actions that seal the bond of marriage.

Photography and Video

As relatively modern inventions, the photographs and video at a wedding do not carry a history of symbolism and meaning. We photograph our weddings to attempt to capture the event forever and share the images with children and grandchildren. Since there is no direct meaning in relation to the wedding day, many women can feel stressed and disconnected during the photographs. Brides I've talked to felt as if they were going through the motions of an act they felt they must check off their list, and that by separating from their guests for forty-five minutes to an hour, the flow and spontaneity of the day was interrupted. To counteract this feeling, I encourage women and their partners to think about ways in which the photos and video can create connection between the couple and their guests instead of removing them from the activity of the day.

φ

CREATIVE IDEA: Ask a friend who is adept at using a camera to tape the ceremony, then interview friends and family during the reception. This brings a meaningful element to the videotaping. Instead of simply documenting the externals of the event, your guests have an opportunity to share their thoughts and offer blessings, and you will enjoy looking back on it in years to come.

CREATIVE IDEA: Hang a beautiful piece of fabric on a tree and place a bench beneath it. As you and your husband enjoy a moment's rest beneath the tree, your guests can spontaneously jump into the scene and spend a quality moment with you as your photographer snaps a shot. This is a way to connect with people, bypass the forced structure of formal photographs, and obtain an authentic and meaningful picture with your guests. To increase the range and authenticity of your photos, place disposable cameras around the reception site and encourage your guests to use them. This will not only save money but will most likely produce great photos, as the best photographs are usually those that are unplanned and natural.

Setting the Reception Details

Receiving is intimately linked to connecting, and as you plan the details of your reception, ask yourself this question: Will including this element help us feel more connected to ourselves, each other, our guests, and Spirit? Because the emphasis in our culture is on creating an externally perfect event, where napkins match flowers, which match cake tops, it's all too easy to lose sight of the internal meaning in this part of the day. As a result, many newlyweds report feeling a sense of disconnection during their reception. Some of this is a normal part of the transition process (as you will see in chapter 8), but when the disconnection outweighs the joy of the event, something is wrong.

It's also important that you set an intention to stay connected to your partner while making reception decisions. As I discussed earlier, planning a wedding is a testing and training ground for the skills that are necessary for a healthy marriage. One of the foremost important skills is that of negotiation and compromise. For example, if you are married to the idea of having a band and your fiancé loves the idea of a DJ, what do you do? Do you bulldoze right over him and insist on implementing your desires? Do you step aside and squelch your voice to avoid a conflict? Or do you begin a dialogue about how to negotiate and compromise in a way that is acceptable to both of you? Your engagement and wedding day will be much more enjoyable if you view each decision as a joint venture where you are practicing one of the most important skills of your marriage. Remember, in the end it's not about the band or the DJ—it's about creating a solid foundation on which your marriage can blossom.

The best way to find caterers, bakers, florists, musicians, and photographers is through personal referrals. Ask your friends who have married or thrown parties in your area who they would recommend. The Internet is also excellent way to find local resources (80 percent of engaged couples use the Internet for some aspect of their planning). You can also contact national organizations for reputable referrals, such as the Society of American Florists (703-836-8700). Finally, you can always consult your phone book and make the rounds of local artisans.

The Food

How important is food to you? What role does it play in your life? What are your associations to food? Is it comfort? Functional? A delight? A chore? Answering these questions will help you determine how much time, energy, and money you want to devote to your wedding meal. Some planners assert that the food will be your biggest expense and the part of your reception that your guests will remember most. I hold a different position: when your guests reminisce about your wedding, will they remember if they had green beans or broccoli? Fish or chicken? Probably not. They'll remember how they felt on that day. They'll remember the joy that filled the room and the connection between people. As with every aspect of your reception, the details are only important if they matter to you. This is not about impressing others; it's about offering a meal that is in alignment with your values. Remembering this will help you stay centered as you begin this task.

PRACTICAL TIPS

There are many ways to save on food and alcohol:

- Select the less-expensive items on the menu: chicken and pasta versus fish or beef.

- For an afternoon wedding, serve a variety of hors d'oeuvres in place of a full meal. At a 3 P.M. wedding your guests will not be expecting lunch or dinner.

- Have the catering staff serve the buffet food. This will limit the amount guests put on their plates and avoid the embarrassment of running out of food.

- For a casual, backyard wedding, consider having a potluck or barbecue.

- Buy your own alcohol and have it served by a staff member.

- If you buy the alcohol from a wholesaler, make sure they will let you return unopened bottles.

- To greatly reduce costs, avoid serving alcohol altogether. Sparkling cider and other non-alcoholic drinks make a suitable replacement, especially for a daytime wedding.

The Rehearsal Dinner and the Postwedding Brunch

As long as you're researching food, think about what kinds of meals, if any, you're considering for the rehearsal dinner and the postwedding brunch. Even if you're planning a simple event, these two meals are a wonderful way to cushion the wedding: the rehearsal dinner as preparation for the ceremony, and the postwedding brunch as a continuation of the celebration. In many cultures around the world the wedding lasts from three days to a full week. This allows the bride and groom to transition more naturally into the roles of husband and wife, then out of the fold of the community and into their more private life as a married couple. It also helps take the pressure off you to see all of your out-of-town guests and connect with people closest to you in a span of five hours on the wedding day.

The plans for both meals can range from simple and casual (ordering take-out, serving scrambled eggs and bagels, or asking a family friend or your parents to host them), to a more formal event at a restaurant or country club.

Use the sheets in the back section to record your final choices.

The Cake

Are you a cake lover, or do you generally pass on sweets? Have you dreamed about a five-tiered wedding cake, or have you never given it a thought? Some brides feel strongly that their cake must match their dress style and their wedding colors, while others are content to find a reasonably priced cake that tastes and looks great. Searching for your cake can be a fun, light day that you can share with your partner. Make a few appointments, set aside an afternoon, and enjoy! How can you go wrong when you're tasting cakes?

PRACTICAL TIPS

- Most bakeries charge between $1.50 and $10 a slice. For a fifty-person wedding, expect to pay at least $100 for your cake.

- If you fall in love with a particular cake but it's out of your budget, you can order a small cake to be presented and several sheet versions to be cut in the back kitchen. The flavors will be the same, but you'll save on tier costs.

- If you are attached to a specific cake style, bring a photo to show the designer. If you're more flexible, look through their photos and, of course, sample the actual cake.

- Make sure the baker is licensed by the state health department.

- Ask about delivery: will it cost extra, or is it included in the price?

The Flowers

Depending on your ceremony and reception sites and your personal sentiment toward flowers, your choices will range from the simple to the ornate. It's difficult to improve on nature's majesty: if you're marrying outdoors, surrounded by the natural beauty of nature, you can forgo spending the money to decorate with flowers. If you're marrying in a reception hall or religious site, you may choose to decorate the aisles or have two or three large bouquets near the altar and around the room. You will also need to decide on your bouquets, corsages, and boutonnieres, as well as flowers for the tables and the cake.

Use the following worksheet to determine the who, what, where, and how much for your flowers.

PRACTICAL TIP

You can save money on flowers by buying directly from a flower mart or a farmer's market. Ask a bridesmaid to be in charge of flowers, and have her arrange your selections in vases around the ceremony and reception sites. Consider purchasing live plants (such as orchids), which you can take home or give away at the end of the day.

WORKSHEET: YOUR FLOWERS

QUANTITY	DESCRIPTION	COST

BOUQUETS

. . . . BRIDE: . . . . $ . . . .

. . . . BRIDESMAIDS: . . . . $ . . . .

. . . . THROWAWAY BOUQUET (FOR TOSS): . . . . $ . . . .

. . . . **TOTAL** . . . . $ . . . .

CORSAGES

. . . . MOTHERS: . . . . $ . . . .

. . . . GRANDMOTHERS: . . . . $ . . . .

. . . . BRIDAL CONSULTANT: . . . . $ . . . .

. . . . OFFICIANT: . . . . $ . . . .

. . . . OTHERS: . . . . $ . . . .

. . . . **TOTAL** . . . . $ . . . .

BOUTONNIERES

. . . . GROOM: . . . . $ . . . .

. . . . GROOMSMEN: . . . . $ . . . .

. . . . DAD: . . . . $ . . . .

. . . . OFFICIANT: . . . . $ . . . .

. . . . **TOTAL** . . . . $ . . . .

FLORAL HEAD WREATH

. . . . FLOWER GIRL: . . . . $ . . . .

. . . . BRIDE: . . . . $ . . . .

. . . . **TOTAL** . . . . $ . . . .

CEREMONY SITE

. . . . ARCH: . . . . $ . . . .

. . . . AISLES: . . . . $ . . . .

. . . . ALTAR: . . . . $ . . . .

. . . . OTHER: . . . . $ . . . .

. . . . **TOTAL** . . . . $ . . . .

RECEPTION SITE

. . . . COUPLE'S TABLE: . . . . $ . . . .

. . . . PARENTS' TABLES: . . . . $ . . . .

. . . . GUESTS' TABLES: . . . . $ . . . .

. . . . CAKE TABLE: . . . . $ . . . .

. . . . TOP OF CAKE: . . . . $ . . . .

. . . . OTHER: . . . . $ . . . .

. . . . **TOTAL** . . . . $ . . . .

SUBTOTAL $ . . . .

TAX $ . . . .

TOTAL $ . . . .

DEPOSIT $ . . . .

BALANCE DUE $ . . . .

The Music

Music can be an integral or peripheral part of your ceremony and reception. For some women, the music played during the processional helps bring them back into their body. Other women are content allowing the church organist to make the selections. How important is music in your life? Are you uplifted by music, your mood transformed simply by listening to a favorite song? Or do you pay little attention to sound and leave the radio tuned to the station that happened to be playing? And, most importantly for your reception, do you love to dance? Do you hope people will dance at your wedding, or is it irrelevant to you? Answering these questions will help you select your music. For more detailed help see www.consciousweddings.com.

Ceremony Music

Music is generally played at four points during the ceremony: prelude, processional, ceremony, and recessional. If you are hiring musicians, they will be able to suggest selections. If you are a music aficionado, you may have specific pieces in mind.

PRACTICAL TIP

If you love the idea of a live musician or vocalist performing for your ceremony but cannot afford a professional group, consider hiring students from a local music conservatory. You can find classical guitarists, harpists, flautists, and vocalists for a reasonable rate: from $50 to $75 per hour, depending on their level of experience and your geographic location.

Reception Music

The reception music—DJ, band, or burning your own CDs—is determined by your vision of how you see your guests spending their time. Do you see them mostly socializing, eating, and drinking, with the music creating atmosphere? Or do you see them hitting the dance floor, letting loose to their favorite tunes? For atmospheric music, consider burning your own CDs (or making mixed tapes). If you want to dance, a DJ or band is the way to go.

PRACTICAL TIPS

- A DJ costs about half as much as a band, with costs ranging as follows:

  DJ: $500 to $1,500

  Band: $1,200 to $3,000

- If you want your entertainment to announce the reception events, be sure to give them the schedule. Conversely, if you don't want events announced, communicate this as well.

- Consider the size of your reception hall when making your band decision. A large, outdoor space is more suitable for a large band, with a smaller orchestral group conducive to an intimate, indoor space. If the band is too large for the space, it will make it very difficult for people to hear each other.

The Photographs

Photography generally rates high on most brides' priority list, competing only with the dress for the number one slot for allocation of time and money. They are aware that, unlike the flowers, food, cake, and music, photographs have a shelf life that extends far beyond the wedding day. Given that you will want to immortalize your day and capture its essence as beautifully as possible, it's easy to be seduced by the wedding photographers who charge upwards of $5,000 for their services. But before you sign that contract, be sure to take the time to do your research.

PRACTICAL TIPS

- To save money, hire the photographer for the ceremony and the first hour of the reception. Most of the shots you need can be taken within that time frame.

- Read the contract carefully and be sure you know what you are signing. For instance, will the studio send a staff photographer to your wedding? Will the photographer keep his or her own negatives? (Most do, then charge for every additional print.) What, exactly, is included in the fee—how many shots, how many prints, how many albums, how many hours?

- Choose someone whom you genuinely like. A great photo is the result of art and chemistry. If your photographer rubs you the wrong way, it will show.

- Do you want posed or photojournalistic shots? Be sure to communicate your preference. Some brides are clear that they do not want a single posed shot but want to capture the essence of the event in spontaneous moments.

- For posed shots, be sure your photographer has a checklist of all the configurations you want (for example, bride alone, bride and groom, groom alone, groom with parents, bridesmaids alone, bride with bridesmaids, etc.). I've heard several stories of women who became swept up in the day and only realized afterward that there were no photographs taken of her groom with his parents, for example.

The Wedding-Night Accommodations

Unless you're leaving immediately for your honeymoon from your reception, you will probably reserve a room at a nearby hotel or bed-and-breakfast. You will spend your first night as a married couple in this room and, while I highly encourage you to keep expectations low, you will want it to be comfortable and have a magical touch. Consider creating a change of scenery, so if you are getting married in a city hotel, you spend the night on the beach; or if you're marrying in the woods, you head off to the city. This will separate your wedding from your honeymoon and begin to create the cocoon that will further develop as the two of you come down from the wedding high and begin to make the adjustments of the first year of marriage.

φ

Remembering to Breathe

Have you allowed yourself to become possessed by the wedding devil? Has Bridezilla managed to sneak into your body? It's very easy to allow these characters to sidle up into your consciousness and begin running the show. If the details of the reception are out of alignment with your wedding vision, step back for a moment and reevaluate your intention. Why are you having this reception?

Remembering to breathe is both a metaphorical and literal practice. When you find yourself feeling swallowed by brain fog because of the overload of details, bringing your focus back to your wedding intention and vision will help clear the air. The simple task of withdrawing your mental energy from the outer to-do list and redirecting it to the inner motivator of "why are we doing this?" will remind you that in the big picture none of those details matter. This redirection of energy will help keep you calm, clear, and focused by "breathing" space around the practical tasks.

Your physical breath is the most powerful grounding tool you can utilize throughout your planning and into your wedding day (and through any significant life transition). Just as a pregnant woman learns how to breathe in preparation for her delivery, so an engaged woman can learn to rely on her breath to ease her transition into marriage. Few of us learn how to breathe properly. This is unsettling, given that our breath is an accessible, effective, and free tool to counteract anxiety. But we live in a culture that promotes the quick fix and expensive reliance on antianxiety medication. When women become overwhelmed by wedding planning, they may rush to obtain a prescription for one of the plethora of medications currently available. When women seek counseling with me, one of the first skills I teach them is how to breathe. For the conscious bride, getting married is often the time when they learn about the power of their breath.

You can use the following exercise as often as you feel your mind constricting and the sense of being overwhelmed entering your body. It can also be used on your wedding day to maintain connection and grounding.

EXERCISE: LEARNING TO BREATHE

Stand with your feet hip-distance apart, knees slightly bent, hips tucked under. Let your arms hang naturally at your sides. Close your eyes. Stand for a few minutes and feel the soles of your feet grounding into the earth. Imagine that you're standing on a wide stretch of land or on a warm, sandy beach. Feel the heat of the sun on your body and the clean air of the summer breeze on your face. When you are ready, slowly stretch your arms toward the sky. Hold them fully extended for a moment, then slowly bring them back down. Do this again, but this time follow your breath: on the inhale, reach your arms toward the sky, and on the exhale, bring them back down toward the earth. Breathe deeply and slowly, in and out, through your nose, listening for the sound of the ocean down the back of your throat. Continue for several minutes, inhaling your arms up toward the sky and exhaling back down to the earth, until your feel yourself settle back into your body.

Honoring the Loss

At extraordinary life events, such as weddings, births, and funerals, the extraordinary range of human emotions is present. This means that grief is often a wedding guest and joy may find its way to a funeral gathering. In the context of mainstream ideology, which says that weddings are joyous, funerals are sad, and to express any other emotions is rude, the idea of actually inviting loss to a wedding is blasphemous. But in the context of a consciousness where we understand that weddings, births, and funerals are rites of passage in which there is both a birth and a death, the panoply of emotions make sense. And the more your losses are consciously invited to the reception, the more space is opened for joy to fill the room.

It's a gross misconception that welcoming the loss will distract from the joy. Contrary to our cultural message, the more we acknowledge the sadness and loss, the more joyous the wedding will be. Why? Because defending against and ignoring loss requires a significant amount of energy, and this prevents us from being fully present for the event. On the other hand, the simple action of honoring loss through symbol or ritual creates a place for it and allows the rest of the reception to continue. Think of loss like the quirky aunt that no one wants to invite to the wedding. If you ignore her and act like she doesn't exist, she may crash your reception and cause a dramatic stir. But if you extend your welcome and send her an invitation, she will know that her place is secure and she can act like a respectable guest. The same is true for loss.

WORKSHEET: HONORING THE LOSS

1. **NAME THE PEOPLE YOU HAVE LOST.** This includes those who have passed over as well as significant friends or family members who are no longer in your life.

. . . .

. . . .

. . . .

. . . .

2. **DOES YOUR GRIEF AROUND THESE LOSSES FEEL COMPLETE?** In other words, have you let yourself cry, scream, write, and talk about the losses until they feel healed? Which losses feel complete and which still need attention?

. . . .

. . . .

. . . .

3. **FOR THOSE LOSSES THAT HAVE NOT BEEN ADEQUATELY GRIEVED WHAT DO YOU NEED TO DO TO COMPLETE THE GRIEF PROCESS?** (talk to a friend or counselor, journal about it, join a grief group, etc.)

. . . .

. . . .

. . . .

. . . .

4. **WHAT WOULD PREVENT YOU FROM HONORING THESE LOSSES AT YOUR WEDDING?** (fear of disapproval from guests, pain of admitting the losses, etc.)

. . . .

. . . .

. . . .

. . . .

5. **WHAT ARE SOME WAYS YOU COULD HONOR THESE LOSSES AT YOUR WEDDING?**

. . . .

. . . .

. . . .

. . . .

If you decide to honor these losses at your wedding, talk to your fiancé, officiant, and relevant family members about how you would like to do so. The conversations themselves may sufficiently create the space that your loss needs, but if not, opening the dialogue will help you arrive at what feels right for you.

φ

Crossing the Threshold: The Wedding Night

As the reception unwinds and the guests slowly depart, the bride and groom, now husband and wife, head to the room where they will spend their first night as a married couple. They kiss and hug on their way over, cushioned in the back of a limousine, slowly sipping champagne, encased in an air of rosy bliss. As they approach the door, the husband sweeps his new wife off her feet and gallantly carries her over the threshold. They enter a gorgeous suite and fall onto a king-sized bed that has been decorated with red rose petals. And then they begin their first night of conjugal bliss. They fall asleep wrapped in a silky embrace, blissed out and beautiful.

Cut! What film are we watching? This isn't reality, it's the fantasy that we are fed by our culture. Of the hundreds of women I have spoken with about their wedding night, a scant few actually had a great sexual experience. Many felt obligated to abide by the tradition and they worried about the ramifications of breaking it. Just as we are imprinted with the message that a perfect wedding will lead to a perfect marriage (and an imperfect wedding to an imperfect marriage), so we consciously or

unconsciously carry the belief that if we don't have sex on our wedding night, we are beginning the marriage on the wrong foot. But if you ask women how they honestly felt that night, after experiencing one of the most emotionally and spiritually profound days of their life, they will say, "I was exhausted. All I wanted to do was fall into bed and sleep for a week." Still, some women felt inspired to make love, others blindly followed tradition, and still others decided to ignore the tradition and create another meaningful ritual of their own.

Before you completely cast aside the tradition, it's important to recognize that there are two meaningful elements embedded into it: the threshold and the "consummation." As I mentioned in the previous chapter, the idea of crossing a threshold is a beautiful symbol of the transition from one way of life to the new life phase. You may choose to include a threshold symbol, like a flowered arch or jumping the broom, during your ceremony. And you may choose to honor the "crossing the threshold" tradition in your own way, like the two of you crossing together while verbally articulating the meaning of the act. What matters is that the action becomes conscious, as opposed to a rote and meaningless act that you blindly follow.

Just as we have to modernize our understanding of the wedding gown so that it is in alignment with our current values, so we must expand our understanding of the word "consummate." Until recently, the bride and groom were virgins on their wedding night, and the marriage was not considered valid until it was physically consummated. In this sense, to consummate meant to have sex. But the full definition of the word actually means to bring an element of completion or culmination. We find several ritual acts of completion during the reception—eating and drinking together, holding hands, kissing—and nothing is lost if the couple chooses to forego the sexual act. If the ceremony and reception are created with the intentions of meaning and connection forefront in the couple's mind, they will feel more than complete at the day's end.

Sometimes, following the wedding-night ritual of physically consummating the marriage may be inspired by fear or obligation, and sometimes it stems from the beautiful human need to enact a final closing ritual for the day. In the context of transitions, making love on your wedding night is a significant rite of incorporation. You are literally inviting one another into the deepest layers of your physical, emotional, and spiritual bodies, incorporating your new husband or wife and closing the circle of the wedding day. In many cultures around the world, the act signifies that bride and groom have transformed into wife and husband, and we carry this worldwide tradition in our bones. So while many newlyweds are not virgins on their wedding night, the sexual act still carries the symbolic resonance of its underlying meaning: breaking the seal of singlehood and initiating them into the realm of a married couple.

Whatever rituals you decide to enact or ignore, I strongly encourage couples to communicate their expectations about this night to each other. All too often, one or both partners is worried about disappointing the other and so denies their true desire in order to please their partner. Do you really want to begin your marriage on the foundation of deceit and self-sacrifice? If you explore your expectations and communicate your fears to each other beforehand, your wedding night can unfold naturally and authentically. You may want to take a bath. You may want to open your gifts. You may want to hold each other and talk about the day. You may need some time alone to digest the intensity of the experience you just had. Laying the groundwork for a healthy marriage doesn't mean following a tradition because you are supposed to; rather, it means honoring your body, communicating your truth to your partner, and staying in alignment with the principles and commitments that have brought the two of you to this moment in your life.

WORKSHEET: YOUR WEDDING-NIGHT BELIEFS AND EXPECTATIONS

1. **WHAT ARE YOUR EXPECTATIONS OF THE WEDDING NIGHT?** What do you hope will happen?

. . . .

. . . .

. . . .

. . . .

2. **WHAT ARE YOUR BELIEFS OR STORIES ATTACHED TO NOT MAKING LOVE THAT NIGHT?** In other words, are you afraid something bad will happen if you break the tradition?

. . . .

. . . .

. . . .

. . . .

3. **WHAT DO YOU THINK YOUR FIANCÉ'S EXPECTATIONS OF THIS NIGHT ARE?**

. . . .

. . . .

. . . .

. . . .

4. **HOW DO YOU THINK YOUR FIANCÉ WILL RESPOND IF YOU TELL HIM THAT YOU MIGHT NOT WANT TO MAKE LOVE ON YOUR WEDDING NIGHT?**

. . . .

. . . .

. . . .

. . . .

5. **WHAT ARE OTHER RITUALS OR PHYSICAL ACTS THAT SYMBOLIZE THE CHANGE AND NEW BIRTH THAT YOUR RELATIONSHIP WILL UNDERGO?** Some couples choose to refrain from sexual contact for a specified time period. Some begin trying to create a baby, thereby having unprotected sex for the first time in their relationship. Some decide to dance together, give each other massages, or light a candle and hold each other in silence.

. . . .

. . . .

. . . .

. . . .

6. **ASK YOUR FIANCÉ ABOUT HIS EXPECTATIONS TO CHECK YOUR ASSUMPTIONS AGAINST THE REALITY.** If you have different needs for that night, continue the dialogues until you find a reasonable compromise. It's better to spend the time having these discussions now instead of having a fight or silencing your true needs on your wedding night. These conversations, like all the conversations you will have throughout your engagement, can help pave the way for a more graceful and joyful experience.

φ

CHAPTER 7

The Final Weeks

Emotional Tasks

Staying Connected to Loved Ones φ
Handling Blended Families

Practical Tasks

Solidifying the Seating Arrangements

As the wedding nears, tension between the members of the inner wedding circle often escalates. Unless the underlying feelings have been consciously addressed, this tension usually manifests as mothers of brides obsessing about practical details, fathers freaking out about financial matters, mothers of grooms pointing an incessantly critical finger at the bride and her family, girlfriends flaking out or lashing out at their betrothed friend, and fiancés checking out. The bride and her party, in a frantic attempt to keep the peace, focus ever more diligently on trying to create perfection, hoping they can find just the right seating arrangements and food selections so everyone will be happy and the wedding day will unfold without a wrinkle. But this hope rarely translates to reality. Just as finding the "perfect" dress will not allay a woman's grief about letting go of singlehood, so attending to the externals will not help your mother grieve her loss or your girlfriends address their fears.

φ

It's Not about the Dress!

Once again, I'm here to remind you that no matter how much energy you devote to the external details of your day, the emotional undercurrents that are being unleashed have a force of their own that, unless acknowledged, can potentially wreak havoc on your carefully laid plans. We've all heard about wedding disasters that erupt on the eve or day of the wedding—screeching fights between bride and mother, bride and girlfriends, and, most painfully, bride and groom. Most of these arguments can easily be avoided if people take the time to do one simple thing: talk. Talk about how they're feeling, talk about their fears, talk about their anxieties. But in our consumer culture that pushes products as the antidote to all of life's problems, most wedding parties are left no time to talk. They are so consumed with making their last purchases and finalizing the endless list of details—a list that seems to grow, not shrink, as the wedding nears—that their emotions are, once again, pushed underground until they are forced to volcanically erupt around the wedding day.

Not only is time eaten up by "doing," but the advice women receive about how to handle the inevitable family tensions is focused on externals. Our culture tells us, and we readily believe, that if we follow the proper seating etiquette and strategically place the stepmother on the north side of the hall in an exact parallel relation to the mother, then the two can successfully avoid each other and, thus, avoid their feelings. This may work; that is, until you run into your mother in the bathroom and she lashes out at you because you had promised to serve beef and there was only chicken on the menu. A more poignant example comes from Alexis, who opened up a bridal magazine in search of guidance on how to handle her dad's new girlfriend. This woman, who was just a few years older than the bride and clearly jealous of the attention Alexis was receiving from her father, was pushing herself front and center on the wedding stage. She had even gone so far as to inform the bride that she was planning on wearing a bright red slip dress and the same

pearl necklace as Alexis's to the wedding. The magazine advised Alexis to appeal to the girlfriend's more compassionate side, simply reminding her that a wedding is the bride's day and that she really shouldn't wear that dress or those pearls. The reasoning behind this advice is that if the woman were to replace the red dress with a nice pastel, the red-hot feelings would vanish.

It would be nice to think that if we wore the right dress, all would be well. Unfortunately, life is a bit more complicated than that. No matter how much money you spend on external items or how perfectly you follow the etiquette guidelines, the feelings your mothers (biological, step, in-law), fathers, friends, and groom are experiencing during this transition are sometimes as intense as your own. And just as you need an alternative guide to walk you through the emotional landmines of your engagement, they need the same. Most likely, your loved ones have no idea that they are also in a process of transition, which means that they are also letting go of ties and grieving losses. Once this information is brought to their attention and they are given a safe space inside which to express it, the dark clouds of tension break and the sun of clarity shines through. I am continually amazed by how much joy and serenity can result from a simple drop of consciousness. But unless your loved ones have been doing "conscious wedding" research on their own, they will need you to turn on the light for them and give them permission to express their less-than-blissful feelings. Having educated yourself with this important information and completed your own conscious work, you are now in position to guide others down the same road.

φ

The Final Task

If you've made it this far into this planner, you have hopefully been attending to the emotional and practical details of your day with your sanity intact, which will leave you some time and serenity as your wedding nears to address this final task. There are three steps I recommend you take now:

1. Offer educational material to your loved ones informing them of what may be occurring for them emotionally and giving them permission to express these feelings appropriately. (I've provided some examples on the Conscious Weddings Web site.)

2. Write a letter to those you feel called to write to, expressing some of your own feelings toward them and what this transition means to you.

3. Set aside some time several weeks before the wedding to talk with family members and friends about their feelings.

My clients are amazed at the intimacy and joy that arise from executing these simple steps. Julia felt compelled to write separate letters to each of her girlfriends expressing what they meant to her, her fears about marriage, and what she needed from them during this time. She also wanted to let them know that if they had any uncomfortable feelings—jealousy, fear of losing her to marriage, inadequacy about their own life or marital status—that she welcomed them telling her. Prior to writing the letters, she had begun to feel a vortex of subtle tension spiraling around her. Her girlfriends were typically complaining about bridesmaids' gowns and other small details. She knew that if she didn't name the elephant in the room, the tension could easily spiral out of control. Her willingness to take the risk and send the letters really paid off. Each of her girlfriends called her to express their gratitude, and she got together with them individually to have a heart-to-heart talk. The tension immediately dissolved and she felt closer to them than ever. On her wedding day and into her marriage she felt lovingly supported by the circle of her female friends.

These steps are simply a guideline and may not apply to every member of your inner circle. The point here is to take some time to notice and name any tension that may be brewing and take the necessary action that will help dissolve it. To help you along the way, I have included a handout on the Conscious Weddings Web site for each of the significant people in your life—mother of the bride, mother of the groom, father, and girlfriends—explaining what this time is about and alerting them to the different emotions that may be surfacing. If a stepparent or other caregiver has been largely responsible for raising you, replace the word "mother" or "father" with the term you use to address your loved one. Sometimes it's easier for family and friends to hear about their experience from an expert, but if you think it would be more effective to educate them with your own words, please do so. As with every element of your wedding, there is no "right" way to approach this task. If the end result is more consciousness, serenity, and joy, then you are on the right track!

φ

Writing Letters to Loved Ones

After offering your family and friends information about the process of transition, the next step in staying connected is to write them each a letter. The purpose of these letters is to give yourself an opportunity to articulate and express how you're feeling during the engagement and what you need from them to facilitate a smooth and healthy transition. As I mentioned earlier, writing these letters has been one of the most powerful exercises for my clients and their inner circle. The art of letter writing—the act of putting a pen to paper and contemplatively formulating thoughts, which is nearly lost due to the popularity of e-mail—encourages the writer and the reader to share and listen from a heartfelt place. When is the last time you sat down at your desk or in your garden and wrote a letter? When is the last time you opened your mailbox and received a letter from a friend or family member? Letters are special; they are tangible documents from the soul representing a specific moment in a person's life. Because they are written with care, they are often received with care. They are a beautiful and effective way to open the dialogue about expression and needs around a wedding. They can help open the doors to crucial conversations so that your loved ones can help guide you into the arms of your marriage.

As you write these letters, think about addressing the following points:

- What this person means to you

- How they have supported you in your life

- The feelings that have been emerging since you became engaged

- Specific exercises from this planner that you would like to share

- How you understand the process of transition

- How they can support you on your wedding day

- How they can support you in the first days and weeks of marriage (both emotional and practical support)

- Ask what they may need from you during this time

Consider writing a letter to your mom, dad, future mother-in-law, girlfriends, and any other important person in your life. You may choose to utilize these letters as springboards for the conversations you have as the wedding nears.

φ

Handling Blended Families

In a perfect world, parents stay happily married for life. In a slightly less-than-perfect world, blended families unite under the lovely roof of the Brady Bunch. In reality, relationships with stepparents range from loving and peaceful to awkward or combative. If your stepmother entered your life when you were young and was largely responsible for raising you, you may have a very close and healthy relationship with her. But if your dad has recently remarried, the term "stepmother" can barely apply. While I strongly encourage you to address the latent emotional issues that may arise as the wedding day nears, there is a practical element to blended families that needs attention. These days, the bridal couple often needs extra help deciding who sits where and does what on the wedding day.

The bottom line when dealing with stepparents is to communicate. When it comes to wording on invitations, ceremony and reception seating, and walking down the aisle, your primary intention should be to help people feel as comfortable as possible on your wedding day. If you are wondering where to seat your stepmother during the ceremony and reception, talk to both your mother and stepmother and find out where each would feel most comfortable. You might think you are pleasing your stepmother by seating her in the first row when actually she would feel more comfortable in row three. So the first step in making any practical decision is to avoid making assumptions and bring the given subject out onto the table. If your mothers and fathers—both biological and step—are reasonable people, you should be able to come to a reasonable solution together. You do not have to guess and make these decisions alone.

But remember that even the most reasonable, levelheaded people can become irrational around a wedding. Your mother's twenty-year resentment of your stepmother's role in your life might come to an explosive head. Or your stepmother's long-held resentment of the intimacy you share with your dad might suddenly appear. You can make a preemptive strike by appealing to their more rational side and simply remind them that they are all adults and you hope that they can put their unresolved feelings aside to support you during one of the most important times of your life. Never underestimate the power of rational communication!

Above all else, remember that you're not required to play therapist and try to assuage your elders' unconscious emotions; the best you can do is remind yourself of what you've learned about the emotional underbelly of weddings, then make sound and strategic practical decisions that will help divert their conflict.

Invitations

Invitation wording is largely dictated by who is hosting the wedding. However, if your father and stepmother are paying but your mother primarily raised you and is helping plan the wedding, you will probably want to acknowledge her as well.

Walking Down the Aisle

Unless you are committed to abiding by tradition, this decision is determined by who raised you. One client's older brother walked her down the aisle, as he was the person who participated most actively in her upbringing after her parents divorced. If you were raised by both your dad and stepfather, ask one to walk you down the aisle and the other to participate in the ceremony by doing a reading or giving the rings. And if your mother primarily raised you, it will make most sense for her to assume that honored role. Again, the gauge is to ask yourself what makes the most sense given the shape and circumstances of your life.

Seating Arrangements: Ceremony

The first three rows are usually reserved for family. For divorced parents, consider seating the parent who raised you in the front row with his or her spouse and the other parent in the third row. Siblings, grandparents, and other honored guests sit in the second "neutral zone" row. Of course, if both sets of parents are on good terms, you can seat them together or let them choose their own seats. Whatever arrangement you decide on, remember to ask both sets how they feel before solidifying your decision.

Seating Arrangements: Reception

For a formal, sit-down dinner, have each set of parents host their own table. If tension is high, consider seating them at opposite sides of the dance floor. Again, communicate your plans with all parties involved before confirming them.

- Seat people with similar interests together. Usually people who are close in age will have something in common.

- Put guests who love to dance close to the dance floor. They will be more inclined to stir things up if the floor is only a few feet away.

- Try to place an even number of guests at a table to avoid leaving someone out of a conversation.

- Put family members who have traveled a long distance with other family members. This is probably one of the only opportunities they will have to catch up.

Solidifying the Seating Arrangements

*N*ow that you have the basic wisdom of blended-family etiquette regarding seating arrangements, you are ready to decide who will sit where at your reception. Of course, if you are having a more casual wedding, your guests will decide on their own where to plant themselves. But if you're having a large wedding with many guests who don't know each other, they will appreciate the comfort of knowing where to sit. One of the aspects of your wedding that your guests will most remember is how well they connected to the people around them. Use the boxed tips when planning the seating, then grab a pencil and draw in the type of tables and arrangement you'll have (round tables, U-shaped head table, etc.). Play with the arrangement until it feels right. When you've finalized the setup, fill in the final seating arrangement worksheet in the back of the book. I've also included a sample seating arrangement just so you get the idea.

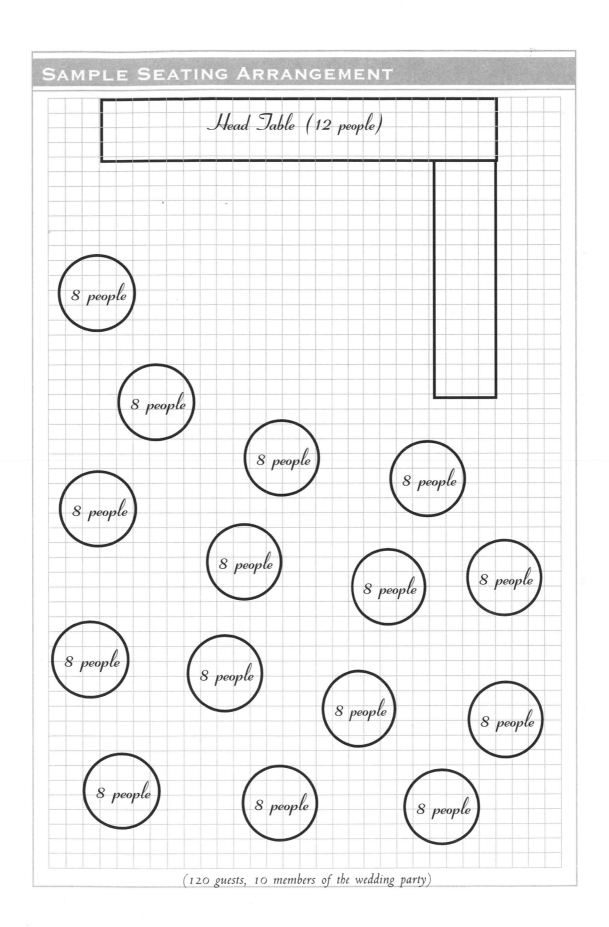

Head Table (12 people)

8 people
8 people
8 people
8 people
8 people
8 people
8 people
8 people
8 people
8 people
8 people
8 people
8 people
8 people
8 people
8 people

(120 guests, 10 members of the wedding party)

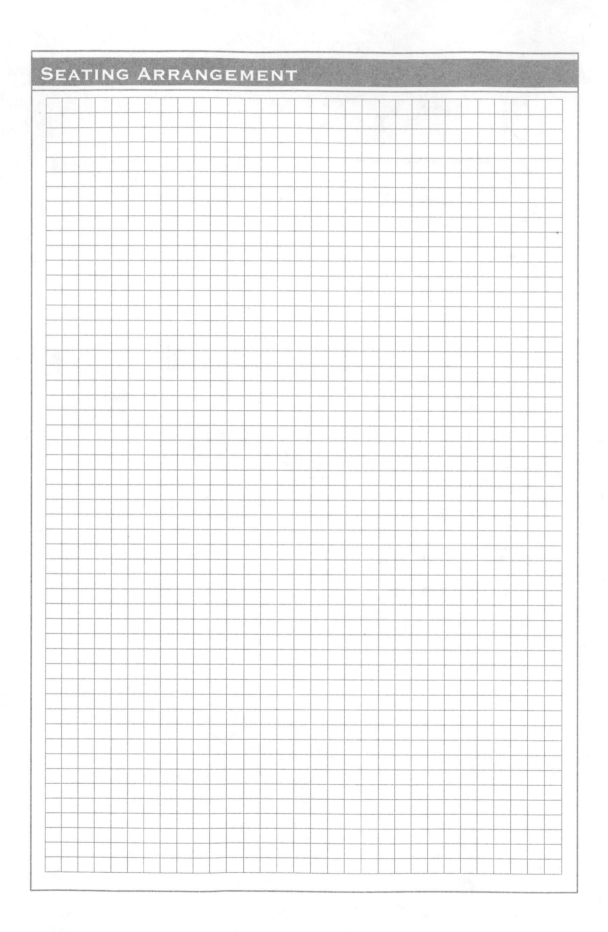

The Man You're Marrying

We discussed staying connected to your loved ones and have now addressed every practical issue around your wedding. But there is one piece we have left out—your groom! As noted earlier, it's frightfully easy to become so caught up in the planning that you forget about the most crucial person in this entire affair. For, while it's important to stay connected to your family and friends and attend to your practical tasks, the person with whom it's most essential, and most challenging, to maintain connection is your fiancé.

Your fiancé, like your mother, stepmother, and everyone closest to you, is an easy target, the perfect place to dump your unexamined and misunderstood fear, loneliness, confusion, grief, disappointment, and anger. After all, if he didn't ask you to marry him, you wouldn't have to be feeling all of these difficult feelings! As you worked through the other pieces of the emotional engagement pie, you probably found that your negative feelings toward your fiancé dissipated.

However, as the wedding nears, each remnant shard of irritation and resentment that you have ever felt toward your intended often comes tumbling through your body with renewed strength and velocity. As with every other area around the engagement, if you don't shine your flashlight of consciousness onto these emotions, making room for them and handling them responsibly, they can easily grow into giant snowballs and pummel you in an avalanche of anger. But, if you remind yourself that they are normal, invite them to your tea table, and give them the attention they need, you will circumvent many prewedding arguments and keep your heart open to the love and commitment that has led you to this moment in your lives.

It's important to keep reminding yourself that your fiancé is not the cause of your emotional state. Given that you have made sure that you are making the right decision, most annoyances and grievances toward your fiancé that develop during the engagement are a result of your transitional emotions being transferred onto him. You would be feeling these feelings no matter who you married. They are a normal, necessary part of your transition and actually have very little to do with your partner. It takes a lot of courage to admit to the less-than-romantic feelings you may be having right now. Let them in, recognize them for what they are, then see if you can trace them to their root.

Use the following checklist to help you put words to your experience toward your fiancé:

- ○ I feel annoyed at my fiancé. Little things, like the way he eats or the way he mumbles his words, bother me now when they never bothered me before.

- ○ Sometimes it hits me, "Oh my god. This is the man I'm going to be married to for the rest of my life!" And it scares the . . . . out of me.

○ I think a lot of my disappointment around the engagement—that I'm not feeling perfectly joyous all of the time—is displaced onto him.

○ Sometimes I feel so separate from him. It's strange that we are walking toward the same event—the wedding—yet we seem to be having vastly different experiences.

○ I feel lonely around him, especially when I'm in touch with my grief and what I'm letting go of. As much as I try to communicate what I'm feeling, I'm not sure that he can really understand.

○ Sometimes I feel angry at him for no reason.

○ Sometimes I feel angry at him for "taking me away" from my single life and my family of origin and "making" me grow up.

φ

Handling Your Emotions

As your wedding nears, the sense of feeling out of control and out of sorts will intensify. If the wedding is the birthday of your marriage, then these last days are like the pains of labor. Like two babies, you and your fiancé are traveling down the birth canal, sometimes together, sometimes separately, experiencing the out-of-control, mysterious, and beautiful transition into a new life. The last vestiges of your singlehood identity are falling away; you are trembling on the precipice of the great unknown, wondering who the two of you will become on the other side of the wedding. Although you have chosen the date of your birth, this conscious choosing does nothing to alleviate the bewildering sense of slipping away from solid ground and diving headfirst into the unknown.

When we feel out of control, when a major life transition squeezes in from all sides and threatens our illusory sense of security, we either feel like we're combusting or exploding. With a wedding, not only are you experiencing the normal emotional components of transition, but you're most likely finalizing the outer details as well as dealing with family and out-of-town guests. Feeling overwhelmed is to be expected. And when we feel overwhelmed, we often lash out at the person with whom we have our most intimate relationship.

How can you manage feeling overwhelmed so that you can avoid unnecessary conflicts with your fiancé? My clients have found the following suggestions helpful in finding release and maintaining at least a semblance of equanimity:

- Remind yourself that it is normal and natural to feel overwhelmed as the wedding approaches.

- Be kind to yourself when the two of you do have an argument. No matter how many precautions you take, it's almost inevitable that you will have a couple of spats as the wedding nears.

- Make a commitment to do one of the following every day: take a short walk; meditate for ten minutes; do yoga at home; dance! Physical exercise and meditation release stress and create equanimity.

- Go to nature: the beach, the mountains, the desert. Connecting with something larger than yourself will help cradle and comfort your large emotions.

- Scream, cry, beat up your pillows—the point here being that the emotions are stored in your body, and they need to be released.

- Pray, or connect with your spiritual source in the way that works for you. Ask for guidance and support as you walk through one of the most important transitions of your life.

- Connect with your fiancé.

φ

Opening Your Heart

One of the most effective ways to stay connected to your fiancé and ground yourself when you are feeling overwhelmed is to connect to the gratitude you feel toward him. When two people fall in love, they often feel like they are returned to a state of innocence and purity where they see themselves, each other, and the world as if for the first time. They feel thankful for each moment on earth. They notice nuances and subtleties in their familiar surroundings that had previously escaped their attention. It's as if their eyes have been cleansed of the film of falsity by the clear waters of truth and wonder.

As time moves on, this open feeling of gratitude often wanes, and around a wedding, it can easily be replaced by resentment and distance. But it only takes a moment to reposition your spiritual compass and align yourself with gratitude. Focusing our intention on noticing and expressing gratitude opens a direct pathway to the soul, like a rush of water that washes away the tentacles of fear and leaves an open heart in its wake.

An effective and simple way to express your gratitude toward your fiancé is to make an appreciation list and give it to him once a day, every few days, or once a week. We all need to know that we are loved and appreciated, and there is no greater heart opener than one person saying to another, "This is why I love you ..." Of course, as with most exercises in this book, the pendulum swings in both directions. I encourage you to give this page to your partner so that you can exchange mutual appreciation during these final days. These can range from the simple to the extraordinary—from "I love the way you stroke my hair," to "I love the commitment you show to our relationship." What matters is that you find the few minutes to search your heart, find the truth, and offer these gifts to your partner. Use the following page as a template for your lists.

WORKSHEET: APPRECIATING YOUR PARTNER

This is what I appreciate about you:

1. . . . .

. . . .

2. . . . .

. . . .

3. . . . .

. . . .

4. . . . .

. . . .

5. . . . .

. . . .

6. . . . .

. . . .

7. . . . .

. . . .

8. . . . .

. . . .

9. . . . .

. . . .

10. . . . .

. . . .

Soon you will experience the gift of standing beside one another at the altar and spiritually offering your love and commitment. You will be showered on your wedding day by the love of your community and uplifted by their support on one of the high days of human life. A wedding, like the birth of a child, is a great mystery and an awesome experience. You have done the hard emotional, spiritual, and practical work of the engagement that will allow you to be present for your ceremony and receive the support and joy of your reception. You have become aware of your intentions and have ensured that you are aligned with your partner about the vision of your wedding. The work is done. Now you only need to breathe, surrender to the majesty of this time, and walk into your wedding day, prepared and serene, ready to step into this new and wondrous phase of your life.

CHAPTER 8

The Wedding Day

Emotional Task

Showing Up

Practical Task

Packing Your Wedding Bag

You've made it! Your wedding is near. As you can see, this is one of the shortest chapters in the book. That's because your work is done. You have completed the tasks to create a meaningful and joyous day, and now all you have to do is show up. Showing up means that you are present in the arc of the day. It means that you embrace the joy and surrender to the chaos. As you enter the day, it's important to remember what you have learned about transitions so you can place the wedding in its appropriate context. This will bring clarity in the event that chaos and confusion invite themselves to your wedding. It will also help you to remain present so that you can ride the emotional waves with grace and enjoy your day.

φ

The In-Between Zone

In every transition, there is an in-between zone. With the wedding, it is the time when you are no longer single and not quite married, as if you're in limbo. We say that someone is in limbo when she is in between jobs, relationships, or any time one state ends and the next has yet to begin. This is a time of formlessness in that the woman stands between two identities without being firmly attached to either one *and* she bows to both the past (life as a single woman) and the future (life as a married woman), thus acknowledging and incorporating two states of being. She is at once *leaving being* and *coming into being* as she waits in a timeless, empty holding space. This can explain the sense of "walking through a dream" that many women feel at some point on their wedding day. The sense of fading in and out of presence is the experience that characterizes the day for brides.

When we understand that the wedding serves a real and ancient psychological and spiritual function, we move away from the culturally fostered assumption that the day is supposed to be perfect. Paradoxically, releasing the expectation of perfection is actually what allows the joy to enter the day. Think about it: you enter your wedding day believing that you must feel more beautiful, loved, and in love than you have ever felt in your life. Suddenly, you feel floaty, like you're in a dream; you can't feel your love for your fiancé, and you panic. You may think, "What's wrong with me? What's wrong with us?" If you don't understand that these sensations are a normal and necessary part of the transformation, you will berate yourself for failing to experience pure joy. On the other hand, if you simply remind yourself that you are in the in-between zone and that whatever you feel on this day is normal, you can allow the feelings to pass and make room for the joy to enter.

When you are in limbo, you know it, and using words and metaphors can help ground you during this predominantly groundless experience. Use the following checklist and worksheet to help you identify how you are feeling as the wedding nears.

CHECKLIST & WORKSHEET: IN-BETWEEN ZONE

The in-between zone can begin several days or weeks before the actual wedding day. Your singlehood identity is loosening, you are entering the caterpillar's cocoon, and you have no idea what being a wife will feel like. Diving into the mystery of an identity transformation creates the sense of being in limbo. The sooner you can name the state with specific words ("Oh, I'm in the limbo phase and I'm feeling . . . ."), the more readily you can surrender to the sensations and move closer to joy. Below are some hallmark emotions of liminality. Check off the ones that you're feeling.

- ◯ Disoriented
- ◯ Groundless
- ◯ Untethered
- ◯ Unreal
- ◯ Numb
- ◯ People feel unfamiliar
- ◯ Difficulty feeling love
- ◯ Floating
- ◯ Asking yourself, "Who am I? Where am I?"
- ◯ Sense of being in a void
- ◯ Vulnerable
- ◯ Skinless
- ◯ Feeling nothing and everything; collision of serenity and chaos
- ◯ Desire to be with your mother, or whomever or whatever symbolizes the womb, familiarity, ground, safety, comfort

Which metaphor works for you?

- ◯ The old structures have crumbled, and the new structures have not been erected.
- ◯ The old skin has been shed, and I have not yet grown the new skin.
- ◯ I am in the middle of the ocean without a compass or rudder.
- ◯ I feel like an infant, and I'm longing for the safety of my mother's warm embrace.

Using one of these statements as a first line, write a paragraph expanding on the metaphor:

. . . .

. . . .

. . . .

. . . .

. . . .

. . . .

. . . .

. . . .

. . . .

. . . .

φ

What to Expect

*C*ontrary to our cultural messages that encourage us to expect a day of pure bliss (despite the pervasive images of wedding-day disasters), there is an arc to a wedding day that includes many varying emotional states. Westerners typically have difficulty accepting the paradox that nothing and everything, chaos and calm, joy and grief can coexist in a single day. Occasions like a wedding or funeral are seen as either joyous or somber, without shades of gray and without the possibility that two or more emotions could live in a single moment. But a wedding is a unique event in human life. As you saw during your engagement, allowing the loss and grief helps open the doors to the joy and excitement. A wedding, as a day of transition that encompasses both a letting go and a joining, invites its participants to span the spectrum of human emotions, encouraging them to grieve and tremble as well as laugh and rejoice.

There is natural and normal ebb and flow on a wedding day. Moments of calm in the bridal suite surrounded by women friends and encased in the serenity of the feminine can be juxtaposed with the internal chaos of preparing to walk down the aisle. The floating, dreamlike quality of the ceremony can be followed by the raucous joy of the music and dancing. There is no one way, no "right" way, to experience your wedding. You cannot prepare for how you will feel in each moment. But you can find reassurance in the information that whatever happens on your wedding day is exactly what is supposed to happen.

No matter how much information and reassurance I give you, a lifetime of living in this culture has no doubt affected your beliefs and expectations about the day. Bringing these into the light will help you to see which ones you wish to follow and which you will replace with more healthy and helpful beliefs. When thinking about the wedding day and night, you may experience an array of conflicting thoughts and emotions. Use the following worksheet to help you identify the thoughts and emotions that are most prominent for you.

WORKSHEET: THE WEDDING DAY

- ○ I feel excited about my wedding day.

- ○ I feel [scared, anxious, terrified] about my wedding day.

- ○ Every time I think about the wedding, I want to . . . .

- ○ It's okay if I cry on that day.

- ○ It's not okay if I cry on that day.

- ○ I hope I look like a princess on that day.

- ○ I hope I look more beautiful than I've ever looked in my life.

- ○ I hope I feel more present and alive than I've ever felt in my life.

- ○ I have low expectations for how I'm going to look and feel on that day.

- ○ I hope my partner and I feel connected and in love on that day.

- ○ I want only [names of friends and family] . . . ., ..., ..., and . . . . with me while I'm getting ready (add more if necessary).

- ○ I feel like this is very much *our* wedding.

- ○ I wonder how I'll feel when the day is over and I have to take off my wedding gown. I imagine I will feel [sad, relieved, regretful, joyous, a sense of loss].

- ○ If we don't feel perfectly in love throughout the day it means that

  . . . .

- ○ Other: . . . .

My biggest fear about my wedding day is . . . .

. . . .

. . . .

. . . .

. . . .

The thing I am most excited about is . . . .

. . . .

. . . .

. . . .

. . . .

Remembering Dreams

As you recall, your dreams can bring greater understanding throughout your engagement and especially in the days shortly before the wedding. Most of my clients share fascinating

and revealing dreams about their wedding day. Dreams are a direct source of wisdom, messages from your unconscious that provide a window into your conscious life. If you take some time to attempt to decipher the dream code, you will often be rewarded with a clear direction about a current issue or internal conflict. Pay attention to your dreams. They will lead the way.

DREAM LOG: *The Wedding*

(Use this space to record your dreams pertaining to the wedding.

. . . .

. . . .

. . . .

. . . .

. . . .

. . . .

. . . .

. . . .

. . . .

. . . .

. . . .

. . . .

. . . .

. . . .

. . . .

. . . .

. . . . φ

Letting Go of Control

Nearly every bride has at least one story to tell about a glitch in her wedding day. The gown rips, the crazy uncle makes a drunken fool of himself, it rains, it hails, the chicken is overcooked, the flowers are wrong. The truth is that no matter how carefully you plan, human beings are fallible and Mother Nature works on her own timetable. If you allow your perfectionism to rule, the glitch will assume monstrous proportions, pulling you out

of your body and out of the flow of your day. But if you enter your wedding day with the expectation that something is likely to go wrong and you keep your intention for marrying at the forefront of your consciousness, you will be able to keep the glitches in perspective, handle them with grace, and continue experiencing the joy of your day.

Now is a good time to recall your intention. Remember that you're not getting married so you can have a wedding; you are having a wedding to consecrate and celebrate the beginning of your marriage. The dress, the food, and the flowers have nothing to do with the intentions and commitment that have led the two of you to this day. In other words, a ripped dress is not calamitous; overcooked chicken does not qualify as a wedding-day disaster. And since these elements are largely out of your control, the only sane response is to smile—or not!—and surrender.

The more you remember your intention, check your expectations, rein in your perfectionism, and practice your relaxation techniques, the more likely it is that you'll experience the joy and be able to fully celebrate. In chapter 6, I offered techniques to help you learn how to breathe and surrender to the stress of planning a wedding. The Bride's Wedding Day Meditation, which my clients receive on CD and have found particularly helpful, can be used to create a calm and centered space preceding the wedding and on the day itself. You can download this meditation, set to music, at www.consciousweddings.com. Soon, the words will begin to reverberate in your mind and body, sending a soothing signal to your cells, informing them that it's okay to let go and receive whatever is meant to arise on your wedding day.

φ

Wedding-Day Tips

There are some very practical ways to stay grounded and present in your body. In preparation for this planner, I put out a call to the conscious brides with whom I've worked and asked them to share tips and advice on how they stayed present for their wedding day. Their responses ranged from the emotional and spiritual to the practical. Think about which ones might work for you, then write them down at the end of this section.

Wendy

One thing I did throughout the day that helped me soak it all in was to close my eyes and take deep breaths. Every time I closed my eyes, I told myself to "remember exactly the way you feel right now." These were cherished little gifts to myself that I knew I would want to hold forever. I look back on my wedding day and remember those particular moments as if they were beautiful packages tied up with ribbons, and each time I think of them, I get to unwrap them again. When I watch my wedding video or look at pictures, I can show the exact times when I took those moments for myself: dancing with my husband, dancing with my father. My expressions at those times were completely peaceful and brimming with happiness. I know that time will fade the memories from that unforgettable day and night, but the moments I took for myself, the way I felt, will always have an indelible imprint in my mind.

Ashley

I brought a vial of lavender oil with me and every time I felt stress creeping up, I opened it and took a deep, long breath. Breathing always helps me to calm down, and lavender is a scent that I use a lot around my house and in my bathtubs. Each time I breathed it in on my wedding day, it reminded me of lying in a bubble bath, feeling calm and peaceful. Then I would open my eyes, see all this beauty before me, remember what's important, and smile.

Jane

I brought a high-school friend (whom I hadn't seen for ten years) and my best friend to the salon the morning of the wedding. I felt very quiet, kind of weepy, and I realized I had to completely relinquish control of everything and be carried through the day by the wedding energy and by the work of other people. It was an adjustment to get used to that feeling. It helped so much to have just a couple of very intimate friends with me for the first part of the day.

Also, eat a big breakfast and have some snacks in the dressing room! You probably won't really eat enough on the wedding day and don't expect to eat at the reception at all. The breakfast and snacks are a very concrete and essential way to help you stay present and grounded in your body.

Sara

My journal always helps me to find myself and stay connected, so I decided to bring it with me and check in with myself every few hours. I actually managed to sneak away amidst the flurry of the reception, and each time I did, I wrote down just a few quick sentences about how I was feeling and thinking. I look back on those entries as little gems, like snapshots of my soul, capturing moments on one of the most incredible days of my life.

Eleanor

Jake and I wanted to honor the Jewish tradition of Yihud (meaning "union"), which is a brief respite after the ceremony where the bride and groom take about ten to fifteen minutes to connect. This was a real grounding point for us. It was our way of acknowledging that this wedding was about and for us. We went into a private room and let the magic and depth of what just transpired in the ceremony sink in. This was our first moment as husband and wife! We held each other, kissed, ate a little, and breathed. And then we felt ready to greet our guests and join in the community celebration of our union. I look back at those few minutes as some of the most profound and spiritual of our day.

Victoria

Early on the morning of our wedding, before we were dressed in our wedding clothes, the Master of Blessings, who married us, gathered the two of us into a private room. He sat us knee to knee, holding hands, with our eyes closed. He led us through a guided meditation where he spoke of each of us from infancy to old age and asked us if this was truly the person we wished to be married to. We each said "yes." He also did a muscle test along the same lines, where he had us pull on a piece of material if we wanted this person in marriage. We had to answer with our physical strength, while he pulled the fabric in the opposite direction. This was powerful in that it made us fight for it, use our bodies and our strength, not just our hearts, head, lust, and emotion. Both of these actions—the meditation and the physical test—brought us into our bodies and set the tone for the wedding and our glorious day.

How can you plan to stay present at your wedding?

. . . .

. . . .

. . . .

. . . .

. . . .

. . . .

. . . .

. . . .

. . . .

. . . .

. . . .

. . . .

φ

Clearing your mind of the clutter of practicalities can help you to be more emotionally present on your wedding day and wedding night. Check the items on the following comprehensive list that you think you'll need on your wedding day. Write additional items down as they occur to you, to lessen the pressure to remember everything on that day. When your list is complete, fill in the sheet entitled "To Pack: Wedding Day" in the back section of this planner.

You don't have to carry this burden alone; your groom and attendants can also be responsible for bringing items to the wedding. Make photocopies of the following sheets, fill in the appropriate name, and communicate what you would like this person to pack. They can also use the space provided to write down their special duties for the day.

There's a bittersweet quality to the end of a wedding, for it signals the end of a long phase of your life. But just around the corner you sense the dawn of a new day, the sun's golden rays reminding you of the new beginning. And as you unpack your honeymoon bags, you realize that the next important phase of your life has begun. Welcome to your marriage, the next phase of your relationship journey.

φ

General:

- ○ This planner (which will contain all vendor and wedding party contact information and a space to journal)
- ○ Cell phone
- ○ Water
- ○ Protein bars
- ○ Disposable camera
- ○ . . . .
- ○ . . . .
- ○ . . . .

Attire and Beauty:

- ○ Dress
- ○ Veil or headpiece
- ○ Shoes
- ○ Stockings
- ○ Makeup
- ○ . . . .
- ○ . . . .

Ceremony items:

- ○ Vows
- ○ Rings
- ○ Unity candle

- ○ Chuppah
- ○ Guestbook
- ○ Ring pillow
- ○ Ketubah
- ○ Yarmulke
- ○ Wine glass
- ○ Wine glass holder (for breaking the glass)
- ○ Broom (for jumping the broom)
- ○ . . . .
- ○ . . . .
- ○ . . . .

Reception Items:

- ○ Checkbook to pay vendors
- ○ . . . .
- ○ . . . .

Emergency Kit:

- ○ Hairspray
- ○ Brush or comb
- ○ Bobby pins
- ○ Extra stockings
- ○ Clear nail polish
- ○ Nail file

- ○ Dental floss
- ○ Toothbrush/paste
- ○ Tampons/pads
- ○ Tissues
- ○ Safety pins
- ○ Needle and thread
- ○ Breath mints
- ○ Medications (asthma inhaler)
- ○ Aspirin or ibuprofen
- ○ Clear Band-Aids
- ○ Lavender oil (to calm your nerves)
- ○ Sage stick (to cleanse)
- ○ Warm shawl
- ○ . . . .
- ○ . . . .

Wedding Night:

- ○ Lingerie
- ○ Toothbrush/paste
- ○ Next-day clothes
- ○ Birth control
- ○ . . . .
- ○ . . . .

Groom's Wedding-Day Packing List

○ . . . .
○ . . . .
○ . . . .
○ . . . .
○ . . . .
○ . . . .
○ . . . .
○ . . . .
○ . . . .
○ . . . .
○ . . . .
○ . . . .
○ . . . .

OTHER RESPONSIBILITIES: . . . .

. . . .

. . . .

. . . .

. . . .

. . . .

. . . .

. . . .

. . . .

. . . .

. . . .

Attendant's Wedding-Day Packing List

○ . . . .

○ . . . .

○ . . . .

○ . . . .

○ . . . .

○ . . . .

○ . . . .

○ . . . .

○ . . . .

○ . . . .

○ . . . .

○ . . . .

○ . . . .

OTHER RESPONSIBILITIES: . . . .

. . . .

. . . .

. . . .

. . . .

. . . .

. . . .

. . . .

. . . .

. . . .

. . . .

CHAPTER 9

The First Year

Emotional Tasks

Coping with Postbridal Blues φ *Being Reborn* φ
Adjusting to Marriage

Practical Tasks

Thank-You Notes φ *Last-Name Change*

*Y*ou did it! You passed through your engagement and you crossed the threshold into marriage. Externally, you planned a ceremony and reception and made it through the wedding day. Internally, you have done the work that allowed you to arrive at your wedding feeling ready for what the day would bring and prepared for the metamorphosis in the first year of marriage. You have shed the old skin and transformed from a single person to a wife. The letting-go process of your engagement has now opened to a new beginning. And that's what the first year is about: beginning anew. The transformation is not complete until you have experienced the rebirth of yourself as a wife and adjusted to the changes in your relationship with your husband. Most of the hard work is done. The autumn leaves have fallen. Spring is here!

While in many ways the first year is an exciting time, it's also a time of tremendous adjustment. These challenges are compounded when we operate under the false belief that, now that you're married, you should feel only blissful. As with the engagement and wedding, we live with a cultural message that assumes that from your wedding night through your honeymoon and into the first year, you and your beloved should be floating through the enchanted forest of marital happiness. While this can be a joyous time, nothing in our culture prepares newlyweds for the challenges that lie ahead. In the context of a rite of passage, you have just undergone one of the biggest transformations of your life, and transformations require adjustments.

As explained in earlier chapters, van Gennep referred to this last phase of a rite of passage as "incorporation." This is the time to adjust to the new identity of "wife" and "husband" and to incorporate your partner at this new level of commitment. The adjustment takes time; we cannot expect to wake up on the first morning of marriage and feel fully confident in our new roles. For even if nothing changes on the outside—if you've been living together for years and already felt married—on the inside everything feels different. You have just entered one of the most complicated, mysterious, and beautiful relationships that human beings engage in. Your mind will be wondering, "What does it mean to be a wife or husband? What does it mean to be married? What have we just done?!"

Before you can answer these questions, you'll be faced with the reality that your wedding—the day that you have been planning for months, years, or your whole life—is over. The first emotional task of the first year of marriage is to come down off the high of the wedding and find your way back to earth.

*P*ostbridal *B*lues

A wedding is one of the most important events in human life. When women have done their prewedding emotional work and are able to enter the day with realistic expectations, they often feel joyous, present, and magical throughout the day. Their diligent preparation coalesced to create the external vision that expressed their love and commitment. Family and friends cried and rejoiced. Their transformation was witnessed and honored. The day was complete.

But where there is a high there is also a low, and what goes up must come down. If we listen to this basic law of nature we will be able to anticipate the natural low that follows the high of a wedding. This cycle of high and low, ebb and flow, is true for all condensed experiences in life into which significant thought, energy, and time have been invested. Have you ever been a part of a play, planned a special dinner, or written a book? Do you remember the anticipation, excitement, and tension that builds to a crescendo when the event is complete, then waking up the next morning feeling depressed? When focused energy culminates in a single event, a natural release follows. With an inhale comes an exhale. With a tension comes a release.

The days and weeks immediately following the wedding are the time to release and exhale. This is the time to allow yourselves to adjust to the enormity of this transition. Often the way that we adjust to large events is to temporarily withdraw from life, creating a cocoon inside which the change can find completion. Our rhythm slows down, our senses are dulled. We become very quiet inside. The time and attention that we have blown into the balloon of the wedding comes to an end, and, without our breath, the balloon begins to deflate. This deflation, this natural inner quietude, is also known as depression.

Making Room for the Blues

Given that a low is a natural and normal response to a high, one might assume that we would expect some depression after a wedding. But, given the unilateral "joy only" view around weddings, coupled with a cultural fear of depression, it would make sense that we would deny that the words "depression" and "newlyweds" could exist in a single sentence.

When newlyweds experience depression after a wedding, they immediately wonder if something is wrong: "Isn't this supposed to be the most blissful time of our lives? Aren't we supposed to be floating through our days until we rush into each other's arms each

evening with a welcome kiss and a bouquet of roses?" Like the engagement, when newlyweds feel anything less than pure joy, they wonder, "Did I make a mistake? Is there something wrong with our relationship? Is there something wrong with me?"

In rare cases, depression could indicate that the decision to marry was out of alignment with your truth. However, if you have made it to this point in the book and have done your conscious work, it's much more likely that your depression is the natural low that follows the high. This low may last three days or three weeks. It's the body's way of slowing back down to a human pace and adjusting to the changes of marriage. As with all difficult emotional states, the more you let it in, the more quickly it will pass. (If you feel uncomfortable with the word "depression," find a word or phrase that works for you: "blue," "quiet," "deflated," "I'm hibernating," "I'm in winter," "I'm under the weather.") Removed from the highly negative connotations it carries in our culture, depression is actually a beautiful and feminine way of honoring rhythms and restoring balance. It's nothing to be afraid of, but simply a natural part of this large transition. Depression is your body's way of finding balance, and many believe that by allowing the natural progress of the depression to move through, you will avoid a more dramatic balancing act, like catching the flu. One way or another, your body will force you to slow down, climb into the cocoon of your bed, and allow your being to process what just happened.

If your depression lasts longer than two months, it could indicate that the emotional work of your engagement is incomplete. You may need to revisit certain exercises in this book or seek the guidance of a counselor who understands transition.

Blue Honeymoon?

There is a reason why most people choose a tropical, lie-on-the-beach location for their honeymoon over the backpacking-across-Europe option. When you've spent months planning your wedding and then have undergone a spiritually transformational experience, you become exhausted. The honeymoon is the time to release, to unwind, to let your body and soul bask in sunshine and rest. It's not uncommon for couples to spend the first several days of their honeymoon sleeping! It's important that you and your partner honor your bodies' rhythms and let yourselves do absolutely nothing if that is what you need. The spectacular hike can wait; the ruins will be there for another thousand years. This is your time to just be.

Again, problems arise when we cannot let go of a rigid expectation of how the honeymoon should be. We may imagine ourselves frolicking with our new spouse, kissing in the surf, and staring at each other misty-eyed over dinner. This may happen—and it may not. The more you can release the expectation that the two of you must be perfectly in love every day of your honeymoon, the more likely it is that you will be. It's important that you be able to communicate with each other about what you're feeling and needing. If you are just too exhausted and spiritually shocked to engage in deep levels of intimacy, tell each other. Reading this paragraph and having the conversations ahead of time may help avoid a conflict, as it will reduce the fantasy and expectation of perfection and allow you to show up for whatever the honeymoon brings.

Doing versus Being

We are a culture addicted to doing. We go to work, we attend meetings, we make lists, we check e-mail, we make phone calls, we exercise, we do, do, do, filling every available time slot in our days and evenings. This kind of schedule stuffing often continues until our bodies make us rest by getting sick or we can finally drag our way to our two-week annual vacation, where we collapse on a beach in some faraway place. We deny our bodies, ignoring the natural rhythm that calls for rest, silence, and solitude. Most of us live chronically out of balance.

Nowhere is this more true than around a wedding. As much as you have attended to your internal needs, you have also been preparing for the external events. Even a simple wedding requires a guest list, invitations, a dress, rings, a ceremony, photographs, a cake, flowers ... and that's keeping it simple! One would think that the compulsion to "do" would end on the wedding day, but when you return from your honeymoon you may feel pressure to continue in the vein of doing as you attend to the follow-up details. This may even appeal to you as a way to avoid the emptiness that you may be experiencing. If you write those thank-you notes, put away all the presents, get your dress cleaned and boxed, and organize your receipts, you simply won't have time to feel depressed. Let me rephrase that: you'll have no time to consciously feel depressed. In other words, your body and psyche will be experiencing a depression but you'll be too busy to recognize it. In this case, what ends up happening is that you actually prolong the unwanted experience by avoiding it. If, on the other hand, you recognize its positive purpose (bringing you into balance) and let it into your life, it will pass through more quickly.

The thank-you cards can wait. The gifts will still be there, sitting patiently until they are unwrapped and put away. No one will collapse if you don't return a phone call for a few days. The world will wait for you. This is your time to be still—to decompress, to cocoon, and to reflect on the magnificent, life-altering journey that has landed you in the beginning of your marriage.

Actively Processing the Wedding

When you return from the honeymoon, you will need to consciously make time to unwind. Our lives tend to move at a very fast pace, and if we don't set an intention and commitment to allow ourselves downtime, the spaces in our days are easily filled.

This is your challenge: Can you take fifteen minutes a day to lie on your bed, in your backyard, or on the floor and just be? It sounds simple, but when you have spent the last year moving quickly, it can be difficult to slow down. See what happens when you give yourself this time and space. Resist the temptation to make a phone call, read a book, flip through a magazine, or watch television. If you've been holding your depression at bay, now is the time when it may crash over you. You may feel overwhelmed at first, but if you stay with it, the emotion embedded in the depression will break through, and after a good scream or cry, you will feel renewed.

In this still place, after you've released your emotions, watch as your wedding washes over you. Allow yourself to bask in the images that come to mind. Some images may fill your body with joy; others may be painful. Most women express regret about at least one aspect of the day. Make room for this as well.

As you return to your body, take a few minutes to consider the following worksheet.

WORKSHEET: PROCESSING THE WEDDING

1. WHAT STANDS OUT MOST ABOUT MY WEDDING DAY IS

. . . .

. . . .

. . . .

2. THE IMAGE THAT KEEPS RECURRING IN MY MIND IS

. . . .

. . . .

. . . .

3. MY BIGGEST REGRET ABOUT MY WEDDING DAY IS

. . . .

. . . .

. . . .

4. MY HAPPIEST MEMORIES OF MY WEDDING DAY ARE

. . . .

. . . .

. . . .

5. WHENEVER I THINK ABOUT MY WEDDING DAY I FEEL

. . . .

. . . .

. . . .

Fifteen minutes a day of simply "being" gives your body and mind the rest it needs to unwind to its natural pace. Whenever you feel your rhythm quickening past your comfort zone, step away from your task at hand, close the office or bedroom door, and let yourself just be.

φ

The "I" within the "We"

As you enter more deeply into your marriage, you may experience confusion about how to retain your independence after making the biggest public commitment of togetherness that you will ever make. The question often becomes: "Now that I've just sacrificed a part of my independence, perhaps even giving up my last name, how do I maintain my separateness, blossom as an individual, and not lose myself within the marriage?" This is one of the most important questions that you'll be asking not only during this first year but throughout your marriage.

Many of the great poets, prophets, and philosophers have written about the necessity of establishing a healthy separateness between partners in marriage. The enmeshed, symbiotic relationship that occurs during the initial "in love" phase of a relationship can only be sustained for so long; eventually one person in the partnership will crave their individuality and claim a degree of the separateness that existed prior to their union. This doesn't mean that the intimacy has to suffer. On the contrary, true intimacy can only exist if each partner has a strong relationship with their solitude. If I define myself exclusively by my relationship to you, you will likely feel stifled by this need and pull back. A healthy marriage is predicated upon two healthy individuals coming together and creating a third entity—the marriage. One way to support this health is to actively nurture one's relationship to self. As Rainer Maria Rilke writes in *Letters to a Young Poet* (1934):

> It is a question in marriage, to my feeling, not of creating a quick community of spirit by tearing down and destroying all boundaries, but rather a good marriage is that in which each appoints the other guardian of his solitude, and shows him this confidence, the greatest in his power to bestow. A togetherness between two people is an impossibility, and where it seems, nevertheless, to exist, it is a narrowing, a reciprocal agreement which robs either one party or both of his fullest freedom and development. But, once the realization is accepted that even between the closest of human beings infinite distances continue to exist, a wonderful living side by side can grow up, if they succeed in loving the distance between them which makes it possible for each to see the other whole and against a wide sky!

Answering the question of separateness may require battling the centuries-old definition of what it means to be a wife. There can be no doubt that the archetypal and ancient expectation of traditional wifehood carries a powerful magnetic force. You may find yourself slipping into behaviors without even noticing. For example, suddenly you feel compelled to have dinner ready when your husband comes home from work. Prior to your wedding, you may have spent that hour catching up on reading, taking a bath, talking on the phone to your girlfriends, writing in your journal, or doing artwork. Now you feel something strange happening inside, almost as if you are sleepwalking to the kitchen to the beat of the unconscious mantra, "Must have dinner ready for husband. Must have dinner ready for husband." Wake up! You don't have to have dinner ready! If you and your partner have been in agreement about your needs and expectations around household chores and cooking, then those agreements still hold. The externals do not need to change after the wedding.

Marriage doesn't have to steal your sense of self or dampen your fire. That is an old model, an old belief, and it's time to set those archaic models aside so that the new models can take root and grow. For many women today, marriage actually provides an increased stability, a stronger foundation from which they can pursue their dreams and actualize their potential. They are no longer expending energy in the single world of trying to find a mate, and they have worked through the fears that consumed their energy during the engagement. When the marriage settles into its groove, a calm stability can arise that is quite conducive to nurturing one's creative self. The loss of the single self that occurred during the engagement has now cleared the field, allowing room for a new, expanded self to develop.

Through your marriage, you have moved into the next level of mature adulthood. If you have successfully completed the conscious work of your engagement, you're now in a position to welcome in the next phase. The old self had to die in order for the new to be born. And who will this new self be? Who are you in this marriage, as an adult woman beginning a family unit of your own?

After the initial phase of postbridal blues or depression lifts, many of my clients find that this is an exciting time. They begin to notice that several things are shifting inside of them. They are not the same women they were before. Unrealized dreams begin to surface. Suddenly the job that satisfied them for years is no longer fulfilling. This is good! This is a sign of growth. You are bursting out of the person you have been and a new self is beginning to emerge. Pay attention to the dreams and longings that emerge. They will pave the way to the new self, the new job, the manifestation of your dreams. You may find your life taking an entirely unexpected and very fulfilling direction.

The following worksheet will help you get in touch with the thoughts and dreams that may be emerging as your new identity and sense of self develops. As human beings, we are continually growing and unfolding, accessing undiscovered aspects of ourselves and reaching into uncharted territory, so this is by no means a finite process. But the phase following your wedding is a rich and pure time when your passions and the visions for your life often become startlingly clear. This is the rebirth, the spring that follows the quiet of winter, which followed the death of autumn. You are the butterfly emerging from the caterpillar's cocoon, trying out her wings for the first time. You are being reborn!

WORKSHEET: THE WOMAN I AM BECOMING

1. I FEEL SATISFIED/UNSATISFIED WITH MY WORK.

2. I FEEL CREATIVELY FULFILLED/UNFULFILLED.

3. I FEEL SPIRITUALLY CONNECTED/DISCONNECTED.

4. WHEN I'M FEELING UNSATISFIED WITH MY WORK, I OFTEN THINK ABOUT DOING SOMETHING ELSE LIKE

. . . .

. . . .

5. I'VE ALWAYS HAD A DREAM OF . . . .

. . . .

. . . .

6. I FEEL MOST CREATIVELY FULFILLED WHEN I'M . . . .

. . . .

. . . .

7. I FEEL MOST SPIRITUALLY FULFILLED WHEN I'M . . . .

. . . .

. . . .

8. SINCE THE WEDDING, I'VE BEEN THINKING ABOUT DOING THINGS I'VE NEVER THOUGHT OF BEFORE LIKE

. . . .

. . . .

Have You Forgotten Yourself?

Another common symptom of the first year is "self-amnesia." The pull toward togetherness is so strong, the bond and commitment that you have just made is so profound, that you may find it difficult to even remember what you enjoyed doing in your separateness before you were married. Who was that independent, self-contained person that your partner fell in love with? Where has she gone? She's still there, just beneath the surface, perhaps needing a few reminders about how she used to spend her time when she was single.

CHECKLIST: COUNTERACTING "SELF-AMNESIA"

What nurtures you? How do you spend your time when you're away from your husband? Check the boxes that resonate for you:

O Reading

O Taking a bath

O Lighting candles

O Listening to music

O Playing a musical instrument

O Having lunch or dinner with a friend

O Dancing

O Hiking

O Walking

O Going to the beach

O Watching the sunset

O Doing yoga or stretching

O Cooking

O Gardening

O Doing a creative project

O Spending time with my family

O Spending time with my pet(s)

O Writing in my journal

O Watching my favorite films

O Listening to spiritual tapes

O Writing a letter (a real letter—not an e-mail!)

O Getting organized—going through files, cleaning my desk

O Looking through old photo albums and journals

O Drawing or painting

O Talking to my friends on the phone

O Sitting in the sun

O Going for a long drive

O Other: . . . .

. . . .

. . . .

O Other: . . . .

. . . .

What Is a Marriage?

The next major question that emerges after the wedding is, "What is a marriage?" Hopefully, this is a question that you contemplated during the engagement as you worked through the exercises in chapter 1. But thinking about marriage and actually being married are two entirely different experiences, and the question actually transforms from "What is a marriage?" to "What is our marriage?"

Your marriage, like your wedding, is a unique alchemical combination of the being that is him and the being that is you. It is a complex dance of each of your thoughts, feelings, experiences, beliefs, fears, joys, idiosyncracies, house-care habits, money practices, child-raising values, and sexual needs. Each of you comes to the relationship as a fully formed adult, and no matter how much training and knowledge you have had about marriage, nothing can actually prepare you for the chemical reactions that occur in this brand-new relationship. A marriage, like a child, is born from two unique individuals. In this sense, we can view the marriage itself as its own entity. One plus one does not equal one and, in this case, it doesn't equal two. It equals three. The wedding births the marriage, which is the third enitiy in your relationship. And, like a child, it takes a while to adjust to what this actually means and what this third entity needs in order to survive and thrive.

Nothing Changes and Everything Changes

One of the most common questions I hear around the wedding and marriage topic is, "If a couple has been living together prior to the wedding, what actually changes?" I find this to be a fascinating question, and I often counter it with, "How many times have you heard about couples who were together for years, got married, and divorced almost immediately?" It's true that not much changes externally if you've already been living together. But the question ignores the reality that getting married is a spiritual, life-altering experience, and the changes that occur happen not in the physical realm but in the psychological, emotional, and spiritual realms. The question is indicative of a culture that doesn't recognize change unless we can see it and touch it.

On the internal, invisible plane, marriage changes everything. How can it not when two people have each relinquished an identity and entered into one of the most complicated of human relationships? For some couples, the change is felt almost immediately; others start to feel it when they return from their honeymoon. But for those that are deeply in touch with their physical bodies and emotional lives, the change is felt at some point. And by "change" I don't mean anything negative. Many couples share that they felt stronger and more solid after they married. But there is a change nevertheless, and it should be recognized.

When couples struggle with the changes that marriage brings, it's often because they haven't taken enough time prior to the wedding to process their fears, beliefs, and expectations about marriage. It is crucial that both partners take time to examine their views of marriage so that they can take a proactive approach to working with their fears and not wait until the fears act on them. For example, if you carry the belief that marriage means a complete death of individuality because that's what was modeled for you in your parents' relationship, you need to bring this belief to consciousness and work with it actively. Otherwise, every time your partner asks you to pick up some food at the market or take out the garbage, you will not hear it as a simple request but through the lens of "marriage equals death." If you haven't already, I encourage you to do the worksheets in chapter 5 on addressing and exploring your fears and expectations about marriage. Again, bringing your beliefs to consciousness will help you see what you're working with and allow you to rationally determine whether or not they're true.

Marriage as a Spiritual Path

Working with deeply ingrained fears and exploring your beliefs about marriage are not easy. As this is not a book on marriage, I can only touch on the intricacies involved in working with the issues that arise. But I will say this: I hold the perspective that marriage is one of the most challenging and rewarding spiritual paths on this planet. I share the viewpoints of such spiritual thinkers and psychologists as Gary Zukav, John Welwood, Harville Hendrix, and Terrence Real, who maintain that your marriage partner will push every single one of your buttons for the purpose of spiritual growth. Marriage is hard, just as being a monk or a priestess is hard—but it's hard for a reason. Nowhere else are we so challenged to work through our deepest fears and false beliefs and learn the most important lesson where we can learn: how to give and receive love. Patricia expressed it beautifully in *The Conscious Bride* (Paul Nissinen 2000, pp. 201–202):

> *The journey of getting married and being married has been so different than I ever would have imagined. Peter and I both hold the view that marriage is not just to have fun or to have kids, but it's something that helps us evolve on a spiritual level. It is as important a vocation as it is to be a religious person. Supposedly, in the ideal sense, the married couple is evidence of God's love in the world. Someone said that being married is a crucible, and I think that is very true. We feel like in being married each of us is helping the other to strip away the ego. All of our issues are coming up and we are learning, in some fundamental way, how to be less selfish and more loving. We very much see a spiritual purpose behind this whole thing and believe that is why we are together.*

There is no doubt that several issues will surface in the course of a marriage. These issues could be psychological and emotional (confronting the ways in which we attempt to control or feel controlled, coming to terms with our fears of abandonment and suffocation), and they could be ways that the external world creates obstacles (issues around money, work, living environment, illness, death). If we enter marriage with the belief that we will live "happily ever after," each time a challenge comes up, we'll view it as a problem that we must get rid of. If, on the other hand, we accept that part of the function of mar-

riage is to learn more about ourselves and others and to become more loving and fulfilled people in the world, then each difficult situation becomes an opportunity for growth.

It's frightfully easy to fall into the illusion that marriage is supposed to be effortless. Despite the fact that most of us grew up in families where conflict was alive and well, we still harbor the belief that it will be different for us. The belief that conflict is a sign of disease is actually part of the cause of a diseased marriage. The more you can break down your fantasies and create a realistic view of what marriage entails, the easier it will be for you to stomach it when the inevitable conflicts arise.

One effective way to foster a realistic vision is to ask other married couples about their experience of marriage. Our fantasies of effortless marriage are partially fed because we live in cloistered situations, removed from witnessing the day-to-day interactions of real-life couples. Our role models largely stem from the media where, if a married couple has problems, they are either tidily resolved in half an hour or the relationship suffers an affair or a divorce. As adults, we have no idea what other couples are dealing with, so we assume that Jen and Jake, the lovely couple who lives next door, must be having an easier time. Asking couples who have been married longer than five years about their marriage will help dispel your unhelpful fantasies. Approaching marriage from a realistic perspective will go a long way toward the health of your relationship.

Just as you did with the idea of what a wife could be, actually interviewing other people can help put marriage in its proper perspective and let you adjust your expectations accordingly. These two questions come from Victoria and Miles. At a family dinner that preceded the rehearsal dinner, they interviewed couples by asking two specific questions: What is the best part about being married? What is the hardest part of being married? They wrote down their answers in what would prove to be quite an unusual guest book.

Set an intention to encounter at least four couples—parents, friends, relatives, parents of friends—who are willing to speak honestly about their relationship. Compile your answers on the next page to create a realistic tapestry about the beauty and challenges of marriage. I encourage you to refer to it when you find yourself stuck in the darkness wondering, "Are we the only ones who are struggling?"

INTERVIEW: THE REALITY OF MARRIAGE

COUPLE 1: . . . . AND . . . .

MARRIED . . . . YEARS.

BEST: . . . .

. . . .

. . . .

HARDEST: . . . .

. . . .

. . . .

OTHER THOUGHTS ON MARRIAGE: . . . .

. . . .

. . . .

COUPLE 2: . . . . AND . . . .

MARRIED . . . . YEARS.

BEST: . . . .

. . . .

. . . .

HARDEST: . . . .

. . . .

. . . .

OTHER THOUGHTS ON MARRIAGE: . . . .

. . . .

. . . .

COUPLE 3: . . . . AND . . . .

MARRIED . . . . YEARS.

BEST: . . . .

. . . .

. . . .

HARDEST: . . . .

. . . .

. . . .

OTHER THOUGHTS ON MARRIAGE: . . . .

. . . .

. . . .

COUPLE 4: . . . . AND . . . .

MARRIED . . . . YEARS.

BEST: . . . .

. . . .

. . . .

HARDEST: . . . .

. . . .

. . . .

OTHER THOUGHTS ON MARRIAGE: . . . .

. . . .

. . . .

The Last Tasks

The emotional tasks of the first year do not occur in a linear fashion. The development of your identity as wife dovetails with the creation of your marriage, and each feeds off the other as you and your partner grow into this next phase of life. Marriage, like life, is a continual learning process; as the Buddhists say, "It is not about the destination—it's about the journey." The work you did during your engagement cleared the field and laid the foundation upon which your marriage will grow. It was the ending that paved the way for this beginning. You stand now at year one. No matter how old you are, your marriage is an infant and your identities as wife and husband are as vulnerable as newborns. Take

care with yourselves and with each other. Remember that if the garden is to flourish, the weeds need to be pulled, and the flowers need be watered and attended to with love. This journey of marriage is, at its core, a journey of love. You have the rest of your lives to learn what this most complicated of relationships really means.

The primary practical tasks of the first year are the thank-you notes and changing your last name. These tasks should be done only when you've had significant time to process the internal shifts. Even traditional etiquette allows for a full year within which to send the thank-you cards. Give yourself as much time as you need. If it will reduce your stress to write them as soon as possible, then go ahead and get them out of the way. But if you need time, if you are recuperating from the earthquake of your wedding, then give yourself some breathing room. Nothing is more important than giving yourself and your partner the time and attention you both need to flourish. As with the engagement, the practical tasks are important, but they mean nothing if the roots of your union are not receiving the attention they need.

Sending Thanks

In the back section is a gift log, which will help you organize your thank-you-note duties. Remember, though it's important to acknowledge your guests' generosity, you may need some time to settle into your new marriage. Try not to use tasks like thank-you notes to avoid any uncomfortable feelings that may be coming up now. You owe it to yourself and to your marriage to honor your feelings.

Changing Your Last Name

It's no longer automatically assumed that you will change your last name after you marry. The decision is yours and comes with many options: you and your husband can both change your name to a completely new name, you can hyphenate to retain both names, your husband can assume your name, you can take on his name, or you can keep your maiden name. As with every other wedding decision, it is important that you check in with yourself and find the action that feels right for you.

If you do decide to change your last name, you will need to complete official forms in order to legalize the change. Some of your identification papers, like your Social Security card, will require a certified copy of your marriage certificate, which you should receive two to four weeks after the ceremony. The Internet can provide most of the legal documents you need to complete the change. Each state has different requirements, so make sure you click on your appropriate state. Some good Web sites are: www.uslegalforms.com/namechange.htm and www.namechangelaw.com/.

CHECKLIST: CHANGING YOUR NAME

You will need to change your name on all of the following:

- ◯ Driver's license
- ◯ Social Security card
- ◯ Passport
- ◯ Credit cards

- ◯ Health insurance cards
- ◯ Car insurance
- ◯ School ID
- ◯ Other: . . . .

Closing the Circle

Living Gracefully

The one-year anniversary is a milestone of the wedding journey. (For creative one year anniversary rituals, see the Conscious Weddings Web site.) It is around this time that women begin to integrate the larger life lessons they learned through the wedding experience. The passage of a full year offers the perspective necessary to look back and make sense of what exactly happened through this process.

One of the primary lessons, one that you can carry with you for the rest of your life, is how to gracefully and skillfully navigate transitions. Life is unpredictable; in fact, the only truly predictable element of life is that change will be a constant companion on the journey. As we saw through the wedding-preparation process, our culture does very little to help us handle change constructively. We are expected to pass through the myriad of life's small and large transitions without many guides or a recognition of the importance of community.

You have a series of changes that may lie ahead of you: motherhood, buying a home, moving to a new city, changing jobs, the loss of a parent, the end of a friendship, your child's first day of kindergarten and last day of high school, and then, eventually, their wedding! Some of these changes have names—"empty nest," "mother of the bride or groom," "midlife," "menopause"—but most fall under the vast umbrella of nameless transitions that, without consciousness, we generally pass through blindly and alone.

Having done your conscious wedding work, you are amongst a small portion of our population that will be able to meet change with courage and deepen your learning with each of life's passages. This time has provided you with a road map that you can use to navigate all future transitions. Not only do you now possess an intellectual understanding of the three phases of change, but you also have a direct experience in your body of what to expect in each of these phases. Together, your mind and body will act as your guide. You now understand that where there is a loss, there is a gain; where there is a death, there can be a magnificent rebirth. Just as nature effortlessly passes through her seasons, so you now have the experience to be able to pass through the seasons of your life with grace, gaining wisdom with each spiral until you arrive at old age without fear and flooded in the light of consciousness.

With each rite of passage, the same life lessons appear in new forms. If you struggled with the "need to please" around your wedding, this life lesson will most likely reappear around motherhood or at the workplace. If you recognized for the first time how deeply ingrained your perfectionism is, you will notice it again if you become pregnant or buy your first home. Sometimes the regrets after a wedding are that these lessons couldn't have been learned prior to the event. The paradox is in wishing we could have learned the lessons earlier, yet knowing that it was the wedding that illuminated the areas of ourselves that need attention. And the beauty is in realizing that we can apply this awareness to every rite of passage in our lives.

It's important to spend some time summarizing for yourself what you have learned from your wedding and early marriage experiences, both intellectually in terms of the mechanics of a rite of passage and psychologically in terms of your life issues. Bringing your new information to full consciousness will help you approach your next transition fortified with the guidance of context and an awareness of your probable pitfalls.

WORKSHEET: NAVIGATING TRANSITIONS

1. WHAT ARE THE THREE PHASES OF A RITE OF PASSAGE?

   A. . . . .

   B. . . . .

   C. . . . .

2. WHAT IS THE BASIC TASK INHERENT TO EACH PHASE?

   A. TASK OF RITES OF SEPARATION: . . . .

   B. TASK OF TRANSITION RITES: . . . .

   C. TASK OF RITES OF INCORPORATION: . . . .

3. WHAT FEELINGS CAN YOU EXPECT TO FEEL IN EACH PHASE?

   A. FEELINGS IN RITES OF SEPARATION: . . . .

   B. FEELINGS IN TRANSITION RITES: . . . .

   C. FEELINGS IN RITES OF INCORPORATION: . . . .

4. WHAT CORE EMOTIONAL OR PSYCHOLOGICAL ISSUES SURFACED DURING YOUR ENGAGEMENT, WEDDING, AND FIRST YEAR OF MARRIAGE THAT IMPEDED THE PROCESS OF A SMOOTH TRANSITION?

   . . . .

   . . . .

5. WHAT WOULD YOU TELL A RECENTLY ENGAGED WOMAN ABOUT WHAT TO EXPECT DURING THIS JOURNEY?

   . . . .

   . . . .

A Parting Word

With this page, your wedding and this book come to a close. As I tell each of the women who contacts me with e-mails of gratitude or inquiries about counseling sessions, you are among a growing segment of our population who are courageous enough to go

against the grain and recognize that the wedding is much more than a unilaterally joyous party. You have had the advantage of realizing that your wedding can be one of the most meaningful and transformative rites of passage in your life. I commend you for honoring yourself and spending your time on more than making phone calls to florists and consulting with caterers.

Through your willingness to feel your sadness and confront your fears, you have widened your capacity for joy and courage. Through your commitment to communicate your inner world to those around you, you have deepened your intimacy with your loved ones. Through your honesty with yourself in the face of a culture that tells you to put on a happy face, you have joined the community of conscious brides who are role models for each woman who stands on the precipice of marriage. The light of consciousness is spread by each woman and man passing the torch of information with loving action.

You are the torchbearers. May you pass it wisely.

φ

Recommended Books and Films

I often recommend books and films to my clients to help elucidate a specific aspect of the emotional wedding journey, provide comfort, invite validation by identifying with a character's challenges and joys, or just for a good laugh. Some of these books and films relate to weddings and others to marriage. While you may not have much time to read during your engagement, keep this list in mind when you pack your honeymoon bag or when you're looking for a good book to comfort you during those first months of marriage. There's nothing like an insightful book or film to help us make sense of and appreciate the profound beauty of our life's journeys.

Books

Dearly Beloved (2003, reprint edition) by Anne Morrow Lindbergh
An insightful fictitious work that explores a wedding ceremony and reception through the eyes of family, friends, and the bride.

Gift from the Sea (1955) by Anne Morrow Lindbergh
A "spiritual compass" about youth and age, love and marriage, solitude, and contentment, written by one of America's most poetic writers. A great honeymoon read!

How Can I Get Through to You?: Reconnecting Men and Women (2002) by Terrence Real
In this groundbreaking book by one of the foremost writers on human relationships, Real examines the disconnect between men and women and offers tangible tools for how to find our way back to each other.

She: Understanding Feminine Psychology (1989) by Robert Johnson
A bride's journey to consciousness and wholeness as seen through the myth of Psyche and Eros.

The Dance of Intimacy: A Woman's Guide to Courageous Acts of Change in Key Relationships (1989) by Harriet G. Lerner.
A guide to maintaining intimacy, with an excellent discussion in chapter 12 on the mother-daughter relationship.

The Divine Secrets of the Ya-Ya Sisterhood (1997) by Rebecca Wells
A beautiful story of how a woman's impending wedding sets her on a journey of unraveling the complexities of the mother-daughter relationship.

The Good Marriage: How and Why Love Lasts (1995) by Judith Wallerstein and Sandra Blakeslee
An interesting examination of the four types of partnerships, including in-depth interviews with couples who have healthy, loving, long-term marriages.

The Illuminated Rumi (1997) translated by Coleman Barks and illustrated by Michael Green
This book is a treasure that should grace the bookshelf of anyone who responds to the healing and spiritual qualities of art and poetry.

The Road Less Traveled: A New Psychology of Love, Traditional Values and Spiritual Growth. (1997) by M. Scott Peck.

The Seat of the Soul (1989) by Gary Zukav
A roadmap for the spiritual seeker with a particularly clear explanation of the concept of "intention."

The Toaster Broke, So We're Getting Married: A Memoir (2002) by Pamela Holm
A funny, poignant, fresh read for anyone caught in that mysterious "bridal vortex" that can consume even the sanest of brides. Also a great honeymoon read.

The Unimaginable Life: Lessons Learned on the Path of Love (1997) by Kenny and Julia Loggins
Through journal entries, poetry, song lyrics, and dialogue, the Loggins tell the story of the lessons learned and joys experienced in their conscious relationship.

We: Understanding the Psychology of Romantic Love (1983) by Robert Johnson
A clear explanation of the roots of our belief that marriage is supposed to provide the answers to all of our questions. A great book to read when you find yourself caught in the common fantasy of thinking that your partner is supposed to be perfect.

Films

Dinner with Friends (2001): This funny and painfully honest film tells the story of two couples, long-time friends, who reevaluate their relationships when one marriage breaks up. Adapted from a play, the film contains powerful dialogue about the challenges, joys, and commitment of marriage and family.

Father of the Bride (1991): A tearjerker comedy about a father, played by Steve Martin, who has a hard time letting go of his daughter and admitting that she's grown up. It also depicts the stresses of planning a wedding, with the final message that weddings are really about two people who are deeply in love joining together as a family. A great film to watch if you have a close relationship with your dad—and a great recommendation for him, as well.

Monsoon Wedding (2001): A beautiful and accurate depiction of the family dynamics that can explode and resolve as a wedding nears. This Indian film also portrays the elaborate, ancient, and meaningful rituals that brides, grooms, and their families participate in to help them gracefully move through the transition.

My Big Fat Greek Wedding (2002): A lighthearted yet insightful film about one woman's attempt to break away from her family's rules and regulations when she falls in love with a man outside her culture. The film delivers an important message about how to separate from family of origin and stand up for one's own needs in way that still invites family into the fold of the wedding and marriage.

The Divine Secrets of the Ya-Ya Sisterhood (2002): Less about a wedding than is the novel on which it's based, the film tells the story of a woman's need to explore her past (especially her relationship to her mother) before she can move forward with her wedding plans.

Walking and Talking (1996): A story of the friendship between two women and the earthquake that hits when one becomes engaged.

References

Baldizzone, Tiziana, and Gianni Baldizzone. 2001. *Wedding Ceremonies*. Paris: Flammarion.

Campbell, Joseph. 1949. *The Hero with a Thousand Faces*. Princeton, NJ: Princeton University Press.

———. 1991. *Reflections on the Art of Living: A Joseph Campbell Companion*. Edited by Diane K. Olsen. New York: HarperCollins Publishers.

Hass, Robert, and Stephen Mitchell, eds. 1993. *Into the Garden: A Wedding Anthology*. New York: Harper Perennial.

Horn, Gabriel. 2000. *The Book of Ceremonies: A Native Way of Honoring the Sacred*. Novato, CA: New World Library.

Lindbergh, Anne Morrow. 1955. *Gift from the Sea*. New York: Pantheon.

Loggins, Kenny, and Julia Loggins. 1997. *The Unimaginable Life: Lessons Learned on the Path of Love*. New York: Avon Books.

New Webster's Dictionary: College Edition. 1975. Chicago: Consolidated Book Publishers.

Nissinen, Sheryl. 2000. *The Conscious Bride: Women Unveil Their True Feelings about Getting Hitched*. Oakland, CA: New Harbinger Publications.

Rilke, Rainer Maria. 1934. *Letters to a Young Poet*. New York: W. W. Norton and Co.

Rumi. 1997. *The Illuminated Rumi*. Translated by Coleman Barks; illustrated by Michael Green. New York: Broadway Books.

van Gennep, Arnold. 1960 *The Rites of Passage*. Chicago: University of Chicago Press.

Wells, Rebecca. 1997. *The Divine Secrets of the Ya-Ya Sisterhood*. New York: HarperCollins Publishers.

Whitman, Walt. 1993. *Leaves of Grass*. New York: Random House.

Williamson, Marianne. 1993. *A Woman's Worth*. New York: Ballantine Books.

Zimmerman, Jack, and Virginia Coyle. 1996. *The Way of Council*. Las Vegas: Bramble Books.

CHECKLIST: A BASIC TIMETABLE

While I am generally against planning your wedding according to a timetable, there are some basic guidelines that will help you keep your head clear and stay organized. After all, you don't want to arrive on your wedding day and realize that you forgot to pick up Aunt May at the airport! If you are planning a large, formal wedding, you will need to begin preparations well in advance as locations, photographers, caterers, and florists tend to book early. If you are planning a smaller, more intimate event, you can plan in considerably less time. Also, the earlier you get your planning details out of the way, the more time you will have to attend to the emotional and spiritual aspects that will arise in waves of intensity as the wedding nears.

Six to Twelve Months

- ○ Decide your budget
- ○ Decide what type of wedding you want
- ○ Create a guest list
- ○ Choose a date
- ○ Choose a location for the ceremony and reception
- ○ Make honeymoon plans
- ○ Select your dress
- ○ Select a caterer
- ○ Select a photographer
- ○ Select a florist
- ○ Select ceremony music
- ○ Select reception music (band, DJ, mixed tapes or CDs)
- ○ Find wedding-night accommodations
- ○ Choose your officiant (if it's not your priest, minister, or rabbi)
- ○ If you're having a destination wedding, send a save-the-date card to your guests
- ○ Other: . . . .

Four to Six Months

- ○ Order or make invitations
- ○ Buy wedding rings

○ Prepare and print a map to include with the invitations

○ Reserve accommodations for out-of-town guests

○ Register for gifts

○ Select your bridesmaids' dresses

○ Get passports for your honeymoon

○ Other: . . . .

Two to Four Months

○ Start writing your vows

○ Order the wedding cake

○ Address invitations

○ Buy your headpiece, shoes, stockings, and personal accessories

○ Hire wedding-day transportation (limousine, carriage, rental car)

○ Arrange the rehearsal dinner

○ Arrange the postwedding brunch

○ Experiment with your hairstyle and makeup

○ Have your wedding dress altered if necessary

○ Select men's formal wear

○ Other: . . . .

One to Two Months

○ Mail invitations four to six weeks before the wedding

○ Make marriage license appointment for three weeks before the wedding (see this section)

○ Have a blood test, if necessary in your state

○ Buy ceremony items: candles, ring pillow, guest book

○ Call your vendors to confirm

○ Confirm honeymoon arrangements

○ Have a massage (I highly recommend nurturing yourself by scheduling at least two massages during your engagement)

○ Other: . . . .

Two Weeks

○ Pick up your wedding dress

○ Schedule appointments with hair stylist, manicurist, massage therapist, etc.

○ Confirm out-of-town guests' accommodations

○ Give a photo list to your photographer indicating who will be in the formal portraits

○ Give your DJ or bandleader a song list, including special requests and songs you do not want played

○ Record gifts as you receive them

○ Other: . . . .

One to Two Weeks

○ Pick up the wedding rings

○ Give the reception site and caterer a final head count

○ Do the reception seating chart and write table cards

○ Call all vendors to confirm arrangements

○ Remind the men to pick up clothes and shoes

○ Make a wedding-day schedule and give key support people a copy

○ Other: . . . .

Two to Three Days

○ Groom and groomsmen pick up formal wear

○ Arrange for out-of-town guests to be picked up from the airport

○ Get a manicure/pedicure

○ Pack your wedding bag and your emergency kit

○ Pack for the honeymoon

○ Other: . . . .

Day Before

○ Give the marriage license to the officiant

○ Attend the wedding rehearsal with the wedding party, family, and officiant

○ Give the maid of honor or best man your wedding rings

○ Give the officiant's fee to the best man (so he can pay the officiant after the ceremony)

○ Write checks for final balances to give to vendors after the reception

○ Attend the rehearsal dinner

○ Have a massage

○ Other: . . . .

Wedding Day

○ Breathe ... show up ... and enjoy! (see this section for final Wedding-Day Schedule)

Postwedding

○ Send out thank-you notes

○ If applicable, take the necessary steps to change your last name

○ Take your wedding dress to dry cleaner

○ Other: . . . .

About two to three weeks before your wedding you will need to buy a marriage license. Make sure you allow enough time to make the appointment but not too much time so that the license expires! Each state has different requirements in terms of how long a license is valid, so you will need to ask your particular marriage bureau when you call. To locate the marriage license bureau closest to you, look in the blue government section of the phone book under "Marriage or Recorder-Registrar."

Find out the following information:

○ Phone number: . . . .

○ Address: . . . .

○ Hours of operation: . . . .

○ Do you need an appointment? . . . .

○ If an appointment is not needed, what is the best time to come? . . . . . .

○ Do you need blood tests to marry in your state? . . . .

○ How long before the wedding must you apply? . . . .

○ How much will the license cost?　$. . . . .

○ What documents (birth certificate, proof of citizenship) do you need to bring with you? . . . .

○ . . . .

Both of you must go to apply for your license. They will need specific information, including signatures from each of you.

After you receive your license, you need to give it to your officiant on your wedding day (or before). She or he will sign it, then will need to file it with the appropriate office. Approximately two weeks later you will receive a copy in the mail.

Store your license in a safe place. You will need a copy of it if you are planning to change your last name. It is the only legal document you will receive that officially states that you are married. If you do not sign it or if it's filed improperly, your marriage is legally invalid.

FINAL GUEST LIST

NAME(S):	NAME(S):	NAME(S):
1.	25.	49. . . . .
2.	26.	50. . . . .
3.	27.	51. . . . .
4.	28.	52. . . . .
5.	29.	53. . . . .
6.	30.	54. . . . .
7.	31.	55. . . . .
8.	32.	56. . . . .
9.	33.	57. . . . .
10.	34.	58. . . . .
11.	35.	59. . . . .
12.	36.	60. . . . .
13.	37.	61. . . . .
14.	38.	62. . . . .
15.	39.	63. . . . .
16.	40.	64. . . . .
17.	41.	65. . . . .
18.	42.	66. . . . .
19.	43.	67. . . . .
20.	44.	68. . . . .
21.	45.	69. . . . .
22.	46.	70. . . . .
23.	47.	71. . . . .
24.	48.	72. . . . .

73. . . . .   98. . . . .   123. . . . .

74. . . . .   99. . . . .   124. . . . .

75. . . . .   100. . . . .   125. . . . .

76. . . . .   101. . . . .   126. . . . .

77. . . . .   102. . . . .   127. . . . .

78. . . . .   103. . . . .   128. . . . .

79. . . . .   104. . . . .   129. . . . .

80. . . . .   105. . . . .   130. . . . .

81. . . . .   106. . . . .   131. . . . .

82. . . . .   107. . . . .   131. . . . .

83. . . . .   108. . . . .   132. . . . .

84. . . . .   109. . . . .   133. . . . .

85. . . . .   110. . . . .   134. . . . .

86. . . . .   111. . . . .   135. . . . .

87. . . . .   112. . . . .   136. . . . .

88. . . . .   113. . . . .   137. . . . .

89. . . . .   114. . . . .   138. . . . .

90. . . . .   115. . . . .   139. . . . .

91. . . . .   116. . . . .   140. . . . .

92. . . . .   117. . . . .   141. . . . .

93. . . . .   118. . . . .   142. . . . .

94. . . . .   119. . . . .   143. . . . .

95. . . . .   120. . . . .   144. . . . .

96. . . . .   121. . . . .   145. . . . .

97. . . . .   122. . . . .   146. . . . .

FINAL COUNT: . . . .

WEDDING-DAY PHONE CONTACTS

BRIDE: . . . . (HOME) . . . . (CELL)

GROOM: . . . . (HOME) . . . . (CELL)

MAID OF HONOR: . . . . (HOME) . . . . (CELL)

BEST MAN: . . . . (HOME) . . . . (CELL)

MOTHER OF BRIDE: . . . . (HOME) . . . . (CELL)

MOTHER OF GROOM: . . . . (HOME) . . . . (CELL)

FATHER OF BRIDE: . . . . (HOME) . . . . (CELL)

FATHER OF GROOM: . . . . (HOME) . . . . (CELL)

BRIDESMAIDS:

. . . . (HOME) . . . . (CELL)

. . . . (HOME) . . . . (CELL)

. . . . (HOME) . . . . (CELL)

. . . . (HOME) . . . . (CELL)

. . . . (HOME) . . . . (CELL)

GROOMSMEN:

. . . . (HOME) . . . . (CELL)

. . . . (HOME) . . . . (CELL)

. . . . (HOME) . . . . (CELL)

. . . . (HOME) . . . . (CELL)

. . . . (HOME) . . . . (CELL)

VENDORS AND HELPERS:

BEAUTY SALON: . . . .

CEREMONY SITE: . . . .

CEREMONY MUSICIANS: . . . .

OFFICIANT: . . . .

TRANSPORTATION: . . . .

RECEPTION SITE: . . . .

CATERER: . . . .

CAKE DESIGNER: . . . .

FLORIST: . . . .

DJ/BAND: . . . .

PHOTOGRAPHER: . . . .

VIDEOGRAPHER: . . . .

WEDDING-NIGHT HOTEL/B&B: . . . .

OTHER: . . . .

. . . .

. . . .

. . . .

. . . .

. . . .

. . . .

. . . .

. . . .

. . . .

The Ceremony Site

CEREMONY SITE: . . . .

SITE COORDINATOR: . . . .

ADDRESS: . . . .

. . . .

ROOM RESERVED: . . . .

PHONE NUMBER: . . . .

FAX NUMBER: . . . .

WEB SITE: . . . .

E-MAIL: . . . .

DEPOSIT OF $ . . . .   PAID ON: . . . .

BALANCE OF $ . . . .   PAID ON: . . . .

FINAL GUEST COUNT: . . . .

NOTES: . . . .

. . . .

. . . .

. . . .

. . . .

. . . .

. . . .

. . . .

. . . .

. . . .

attach business card here

. . . .

The Reception Site

RECEPTION SITE: . . . .

SITE COORDINATOR: . . . .

ADDRESS: . . . .

. . . .

ROOM RESERVED: . . . .

PHONE NUMBER: . . . .

FAX NUMBER: . . . .

WEB SITE: . . . .

E-MAIL: . . . .

    DEPOSIT OF $ . . . . PAID ON: . . . .

    BALANCE OF $ . . . . PAID ON: . . . .

    FINAL GUEST COUNT: . . . .

NOTES: . . . .

    . . . .

    . . . .

    . . . .

    . . . .

    . . . .

    . . . .

    . . . .

    . . . .

    . . . .

attach business card here

Travel Agent

NAME: . . . .

ADDRESS: . . . .

. . . .

PHONE NUMBER: . . . .

FAX NUMBER: . . . .

WEB SITE: . . . .

E-MAIL: . . . .

APPT DATE: . . . ./ . . . ./ . . . .

TIME: . . . .

NOTES: . . . .

. . . .

. . . .

. . . .

. . . .

. . . .

. . . .

. . . .

. . . .

. . . .

attach business card here

. . . .

. . . .

. . . .

. . . .

My Wedding Dress

SALON OR DESIGNER: . . . .

ADDRESS: . . . .

. . . .

CONTACT NAME: . . . .

PHONE NUMBER: . . . .

FAX NUMBER: . . . .

EMAIL: . . . .

WEB SITE: . . . .

DRESS DESIGNER: . . . .

STYLE NUMBER: . . . .

PICK-UP DATE: . . . . / . . . . / . . . .

FITTING DATES:

   FIRST . . . . / . . . . / . . . .

   SECOND . . . . / . . . . / . . . .

   THIRD . . . . / . . . . / . . . .

attach business card here

ALTERATION ESTIMATE: $ . . . .

ACCESORIES:

SHOES: $. . . . .

BRA: $. . . . .

HEADPIECE: $. . . . .

GARTER: $. . . . .

STOCKINGS: $. . . . .

GLOVES: $. . . . .

CAPE OR SHAWL: $ . . . .

JEWELRY: $. . . . .

TOTAL ACCESSORIES: $ . . . .

TOTAL PRICE: $. . . . .

DEPOSIT OF $ . . . .   PAID ON: . . . .

BALANCE OF $ . . . .   PAID ON: . . . .

The Officiant

NAME: . . . .

ADDRESS: . . . .

. . . .

PHONE NUMBER: . . . .

FAX NUMBER: . . . .

E-MAIL: . . . .

FEE OF $. . . . .   DUE ON: . . . .

NOTES: . . . .

. . . .

. . . .

. . . .

. . . .

. . . .

. . . .

. . . .

. . . .

. . . .

. . . .

. . . .

. . . .

attach business card here

Postwedding Brunch

DATE AND TIME: . . . .

LOCATION: . . . .

PHONE NUMBER: . . . .

TYPE OF FOOD: . . . .

. . . .

. . . .

NOTES: . . . .

. . . .

. . . .

. . . .

GUESTS:

. . . .

. . . .

. . . .

. . . .

. . . .

. . . .

. . . .

. . . .

. . . .   TOTAL # . . . .

The Caterer

CATERING COMPANY: . . . .

ADDRESS: . . . .

. . . .

CONTACT NAME: . . . .

PHONE NUMBER: . . . .

FAX NUMBER: . . . .

E-MAIL: . . . .

DEPOSIT OF $ . . . .   PAID ON: . . . .

BALANCE OF $ . . . .   PAID ON: . . . .

FINAL GUEST COUNT: . . . .

NOTES: . . . .

. . . .

. . . .

. . . .

. . . .

. . . .

. . . .

. . . .

. . . .

attach business card here

. . . .

. . . .

. . . .

φ *219*

The Cake

CAKE DESIGNER OR STORE NAME: ....

ADDRESS: ....

....

CONTACT NAME: ....

PHONE NUMBER: ....

FAX NUMBER: ....

E-MAIL: ....

    DEPOSIT OF $ ....   PAID ON: ....

    BALANCE OF $ ....   PAID ON: ....

NUMBER OF SLICES: ....

NOTES: ....

....

....

....

....

....

....

....

....

....

....

attach business card here

The Flowers

FLORIST: . . . .

ADDRESS: . . . .

. . . .

CONTACT NAME: . . . .

PHONE NUMBER: . . . .

FAX NUMBER: . . . .

E-MAIL: . . . .

DEPOSIT OF $ . . . .   PAID ON: . . . .

BALANCE OF $ . . . .   PAID ON: . . . .

PICK-UP DATE: . . . . . / . . . . . / . . . . . .

TIME: . . . .

NOTES: . . . .

. . . .

. . . .

. . . .

. . . .

. . . .

. . . .

. . . .

. . . .

. . . .

. . . .

attach business card here

φ *221*

The Ceremony Music

MUSICAL GROUP: . . . .

MUSICIANS' NAMES: . . . .

ADDRESS: . . . .

. . . .

CONTACT NAME: . . . .

PHONE NUMBER: . . . .

FAX NUMBER: . . . .

E-MAIL: . . . .

DEPOSIT OF $ . . . .   PAID ON: . . . .

BALANCE OF $ . . . .   PAID ON: . . . .

START TIME: . . . .

END TIME: . . . .

NOTES: . . . .

. . . .

. . . .

. . . .

. . . .

. . . .

. . . .

. . . .

. . . .

. . . .

attach business card here

The Reception Music

MUSICAL GROUP: . . . .

MUSICIANS' NAMES: . . . .

ADDRESS: . . . .

. . . .

CONTACT NAME: . . . .

PHONE NUMBER: . . . .

FAX NUMBER: . . . .

E-MAIL: . . . .

DEPOSIT OF $ . . . .   PAID ON: . . . .

BALANCE OF $ . . . .   PAID ON: . . . .

START TIME: . . . .

END TIME: . . . .

NOTES: . . . .

. . . .

. . . .

. . . .

. . . .

. . . .

. . . .

. . . .   *attach business card here*

. . . .

. . . .

. . . .

The Photographer

NAME: . . . .

ADDRESS: . . . .

. . . .

CONTACT NAME: . . . .

PHONE NUMBER: . . . .

FAX NUMBER: . . . .

E-MAIL: . . . .

PACKAGE CHOICE: . . . .

DEPOSIT OF $ . . . . PAID ON: . . . .

BALANCE OF $ . . . . PAID ON: . . . .

START TIME: . . . .

END TIME: . . . .

NOTES: . . . .

. . . .

. . . .

. . . .

. . . .

. . . .

. . . .

attach business card here . . . .

. . . .

. . . .

. . . .

Wedding-Night Accommodations

NAME: . . . .

ADDRESS: . . . .

. . . .

CONTACT NAME: . . . .

PHONE NUMBER: . . . .

FAX NUMBER: . . . .

E-MAIL: . . . .

OF NIGHTS RESERVED: . . . .

CONFIRMATION #: . . . .

   DEPOSIT OF $ . . . . PAID ON: . . . .

   BALANCE OF $ . . . . PAID ON: . . . .

CHECK-IN: . . . .

CHECK-OUT: . . . .

NOTES: . . . .

. . . .

. . . .

. . . .

. . . .

. . . .

. . . .

attach business card here

. . . .

. . . .

. . . .

Honeymoon Accommodations

NAME: . . . .

ADDRESS: . . . .

. . . .

CONTACT NAME: . . . .

PHONE NUMBER: . . . .

FAX NUMBER: . . . .

E-MAIL: . . . .

OF NIGHTS RESERVED: . . . .

CONFIRMATION #: . . . .

DEPOSIT OF $ . . . .   PAID ON: . . . .

BALANCE OF $ . . . .   PAID ON: . . . .

CHECK-IN: . . . .

CHECK-OUT: . . . .

NOTES: . . . .

. . . .

. . . .

. . . .

. . . .

. . . .

. . . .

. . . .

. . . .

attach business card here

Ceremony Rehearsal

NAME: . . . .

ADDRESS: . . . .

DATE & TIME: . . . .

PHONE NUMBER: . . . .

LOCATION: . . . .

WHAT TO BRING: . . . .

NAMES OF EVERYONE INVOLVED:

. . . .

. . . .

. . . .

. . . .

. . . .

. . . .

. . . .

. . . .

. . . .

. . . .

. . . .

. . . .

. . . .

. . . .

Rehearsal Dinner

NAME: . . . .

ADDRESS: . . . .

DATE & TIME: . . . .

PHONE NUMBER: . . . .

LOCATION: . . . .

WHAT TO BRING: . . . .

NAMES OF EVERYONE INVOLVED:

Wedding Day

ACTIVITY: . . . .

CONTACT NAME: . . . .

ARRIVAL TIME: . . . .

PHONE NUMBER: . . . .

LOCATION: . . . .

WHAT TO BRING: . . . .

COMMENTS: . . . .

. . . .

. . . .

. . . .

. . . .

ACTIVITY: . . . .

CONTACT NAME: . . . .

ARRIVAL TIME: . . . .

PHONE NUMBER: . . . .

LOCATION: . . . .

WHAT TO BRING: . . . .

COMMENTS: . . . .

. . . .

. . . .

. . . .

. . . .

Contact Sheet for _____

NAME: . . . .

ADDRESS: . . . .

. . . .

CONTACT NAME: . . . .

PHONE NUMBER: . . . .

FAX NUMBER: . . . .

E-MAIL: . . . .

ESTIMATE: $ . . . .

OPTIONS: . . . .

. . . .

. . . .

PROS: . . . .

. . . .

. . . .

. . . .

. . . .

. . . .

CONS: . . . .

. . . .

. . . .

attach business card here

. . . .

. . . .

. . . .

WEDDING DAY PACKING LIST

○ . . . .   ○ . . . .
○ . . . .   ○ . . . .
○ . . . .   ○ . . . .
○ . . . .   ○ . . . .
○ . . . .   ○ . . . .
○ . . . .   ○ . . . .
○ . . . .   ○ . . . .
○ . . . .   ○ . . . .
○ . . . .   ○ . . . .
○ . . . .   ○ . . . .
○ . . . .   ○ . . . .
○ . . . .   ○ . . . .
○ . . . .   ○ . . . .
○ . . . .   ○ . . . .
○ . . . .   ○ . . . .
○ . . . .   ○ . . . .
○ . . . .   ○ . . . .
○ . . . .   ○ . . . .
○ . . . .   ○ . . . .
○ . . . .   ○ . . . .
○ . . . .   ○ . . . .
○ . . . .   ○ . . . .
○ . . . .   ○ . . . .
○ . . . .   ○ . . . .
○ . . . .   ○ . . . .
○ . . . .   ○ . . . .
○ . . . .   ○ . . . .
○ . . . .   ○ . . . .

WEDDING-DAY SCHEDULE

Use this sheet to fill in the events of your day, beginning with wake-up time, a nourishing breakfast, and perhaps meditation or a short walk, and continuing with your hair appointment, arrival times of vendors, and start times of key events (first dance, cake cutting, etc.). Remember, however, that as much as you would like your wedding to proceed according to schedule, the most joyful brides are those who are willing to improvise and go with the flow. No one will mind if the cake cutting occurs at 3:30 instead of 3:00, but if you allow the inevitable mishaps or miscommunications to ruffle your feathers, you'll miss out on the overarching point of your day: to be present, connect, receive, and have fun. Also, be sure to create time to meditate, breathe, or write in your journal, even if only for a few minutes. These small but important actions will help you feel present for the emotional intensity and activities of the day. Make as many photocopies as you need to give one to each of your attendants.

7:00 A.M. . . . .

7:30 A.M. . . . .

8:00 A.M. . . . .

8:30 A.M. . . . .

9:00 A.M. . . . .

9:30 A.M. . . . .

10:00 A.M. . . . .

10:30 A.M. . . . .

11:00 A.M. . . . .

11:30 A.M. . . . .

12:00 P.M. . . . .

12:30 P.M. . . . .

1:00 P.M. . . . .

1:30 P.M. . . . .

2:00 P.M. . . . .

2:30 P.M. . . . .

3:00 P.M. . . . .

3:30 P.M. . . . .

4:00 P.M. . . . .

4:30 P.M. . . . .

5:00 P.M. . . . .

5:30 P.M. . . . .

6:00 P.M. . . . .

6:30 P.M. . . . .

7:00 P.M. . . . .

7:30 P.M. . . . .

8:00 P.M. . . . .

8:30 P.M. . . . .

9:00 P.M. . . . .

9:30 P.M. . . . .

10:00 P.M. . . . .

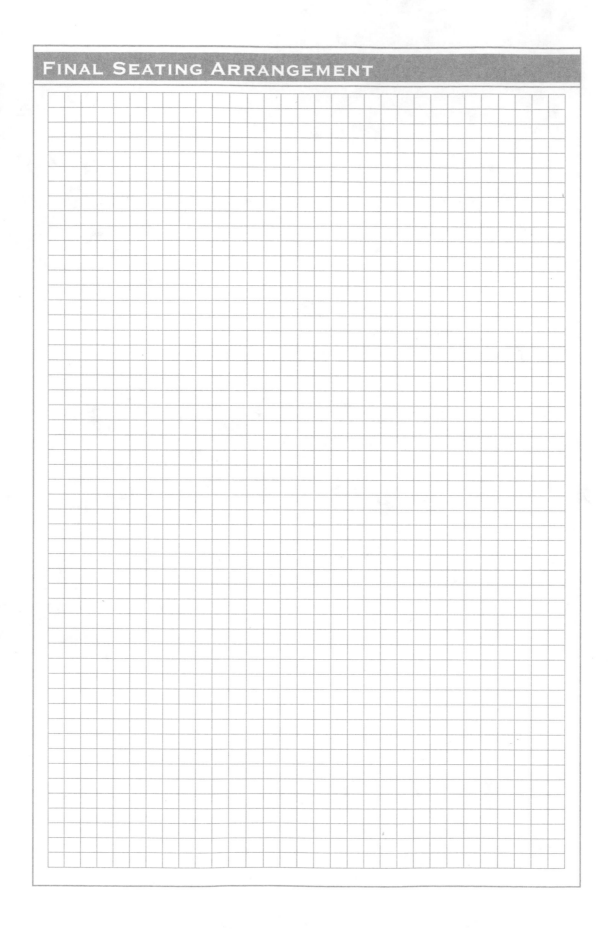

BUDGET BREAKDOWN

TOTAL BUDGET: $ . . . .

WEDDING ITEM	AMOUNT BUDGETED	AMOUNT SPENT
EMOTIONAL PLANNING:		
Bridal counseling	$	$. . . . .
Premarital counseling	$	$. . . . .
Books	$	$. . . . .
. . . .	$	$. . . . .
TOTAL:	$	$. . . . .
INVITATIONS:		
Save-the-date notices	$	$. . . . .
Invitations and envelopes	$	$. . . . .
Postage	$	$. . . . .
Thank-you notes	$	$. . . . .
. . . .	$	$. . . . .
TOTAL:	$	$. . . . .
WEDDING CLOTHES:		
Wedding dress	$	$. . . . .
alterations	$	$. . . . .
cleaning	$	$. . . . .
Veil or headpiece	$	$. . . . .
Groom's suit or tux	$	$. . . . .
. . . .	$	$. . . . .
TOTAL:	$	$. . . . .

WEDDING ITEM	AMOUNT BUDGETED	AMOUNT SPENT
ACCESSORIES:		
LINGERIE	$	$ . . . .
SHOES	$	$ . . . .
GROOM'S SHIRT	$	$ . . . .
GROOM'S TIE	$	$ . . . .
GROOM'S SHOES	$	$ . . . .
. . . .	$	$ . . . .
TOTAL:	$	$ . . . .
CEREMONY:		
SITE FEE	$	$ . . . .
OFFICIANT FEE	$	$ . . . .
CHUPPAH	$	$ . . . .
CANDLES	$	$ . . . .
MARRIAGE CERTIFICATES	$	$ . . . .
. . . .	. . . .	$ . . . .
TOTAL:	$	$ . . . .
RINGS:		
BRIDE'S RING	$	$ . . . .
GROOM'S RING	$	$ . . . .
ENGRAVING	$	$ . . . .
. . . .	$	$ . . . .
TOTAL:	$	$ . . . .

Budget

Wedding Item	Amount Budgeted	Amount Spent
Reception:		
Site fee	$.	$. . . . .
Food	$.	$. . . . .
Beverages	$.	$. . . . .
Cake	$.	$. . . . .
. . . .	$.	$. . . . .
Total:	$.	$. . . . .
Rentals:		
tables and chairs	$.	$. . . . .
linens and silverware	$.	$. . . . .
. . . .	$.	$. . . . .
Total:	$.	$. . . . .
Flowers:		
Bridal bouquet	$.	$. . . . .
Bridesmaid's bouquets	$.	$. . . . .
Boutonnieres	$.	$. . . . .
Corsages	$.	$. . . . .
Centerpieces	$.	$. . . . .
Reception arrangements	$.	$. . . . .
Delivery fees and setup	$.	$. . . . .
. . . .	$.	$. . . . .
Total:	$.	$. . . . .

WEDDING ITEM	AMOUNT BUDGETED	AMOUNT SPENT
HAIR AND BEAUTY:		
HAIR	$	$ . . . .
MAKEUP	$	$ . . . .
MANICURE	$	$ . . . .
PEDICURE	$	$ . . . .
MASSAGE	$	$ . . . .
. . . .	$	$ . . . .
TOTAL:	$	$ . . . .
MUSIC:		
CEREMONY MUSICIANS	$	$ . . . .
BAND OR DJ	$	$ . . . .
. . . .	$	$ . . . .
TOTAL:	$	$ . . . .
PHOTOGRAPHY/VIDEO:		
PHOTOGRAPHY PACKAGE	$	$ . . . .
DISPOSABLE CAMERAS	$	$ . . . .
ADDITIONAL PRINTS	$	$ . . . .
PHOTO ALBUM	$	$ . . . .
VIDEO PACKAGE	$	$ . . . .
ADDITIONAL VIDEOS	$	$ . . . .
. . . .	$	$ . . . .
TOTAL:	$	$ . . . .

Budget

Wedding Item	Amount Budgeted	Amount Spent
Other Meals:		
Rehearsal dinner	$.	$. . . . .
Postwedding brunch	$.	$. . . . .
. . . .	$.	$. . . . .
Total:	$.	$. . . . .
Transportation/Wedding Night:		
Limousine or car	$.	$. . . . .
Guest parking	$.	$. . . . .
Hotel room	$.	$. . . . .
. . . .	$.	$. . . . .
Total:	$.	$. . . . .
Honeymoon:		
Transportation	$.	$. . . . .
Accommodations	$.	$. . . . .
Food	$.	$. . . . .
Activities	$.	$. . . . .
. . . .	$.	$. . . . .
Total:	$.	$. . . . .
Grand Total:	$.	$. . . . .

Gift Log

GUEST'S NAME(S)	GIFT RECEIVED	THANK-YOU SENT
. . . .	. . . .	. . . ./. . . . . . ./. . . . . . .
. . . .	. . . .	. . . ./. . . . . . ./. . . . . . .
. . . .	. . . .	. . . ./. . . . . . ./. . . . . . .
. . . .	. . . .	. . . ./. . . . . . ./. . . . . . .
. . . .	. . . .	. . . ./. . . . . . ./. . . . . . .
. . . .	. . . .	. . . ./. . . . . . ./. . . . . . .
. . . .	. . . .	. . . ./. . . . . . ./. . . . . . .
. . . .	. . . .	. . . ./. . . . . . ./. . . . . . .
. . . .	. . . .	. . . ./. . . . . . ./. . . . . . .
. . . .	. . . .	. . . ./. . . . . . ./. . . . . . .
. . . .	. . . .	. . . ./. . . . . . ./. . . . . . .
. . . .	. . . .	. . . ./. . . . . . ./. . . . . . .
. . . .	. . . .	. . . ./. . . . . . ./. . . . . . .
. . . .	. . . .	. . . ./. . . . . . ./. . . . . . .
. . . .	. . . .	. . . ./. . . . . . ./. . . . . . .
. . . .	. . . .	. . . ./. . . . . . ./. . . . . . .
. . . .	. . . .	. . . ./. . . . . . ./. . . . . . .
. . . .	. . . .	. . . ./. . . . . . ./. . . . . . .
. . . .	. . . .	. . . ./. . . . . . ./. . . . . . .
. . . .	. . . .	. . . ./. . . . . . ./. . . . . . .

GUEST'S NAME(S)	GIFT RECEIVED	THANK-YOU SENT
. . . .	. . . .	. . . . . . / . . . . . . / . . . . . .
. . . .	. . . .	. . . . . . / . . . . . . / . . . . . .
. . . .	. . . .	. . . . . . / . . . . . . / . . . . . .
. . . .	. . . .	. . . . . . / . . . . . . / . . . . . .
. . . .	. . . .	. . . . . . / . . . . . . / . . . . . .
. . . .	. . . .	. . . . . . / . . . . . . / . . . . . .
. . . .	. . . .	. . . . . . / . . . . . . / . . . . . .
. . . .	. . . .	. . . . . . / . . . . . . / . . . . . .
. . . .	. . . .	. . . . . . / . . . . . . / . . . . . .
. . . .	. . . .	. . . . . . / . . . . . . / . . . . . .
. . . .	. . . .	. . . . . . / . . . . . . / . . . . . .
. . . .	. . . .	. . . . . . / . . . . . . / . . . . . .
. . . .	. . . .	. . . . . . / . . . . . . / . . . . . .
. . . .	. . . .	. . . . . . / . . . . . . / . . . . . .
. . . .	. . . .	. . . . . . / . . . . . . / . . . . . .
. . . .	. . . .	. . . . . . / . . . . . . / . . . . . .
. . . .	. . . .	. . . . . . / . . . . . . / . . . . . .
. . . .	. . . .	. . . . . . / . . . . . . / . . . . . .
. . . .	. . . .	. . . . . . / . . . . . . / . . . . . .
. . . .	. . . .	. . . . . . / . . . . . . / . . . . . .
. . . .	. . . .	. . . . . . / . . . . . . / . . . . . .
. . . .	. . . .	. . . . . . / . . . . . . / . . . . . .

Notes

Wedding Planner Calendar

MONTH . . . . **YEAR** . . . . . . **MONTHS BEFORE WEDDING** . . . .

Sunday	Monday	Tuesday	Wednesday	Thursday	Friday	Saturday

REMINDERS: . . . .

. . . .

. . . .

. . . .

Wedding Planner Calendar

MONTH . . . . YEAR . . . . MONTHS BEFORE WEDDING . . . .

Sunday	Monday	Tuesday	Wednesday	Thursday	Friday	Saturday

REMINDERS: . . . .

. . . .

. . . .

. . . .

Wedding Planner Calendar

MONTH . . . . YEAR . . . . MONTHS BEFORE WEDDING . . . .

Sunday	Monday	Tuesday	Wednesday	Thursday	Friday	Saturday

REMINDERS: . . . .

. . . .

. . . .

. . . .

Wedding Planner Calendar

MONTH . . . . YEAR . . . . MONTHS BEFORE WEDDING . . . .

Sunday	Monday	Tuesday	Wednesday	Thursday	Friday	Saturday

REMINDERS: . . . .

. . . .

. . . .

. . . .

Wedding Planner Calendar

MONTH . . . . YEAR . . . . MONTHS BEFORE WEDDING . . . .

Sunday	Monday	Tuesday	Wednesday	Thursday	Friday	Saturday

REMINDERS: . . . .

. . . .

. . . .

. . . .

Wedding Planner Calendar

MONTH . . . . YEAR . . . . MONTHS BEFORE WEDDING . . . .

Sunday	*Monday*	*Tuesday*	*Wednesday*	*Thursday*	*Friday*	*Saturday*

REMINDERS: . . . .

. . . .

. . . .

. . . .

Wanna Be Conscious for the Wedding?

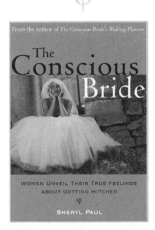

For this frank look at a bride's inner life, author Sheryl Paul interviewed a diverse group of women who share their true feelings about such issues as being given away, changing their names, and other concerns that can make an engagement a roller coaster of emotional ups and downs. Along with practical advice to help any bride-to-be think through the traditions of the dress and the vows and the ring, she'll find much-needed support and welcome acknowledgment of the shared doubts and fears that so often run amok as wedding bells take their toll.

Only from women who have done the "do's" can you learn the truth about:

- the jumble of pre-wedding emotions

- what all those "big day" traditions really mean

- staying true to yourself and still walking down the aisle

$12.95   220 pages   ISBN 1572242132

Call toll free, 1-800-748-6273, or log on to our online bookstore at www.newharbinger.com to order. Have your Visa or Mastercard number ready. Or send a check for the number of copies you want to New Harbinger Publications, Inc., 5674 Shattuck Ave., Oakland, CA 94609. Include $4.50 for the first book and 75¢ for each additional book, to cover shipping and handling. (California residents please include appropriate sales tax.) Allow two to five weeks for delivery.

Some Other New Harbinger Titles

Eating Mindfully, Item 3503 $13.95

Sex Talk, Item 2868 $12.95

Everyday Adventures for the Soul, Item 2981 $11.95

A Woman's Addiction Workbook, Item 2973 $18.95

The Daughter-In-Law's Survival Guide, Item 2817 $12.95

PMDD, Item 2833 $13.95

The Vulvodynia Survival Guide, Item 2914 $15.95

Love Tune-Ups, Item 2744 $10.95

The Deepest Blue, Item 2531 $13.95

The 50 Best Ways to Simplify Your Life, Item 2558 $11.95

Brave New You, Item 2590 $13.95

Loving Your Teenage Daughter, Item 2620 $14.95

The Hidden Feelings of Motherhood, Item 2485 $14.95

The Woman's Book of Sleep, Item 2493 $14.95

Pregnancy Stories, Item 2361 $14.95

The Women's Guide to Total Self-Esteem, Item 2418 $13.95

Thinking Pregnant, Item 2302 $13.95

The Conscious Bride, Item 2132 $12.95

Juicy Tomatoes, Item 2175 $13.95

Facing 30, Item 1500 $12.95

The Money Mystique, Item 2221 $13.95

High on Stress, Item 1101 $13.95

Perimenopause, 2nd edition, Item 2345 $16.95

The Infertility Survival Guide, Item 2477 $16.95

After the Breakup, 1764 $13.95

Claiming Your Creative Self, Item 1179 $15.95

The Self-Nourishment Companion, Item 2426 $10.95

Serenity to Go, Item 2353 $12.95

Call **toll free, 1-800-748-6273,** or log on to our online bookstore at **www.newharbinger.com** to order. Have your Visa or Mastercard number ready. Or send a check for the titles you want to New Harbinger Publications, Inc., 5674 Shattuck Ave., Oakland, CA 94609. Include $4.50 for the first book and 75¢ for each additional book, to cover shipping and handling. (California residents please include appropriate sales tax.) Allow two to five weeks for delivery.

Prices subject to change without notice.

RACE
RELATIONS

RACE
RELATIONS

HARRY H. L. KITANO
University of California, Los Angeles

PRENTICE-HALL, INC., ENGLEWOOD CLIFFS, NEW JERSEY

Library of Congress Cataloging in Publication Data

KITANO, HARRY, H. L.
    Race relations.

    Includes bibliographies.
    1. United States—Race question.   2. Prejudices and
antipathies.   I. Title.
E184.A1K47   301.45′1′0420973   73–14775
ISBN   0-13-750067-X

PHOTO CREDITS
Chapter 1: Black Star; Chapter 2: Black Star;
Chapter 3: Wide World Photos; Chapter 4: Herb Taylor/Editorial
Photocolor Archives; Chapter 5: United Press International; Chapter 6:
Black Star; Chapter 7: Wide World Photos;
Chapter 8: Wide World Photos; Chapter 9: Wide
World Photos; Chapter 10: Wide World Photos;
Chapter 11: Doug Magee/Editorial Photocolor Archives; Chapter 12:
Jim Marshall/BBM; Chapter 13: Black Star

PRENTICE-HALL SOCIOLOGY SERIES
Neil J. Smelser, Editor

© 1974 by Prentice-Hall, Inc., Englewood Cliffs, New Jersey

PRINTED IN THE UNITED STATES OF AMERICA

10 9 8 7 6 5 4 3 2 1

PRENTICE-HALL INTERNATIONAL, INC., *London*
PRENTICE-HALL OF AUSTRALIA, PTY. LTD., *Sydney*
PRENTICE-HALL OF CANADA, LTD., *Toronto*
PRENTICE-HALL OF INDIA PRIVATE LIMITED, *New Delhi*
PRENTICE-HALL OF JAPAN, INC., *Tokyo*

To all Americans,
especially of ethnic and minority descent,
who have carved a position for themselves
by overcoming the barriers
of prejudice and discrimination.

CONTENTS

PERSPECTIVES AND PROBLEMS IN RACE RELATIONS I

PREFACE

This book is about race relations in the United States. It traces the racial attitudes of early European immigrants and shows how their perceptions shaped the basic character of American race relations. Early definitions of citizenship, desirability, control, and power emphasized the central role of Europeans and assigned peripheral positions to native Americans and Africans. Later immigrants reinforced these basic structures, and American citizenship and democracy came to mean one thing for white people and another for people of color.

Against this background, part one of the book presents theories of racial interaction and perspectives on discrimination, prejudice, and segregation; analyzes the adaptation of dominated groups to their low-power positions; and explores the question, "Is conflict inevitable?" It looks at the goals of American society—the melting pot, pluralism, integration, and acculturation—and discusses the consequences of each. Part one closes with a chapter on identity which discusses the difficulties a nonwhite encounters in forming a positive self-image in a white-dominated society.

Part two tests these perspectives by analyzing experiences of selected ethnic groups. Their culture, power, styles, and goals are pre-

sented within the context of their "acceptability and desirability" to
the group in power. The interrelationship between the ethnic group and
the dominant group is established as a basis to explain where minority
groups were, where they are now, and where they may be in the future.
The power relationships between the whites and nonwhites have significantly altered most ethnic cultures so that cultures of "poverty,
powerlessness, and deprivation" have developed instead of intact social
systems.

Most textbooks on race relations have been written from the point
of view of the white, dominant majority. They generally advocate a universalistic view: there is one truth, there are clear standards, and there
are "normal" and "abnormal" behaviors. Most of these spokesmen, no
matter how sympathetic to the minorities, ignore the fact that these
"universals" are prescribed by those in a dominant position and are
maintained and enforced by their power.

I have looked at race relations from another position—that of a
minority group member. From this position many of the universals advocated by majority group social scientists look different. For in most
instances, universal standards mean that only those individuals and
minorities who look and act like the group in power become acceptable
and can be labelled successful, or that those who answer test questions
on the basis of these "universalistic criteria" are normal. In extreme
cases, the culture of minorities that deviates widely from the universal
standards becomes the target for attack; one prescribed solution is drastic
change, which may include the destruction of that culture.

I have experienced racism from very early days. I spent my adolescent years behind barbed wire with 110,000 other Japanese Americans
for the crime of being of Japanese ancestry. Like countless others of all
colors, races, nationalities, and religions, I was the victim of "national
security," as defined by those who wished to maintain their dominance.
Massacres, genocide, and incarceration can all be rationalized for the
sake of "security;" illegal wiretaps, bribery, and outright lying are
minor or nonexistent crimes when "national security" is at stake.

I changed my name to Lee in order to find employment. I became the only Asian in all white dance orchestras performing throughout the Midwest. Later I joined black bands to become the only non-
black in such groups. I have taught at the University of Hawaii (Manoa
and Hilo), at the International Christian University in Tokyo, and at
UCLA. What brings nods of assent in one setting does not necessarily
invite the same reaction in others. What is assumed in Tokyo is debatable in Hawaii, and racism from one perspective is a different phenomenon from another.

But there is one common denominator that cuts across ethnicity,
color, or nationality. Majority groups everywhere advocate a more universalistic perspective (theirs), while the less powerful hold to more par-

ticularistic and relativistic positions. However, no matter what the perspective, nor how the issues are presented, problems of race are live and real. Preaching for more brotherly love, understanding, and acceptance ignores the basic issue of the inequality of racism. Unless there is real change in the economic, legal, political, and social structures that maintain racism, the promise of justice, liberty, and equality for all will remain unfulfilled.

ACKNOWLEDGMENTS

I would like to acknowledge the assistance of the following people. John Longres of Portland State University helped on the Puerto Rican chapter; Dorothy Miller, Director of Scientific Analysis Corporation, and Anthony Purley, Director of the Native American Center at UCLA provided information on the Indians; Art Smith, Director of the Afro-American Center at UCLA analyzed the chapter on the blacks. Lowell Chun Hoon and Buck Wong, both of the Asian American Study Center at UCLA read the Chinese chapter, and Deluvina Hernandez of the Department of Social Welfare, UCLA, was helpful in analyzing the Mexican American. The cooperation and comments from each of these scholars is gratefully acknowledged.

In addition I would like to acknowledge the work of historian Roger Daniels with whom I wrote *American Racism: Exploration of the Nature of Prejudice* (Prentice-Hall, 1970). Our collaboration on that volume provided much of the background material for this book.

Ms. Jeannie Tanaka provided helpful editorial assistance in Japan, and Ms. Akemi Kikumura served as a most capable research assistant, bibliographer, and organizer. Finally, the perspective and helpful comments of editor Neil Smelser were essential in shaping the manuscript into its final form.

INTRODUCTION

We are a large country blessed with abundant natural resources and populated by people with big physiques. Almost everything we do is on a grand scale: our technology produces tanklike cars in inexhaustible numbers; our movies require bigger and wider screens; and our athletic heroes seem to grow taller and heavier year by year.

Our problems and failures also reflect this American ethos: we pollute and destroy at rates that can only be described as monumental; and the inability to deal successfully with our racial problems has led to riots, killings, and such incredible internal strain that even the most appropriate term—"crisis"—seems weak.

This is how America looks to many people abroad and, in a comparative sense, their perceptions are not totally erroneous: we are oversized, and one of our biggest unsolved problems is that of race relations. Yet, many of our most vociferous critics come from nations that are not only more racially homogeneous, but from those that have formidable barriers against large-scale immigration of different racial groups. Such countries will probably never experience the racial diversity and tensions that have become a way of life in the United States.

This is not to say that prejudice, discrimination, and segregation are 1 peculiar to the United States. Many nations use stratification systems other than those based on color—religion, social class, nationality, age, and sex are other examples of forms of social stratification. The reasons other nations give for justifying the maintenance of their inequalities sound familiar: "certain classes are inherently lazy and backward;" "there are inferior people and cultures;" "pariah group themselves are responsible for their lower position in society."

We emphasize, however, that the racial divisions in our society are the most inflammable. Racism is, theoretically, a form of social stratification, and the appeals to racism—both overt and covert—that have characterized many of our recent political elections are a symptom of the unresolved nature of the problem.

A SEARCH FOR SOLUTIONS

Authoritarian solutions enforced by the arbitrary use of power are the simplest, the most direct, and often the most unjust means of resolving racial problems. They have often been used in the past and will without doubt continue to be used in the future. The perpetrators and victims of such solutions will represent the entire spectrum of colors and races. These solutions are not the sole province of autocratic systems, nor of any one race or color: under certain conditions, all societies appear capable of such actions. Groups will be expelled from countries on the basis of race, others will be denied equality, while still others will be prevented from entering a country primarily because of race undesirability. More extreme solutions such as extermination and genocide have dotted our history books (Daniels and Kitano, 1970).

The basic platform in the search for an American solution relates to our stated goals and expectations: "equality of opportunity," "fair play and the maximum development of each individual's capacities." Because these guidelines underlie our values, it would be difficult to argue against them; and believing in their validity should preclude those solutions based on the arbitrary use of power (e.g., "send them back where they came from"), although native Indians could not be blamed too much for having these thoughts in mind. But because we place high value on individualism, our solutions may be more difficult to achieve— certain actions that may be ameliorative in societal terms may threaten the rights of the individual.

OPPOSING VIEWS OF MAN

A study of race relations is related to the two opposing views of man (with all the subvariations) that are reflected in any analysis.

One view emphasizes that man is a conscious agent, striving after goals. In this view, concepts such as motivation, desire, and will play an   2 important part in any explanation of race relations. Prejudice and discrimination, then, are aspects of consciousness and remain as a part of man's attitudinal system that can be altered and changed under appropriate conditions. In other words, man does what he wants to do because he thinks it will bring him closer to what he wants, or to avoid something he dislikes. Prejudice and discrimination are a part of the will of the individual, and his expressions of contempt for other races reflect his solution to the racial problem.

On the other hand, a physiological view and an analysis of "structures" encourage a much more deterministic point of view. The human being can be described in physiochemical terms which make concepts such as desires, beliefs, and anxieties' seem unimportant when compared to the neural processes of the body and brain which determine what man is going to do. Or on a sociological level, the structures and organizations of a society will predetermine man's behavior much more significantly than his own will. That is, man does what he does, not because of any conscious desire but because his role, position, and place in a reference group, structure, or organization "determine" his actions. Therefore, his "solutions" are determined by those organizations and structures that have influenced him.

LEVELS AND ORDERS OF RACISM

Our presentation throughout the book will indicate that racism can be viewed in terms of levels and orders, and that "solutions" designed for one level will not prove effective if the major racial issues lie at another level. For example, if racism were a direct phenomenon between people of different colors, then the most reasonable solution would be for the groups to meet each other, become acquainted, and eventually work together. Confrontation, discussion, and therapy might be appropriate techniques for bringing about the desired change. However, if racism is, for example, the byproduct of a competitive industrial system, then it is at a different level, and direct contact situations may have only a minimal effect upon the problem.

We hypothesize three levels of racism and a variety of different orders. The increasing complexity of the problem is illustrated in our model (see Table 1), as we approach Levels II and III. Rather than being a "pure" phenomenon, the deeper levels indicate that racism is intertwined with a host of other variables, and is extremely difficult to isolate.

Level I

The simplest level and order of racism is the one-man, one-perception point of view. An individual sees a person of color and is repelled by him; he reacts with prejudice and discrimination. Color may be the primary

TABLE 1
THREE LEVELS OF RACISM

Level	Racism as Product of:	Basis	Solution
I	Color and its variations (culture, ethnocentrism).	Fear of difference, strangeness, foreignness.	Equal status contact, knowledge, attitudinal change.
II	Economic system (e.g., capitalism, competitiveness). Psychological system (frustration-aggression, socialization). Social system (status). Political system (power).	Racism is intertwined with a host of other variables and is one product of the various structures. Therefore a direct attack on racist attitudes may prove to be effective.	Change in the various systems.
III	Urbanization, industrialization. Technology.	Rapid social change and changing needs of the society.	Wholesale modification of the culture.

trigger for avoidance; other "orders" and variations may include an abhorrence of the other's culture, life style, or even the way he smells. The basis may lie in ethnocentrism, in a fear of strangers, in ignorance, or it may be a result of directly negative experiences—the important point is that it is a direct interaction between the subject and the racial object.

Some preferred solutions on Level I are to overcome the fear and the attitude through equal-status contact, additional knowledge, and increased familiarity. Direct confrontation of one's racial feelings and psychotherapy may be other reasonable solutions.

It would be difficult to defend a hypothesis that places the major portion of our current racial problems on Level I. Modern communication has provided constant exposure of various groups so that few remain unheard of; increased knowledge and the contributions of ethnic groups to our culture has also risen dramatically in the past decade. Chapter 1, on prejudice, concentrates on this Level I point of view.

Level II

Level II hypothesizes that racism is primarily a byproduct of the economic, political, and other systems. For example, it may be one outcome of the capitalistic economy and its stress on competitiveness; or it may be intimately associated with social status or power. The important difference from Level I is that there will not necessarily be a direct hate relationship with the object, although such an attitude may eventually develop.

The solutions on this level lie primarily with the institutional structures rather than with the individual racist. However, the problem   4 is compounded by the fact that the "free enterprise" system may be meeting the needs of the majority who are willing to "tolerate" some of the negative effects (i.e., racism) unless it gets out of hand. As one consequence, the majority-group scholar will probably tend to analyze the cluster of variables associated with racism as a higher priority than racism itself, whereas the ethnic scholar will probably focus on racism as the most important variable.

The strategy for changing this perspective is an analysis of those systems that comprise the culture. Since there are many interacting variables within each institution and structure, race can no longer remain a simple "issue." Any program will run into resistance because of its effect on variables other than race.

Level III

Level III hypothesizes that racism is one outcome of urbanization, industrialization, and technology. The connection between these variables and racism is even harder to trace than in Level II and much of the material remains speculative. Nevertheless, the point to be made is an important one: mass society, and the dehumanizing influences of technological change are related to racism. The social structures that accompany urbanization and industrialization create fertile conditions for racist actions. Because any planned solution may have to take into account these broader variables, the simpler solutions on Level I may prove to be relatively meaningless.

Our estimate is that on Levels II and III are found the major variables in racism; Chapters 2 through 6 focus on these variables.

INTERACTION AMONG LEVELS

Our perspective by levels illustrates deeper roots of racism that go beyond the individual will to discriminate solely on the basis of color. As the problem goes deeper, the identification and the hoped-for solutions also become much more complicated since racism is intertwined with many other variables.

The individual who is responding on all three levels by racist actions is a much different person from the solely ethnocentric (Level I) individual who has a vague fear of the person with a different skin color. Conversely, if appropriate societal changes take place (e.g., more job security, less competition) so that other fears and anxieties are resolved, racist actions may diminish. But it is the interaction of all three levels that illustrates the "hard core racist." Although his discriminatory actions may have started on any of the levels, the hard core racist is usually reacting at all three levels. He is a victim of technology and urbanization; he has unsatisfied status needs; he fears competition; recent changes have led him to yearn for the good old days or at least a status quo; he feels powerless, and he hates the uppity minorities with their different styles of life. His current position is vulnerable to minority group "power," and many of his peers are caught in the same position. Discovering the factors that would lead to a change in his racist thinking is an important area for research.

ROLE OF SOCIAL SCIENTISTS

There is little consensus or agreement among social scientists concerning solutions to our racial conflicts. Some respond to immediate pressures by advocating action now, feeling that further research and planning will only tend to delay and exacerbate the problem. Others emphasize the premature nature of any intervention, and feel that unless scientific and objective procedures are rigorously practiced, action programs will be futile.

Both approaches, including their multiple variations and constant overlap, are not necessarily antagonistic (unless their adherents wish them to be). An adversary point of view is developing; one style is more valid than the other, and attacks from the opposite side provide occasions for heated debate, impressive erudition, and questionable illumination.

The issue is directly related to the racial problem. Most minority group writers, having suffered under racist conditions, are likely to write with higher emotion and impatience. These "targets" or "victims" of racism are likely to plead for *action now,* since any change is viewed as better than the status quo.

Conversely, majority group researchers are more likely to look beyond the immediate conflicts for broader and more "scientific" generalizations. Many question the notion that racism is the critical issue, feeling that social class, personality, and other variables are as important. A more detached, objective approach with less emphasis on practical application is advocated.

RASHOMON PERSPECTIVE

We do not subscribe to a "one valid truth" model, but prefer to respect the perceptions of reality from various positions. Some have referred to this as the "Rashomon model," named after the famous Japanese movie where various characters give their own interpretations of a single incident. The basic point is an important one: views of reality are shaped by experiences, emotions, and needs. Therefore, an explanation from one position may be valid from that view, whereas another observation from a different angle may bring forth an equally valid perception.

There should be a common thread of the scientific method to make observations systematic and objective, studies replicable, researchers well-trained, and data carefully recorded. Up to now, however, the scientific method has not solved our racial problems; in fact, social scientists have probably contributed as much to the confusion and hysteria surrounding the issue as any other source.

Part of the problem lies with the social scientist because he remains first of all a human being. His expectations, needs, experiences, racial background, personality, training, class position, reference group, status, and role shape his research efforts, no matter how faithfully he uses scientific techniques. In the arena of race relations, he is constantly challenged by value references—a "good" adaptation, a "successful" ethnic group, a "healthy" personality, a "functional" culture, and a "conflict-free" interaction. These value judgments are impossible to avoid in any serious effort, and social scientists of various identifications will hold to different positions on these issues.

For example, a "good" minority or a "good" Indian from the majority perspective might be one who would tend to follow dominant group role prescriptions. Conversely a "bad" minority or a "bad" Indian would be the "war-like," "deceitful," "cunning," "savage" Apache. Indians were originally given this reputation for one major reason—their skill in resisting the white man. Terrell (1972) suggests that the Apache were not that different from other tribes inhabiting the same area, but because they were successful in fighting back they were given a perjorative label.

The issue remains the same today—a "successful" minority might adapt to a "less than equal citizen" status through passivity, humility, and acceptance. Conversely, a "bad" minority might be dissatisfied with their pariah status and be openly motivated to change the status quo.

It seems clear that the criteria for "success" depend on whether one takes a majority or minority group perspective. Social scientists of one persuasion may objectively assess the facts, conduct their own observations, check the validity and reliability of their results, and come up with one conclusion; whereas others may check the same facts and arrive at a different interpretation. Up to now, the most dominant (and often the sole) perspective has come from the white majority.

We also advocate the Rashomon perspective because of the complexity of the phenomena under observation and the crude instruments used to measure them. Our theory and techniques are simply not precise enough to justify a one-dimensional, universal truth perspective, even if such a goal is highly desirable. Finally, the phenomenon under study is itself undergoing constant change, so it is wise to present the issues of race from a variety of perspectives.

The issue of objectivity and subjectivity raises still another question in a study of race relations. One of the tenets of science is its stress on objectivity. There is little question that objective observation is important but this question remains, how important is it?

A pertinent example involves the assignment of majority-group scientists to observe, record, and write about their experiences with the Japanese in "relocation centers" during World War II. Does the scientist strive to remain neutral and objective while on assignment? What if the Japanese had been herded into death ovens as the Jews were in Germany? Would the objective scientist remain to record the behavior of the inmates under stress, and if necessary, through cremation and then compare his results with appropriate control groups? Is it his role to observe in a meticulous fashion and provide reliable results and a sound theoretical framework for his findings? During an earlier era the answers were tipped on the side of the objectivity of the researcher; times have changed to the extent that if another wartime evacuation were to occur, social scientists would question different things, including the very existence of concentration camps.

Of course, the ethnicity of the researcher is pertinent here. Would a Japanese American social scientist have behaved differently if he had been in a position of power during the relocation? Should only blacks study blacks, and only black females study black females? The question can be drawn to its logical, or perhaps more accurately, to its illogical conclusion—should studies of death and dying be conducted by those who most closely approximate these conditions?

We reemphasize the desirability of various perspectives. Those extremely close to the problem may present more subjective points of view; those further removed may produce more objective research. The principle of triangulation—that is, taking at least three different sightings of the object before charting a path—may be an appropriate model.

But many questions remain. Is there an objective world of facts and figures that can lead to high-consensus generalizations? How do we deal with the feelings that are especially important in racial questions? Are political perspectives and solutions necessarily invalid? Can there be "scientific" studies on race? Is the ethnicity of the researcher an important factor?

WHY THESE QUESTIONS?

The reasons behind these questions deserve some emphasis. Science, as a technique, methodology, or philosophy is not the primary issue—but rather the social scientist, the politician, and others who write, use, inter-   **8** pret, and act upon the material. In the past, majority-group researchers came into minority communities to conduct "scientific" studies. Many ethnics felt they were used and exploited by the researchers first as subjects then as objects of the findings. It was analogous to a colonial situation: the ethnics were the raw material from which data could be extracted; the information was shipped to universities and research institutions to be processed, then returned to the ghettos in the form of advice and recommendations. The feelings of the ethnic groups were generally ignored; white researchers learned their trade and made their reputations on these studies without any subsequent benefit to the minority communities.

Serious questions have also arisen concerning the interpretations and applications of these findings. Minorities have been told that they are disadvantaged; that their family structure is pathological; that their personality patterns are neurotic; that their "culture" is the reason for their low position and status in the American social system. They have felt the sting of prejudice; they have consistently met with discrimination through studies that emphasized both their unassimilability and their general undesirability. Probably most of these findings ended up in research archives with other unused material but because there have been enough instances where "scientific findings of inferiority" were used to back racist arguments, ethnic communities remain realistically wary.

One current "scientific" issue that will be discussed later in the book deals with the genetic inferiority and the uneducability of the black. It should be noted that only a small handful of researchers advocates this point of view, but publicity and reaction have given it prominent display. The notion of an IQ deficiency based on genetic factors has widespread lay appeal, and the additional impetus from reputable scientists advocating this perspective has provided strong emotional backing. Although the Rashomon perspective welcomes various viewpoints, it is our interpretation that those who back theories of genetic inferiority may be unaware of the possible tragic consequences of translating their beliefs into large-scale programs. It is not a distant step from belief in genetic inferiority to elimination of the "inferior" group.

ETHNICS TO STUDY ETHNICS?

Ethnics have reacted to research with a slogan of their own: "only ethnics should study ethnics." Most studies of minorities in the past were conducted by majority-group researchers; white researchers have often ignored the fact that whites have played the major role in shaping the interaction between the races.

Sloganeering aside, an ethnic individual would have several advantages over the white researcher. First, the mood of many ethnic com-

9

munities currently will not allow a white researcher to come in to conduct a study. Second, the experiences of an individual growing up as an ethnic are different from those of a majority-group member, with the result that critical and relevant questions may be ignored or incorrectly assessed. Finally, there can be a black, yellow, brown, red, and white points of view, and an ethnic researcher will be better able to bring out the hereto ignored ethnic perspective.

An example of a differential perspective is the assessment by various researchers of the effect of the California Alien Land Law of 1920. The law forbade ownership of agricultural land by Japanese aliens (most of the Japanese in California were aliens at that time). White scholars sympathetic to the plight of the Japanese, such as Daniels (1962) and Modell (1969), using "hard" data (i.e., land-ownership figures) wrote that the Japanese in California agriculture were not adversely affected by the law.

However ethnic scholars such as Iwata (1962) and Kitano (1969) disagreed and pointed out some of the damaging effects on the Japanese community. They claim it lowered expectations, raised serious questions about the future of the Japanese in California, and heightened feelings of inferiority and difference at a time when the "melting pot" ethos was a part of the American dream. The ethnic researchers, having grown up in the Japanese community, were sensitive to the moods and feelings of the population in a way that would have been difficult for a majority-group professional. As Peterson (1972) remarks, this issue clearly separated the nonethnic from the ethnic researcher, with the former interpreting from "hard," but perhaps less pertinent data. Merton (1972) relates this to the "insider-outsider" perspective. Each side feels it has the exclusive access to the truth which the other side can only approximate. This condition may arise when a subjugated group has heard about the superiority of a dominant group for a period of time. Upon achieving some degree of power, the powerless collectivities experience heightened self-glorification as a response to the belittlement and downgrading of the past.

Better Studies?

Whether an ethnic will provide "better" studies than a nonethnic is beside the point. The problem is exacerbated by the limited supply of nonwhite researchers, although this problem will disappear in the near future as more and more ethnic researchers become available.

Our perspective encourages a variety of approaches to research, of which ethnicity is but one. Ethnic groups often go through a developmental process and at certain stages "want to do it themselves." They want to use only their own talent, researchers, and resources, and their plea is often nonnegotiable. They want to make their own errors and at this stage it would take a highly insensitive majority-group researcher, no matter what his status, not to listen to their message.

The ethnicity of the researchers is also important to the researcher himself—how he feels about himself and his ethnic identification. His motivations for studying his group and his interpretations have significance far beyond his being a member of the ethnic group itself. In addition, as part of an integrated research team, he is often placed in a token position. His name and ethnicity are prominently displayed, but his power to make decisions is generally limited. Both affect the quality of the product.

However, as studies are conducted, research findings published, and more knowledge uncovered, the sloganeering and tokenism usually are discarded. Rather, questions of the competence of the reasearcher, the validity and reliability of the data, and the logic of the design and analysis become more important, and various points of view are welcomed. This is the stage when cooperative research studies can be undertaken.

DEFINITIONS

In order to discuss race, racism, and ethnic identity, we must first define our terms:

Ethnic group refers to any group "which is defined or set off by race, religion, or national origin, or some combination of these categories" (Gordon, 1964: 27).

Race refers to differential concentrations of "gene frequencies responsible for traits which, so far as we know, are confined to physical manifestations such as skin color or hair form; it has no intrinsic connection with cultural patterns and institutions" (Gordon, 1964: 27).

Nationality refers to being American, whereas *national origin* refers to the country of birth of one's ancestors such as England, Japan, or Mexico. *Religion* means the preferred denomination such as Catholic, Protestant, Jewish, or Buddhist.

Racism—the basic tenets of white racism include:

1. There is no such thing as racial equality; some races are demonstrably superior to others.
2. Races can be graded in terms of superiority. The Caucasian is "superior," and this claim is validated by history. Caucasians have constantly shown their physical, mental, and cultural "superiority."
3. Nations and peoples who have interbred with the nonwhite races do not progress, and countries controlled by nonwhites remain backward.
4. Amalgamation would mean the eradication of the "superior" Caucasian race, a process that would lead to the eventual decline of civilization.

11

There are other examples that can be used to illustrate white racism, but generally these tenets are central. The white or European culture, its civilization, people, and inheritance, is presumed superior to all other races of mankind.

One of the dilemmas in any discussion of race is that of definitions. We have used what is generally referred to as a social definition of race which assumes that how people perceive and feel is the most important facet of racial stratification. Therefore, we use terms such as race, ethnicity, and minority interchangeably, acknowledging that from a different perspective the terms may be defined differently.

ORGANIZATION OF THE BOOK

The book consists of two sections. The first section concentrates on prejudice (chapter 1), discrimination, and segregation (chapters 3 and 4). Chapter 2 presents a variety of patterns that are observable when different racial groups meet, and chapter 5 hypothesizes a number of adaptations to prejudice, discrimination, and segregation. Chapter 6, which closes the first section, hypothesizes the stages in the development of an ethnic identity.

The second section focuses on the history, "style," and culture of several of our major ethnic groups. We have included the blacks, Puerto Ricans, Mexican Americans, Indians, and three Asian groups—the Chinese, Japanese, and Filipinos. Each of them has a different history, a different amount of power, a different entrance into American society, and a different adaptive style, yet their treatment at the hands of white America has been remarkably similar.

STUDY OF CHANGE

Finally, a study of race relations reflects the importance of change—time, place, and conditions all shape explanations and actions. Although we may deplore the current state of practice and research in this area, the racial models of yesterday were vastly more frightening. It was not that long ago that such reputable sources as the *Encyclopaedia Brittanica* were publishing blatantly racist explanations of white superiority; that our immigration policies were overt reflections of our views of colored inferiority; and that the only permissible public portrayal of nonwhites such as in the motion pictures was that of servile, less than equal people.

Neither does the current state of affairs warrant wild enthusiasm. There are many, including some in academia, who believe in biological and racial inferiority and who are willing to limit equal opportunity based on these assumptions. There are also institutions that eagerly, will- **12** ingly, or unconsciously perpetuate the inequalities of the past so that their repressive programs can be carried into the future. The situation was aptly summed up by W. E. B. Du Bois over seventy years ago: "The problem of the twentieth century is the problem of the color line—the relation of the darker to the lighter races of men in Asia and Africa, in America and the islands of the sea."

BIBLIOGRAPHY

DANIELS, ROGER (1962). *The Politics of Prejudice: The Anti-Japanese Movement in California and the Struggle for Japanese Exclusion.* Berkeley: University of California Press.

—— and Harry H. L. Kitano (1970). *American Racism: Exploration of the Nature of Prejudice.* Englewood Cliffs, N.J.: Prentice-Hall, Inc.

GORDON, MILTON (1964). *Assimilation in American Life.* New York: Oxford University Press.

IWATA, MASAKAZU (1962). "The Japanese Immigrants in California Agriculture." *Agricultural History,* 36: 27–37.

KITANO, HARRY H. L. (1969). *Japanese Americans: The Evolution of a Subculture.* Englewood Cliffs, N.J.: Prentice-Hall, Inc.

MERTON, ROBERT (1972). "Insiders and Outsiders: A Chapter in the Sociology of Knowledge." *American Journal of Sociology,* 72 (2): 9–47.

MODELL, JOHN (1969). "The Japanese in Los Angeles: A Study in Growth and Accommodation, 1900–1946." Unpublished doctoral dissertation. New York: Columbia University.

PETERSEN, WILLIAM (1971). *Japanese Americans.* New York: Random House, Inc.

TERRELL, JOHN UPTON (1972). *Apache Chronicle.* New York: World Publishing Company.

PERSPECTIVES
AND
PROBLEMS
IN
RACE RELATIONS

I

PREJUDICE I

One point of view emphasizes that prejudice on the part of the individual is the basic "cause" of racism, and the logical cure is to change the individual's attitude. Behind every racist institution and structure lies a prejudiced mind, and behind every racist action lies a racist attitude.

Psychologists have been especially active in analyzing prejudice as the primary independent variable in racism and the number of research studies is large. Nevertheless, there are many unresolved aspects to prejudice, and no single theory can satisfactorily explain it. Furthermore, the linkages between prejudice, discrimination, and racism remain hypotheses that have still to be empirically demonstrated.

DEFINITIONS

There are many definitions of prejudice. It is "a set of attitudes which causes, supports, or justifies discrimination" (Rose, 1951: 5); ". . . an emotionally rigid attitude, or predisposition to respond to a certain stimulus in a certain way toward a group of people" (Simpson and Yinger, 1965: 10); ". . . an antipathy based upon a faulty and inflexible generalization" (Allport, 1958).

Collins, in summarizing the various definitions of prejudice, lists the following common features (1970: 249):

1. Prejudice is an intergroup phenomenon.
2. Prejudice is a negative orientation.
3. Prejudice is bad.
4. Prejudice is an attitude.

From this summary, racial prejudice can be viewed as an attitude towards an ethnic group that is directed in negative and often stereotypic terms, and is based on a social, not a scientific definition of race and groups. An individual is hated, despised, shunned, and avoided because of membership in a particular group.

Our definition of racial prejudice is "a prejudgment of others through negative racial signs." By negative racial signs, we refer primarily to stereotypes and their primary effect in race relations is avoidance. Therefore, our total definition includes the prejudgment (an attitude), the mechanism or technique that maintains or justifies the attitude (stereotyping), and its primary effect on intergroup relations (avoidance).

MEASURING PREJUDICE

Since prejudice is defined as an attitude, researchers have been able to follow the general models of attitudinal research to assess this variable. The basic assumption that attitudes are accurate predictors of behavior remains debatable; nevertheless, without this theoretical linkage, attitudinal research is quite meaningless.

Collins lists and criticizes some of the more common means of measuring prejudice (1970: 253–54).

THE SELF-REPORT

The usefulness of the self-report is limited primarily because of problems of validity. Can a person's response to a paper-and-pencil test measure his actual behavior in interracial situations? Generally, the self-report is gathered through an attitudinal scale. A person responds to a question such as, "By nature the Negro and the white man are equal"; and it is presumed that the prejudices of a person are revealed through his responses. The F (fascism)-scale drawn from *The Authoritarian Personality* (Adorno et al., 1950) and the Bogardus social-distance scale (1933) are examples of the paper-and-pencil self-report.

The self-report can be used to survey a respondent's attitudes toward an ethnic group. The experimenter can then introduce an independent variable by exposing the subject to new information or knowledge about the group, and follow it up with another self-report. The **18** expected change between the first and second reports would illustrate the attitudinal change.

Observations of Overt Behavior

There has been little research linking overt behavior to prejudice. The major limitation is the problem of identifying the appropriate behaviors to be measured and their association with significant attitudes. For example, although a person may hold "liberal attitudes" towards ethnic minorities, it is difficult for a researcher to observe his actual behavior in interracial situations. Perhaps the most valid technique would be for a researcher to live with a family for a period of time, but the time and cost problems present a major barrier. In contrast, the self-report attitudinal scale is easy to administer to large samples.

The La Piere experiment (1934) is one of the prototypes of the measurement of overt behavior. In this study, an Oriental couple traveled around the country, first writing for hotel reservations (high refusal) and then actually showing up (low refusal).

Recent work on nonverbal communication such as proxemics (Hall, 1963; Mehrabian, 1967) introduces behavioral techniques in the measurement of prejudice. Proxemics refers to the degree of closeness, directness, or intimacy of nonverbal interaction between two communicators. The major variables are distance (how far apart the communicators choose to be), eye contact (the percentage of time the communicators look into each other's eyes), and body relaxation (the amount of leaning forward or backward by the communicators). Negative racial feelings were supposed to be shown by remaining at a greater distance, less eye contact, and the tendency to lean away from rather than toward the other party.

Even these behavioral techniques, although objective, reliable, and quantifiable, can be misleading. For example, many Japanese deliberately avoid eye contact. They consider it rude to look directly into another person's eyes, and therefore their avoidance may be unrelated to racial prejudice. A knowledge of various cultural styles is important because similar behaviors may entail different motivations.

THE DE FLEUR-WESTIE STUDY

A laboratory experiment by De Fleur and Westie (1958) linked attitudes and behavior. Subjects who had already taken a written test of attitudes were shown some colored photographic slides of a well-dressed, good-looking Negro man with a well-dressed white woman. Other slides showed a white man with a Negro woman. The subjects were then asked if they would be willing to be photographed with a Negro person of the opposite sex; they were then given a standard photograph release agreement. It was specified that the signature was necessary so that the photograph could be given public exposure. The subjects were to sign the release; those who refused to sign were considered to be prejudiced.

The findings indicated some consistency between behavior and attitudes. By both measurement techniques, eighteen subjects were classified as prejudiced and fourteen as unprejudiced. However the remaining fourteen or nearly a third of the sample, behaved "inconsistently" —that is, they were classified as prejudiced under one measure and unprejudiced under the other.

PHYSIOLOGICAL REACTIONS

Another technique for assessing prejudice employs physiological measures. The galvanic skin response (GSR) has been used to assess prejudice (Cooper and Singer, 1956; Cooper and Siegel, 1956; De Fleur and Westie, 1958). The technique assesses only extreme responses, and not the direction of the attitude. However, with increased sophistication and continued use, this technique may become a valuable indicator.

PROJECTIVE TECHNIQUES

The projective test is a device whereby the subject is asked to respond to an unstructured stimulus such as a set of pictures (TAT) or to ink blots (Rorschach). Its use in the assessment of racial attitudes has been limited, and it remains somewhat unreliable, difficult to interpret, and expensive. The major advantage of this method is its indirectness; the unstructured responses and the lack of obvious "racist" stimuli reveal information that is relatively easy to conceal with a direct approach.

EXPLANATIONS OF PREJUDICE

Most explanations of prejudice are related to the scientific discipline of the observer.

Some theories of prejudice emphasize the historical aspect; they may regard slavery and Reconstruction as important variables in explaining the current Negro problem. Some theories lean toward an economic exploitation approach, emphasizing the functional nature of prejudice in maintaining an exploited group either for its labor or for its resources. A case may be made for urbanization, for industrialization, for the effects of materialism, depersonalization, and the mass culture; another point of view . . . emphasizes mobility in our society, either upward or downward.

Broader theories, based on Hobbesian perspectives, find the roots of prejudice in the unsavory nature of man himself. Some theories emphasize prejudice as one outcome of the frustration-aggression model; others emphasize inadequate socialization and the development of the authoritarian personality; while others stress the importance of stereotypes. Each perspective can probably be partially validated with empirical data. But no one theory can explain every aspect of prejudice (Daniels and Kitano, 1970: 16–17).

Simpson and Yinger (1965) mention that early studies were limited in their usefulness because they attempted to find simple, one-factor explanations. It would be difficult to defend a single causal factor or prejudice when we know that:

1. Groups differ in the direction and amount of prejudice they exhibit.
2. Individuals differ in the direction and amount of prejudice they exhibit.
3. Target groups change over time, and the *kinds* of target groups may also change.

One of the main tasks of the social scientist is to identify the process by which prejudice is acquired, developed, maintained, and transmitted. Hopefully, with this understanding the process can be reversed and prejudice can be reduced, controlled, or eliminated.

CLASSIFICATION OF CAUSES

There are various kinds of explanations for prejudice. Simpson and Yinger (1965) divide and discriminate by: (1) personality functions, (2) weapons in group conflict, (3) cultural factors, and (4) consequences on both the minority and majority groups.

Collins (1970) uses a two-level analysis schema on the causes of prejudice: societal and individual. Societal explanations trace the development of prejudice in a given social system, culture, or group and have been the focus of historians, sociologists, anthropologists, and social psychologists. Individual explanations look for the causes of prejudice in the individual personality and have been the chief domain of psychologists, psychiatrists, and social workers.

There are four categories that encompass most of the explanations on how prejudice develops. We are omitting those views that explain prejudice as an inherited instinct, since our basic assumption is that prejudice is learned. The categories form simple guidelines, and they overlap somewhat: (1) exploitation, (2) ignorance, (3) racism-ethnocentrism, and (4) symbolic.

Exploitation Explanations

According to these theories, one group dominates another sexually, economically, and socially. The "inferior" group must be kept in its place so that the "superior" group can achieve and enjoy the advantages of better employment and social status. The inferior group pays higher rents, is charged higher prices, is denied the use of public facilities, and is paid lower wages. This system has been called "a mask for privilege," and it describes how the economically advantaged are able to use and exclude rising groups from full participation in American life.

21

Slavery is an obvious and dramatic example of the exploitation of one group by another. There are several hypothesized conditions which can lead to this use of other human beings. First, the culture must have one primary goal, the maximization of profit. Second, societal organizations such as the business and educational establishments must also support this primary goal. Third, there must be a large labor force for the unpopular and menial jobs. Fourth, the inferior group must be considered heathen or subhuman and therefore deserving of unequal treatment. Finally, their skin color is also an important factor.

Nonwhite groups have felt the relationship between prejudice and economic exploitation. In California, the Chinese were wanted for labor, later the Japanese, then the Mexicans and the Filipinos. None of these groups was readily accepted into the larger society, and the minute their labors were no longer needed (or they desired to look for other than the menial agricultural positions), they faced heightened prejudice and discrimination.

THE MARXIAN PERSPECTIVE

Marxist writers have proffered the strongest explanation for prejudice as a tool in economic exploitation. Cox (1948) views racial prejudice as an attitude propagated among the public by an exploiting class for the purpose of labeling an inferior class. The inferiority is related to their supposed subhuman nature so that by stigmatizing a group as parahuman or inferior, the capitalist can exploit this group and their resources.

Under capitalism, labor is just another factor of production to be used in maximizing profit. It can be bought or sold on a dehumanized basis so that the importance of individuality and the family is minimized. Human beings are treated as commodities, little different from land and capital. Therefore, in capitalistic countries, the industrialists must proletarianize the masses; and in dealing with colonial, or nonwhite labor, they can go one stage further by denying them even the status of white proletariats.

As Mason states, ". . . the inhabitants of distant or outlying territories could be exploited even more ruthlessly than those at home, and with even less opportunity of revolt, while the domestic labor could be encouraged to take part, up to a point, in the exploitation," (1970: 62).

Race hostility and prejudice in the Marxist perspective are not the central issues of capitalism and imperialism. The central issue is class conflict. White people, in order to bolster their positions in the class structure, have been brought to look at nonwhites as a lower class. The correlation between racism and the development of capitalism however, is one of cause and effect; therefore, the prediction is that race prejudice would disappear with the collapse of capitalism.

Broad theories such as the Marxist perspective are difficult to evaluate. Prejudice is relative—it is not an absolute in that one country or culture has it and another does not. All countries contain varying degrees of racism; it is not a trait peculiar only to capitalistic countries.

Ignorance

Explanations of prejudice based on ignorance cover a wide range. Ignorance can result from a simple lack of information and knowledge, from preset attitudes, false beliefs, selective perceptions and experiences, and from superficial knowledge of groups. Stereotypes and images projected through the mass media such as books, radio, magazines, newspapers, television, and the movies play on the ignorance of large numbers. Each of these factors keeps the ignorance and stereotypes of the past alive for new generations.

The simplest explanation is that prejudice results from pure ignorance. Asians are generally unknown in the eastern and southern states; the northern states have not had much contact with Mexican Americans; and there are rural areas that have had almost no contact with any ethnic group. Under these conditions, information about groups is garnered from whatever existing sources; and the influence and power of the mass media becomes extremely important.

For example there was a recent report of the stereotype of the "sneaky, tricky Jap" in Georgia. There are few Japanese in that state, and intergroup contacts are minimal, but a war movie had been shown on a popular TV time slot, and the World War II stereotype lingered in the minds of many viewers.

The problem is not solely regional. Segregation and separation reinforces a growing insulation between groups. Although there may be some contact in integrated work and school situations, there is seldom any meaningful social and emotional communication across ethnic and racial lines, and people remain generally ignorant of other groups. The mass media provide the only ethnic contact and exposure for many, and this is limited to stereotypes of the Chinese cook, the Mexican bandito, the Italian gangster, the treacherous Japanese, and the "Step n' Fetchit" Negro.

SELECTIVE PERCEPTIONS AND EXPERIENCES

Another series of events often shapes prejudice. When stereotypes of a group are already given wide credence, selective perceptions and experiences can validate the attitude. The term "self-fulfilling prophecy" is an apt one; for example, if a group is labeled loud and pushy, an experience with a member of that group who fits the stereotype reinforces the prejudice. Evidence concerning those who do not fit the label is usually ignored; and making exceptions such as "but he doesn't act like one of them" does nothing to upset the basic prejudice.

A particularly negative experience with a member of an ethnic group is also used to reinforce prejudice. Individuals can "remember when," and these negative feelings remain in spite of numerous other intervening experiences and the passage of time.

The problem of selective perceptions is a constant one and remains a special barrier in attitudinal change. An emotional preset or bias works in such a manner that the viewer selects those incidents in a movie or those examples in a book that reinforce his prejudices and conveniently ignores the rest of the exposure.

Another technique that is related to selective perceptions is to place the blame for minority problems on the minorities themselves. It is referred to as the "earned reputation" approach by Rose (1951). This perspective shifts the responsibility from the dominant to the minority group. "It's their fault," "if only they would change, the problem of prejudice and discrimination will disappear," are statements that enable the majority to ignore the plight of ethnic groups.

A hypothesis by Rokeach, Smith, and Evans (1960) contends that a prejudiced person does not reject a person of another race, religion, or nationality because of ethnic membership per se but rather because he perceives that the other differs from him in important beliefs and values. The question he asks might be, "Can I be friends with that person" rather than "I don't like his color." Stein et al. (1971) devised an experiment that supported Rokeach's theory that the major portion of prejudice was based on belief congruence. They concluded that if different races encountered one another on the basis of equal status, which then led to shared beliefs, then racial prejudice could be substantially reduced. The basic assumption behind the belief congruence approach appears to involve an oversimplification of the problem. Perhaps the qualification, "other things being equal" (e.g., social class, values, goals, power, status, vulnerability) would be necessary; and such conditions are often themselves determined by ethnic group membership.

*

Ethnocentrism–Racism

Simpson and Yinger (1965) feel that the underlying attitude in the use of prejudice as a weapon in group conflict is *ethnocentrism,* the belief that one's own group is unique and "right." They see the phenomenon as almost universal.

As an individual is socialized to the beliefs and behaviors of his own family and society, he begins to feel that what he and his group do is "natural" and so begins to judge others from this standpoint. In this sense, ethnocentrism is almost inevitable since the very standards one uses to judge others are part of the culture he has absorbed. Those who deviate are then viewed as "unnatural" and can become the target of prejudice.

24

The family plays an important part in this process. The way one's family conducts itself is "normal." The food, the conversation, and the life style become a part of a standard, and other families who differ may be judged strange, foreign, or alien.

Ethnocentrism is a part of the "identity" of an individual, and may be linked to other variables such as pride, belonging, standards, and the like. In this sense it is normal, and one may hypothesize that some measure of pride in one's own family and culture is a positive strength. It turns into a negative prejudice only when it becomes overly rigid and intolerant of the behavior of others.

One of the more damaging aspects of racism is the "reverse" ethnocentrism often observed in ethnic groups. An individual may lack even a minimal sense of pride in his own family and culture because of his constant exposure to American models. Therefore, rather than being proud of his family, or his ethnic background, the individual may deny his family, or "lie" about his background so that his immigrant parents are now fluent and acculturated, or he may attempt to pass as a member of the majority culture. This obviously destroys any healthy sense of identity for many ethnic group members. However, there is current evidence (e.g., "black is beautiful") that styles are changing.

Ethnocentrism mainly serves the group in power. The European colonists' self-esteem led them to think of Western civilization as the "best," and to lack respect for the achievements of Asian, African, and South American cultures. Prejudice provides the rationalization for those who want to maintain the equilibrium between the "dominant" and the "inferior."

STRUCTURAL OPPOSITION

Prejudice may also be conceptualized as a product of structural opposition. Prejudice is a part of the "we-they" phenomenon, and the very formation of one unity in contrast to another leads to certain conditions. As Daniels and Kitano say, "[we prefer] . . . an interpretation in which a man is a member of a group of a certain kind by virtue of his nonmembership in other groups. A person belongs to a tribe or its segment, and membership is activated when there is opposition to this tribe. Therefore a man sees himself as a member of a group only in opposition to other groups, and he sees a member of another group as a member of a social unity, however much that unit may be split into opposing segments" (1970: 19). Social groups form because in response to stimuli, people choose to associate with certain persons and not with others. A football team is not really an entity until there is an opponent; once the opposition is present, prejudice between the "enemies" can be predicted.

Although race and color prejudice are the current divisive issues, other conflicts were more central in previous eras. Religious differences

25

were major problems of the Middle Ages, and the world was divided between "superior" and "inferior" religions. Great amounts of prejudice are also found in class and national conflicts.

Symbolic Explanations

Another group of theories views prejudice as a symptom, a symbol, or a byproduct stemming from other concerns. Psychological symptom theories are most often associated with Freudian psychoanalytic thought. The basic assumption in Freudian theory is that all behavior is psychically determined and that prejudice, as a symptom, is a reflection of deeper intrapsychic phenomena.

PREJUDICE AS A DISPLACEMENT OF HOSTILITY—SCAPEGOATING

Social psychological theory has emphasized frustration-aggression as one of the critical variables behind prejudice. The blockage of goal-directed behavior, whether by other people, by natural forces, or by one's own lack of skill or unrealistic expectations, is a frustrating experience and creates hostile impulses. In many instances this hostility cannot be directed against the primary source of the frustration; it may be too powerful and it may retaliate; in other cases, the source of frustration cannot be easily identified. In any case, the individual may then direct his hostile impulses against a more convenient target, or a scapegoat. Less powerful but readily identifiable racial groups can become the unwilling recipients of such hostility. The studies of Dollard and Miller (1939) and their colleagues typify this point of view. The very ineffectiveness of the frustration-hostility-scapegoat cycle can lead to the further development of prejudice. The frustrated individual may feel somewhat guilty about his displaced hostility, and the effectiveness of the outlet may be open to question. Therefore as guilt and anxiety develop, there may be further displacement and hostility towards the scapegoat, which serves to reinforce the vicious cycle.

DISPLACEMENT

Displacement is the process whereby the hostility is directed towards a target that cannot realistically be shown to be the cause of one's difficulties. A classical example of displacement is the case of German anti-Semitism described by Dollard and Miller (1939).

From 1914 to 1933, the Germans developed a policy of overt anti-Semitism. Rather than channeling their hostilities directly toward the all-powerful Allies who had defeated them in war, dictated the Treaty of Versailles, and forced them to relinquish their colonies, the Germans vented their frustrations against the Jews. The subsequent depression, the ruinous inflation, and the collapse of their economic system was blamed on the Jews, and anti-Semitism was one of Hitler's planks in his rise to power.

There is some evidence that the choice of a scapegoat is not a purely random factor. Some are attacked, but not others. The attack is not always against the weakest, but often against those who are stronger and potentially more dangerous.

Both the frustration-aggression and displacement explanations analyze prejudice as an indirect rather than a direct phenomenon. Therefore, any attempt to solve the problem without an attack on the "real causes" may be futile. The theories, although plausible on an expost facto basis, are difficult to validate because of the relativity of such concepts as frustration and aggression and because of the difficulty of operationalizing the terms adequately (see Chapter 6 for other adaptive responses). Nevertheless, these views do not see prejudice as a simple, linear phenomenon, but one involving different levels and orders.

RATIONALIZATION

Rationalization is similar to the "earned reputation" approach. In both the actor attempts to justify actions that he knows to be wrong with the explanation that the victim "deserves what he gets" or "gets what is coming to him." By this process, prejudicial attitudes can be justified, and restrictive acts and outright violence can be rationalized.

Neutralization is a common technique that is used to dehumanize the intended victim. By defining the victim as less than human (animals are a favorite label, especially dogs, rats, and pigs), the actor can permit himself to do what he had previously inhibited himself from doing. Labelling and categorization play an important part in the dehumanization process.

The process is an extremely common one and may be more closely related to discrimination (action) than to prejudice (attitude). The ease with which other human beings can be bombed, burned, and destroyed simply by labelling them "the enemy" is frightening, especially when such behavior is often cloaked in self-righteousness, morality, patriotism, and heroism. Further, there is often a lack of prejudice by those who destroy ("I don't hate them"; "I was just doing my duty") which further removes the act from a sense of emotion, participation, and reality.

PREJUDICE CAUSED BY A "SICK" PERSONALITY

Another explanation of prejudice views the problem as a result of improper socialization and the development of a "sick" personality. The most well-known view from this perspective is found in *The Authoritarian Personality* (1950), which was the joint product of a group of psychologists headed by Adorno, Frenkel-Brunswik, Levinson, and Sanford, who were based primarily in Berkeley several years after the end of World War II. The study focused on the relationship between personality structure and prejudice, especially anti-Semitism.

Although the authors leaned heavily on Freud's structure of the personality, they were guided by academic psychology when discussing the more directly observable and measurable aspects of personality. Their findings encouraged the view that the prejudiced person was closer to a pathological personality than the normal person. For example, the authoritarian was pessimistic, cynical, anti-intellectual, distrustful, suspicious, dogmatic, and lacking in poise and appearance. On the other hand, those low in prejudice were flexible, tolerant, autonomous, self-reliant, and possessed realistic goal orientations.

There have been many criticisms of the interpretations in *The Authoritarian Personality*. Its methodological weaknesses include biased sampling procedures, no control for education and group membership, and the dubious coding procedures of the qualitative material. The interpretations are open to question, and replications of various subscales have brought out conflicting and contradictory material.

Nevertheless, *The Authoritarian Personality* was a valuable addition to the study of race relations. It brought together many of the scattered works of the previous era, provided a series of empirical tools for analyzing prejudice, encouraged research, and served as an impetus for a legion of studies in this vital area.

SOCIAL CHANGE

A more sociological perspective mentioned by Park (1950) relates the "cause" of prejudice to social change. The more rapid the social change, the higher the degree of prejudice. Conversely, the more static a society, the lesser the degree of prejudice. We add that the higher the diversity of groups, the higher the probability of prejudice.

Prejudice, from this perspective is essentially a conservative tool. It is used to retain a social distance and to preserve the social order. In a rigid and static class-caste system, the internal organizations and patterns of communication are established, and most people know their place in the society. Therefore, there are few constant challenges to status and power, and prejudice is hypothesized to be low.

In a rapidly changing culture with multiple and diverse groups there are constant challenges to status. The need to retain social distance becomes higher, and prejudice is hypothesized as one consequence of this state. The great amount of prejudice in our rapidly changing, multigroup culture demonstrates the validity of this perception.

The view of prejudice as a resultant of changing social forces is intriguing but almost impossible to evaluate. Japan's rapid change into an industrial giant may not have been accompanied by a high rise in prejudice since her social institutions (e.g., family "ie" system) are so stable. Thus other variables must be taken into account.

In summary, the "causes" of prejudice are multiple, varied, and interactive. We assume that it is learned and that it has both positive and negative functions. However, race prejudice is primarily a negative phenomenon because it is a prejudgment, a stereotyping, and a condemnation of a whole race. As such, it creates barriers between entire groups and fosters conditions that can lead to more destructive intergroup actions. Therefore, although it is unrealistic to think it can ever be completely eliminated, we should give the highest priority to programs aimed at reducing it through fostering healthier intergroup and interpersonal patterns.

REDUCING PREJUDICE

Prejudice-reducing programs are closely linked to hypothesized causes. Since these differ so widely, it is important that the programs be based on the theories, otherwise the attempts will appear diffuse and unrelated.

Lessening Exploitation: Equal-Status Contact

One of the most common prescriptions for eliminating prejudice is to get rid of the capitalistic system. The basic assumption is that the exploitation and the competitiveness under free enterprise is directly related to prejudicial attitudes. Although this assumption is difficult to validate empirically, it is logical to speculate whether there are any "prejudice-free" societies under other forms of government. As far as we know, there are none. But since the term "prejudice-free" is relative rather than absolute, some societies are considered to be less racially prejudiced than others. South Africa is generally considered to have one of the most highly prejudiced systems, whereas Brazil and the state of Hawaii have among the lowest prejudiced systems.

Bettelheim and Janowitz (1964), along with Dicks (1959), suggest solutions to intergroup conflict through social and economic changes that would reduce the feelings of fear and deprivation by controlling certain sources of prejudice such as unemployment and by guaranteeing security such as extending social welfare. These solutions remain long range rather than immediate and are difficult to assess.

Some advocate increased contact as a means of lessening interethnic fears and anxieties. The contact method has at times proved effective where members of different groups have equal economic and social status. By destroying old stereotypes, the person feels compelled to change his beliefs and attitudes toward the outgroup. He feels uneasy when his feelings and beliefs toward the outgroup are inconsistent, and he tries to bring them into congruence (Rosenberg, 1956).

29

But contact can work both ways. It may confirm stereotypes by actually forcing the outgroup to behave according to the stereotype. For example, a prejudiced person with unfavorable stereotypes of a outgroup may react negatively towards that group, which in turn will induce a member of the outgroup to behave in congruence with the prejudiced person's stereotype. Rosenthal's study (1964) indicated that teacher attitudes toward minority-group children as being "really not educable" had been an important cause in their low academic achievement.

Contact itself may be rather specific. A study by Secord and Backman (1964) shows that contact with certain minority-group members in particular situations destroys only those stereotypes formed in that situation. For example, interaction with minority-group members as neighbors, eventually leads to greater acceptance of those members, but only in that particular role. Another example can be found in the greater acceptance and willingness to work with members of minority groups if there is direct contact on the job. However other prejudiced attitudes may remain scarcely changed.

Studies of occupational contact have shown that reduction of prejudice does not go beyond the work situation. Reed's (1947) and Minard's (1952) studies have indicated that wider community norms have often made off-the-job friendships extremely difficult or impossible. Another factor that may preclude reduction of prejudice beyond the work situation is distance of housing between coworkers due to segregated neighborhoods. Mandelbaum's study (1952) of the air force, where residential segregation does not prevail among personnel, supports this assumption.

Many studies indicate that contact per se is not sufficient in reducing racial prejudice. Cole, Steinberg, and Burkheimer (1968) found that token integration and passive, uninvolved contact did little to reduce the prejudice and hostility of white students toward blacks.

Contact methods in reducing prejudice by unlearning attitudes and reevaluating the outgroup are successful under the following conditions. First, the behavior of the member of the outgroup who comes into contact with the prejudiced person must not conform to the stereotype, and the outgroup member's beliefs must be congruent with those of the prejudiced person. Second, the duration of the relationship must be long and the sample large enough so that the prejudiced person cannot attribute his change in attitude to the specific contact situation or to individual exceptions to the rule. Third, the prejudiced person must be able to perceive those behaviors that are inconsistent with his fixed, stereotyped perceptions of the outgroup (Collins, 1970: 317).

The Shared-Coping Approach

This approach supplements the previously discussed approaches by explaining when and how prejudice is reduced through intergroup contact. It proposes that prejudice can be reduced through intergroup contact involving shared goals and shared-coping to achieve these goals, which in part foster cooperation and interdependence.

The shared goal promotes cohesiveness of the group (whether it be a fund-raising party or survival in a lifeboat), requires group interdependence, and promotes a common fate for all involved. Shared-coping and cooperation is thus deemed necessary to achieve these goals, for it reinforces the unlearning mechanisms and reduces misperception.

Feshbach and Singer (1957) found that the creation of superordinate goals produces a new in-group composed of minority and majority members, and that reduction of prejudice proceeds by having both groups work toward the superordinate goals.

Shared-coping experiences also tend to reduce ethnic prejudice through the development of intergroup friendships. These friendships tend to foster greater acceptance of other members of a minority group and of the group as a whole. It also encourages the prejudiced person to be more receptive to favorable information concerning the minority group; it also tends to close the social distance in other contact situations since the role of a friend is quite varied. Finally, intergroup friendship forces the prejudiced person to bring into congruence and consistency the views that he holds of his friend to those that he holds of the outgroup.

Studies indicate that the more acquaintance one has with members of an outgroup, the more favorable the attitude towards the entire group in general (Orata, 1927; Diggins, 1927; Gray and Thompson, 1953). A study by Stouffer and his colleagues (1949) shows how the interaction between shared goals and shared-coping during World War II between black and white soldiers reduced prejudice. The research was initiated when units were mixed racially due to the extreme shortage of white infantry replacements; black volunteers were then recruited into replacement platoons previously restricted to all-white companies. Those who had closer cooperative intergroup contact with black soldiers were less prejudiced than those who did not.

We believe that the studies indicate some success in reducing prejudice under certain proscribed conditions such as equal status contact. The findings support the attempts to eliminate discriminatory barriers in housing, education, and jobs in order that minorities may eventually have the opportunity to meet their white peers on an equal level.

Ignorance

If ignorance is one of the main reasons for prejudice, then the preferred solution would be to provide information. Prejudice can be reduced by resocializing those who have been exposed to misinformation and thus have made overgeneralizations, formed misconceptions, and made incorrect causal attributions. Therefore, evidence conveying information contrary to this misinformation could reduce prejudice. Two major vehicles useful for conveying such evidence would be propaganda and education.

PROPAGANDA

Although propaganda under certain conditions has been found effective in reducing prejudice, studies have shown that people tend to avoid propaganda (Lazarsfeld, 1944). Even if not avoided entirely, people tend to receive different implications from the propaganda from what was intended. Cooper and Johoda (1947) describe four such mechanisms for propaganda evasion.

1. Although the message may be initially understood and followed, people finally miss the main appeal of the message.
2. People may understand the message but proclaim it invalid or as not revealing the entire picture, or they may rationalize by stating that a few prejudices are permissable.
3. Studies have shown that propaganda aimed at increasing tolerance has instead increased or reinforced prejudice (Bettelheim and Janowitz, 1964). It is believed that those who have strongly cemented prejudiced attitudes often selectively perceive and interpret information and facts to fit their views.
4. Often the person to whom the appeal is being made lacks the education to understand it.

Propaganda has been found successful when projected to captive audiences (especially through motion pictures) and when prejudiced attitudes are initially low. But its effectiveness remains questionable when applied to those already highly prejudiced. Protolerance campaigns in the past have been ineffective because of the great amount of avoidance and evasion.

EDUCATION

Many studies indicate that those who have more education tend to be less prejudiced (Bettelheim and Janowitz, 1964; Harding et al., 1954). However, the variables of income, social status, and intelligence that usually accompany higher education tend to cloud the efficacy of education per se in reducing prejudice.

In other studies, however, higher education has led to more prejudice toward ethnic groups. McNeill's study (1960) showed that prejudice actually increased from the tenth to the twelfth grade; Sims and Patrick (1936) showed that attitudes of prejudice increased among northern students attending a southern university, whereas there was a reduction in the prejudice of southern students attending a northern university, which indicates that geographical location is also an important variable. However, Stember's study (1961) did conclude that less rigid ethnic attitudes were more prevalent among those with higher education than those with less.

The kind of education one is exposed to in elementary school may also be a crucial variable in prejudice reduction. A study conducted by Litcher and Johnson (1969) investigating the effects of curriculum materials on racial attitudes found a marked positive change of attitude of white elementary school students toward Negroes after a multiethnic reader was used.

Special educational programs directly aimed at reducing prejudice have often been successful, but the specific agents responsible for attitude change still remain unknown. Probably the most ambitious and controversial program involving the educational system has been that of school busing (see Chapters 3 and 4 on discrimination). The logic of different racial and class groups working together in school seems valid, especially since de facto segregation will probably limit effective contact at any other time. But so many other issues have entered into the argument that there is little room for calm discussion. The notion that busing is a "sociological experiment" is a defensible one, but interestingly enough, the term is often used disparagingly to imply that it is unworthy of consideration. But unless children get together at some time in their lives, their sole means of communication and interaction may remain at the stereotyped level.

The Symptom Theory Approach

Suggestions offered by those who believe in symptom theories, which claim that the cause of prejudice is maintained by psychological conflict, tend to solve the problem of prejudice by reconstructing the psychological conflicts that underlie prejudice. However, according to Ashmore (Collins, 1970: 298), direct methods to reduce prejudice will not work if one adheres to the symptom theories because of the following reasons:

1. Prejudice functions as a crutch for people to solve inner conflict, tension, and anxiety. Therefore, if prejudice is used in this manner, one encounters high resistance to change of attitudes.
2. Efforts to reduce prejudice may, in fact, increase its intensity since they may increase the psychological conflicts within the individual.
3. If the symptom (prejudice) is removed, but the actual personal conflict that caused it is not removed, the person will in fact find another target on which to vent his hostility.

Therefore Ashmore suggests the following indirect methods as a more successful means for reducing prejudice:

PSYCHOTHERAPY

Perhaps the most effective method of reducing prejudice would be to work on the individual's basic personality structure while attempting to integrate the personality and eliminate the hostility toward target groups. There has been conflicting evidence of the efficacy of this method. Pearl (1955) found psychotherapy to actually increase rejection of target groups, whereas Allport (1958) has found that therapy reduces it.

However, in view of the high expense, time consumption, and questionable efficacy of individual psychotherapy, more attention has been given to group therapy. Studies by Haimowitz and Haimowitz (1950) revealed actual reduction in prejudice by using the Rogerian Group therapy of evaluating change in intergroup attitudes and measuring actual reduction of social distance. But because of the biased nature of their sample of twenty-four highly educated and ethnically mixed people, broad generalizations could not be drawn from their results. As Ashmore points out, one cannot be certain whether "intergroup contact" or group therapy itself improved personality structure and was responsible for reducing social distance. Pearl's studies (1954, 1955) showed that some aspects of group therapy reduced ethnocentric attitudes. Rubin's study (1967) in sensitivity training revealed that improved self-concepts and more self-acceptance increased acceptance of outgroups. This study also involved an ethnically mixed sample of white and blacks so that the change of attitude could also be partially explained by intergroup contact.

The effectiveness of group therapy is probably high, although studies have not yet revealed how it actually does reduce prejudice. Is it, in fact, the group therapy itself or the intergroup contact that is responsible? The independent effects of these two factors must be further analyzed before the effectiveness of group therapy can be assessed.

More recent variations of the group approach include "t" groups, encounter sessions, and interracial confrontations. Because of their recency and the lack of research data, there is little experimental evidence to demonstrate the effectiveness of these approaches.

INSIGHT

Self-insight training has been found effective in several experiments. Katz, Sarnoff, and McClintock (1956) used this technique by reasoning that if prejudice is an attitude that one uses for ego defense, then one can reduce prejudice through insight into its true nature. This insight, which would bring about reorganization of the personality, would make one less dependent on ego-defense mechanisms.

Subsequent studies have also found self-insight procedures to be effective in reducing prejudice, although the role of the reorganized personality has been questioned. Stotland, Katz, and Patchen (1959) found self-insight methods most effective when motivated by an appeal to a consistent pattern in attitude, behavior, and values. This result brings into question the precise mechanisms of attitude change.

How effective this self-insight training will be on the average citizen 34 also remains in doubt, for all subjects in past research have been college students. It is felt that college students are more concerned about self-consistency and are also more skilled in language and logic than the general population, which would produce a bias in the research.

CATHARSIS

The basic assumption of catharsis is that verbal release of hostility reduces aggression. This assumption has been challenged by the research of Bandura and Walters (1963) and by Berkowitz (1962). Overt release of hostility may actually increase prejudice by reinforcing the expression of hostility and may even increase prejudice in other directions.

ALTERNATIVE MEANS OF REDUCING TENSION

Release of tension through one activity may result in decreasing tension in another sphere. Bettelheim and Janowitz (1964) report that under normal conditions, tensions could be handled with greater ease if people could engage in mutually gratifying sexual relations. Pleasing as this alternative may seem, its probability of success remains very tenuous.

CHANGES IN CHILD-REARING PRACTICES

Changes in child-rearing practices have been encouraged by proponents of the authoritarian personality explanation of prejudice as the only permanent way of reducing prejudice. This method would concentrate on eliminating personality conflict before it develops by teaching parents to be more understanding and less capricious and authoritarian in their control over their child. This approach, which was especially popular several decades ago, appears simplistic and naive today. Nevertheless it would be difficult to argue against encouraging the development of healthy children through better socialization techniques.

There is one consistent omission in the study of prejudice which is both welcome and unwelcome at the same time. The majority of studies concentrate on the dominant white group; this is appropriate since their power remains the most important consideration. Nevertheless there is very little about the development and maintenance of prejudice among the ethnics. Is the function and process of prejudice the same in the minority groups? How does one change the attitudes of the minority? The study of prejudice up to now has been primarily from and about the white majority point of view.

In summary, the techniques for the reduction of prejudice are as broad and varied as the "causes." The evidence of the effectiveness of various approaches remains indefinite, and research evidence presents conflicting results. However, there is some agreement that prejudice can be reduced under the broad conditions of equal-status contact, where people work together under cooperative conditions; where role positions are equal and complementary; where past experiences have not been too damaging; where the people have knowledge about the other group so that feedback is positive and negative stereotypes do not develop. But, as we emphasize, such conditions are quite difficult to achieve in modern-day America.

There is one grave concern about the problem of prejudice in our complicated social system. A nonprejudiced leader cannot do much in reshaping an institution in terms of racism; perhaps his power is essentially negative in that he can prevent certain things from happening. Conversely, an extremely prejudiced person can wield a great deal of influence over racist practices. To think of the actions of extremely prejudiced individuals in positions of great power is frightening.[1]

We would also emphasize that very few researchers today would defend the position that prejudice is the sole or the main cause of racist behavior. However, it remains as one important factor among a complex of other factors that contribute to the problem.

BIBLIOGRAPHY

ADORNO, T. W., Else FRENKEL-BRUNSWIK, D. J. LEVINSON, and R. N. SANFORD (1950). *The Authoritarian Personality*. New York: Harper & Row, Publishers.

ALLPORT, G. W. (1958). *The Nature of Prejudice*. New York: Doubleday & Company, Inc.

ASHMORE, R. D. (1969). "Intergroup Contact as a Prejudice-reduction Technique: An Experimental Examination of the Shared-coping Approach and Four Alternative Explanations." Unpublished Ph.D. dissertation. Los Angeles: University of California.

BANDURA, A. and R. H. WALTERS (1963). *Social Learning and Personality Development*. New York: Holt, Rinehart & Winston, Inc.

BANTON, MICHAEL (1967). *Race Relations*. London: Tavistock Publications.

BERKOWITZ, L. (1962). *Aggression: A Social Psychological Analysis*. New York: McGraw-Hill Book Company.

BETTELHEIM, B. and M. JANOWITZ (1964). *Social Change and Prejudice*. New York: The Free Press.

BOGARDUS, E. S. (1933). "A Social Distance Scale." *Sociology and Social Research*, 17: 265–71.

BURNSTEIN, E. and A. V. MCRAE (1962). "Some Effects of Shared Threat and Prejudice in Racially Mixed Groups." *Journal of Abnormal and Social Psychology*, 64: 257–63.

CAMPBELL, E. Q. (1958). "Some Social Psychological Correlates of Direction in Attitude Change." *Social Forces*, 36: 335–40.

---

[1] Our national experiences built upon the prejudices of anti-Communism remain too recent for objective evaluation. Nevertheless it would appear that a high proportion of critical, rational decisions of national policy were built upon prejudiced viewpoints about the nature of the "enemy."

CANTRIL, H. (1941). *The Psychology of Social Movements.* New York: John Wiley & Sons, Inc.

COLE, SPURGEON, JAY STEINBERG, and G. J. BURKHEIMER (1968). "Prejudice and Conservatism in a Recently Integrated Southern College." *Psychological Reports,* 23 (1): 149.

COLLINS, BARRY (1970). *Social Psychology.* Reading, Mass.: Addison-Wesley Publishing Co.

COLLINS, B. E. and B. H. RAVEN (1969). "Psychological Aspects of Structure in the Small Group: Interpersonal Attraction, Coalitions, Communication, and Power." In G. Lindzey and E. Aronson, eds., *Handbook of Social Psychology,* 2nd ed. Reading, Mass.: Addison-Wesley Publishing Co. Pp. 102–204.

COOPER, E. and M. JAHODA (1947). "The Evasion of Propaganda: How Prejudiced People Respond to Anti-prejudice Propaganda." *Journal of Psychology,* 23: 15–25.

COOPER, J. B. and H. E. SIEGEL (1956). "The Galvanic Skin Response as a Measure of Emotion in Prejudice." *Journal of Psychology,* 42: 149–55.

——— and D. N. SINGER (1956). "The Role of Emotion in Prejudice." *Journal of Social Psychology,* 44: 241–47.

COX, OLIVER CROMWELL (1948). *Caste, Class and Race: A Study in Social Dynamics.* New York: Doubleday & Company, Inc.

DANIELS, ROGER and HARRY H. L. KITANO (1970). *American Racism: Exploration of the Nature of Prejudice.* Englewood Cliffs, N.J.: Prentice-Hall, Inc.

DE FLEUR, M. L. and F. R. WESTIE (1958). "Verbal Attitudes and Overt Acts: An Experiment on the Salience of Attitudes." *American Sociology Review,* 23: 667–73.

DEUTSCH, M. and M. E. COLLINS (1951). *Interracial Housing: A Psychological Evaluation of a Social Experiment.* Minneapolis: University of Minnesota Press.

DICKS, H. V. (1959). "Psychological Factors in Prejudice." *Race,* 1: 26–40.

DIGGINS, E. (1927). "A Statistical Study of National Prejudice." Unpublished master's thesis. New York: Columbia University.

DOLLARD, JOHN, LEONARD DOOB, NEAL MILLER, et al. (1939). *Frustration and Aggression.* New Haven: Yale University Press.

FESHBACH, S. and R. SINGER (1957). "The Effects of Personal and Shared Threats upon Social Prejudice." *Journal of Abnormal Social Psychology,* 54: 411–16.

GRAY, J. and A. H. THOMPSON (1953). "The Ethnic Prejudices of White and Negro College Students." *Journal of Abnormal Social Psychology,* 48: 311–13.

HAIMOWITZ, M. L. and N. R. HAIMOWITZ (1950). "Reducing Ethnic Hostility Through Psychotherapy." *Journal of Social Psychology,* 31: 231–41.

HALL, E. T. (1963). "A System for the Notation of Proxemic Behavior." *American Anthropologist,* 65: 1003–1026.

HARDING, J. and R. HOGREFE (1952). "Attitudes of White Department Store Employees Toward Negro Co-workers." *Journal of Social Issues,* 8: 18–28.

————, B. Kutner, H. Proshansky, and I. Chein (1954). "Prejudice and Ethnic Relations." In G. Lindzey, ed., *Handbook of Social Psychology.* Reading, Mass.: Addison-Wesley Publishing Co. II, 1021–61.

Katz, Daniel and Kenneth W. Braly (1958). "Verbal Stereotypes and Racial Prejudice." In Eleanor Maccoby, Theodore Newcomb, and Eugene Hartley, eds., *Readings in Social Psychology.* New York: Holt, Rinehart & Winston, Inc. Pp. 40–46.

————, I. Sarnoff, and C. McClintock (1956). "Ego-defense and Attitude Change." *Human Relations,* 9: 27–45.

Katz, I. (1955). *Conflict and Harmony in an Adolescent Interracial Group.* New York: New York University Press.

La Piere, R. T. (1934). "Attitudes vs. Action." *Social Forces,* 13: 230–37.

Lazarsfeld, P. F., ed. (1944). *Radio and the Printed Page.* New York: Duell, Sloan, Pearce.

Leavitt, H. J. and R. A. Mueller (1951). "Some Effects of Feedback on Communication." *Human Relations,* 4: 401–410.

Litcher, John H. and David W. Johnson (1969). "Changes in Attitudes Toward Negroes of White Elementary School Students after use of Multiethnic Readers." *Journal of Educational Psychology,* 60 (2): 148–52.

Longres, John, C. Roberts, and K. Shinn (1966). "Some Similarities and Differences in Northern-urban Race Riots Involving Negroes During the Twentieth Century." Unpublished Master's thesis. Los Angeles: University of California.

Mandelbaum, D. G. (1952). *Soldier Groups and Negro Soldiers.* Berkeley: University of California Press.

Mann, J. H. (1959). "The Effect of Interracial Contact on Sociometric Choices and Perceptions." *Journal of Social Psychology,* 50: 143–52.

Mason, Philip (1970). *Race Relations.* London: Oxford University Press.

McNeill, J. D. (1960). "Changes in Ethnic Reaction Tendencies During High School." *Journal of Educational Research,* 53: 199–200.

Mehrabian, A. (1967). "Orientation Behaviors and Nonverbal Attitude Communication." *Journal of Communication,* 17: 324–32.

Minard, R. D. (1952). "Race Relationships in the Pocahontas Coal Field." *Journal of Social Issues,* 8: 29–44.

Mussen, P. H. (1950). "Some Personality and Social Factors Related to Changes in Children's Attitudes Toward Negroes." *Journal of Abnormal Social Psychology,* 45: 423–41.

Newcomb, T. M. (1961). *The Acquaintance Process.* New York: Holt, Rinehart & Winston, Inc.

Orata, P. T. (1927). "Race Prejudice." *Welfare Magazine,* 28: 765–75.

Park, Robert E. (1950). *Race and Culture.* New York: The Free Press.

Pearl, D. (1954). "Ethnocentrism and the Self-concept." *Journal of Social Psychology,* 40: 137–47.

————, (1955). "Psychotherapy and Ethnocentrism." *Journal of Abnormal and Social Psychology,* 50: 227–30.

Reed, B. A. (1947). "Accommodation Between Negro and White Employees in a West Coast Aircraft Industry, 1942–1944." *Social Forces,* 26: 76–84.

Rokeach, Milton, Patricia W. Smith, and R. I. Evans (1960). "Two Kinds of Prejudice or One?" In M. Rokeach, ed., *The Open and Closed Mind.* New York: Basic Books. Pp. 132–68.

Rose, Arnold (1951). *The Roots of Prejudice.* Paris: UNESCO.

Rosenberg, M. J. (1956). "Cognitive Structure and Attitudinal Affect." *Journal of Abnormal and Social Psychology,* 53: 367–72.

Rosenthal, R. (1964). "Experimenter Outcome-orientation and the Results of the Psychological Experiment." *Psychology Bulletin,* 61: 405–412.

Rubin, I. M. (1967). "Increased Self-acceptance: A means of Reducing Prejudice." *Journal of Personal and Social Psychology,* 5: 233–38.

Secord, P. F. and C. W. Backman (1964). *Social Psychology.* New York: McGraw-Hill Book Company.

Simpson, George E. and J. Milton Yinger (1965). *Racial and Cultural Minorities,* 3rd ed. New York: Harper & Row, Publishers.

Sims, V. M. and J. R. Patrick (1936). "Attitude Toward the Negro of Northern and Southern College Students." *Journal of Social Psychology,* 7: 192–204.

Singer, D. (1969). "The Impact of Interracial Classroom Exposure on the Social Attitudes of Fifth Grade Children." Unpublished study, 1964. Cited in J. Harding, B. Kutner, H. Proshansky, and I. Chein, "Prejudice and Ethnic Relations." In G. Lindzey and E. Aronson, eds., *Handbook of Social Psychology,* 2nd ed., Vol. 5. Reading, Mass.: Addison-Wesley Publishing Co.

Stein, David, Jane A. Hardyck and M. Brewster Smith (1971). "Race and Belief: An Open and Shut Case." In Freeman, Jonathan, J. M. Carlsmith, and David O. Sears, eds., *Readings in Social Psychology.* Englewood Cliffs, N.J.: Prentice-Hall, Inc. Pp. 132–45.

Stember, Charles (1961). "Education and Attitude Change: The Effect of Schooling on Prejudice Against Minority Groups." New York: Institute of Human Relations Press.

Stotland, E., D. Katz, and M. Patchen (1959). "The Reduction of Prejudice Through the Arousal of Self-insight." *Journal of Personality,* 27: 507–531.

Stouffer, S. A., E. A. Suchman, L. C. DeVinney, S. A. Star, and R. N. Williams (1949). *The American Soldier,* Vol. 1. *Adjustment During Army Life.* Princeton, N.J.: Princeton University Press.

Sykes, G. and D. Matza (1957). "Techmniques of Neutralization: A Theory of Delinquency." *American Sociology Review,* 22: 664–70.

Webster, S. W. (1961). "The Influence of Interracial Contact on Social Acceptance in a Newly Integrated School." *Journal of Educational Psychology,* 52: 292–96.

Westie, F. R. and M. L. DeFleur (1959). "Autonomic Responses and Their Relationship to Race Attitudes." *Journal of Abnormal and Social Psychology,* 58: 340–47.

White, Ralph and Ronald Lippitt (1960). *Autocracy and Democracy: An Experimental Inquiry.* New York: Harper & Row, Publishers.

Works, E. (1961). "The Prejudice-Interaction Hypothesis from the Point of View of the Negro Minority Group." *American Journal of Sociology,* 67: 47–52.

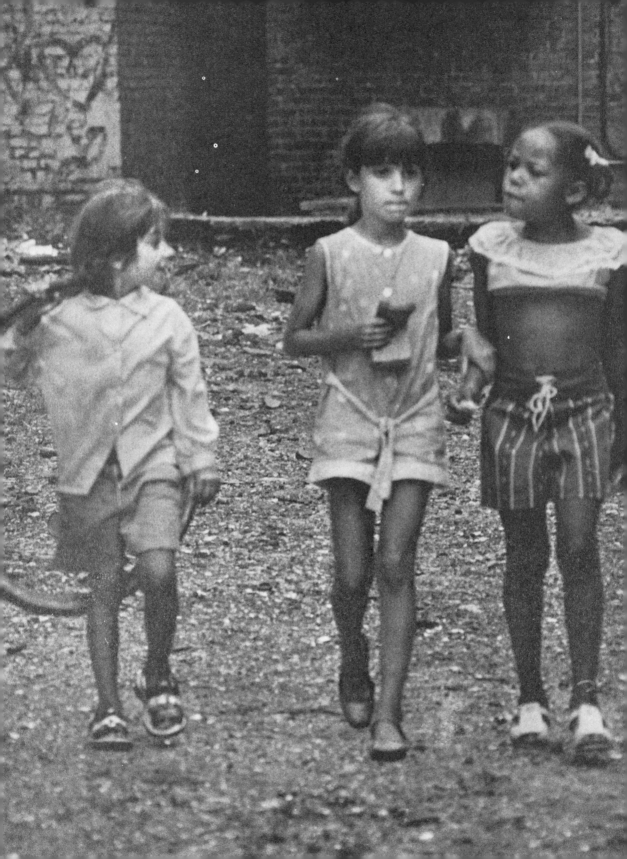

PATTERNS
OF
INTERACTION 2

All race relations begin with some degree of contact, and in the past, these interactions began with either migration or conquest. Some current theories (Blauner, 1971) emphasize the central importance of the first contact on subsequent events.

Whenever various groups mingle in the United States, there is always some kind of change. Static relationships occur under completely closed systems where one group has absolute domination over the other; in more open systems, there is a dynamic relationship that affects both the minorities and the majority. Therefore, the effects of continuous intergroup contact will be different depending on the openness of the system and whether one belongs to the dominating or the dominated groups.

One of the hypothesized consequences of cultural openness is an increase in prejudice. As Park (1950) suggested, prejudice is an expression of conservatism that wishes to maintain the status quo; conversely, the greater the rate of change and the larger the number of ethnic groups, the higher the probability of prejudice in an open system. Prejudice in this sense works to maintain social distance, because constant change poses a threat to the stability of the existing order.

Early theories by sociologists such as Park and Bogardus suggested a cyclical pattern to race relations. Park concluded that this pattern was progressive and perhaps irreversible. The contact stage was followed by competition, which eventually led to some kind of adjustment or accommodation, and finally to assimilation and amalgamation. Park studied the case of Hawaii in 1926 and predicted that the native races would disappear as new peoples came into existence—that individual races and cultures die, but the majority civilization lives on. The common idea of all groups ultimately being absorbed into the American mainstream underscores Park's theory of inevitability.

Shibutani and Kwan (1965: 21) also believe that assimilation is a phenomenon found in all cases of interethnic contact in which one group does not exterminate the other: "In the United States one need only review the history of various immigrant groups—the Irish, the Poles, the Jews, the Italians, the Chinese, the Mexicans—to see the regularity with which many of them have become incorporated into the mainstream of American life." Shibutani and Kwan define assimilation as a change of mental perspective in which the immigrant eventually perceives the world from an American point of view, rather than from that of his previous national background.

Bogardus (1930), focusing primarily on the experiences of the Chinese, Japanese, Filipino, and Mexican immigrants in California, saw sufficient recurrences to propose a race relations cycle. The stages were: curiosity, economic welcome, industrial and social antagonism, legislative antagonism, fair-play tendencies, quiescence, and second-generation difficulties.

Cyclical perspectives provide a broad picture of the relationships between an immigrant group and the host culture. However, one can question the matter of inevitability of certain stages, especially the final one of assimilation, and the universality of such progressions. For immigrant groups vary in size, color, culture, power, and the context of their interaction; and it is too early to specify what kind of interaction will take place or to predict which variables are related.

BANTON'S SIX ORDERS OF RACE RELATIONS

A more sophisticated presentation of interracial contacts is presented by Banton (1967: 68–76), who describes what happens to members of two different societies when they begin to have dealings with one another. He pictures six orders of race relations, with the plausible hypothesis that there may be several kinds of contact with different sequences of stages.

Peripheral contact is the stage where transactions between two societies have no real influence. There is little change in outlook, and both groups remain independent. One example of such contact given by Banton is that between the pygmies of the Ituri forest of the Congo and some

Figure 2-1 Peripheral contact.
Source: Banton (1967: 69).

nearby Negro settlements. One group places piles of goods such as game and forest products at a trading place, then retires. The other group places piles of agricultural and other goods as its exchange. The first group returns and, if the terms are acceptable, picks up what it desires; the second group goes through a similar procedure. Such transactions require little intimate contact and minimal mutual knowledge of customs, habits, and language. Nevertheless, certain logical questions arise: What if one group feels that it has been cheated? How are misunderstandings resolved? What if one group decided that it would be easier to take over the other? The questions pinpoint one generalization about peripheral contacts; they are usually short-lived or maintained in extremely restricted circumstances.

Order II: Institutionalized Contact
and Acculturation

Continuous contact between members of two groups may develop either by institutionalized contact or by acculturation.

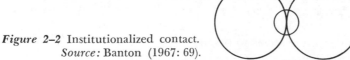

Figure 2–2 Institutionalized contact.
Source: Banton (1967: 69).

Institutionalized contact is most apt to develop under the following conditions:

1. When one of the two groups has a centralized political structure in which a few leaders control the action of their own members and use their power to dominate the other group.
2. When two societies enter into contact primarily through their outlying members, and there is no strong competition for resources.

43

People who live on the social boundaries of the groups are most apt to exchange with each other. These people may begin to occupy positions in both systems, and a new system of interrelations develops between the groups. The roles may be rather crude because the languages and the cultures may be different; but no matter how undeveloped, it is a closer system of interrelations than peripheral contacts.

There is no common political order or integral social system in institutional contacts. Racial awareness occurs only at the point of overlap; the initial relations are important in determining subsequent steps. For example, if the first contact came in the form of trade, the interrelationships probably developed through interpersonal contacts, individual by individual. Expectations are formed by initial individual experiences, and insofar as the expectations continue to be realized, roles are created. If power relationships remain relatively stable, this type of institutional contact (whereby only a few members from each group interact) may remain for some time.

One example used by Banton to illustrate institutionalized contact is drawn from Gluckman (1955, 1958). Gluckman describes the following ceremony that brought together 24 Europeans and 400 Zulus. The opening formalities were followed by a carefully prepared round of speeches. Although they were brought together for the common purpose of the opening of a bridge, the two groups assembled in separate places. Each was bound to his own group; and although a European officer could talk with a Zulu on a common problem, he could not sit down and eat with him. Nonprofessional socialization was kept to a minimum.

The illustration ". . . brings out the way in which the participants all occupied basic racial roles, as Europeans and Africans, but at the same time they had more independent roles to play which brought them together in other respects." Those Europeans most involved with the Zulus alternated between roles that permitted them to associate with Zulus and roles that required them to keep a distance. Thus, there is a patterned and formalized interaction between 2,000,000 whites and 6,500,000 Zulus. Within these institutionalized patterns, a man's dress, stance, location, and form of greeting are all facets of the controlled intergroup interaction.

However, the example seems to be more of a dominant-subordinate relationship than an interaction between equals. Another form of institutionalized contact occurs through consuls and embassies whereby the vast majority of the citizenry has almost no interaction with the representatives from abroad, and where institutionalized patterns remain the primary ones.

ACCULTURATION

One common definition of acculturation is "the process of learning a culture different from the one in which a person was originally raised"

(Berelson, 1964: 646). The term is generally used to specify movement across widely different cultures, whereas learning in the original culture is usually called socialization.

Acculturation most often occurs where societies are small, informal, and noncompetitive. Those who are in contact make adjustments to members of the other society. Members who are not in contact exert few pressures, and eventually the two societies tend to merge, with the "weaker culture" having to make more changes than the "stronger" (Figure 2–3).

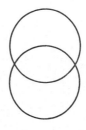

Figure 2–3 Acculturation.
Source: Banton (1967: 70).

ACCULTURATION AND ASSIMILATION

Acculturation is common to intergroup relationships in America. A committee of distinguished anthropologists, Robert Redfield, Ralph Linton, and Melville J. Herskovits, defined acculturation as follows: ". . . those phenomena which result when groups of individuals having different cultures come into continuous first-hand contact, with subsequent changes in the original cultural patterns of either or both groups." But this definition says nothing about the social relationships between the two cultures or the identities of the people involved.

Acculturation is only one of many kinds of assimilation; Gordon (1964) posits differences between cultural, behavioral, structural, and other types. Cultural assimilation (or acculturation) is likely to be the first to occur and consists of a change in the cultural patterns of the two interacting groups. It is not necessary for other types of assimilation to occur, and acculturation by itself can go on indefinitely.

Structural assimilation refers to social interaction between groups— that is, when one group enters into the social clubs, cliques, organizations, and institutions of the other on a peer basis. Once this stage is reached, most of the other kinds of assimilation will follow, including inter-marriage. Although acculturation may not necessarily lead to structural assimilation, structural assimilation will lead to acculturation; and it is possible for an ethnic group as a separate entity to disappear.

Theoretically, prejudice and discrimination would be eliminated, and a person would become a full participant (civic assimilation) in the American system.

However, structural assimilation has not yet occurred in the United   45

States, although cultural assimilation has. We assume that the vast majority of individuals in the United States are acculturated—language, dress, and other American forms are widespread—but racial and intergroup conflicts continue. Ethnic and racial groups (as well as the social classes) remain separated, and structural "pluralism" is a more apt description.

Groups of white, European origin are less separated, although in some areas of the country (e.g. the Swedes in Minnesota; the Germans in Milwaukee; the Poles in Chicago) Europeans still cluster in ethnic groups.

Order III: Domination

Figure 2–4 Domination.
Source: Banton (1967: 71).

Contact and the growth of ties between racial groups (or nations) has often resulted in Order III, the domination of one group by another (Figure 2–4) within a single society. This is a two-category system based on race; all members of one category are subordinated to the other and are responded to not as individuals but as representatives of their category. As Banton says, "This kind of subordination is far harsher, and it provides the most clear-cut illustration of race as a role sign. Whatever their personal qualities, individuals are ascribed to one or the other category, and those in the lower are prevented from claiming the privileges of those in the upper category . . ." (1967: 71).

Simmel (1965), a German sociologist, felt that all social life was characterized by *superordination* and *subordination*. One group or one individual in a social relationship will always dominate, while the other, voluntarily or not, will take the lesser role. Domination is related to power, so that groups with more "power" become the superordinates of that system. In this model, equality is seldom achieved; rather, groups may be constantly attempting to change their subordinate positions.

The two-category system closely resembles the current stage of race relations in the United States (Daniels and Kitano, 1970). To be white is to belong to the upper half of the system with its coresponding social-psychological perspectives. Those in power have hypothesized feelings of superiority, power, and noblesse oblige. They emphasize law and order and gradualism in race relations, and place a high value on rational discussion and scientific studies. They feel that if the "others" would only become more like them, the stratification and the boundaries would disappear.

Obviously, those caught in the subordinate positions view the world **46** differently. They may try to escape their subordinate status by changing their names, undergoing facial operations, and using drugs. They may overidentify with the dominant group, or vent their frustrations on members of other subordinate groups, including their own. They feel a great impatience with the racial status quo and demand immediate action.

In some cases, power, not race alone, determines who plays superordinate and subordinate roles. For example, there are observable differences between West Coast Japanese (subordinated status) and their peers in Hawaii (closer to superordinate status). The less powerful mainland group has acculturated much more rapidly, and is much more respectful and "humble" toward the white man than the Hawaiian Japanese, although this factor is tempered by the retention of many "low posture" Japanese styles in the Islands.

SOUTH AFRICA: A CLOSED, DOMINANT ORDER

South Africa is an example of a two-category racial stratification system based on the dominance of one group over another. The 1970 Census showed a total South African population of 21,282,000, composed of 14,893,000 Africans (blacks); 3,799,000 coloreds (or mixed); 614,000 Asians (nearly all Indians); and 1,996,000 whites (Los Angeles *Times*, 1970).

The ruling Nationalist Party does not regard the Africans as a homogeneous group, but divides them into ten major "nations" and claims that the whites represent the largest nation. However, the 1970 Census figures indicate that the Zulus with 3,970,000 and the Xhosas with 3,907,000 have overtaken the white total.

Although the whites clearly are a numerical minority, they have managed to retain their power and are determined to hold it. How they have managed to do so is described by Mason:

> This they do, first, by laws which forbid marriage between races and also any kind of sexual contact outside marriage. The law further forbids association between the races in many other ways; education is separate, even at the university level, as is travel in public conveyances; trade unions are segregated, and a wide range of posts is reserved for white people only. No African may vote or sit in Parliament. Africans have no right to combine in a strike, and the level of African wages for manual workers varies around one-seventh of that for white manual laborers (1970: 101).

Mason adds that although the Africans outnumber the whites by a wide margin, only 13 percent of the land is reserved for them and only in certain areas. He continues:

> . . . where labor is required, certain areas are set aside for Africans to occupy but they usually live in houses rented from the municipality or from their employers, which they must leave if they lose their job. An African is liable to arrest and punishment if he is without documents to

47

show that he has a valid reason for being outside the African reserves. Employment is a valid reason; he can also for short periods have a permit to seek employment. If no valid reason can be proved, he may be ordered to return to a place of origin, which in some cases he may not have visited for many years. This is enforced even if it divides man and wife (101–2).

The purpose of this legislation ("apartheid") is to keep the black races apart and subordinated; family life and justice have less priority than the insurance that no white person ever has to look upon an African as a peer. Such a system can only be maintained through a vigorous use of force, continuous, up-to-date legislation, a comprehensive police and judicial establishment, and the maintenance of law and order. People suspected of a political offense, such as spreading Communism (and the definition of Communism can be very broad—for example, one can be accused of being a Communist for advocating universal adult suffrage), may be kept in prison for a long time without a trial. And the constant fear of being inundated by superior numbers leads white men to many harsh and brutal acts.

The colored (mixed) and Indian populations complicate the two-category classification system. These marginal groups often absorb the hostility of both the whites and the Africans, but the basic problem remains as the relationship between the numerically superior Africans and the white minority in power. The white group has a monopoly of political power and an enormous advantage in wealth, education, esteem and oportunity and it has no intention of sharing these advantages with the subordinated population.

In summary, South Africa is an example of a dominant order, or a *dominant, closed* system. The technologically "superior" white system, enhanced by its monopolistic control of the political and economic sectors, has enforced a web of laws that has resulted in rigid dominant-subordinate racial stratification. There is a constant movement towards closing any loopholes, and the apartheid policies are even more rigorously enforced. Many observers feel that only a racial revolution can bring about change in South Africa.

Order IV: Paternalism

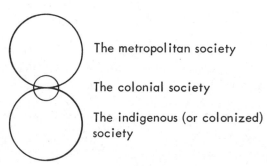

The metropolitan society

The colonial society

The indigenous (or colonized) society

Figure 2–5 Paternalism.
Source: Banton (1967: 72).

48

When subordinates are subject to some control by a home government (e.g. England), there is a high probability that paternalism (colonialism) becomes the established order (Figure 2–5).

Paternalism is a special form of institutionalized contact that maintains the distinctiveness of the interacting societies. Banton says,

> It is exemplified in some forms of colonial rule, such as those that sanctioned and often reinforced the control tribal chiefs exercised over their peoples. In the pure form of paternalism, the only representatives of the metropolitan society who have dealings with the indigenous society are approved agents responsible for their action to authorities in their homeland (1967: 72).

Race, career, education, and training are important in determining specific official roles, and the influx of immigrants and new settlers strain the paternalistic order. The basic difference between the dominative and paternalistic orders is that in the former, the roles are determined by the desire of the upper group to maintain control over all significant spheres of activity, while in the latter, major decisions are made by the metropolitan society and are carried out by the colonial society.

Van den Berghe (1967) writes that the paternalistic system follows a master-servant model. The master group may be small in number but is able to dominate the subordinates. The subordinates are looked upon as childish, immature, irresponsible, and improvident, but are lovable as long as they remain in their place. Subordinated groups often internalize these inferiority feelings through self-deprecation.

Under paternalism, roles and statuses are sharply defined, and social distance is maintained through etiquette, regulations, and repeated demonstrations of power by the dominant group. There may be high rates of miscegenation between men of the ruling group with women of the subordinated population, but very few of these sexual encounters end in marriage. Van den Berghe remarks that racial prejudice on the part of the ruling group is present but appears more related to economic and social position rather than to any deep psychodynamic feelings.

The paternalistic model is often found in relatively complex preindustrial societies in which agriculture and handicraft production constitute the main economic base (Van den Berghe, 1967: 28). Examples of this model include the Southern United States, the West Indies, and the preabolition regimes in Northeastern Brazil.

Paternalistic societies are rigidly stratified into racial castes. The caste barrier is the most important; and although class distinctions exist, the color line limits mobility between castes. Race remains the major factor in social stratification, and elaborate ideologies of the inferiority and superiority of races are developed to maintain the system.

Because there are more servants than masters, part of the longevity **49** and stability of this model comes from the acquiescence of the subordinated. Although there have been constant conflicts engendered by "revolting servants," a symbiotic relationship is often achieved, especially in the economic area. In addition, miscegenation and other forms of unequal, but often intimate social relations (e.g., a black woman mothering white children) may create affective bonds across caste lines.

DOMESTIC COLONIALISM

A special form of paternalism called internal, or domestic colonialism is hypothesized by Blauner (1971). Rather than limiting the dominant-subordinate relationship to colonized countries, Blauner emphasizes the appropriateness of this model to race relations in the United States.

Four basic components make up this colonization complex. The first concerns the racial group's forced, involuntary entry into the country. The slaves were this kind of group. Second, the impact of the interaction is much more dramatic than the slower and perhaps more natural processes of acculturation. The colonizing power "carries out a policy which constrains, transforms, or destroys indigenous values, orientations, and ways of life" such as those of the native Indians and conquered Mexicans. Third, colonization "involves a relationship by which members of the colonized group tend to be administered by representatives of the dominant power. There is the experience of being managed and manipulated by outsiders in terms of ethnic status" (Blauner, 1971: 396). Finally, there is racism. Since one group is seen as inferior, it is exploited, controlled, and oppressed by the dominating group.

The colonization concept helps to explain the differences between various immigrant groups. As Blauner writes:

> The crucial difference between the colonized Americans and the ethnic immigrant minorities is that the latter have always been able to operate fairly competitively within that relatively open section of the social and economic order because they came voluntarily in search of a better life, because their movements in society were not administratively controlled, and because they transformed their culture at their own pace—giving up ethnic values and institutions when it was seen as a desirable exchange for improvements in social position (396).

There are several important differences in the ghetto living of "colonized" immigrants and those from Europe. First, the white immigrants chose to come to the United States and decided to live among other white ethnics. Second, these white immigrants lived in ghettos for only a generation or two until they were acculturated. Those ghettos that still persist have become tourist attractions and business centers.

But Blauner emphasizes that the third major point, that of local

50

control and ownership, may be the vital difference. It was usually less than one generation before these white ethnic groups controlled their own buildings, commercial stores, and other enterprises. The Asian groups have also followed this pattern. However, the black segregated communities have always been controlled from the outside, and political, economic, and administrative decisions have been taken out of their hands. Outsiders come into the ghetto to work, police, and administer. Teachers, social workers, policemen, and politicians represent the establishment, which governs the ghetto as if it were an overseas colony.

One significant effect of this kind of colonialism is to weaken the will of the colonized in resisting oppression. And as Blauner says:

> It has been easier to contain and control black ghettoes because communal bonds and group solidarity have been weakened through divisions among leadership, failures of organization, and a general disspiritment that accompanies social oppression (1971: 399).

Blauner also stresses the point that the cultures of overseas colonies were not destroyed nearly to the extent that the African slave cultures were in America. The language, religion, and family structures of these Africans were almost totally obliterated when they were brought into this country.

Glazer (1972), however, feels that racial ethnic groups are not that trapped and that it is possible for them to move away voluntarily from their pariah status. He cites the increasing number of skilled workers, foremen, professionals, and white-collar workers from among minorities and sees a strong similarity between their situation and that of the European immigrants.

Glazer admits that prejudice and discrimination face racial minorities, but states that these barriers are universal and have to be faced by all who are strangers. The level of prejudice and discrimination is determined by what official assistance it gets and the role of the state. On all levels, he perceives that expressed prejudice has steadily declined and that the percentage of minorities has increasd in all levels of government employment. Therefore, he feels that the colonial analogy, especially as applied to the American Negro, is an invalid one.

Order V: Integration

Figure 2–6 Integration.
Source: Banton (1967: 73).

51

An integrated order of race relations develops when racial distinctions are disregarded (although they may never be ignored completely). Generally, integration occurs where there are several different racial groups and peoples of mixed descent. As Banton says:

> Race is then still used as a social sign, though as a sign indicating an individual's background and probably his claims to deference. It is one sign among many others, being irrelevant in some sectors . . . but of some account in status-sensitive situations of social acceptance or rejection. For nearly all purposes, race has much less significance than the individual's occupation and his other status-conferring roles. Thus, in a racially integrated social order, race is a sign of an independent role, signaling rights and obligations in only a few restricted sets of circumstances (1967: 73).

Integration is similar to Gordon's term of structural assimilation or to the concept of social assimilation whereby racial signs become less important than other cues.

We hypothesize that an open class system will create pressures towards racial integration. For example, in a previous era, the Japanese daughter, after a date might be asked by her parents, "Is he Japanese?" Currently, they might ask, "Is he a doctor?", and make no references to race and ethnicity.

Racial integration is also related to the size, isolation, and cohesion of ethnic groups and the cultural similarities between groups. The stereotypes of groups may also foster or hinder integration.

Integration will also occur under a natural state of interaction among peoples. By natural state, we mean a "barrier-free" system where discrimination and prejudice are at a minimum and where there is high opportunity to advance; for the longer the barriers have been in operation, the more effective they will be in keeping groups apart and sustaining a more "disadvantaged" state. For example, if at the beginning of our country, Indians and Negroes had been given full rights to citizenship, equal oportunity, and equal acceptance, and all subsequent groups had also been treated in this manner, we probably would not have our current racial problems. But generations of domination have widened the gap between the groups. This perspective of course, would not rule out other forms of intergroup conflict, especially that of social class, as racial signs diminished.

Order VI: Pluralism

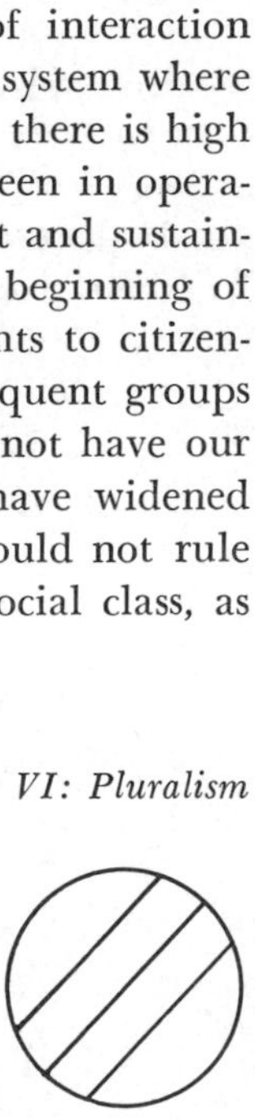

Figure 2–7 Pluralism.
Source: Banton (1967: 74).

52

In a pluralistic order (Figure 2–7) racial differences do signalize variations in expected behavior much more widely than under the model of integration (Figure 2–6). In some pluralistic societies different ethnic groups retain their own language and culture (e.g. Malaysia), but in most modern-day examples, race plays an important part in many, but not all, important situations. The basic difference between a dominative and a pluralistic order is that in the latter the relationship between groups is closer to parity but may not necessarily be equal.

The cultural pluralist views the necessity of subsocietal separation "to guarantee the continuance of the ethnic cultural tradition and the existence of the group, without at the same time interfering with the carrying out of standard responsibilities to the general American civic life" (Gordon, 1964: 158). Widescale intermarriage and extensive primary-group relations across ethnic lines pose the gravest threats towards a pluralistic society.

Gordon feels that the American reality is that of structural pluralism rather than cultural pluralism, although some of the latter remains. The major ethnic and religious groups do provide separate subsocieties that tend to restrict large-scale primary-group interaction, but most of them are carrying out variants of the American culture. The important theoretical problem then is "how ethnic prejudice and discrimination can be eliminated or reduced and value conflict kept within workable limits in a society where the existence of separate subsocieties keeps primary-group relations among persons of different ethnic backgrounds at a minimum" (Gordon, 1964: 159).

Van den Berghe views pluralism from a different perspective. Pluralistic societies are segmented into corporate groups and have different cultures or subcultures; their social structure is "compartmentalized into analogous, parallel, noncomplementary, but distinguishable sets of institutions" (Van den Berghe, 1967: 34). Additional characteristics frequently associated with pluralism are the following:

1. Relative absence of value consensus.
2. Relative presence of cultural heterogeneity.
3. Relative presence of conflict between the significant corporate groups.
4. Relative autonomy between parts of the system.
5. Relative importance of coercion and economic interdependence as bases of social integration.
6. Political domination by one of the corporate groups over the others.
7. Primacy of segmental, utilitarian, nonaffective, and functionally specific relationships between corporate groups, and of total, nonutilitarian, affective, diffuse ties within such groups (Van den Berghe, 1967: 35).

Pluralism is a matter of degree. South Africa, which is divided into four major castes and several unrelated cultural traditions, is more pluralistic than the United States, with its two major racial castes; but 53 where both whites and nonwhites share the same Western culture and the same language.

There are, however, great differences between cultural and social pluralism. Although in practice both go together, cultural pluralism refers to the maintenance of ethnic subcultures with their traditions, values, and styles. Social pluralism refers to the extent that a society is structurally compartmentalized into analogous and duplicatory but culturally alike sets of institutions and into corporate groups that are differentiated on a basis other than culture.

Developmental Sequence

Banton suggests the following sequence among the orders:

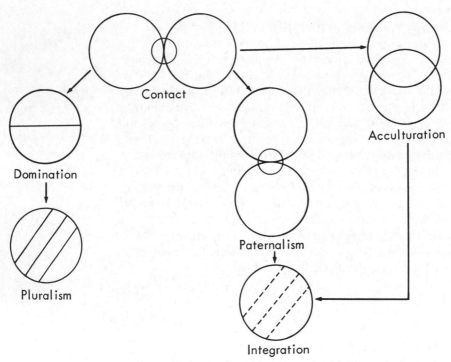

Figure 2–8 Sequence of racial orders.
Source: Banton (1967: 75).

Therefore, there are three major patterns: (1) contact, domination, and pluralism; (2) contact, paternalism, and integration; and (3) contact, acculturation, and integration.

SEQUENCE 1: CONTACT, DOMINATION, PLURALISM

The sequence of contact, domination, and some form of pluralism may be the most appropriate model of race relations in the United 54

States. For most nonwhite groups, the initial contact with the majority group was already that of subordinate to superordinate—slavery, contract labor, and the like meant a two-category system.

The order is so structured that the pattern of dominance is continuously reinforced, and fundamental changes in race relations are difficult to achieve. The superordinate group has the power and ability to limit the entry of more of these "aliens"; it also has the power to maintain the two-category system through prejudice and discriminatory laws such as antimiscegenation; it can also forstall the development of other categories. However, through political, economic, educational, and technological changes, subordinate racial groups have been given some privileges; most of them acculturate, and they eventually acquire some degree of independence and power.

Majority-group resistance towards full integration has forced dominated groups to form a pluralistic structure. This does not mean that the inequalities between groups have been greatly reduced, but it does indicate that a form of unequal pluralism becomes the new order.

SEQUENCE 2: CONTACT, PATERNALISM, INTEGRATION

Contact, followed by some form of paternalism that leads to integration is another sequence postulated by Banton. In a paternalist order, the power of the metropolitan culture may weaken over time, and this is reflected in changes in the roles of the personnel who carry out the orders. "In such ways the transition to an integrated order is facilitated; it may entail the withdrawal of all representatives of the former metropolitan country and the creation of a society without racial minorities" (Banton, 1967: 74).

The examples used by Banton are more appropriate to European-African relationships. As the influence of the paternal power wanes, integration may be achieved, primarily through one overriding factor—the number of natives, who have always comprised the numerical majority.

However, this pattern is not demonstrated in the Southern states. Part of the reason may be the out-migration of numbers of blacks so that a form of domination-pluralism appears to be emerging.

SEQUENCE 3: CONTACT, ACCULTURATION, INTEGRATION

Perhaps the most predictable sequence is that of contact, followed by acculturation, leading to integration. Generally, this has been the pattern of white immigrants to the United States, but not all groups can therefore follow the same pattern. Interestingly enough, most ethnic groups have perceived and desired this sequence, but because of the *barriers of racism,* have been interrupted in the quest. Acculturation has not led to integration but instead has often strengthened domination. However, race relations do not remain static, and there is a continuous process of change.

In the previous section, we discussed some of the goals and outcomes of group interaction. The models were deceptively simple because they were limited to two groups, and the outcomes based on the interaction could be followed without too much difficulty. But what we face in the United States staggers the imagination; rather than two, there are many races that run the entire gamut of colors, as well as nationalities and cultures. We, therefore, are the "great experiment" in bringing diverse peoples under one banner.

GOALS OF AMERICAN SOCIETY

Race relations can also be analyzed by considering some of the broad goals and problems of becoming an American. These involve Anglo-conformity, the melting pot, cultural pluralism, and the "other world" perspectives. The first three variables are based on Gordon (1964).

Anglo-Conformity

Gordon's use of the term Anglo-conformity covers a variety of viewpoints on assimilation and immigration. The central assumption behind this model is the desirability of maintaining the English language and its culture as the standard of American life. This is not to deny that many other influences have also shaped America, but as Gordon says: "as the immigrants and their children have become Americans, their contributions as laborers, farmers, doctors, lawyers, scientists, and artists have been by way of cultural patterns that have taken their major impress from the mold of the overwhelmingly English character of the dominant Anglo-Saxon culture or subculture in America, whose domination dates from colonial times and whose *cultural* domination in the United States has never been seriously threatened" (Gordon, 1964, 73).

From the point of view of the English colonists, the newcomers were a mixed blessing. On the one hand, they were necessary for the growth and development of the country; on the other hand, they were foreigners with alien ways. Nativist organizations often played upon the fear of strangers and riots; immigrants to America were subject to much scapegoating and hostility (Higham, 1955).

Restrictions against the open immigration policies began to appear in the late 1800s, and in 1882 the first effective federal legislation controlling immigration was passed. Phrases similar to "America, Love It or Leave It" were common, and the immigrants were advised to cast off their old skin, not to look back, to forget the old country and adopt the new—and if they didn't like it, they could always go back.

"Adopting the new" clearly meant conforming to Anglo standards; the control of the country was securely in the hands of the descendants of the early English settlers. Madison Grant, in *The Passing of the Great Race* (1916), wrote about inferior breeds in differentiating between the

56

Southern Europeans and the Anglo-Teutons. The Anglo-Saxon concepts of righteousness, law, and order were clearly those of a "superior race"; and it was necessary to break up inferior groups before they could be assimilated.

The height of the Americanization movement occurred during World War I, when the foreigner was stripped of his native culture and made into an American as rapidly as possible. Political loyalty, patriotism, the teaching of American history, and Americanization classes reflected the sentiments of the country and culminated in the restrictions of the Immigration Act of 1924. Desirable and undesirable races and nationalities were fully differentiated in this law—no immigration for Asians, low quotas for Southern Europeans and "less desirable" races, and high quotas for those of Anglo-Saxon background.

Americanization has been successful, especially among Europeans. By the second generation vast numbers had discarded their previous culture, learned English, and become patriotic. They had fought and died for the new country (even against their ancestral homelands), and had become the new Americans.

Racial ethnic groups have also gone through the same process and have often been successfully acculturated. They have learned English and the American way; they have fought and died for America and have subscribed to the tenets of patriotism and love of country. But in one dramatic sense they have not become Anglo—their skin color and visibility have not allowed for this critical step. Therefore, the separatist techniques of prejudice, discrimination, and segregation have kept minority-group Americans at a distance and made a mockery of the goals of Anglo-conformity.

Gordon feels that the critical variable in the Anglo-conformity model is not acculturation but structural assimilation. Acculturation has taken place, but structural assimilation has not. Minority-group members have not been allowed to enter into the more intimate circles of the majority:

> The answer lies in the attitudes of both the majority and the minority groups and in the way in which these attitudes have interacted. A folk saying of the current day is that "It takes two to tango." To utilize the analogy, there is no good reason to believe that white Protestant America ever extended a firm and cordial invitation to its minorities to dance. Furthermore, the attitudes of the minority-group members themselves on the matter have been divided and ambiguous.
>
> With regard to the immigrant, structural assimilation was out of the question. He did not want it, and he had a positive need for the comfort of his own communal institutions. The native American, moreover, whatever the implications of his public pronouncements, had no intention of opening up his primary-group life to entrance by these hordes of alien newcomers. The situation was a functionally complementary standoff (Gordon, 1964: 111).

57

A much more idealistic goal for American society lay in the theory of the "melting pot." The concept proposed that people from all over the world would come to the United States, meet new people and new races, intermix and come up with a new breed called "the American."

Part of the support for the relatively open immigration policy was based on the underlying faith in the effectiveness of the melting pot. Rather than Anglo-conformity and European influence, the uniquely American character could be explained by the intermingling of different people in this new environment. Frederick Jackson Turner (1963), an historian, was especially influential in presenting the thesis that the dominant influence in American institutions was not the nation's European heritage, but rather the experiences created by the ever-changing American frontier. The frontier acted as a solvent for the various nationalities and the separatist tendencies of many groups as they joined in the westward trek. Therefore, the new immigrants would amalgamate and produce a new, composite national stock.

The theme of the melting pot was especially strong during the first third of the twentieth century. In 1908, Israel Zangwill (1909) produced a drama entitled *The Melting Pot,* which brought to popular attention the role of the United States as a haven for the poor and oppressed people of Europe. The major theme of the play concerned the entrance of a myriad of nationalities and races and how their fusion and mixing produces a new individual.

Studies of intermarriage conducted in the 1940s raised questions about the success of the melting pot. Although there was intermarriage across nationality lines, there was also a strong tendency to restrict marriage within the three major religious denominations: Protestant, Catholic, and Jewish. Therefore, instead of a single melting pot, a variant, the "triple melting pot," was proposed (Kennedy, 1944: 1952).

The concept of the melting pot was perhaps a noble one; but in practice it was difficult to form much more than a vague notion of how it would work. Questions as to proportions, power, and the proper blend and mixture could be raised, although the most logical prescription from this model would be intermarriage and the constant intermixing of races, nationalities, and religions. Such a state could have occurred earlier under more "natural" circumstances, but prejudice, discrimination, and segregation had already created barriers and boundaries to free interaction. People of color especially have been denied entrance into any of the white communities; and the idea of a "triple melting pot" becomes an exclusivist concept since it ignores the many individuals who belong to the "other world" that is not Catholic, Protestant, or Jewish.

Perhaps the most successful example of the melting pot has been the American cuisine. Here one can see the contributions of the various

cultures and taste their blending and intermixing. An interesting outcome of this process has been the development of certain "foreign"
dishes (i.e., chow mein, pizza) that have actually been invented in
America.

The melting pot became very similar to the practices of Anglo-
conformity. The contributions of minorities were often ignored, and the
melting process consisted of discarding the ethnic in favor of the
American. Many immigrant groups disappeared completely without
leaving a trace of their own cultures.

> Entrance by the descendants of these immigrants into the social struc-
> tures of the existing white Protestant society, and the culmination of this
> process in intermarriage, has not led to the creation of new structures, new
> institutional forms, and a new sense of identity which draws impartially
> from all sources, but rather to immersion in a subsocietal network of
> groups and institutions which was already fixed in essential outline with a
> general Anglo-Saxon Protestant stamp. The prior existence of Anglo-Saxon
> institutional forms as the norm, the pervasiveness of the English language,
> and the numerical dominance of the Anglo-Saxon population made this
> outcome inevitable (Gordon, 1964: 127).

Cultural Pluralism

Both Anglo-conformity and the melting pot assumed the absorption and
eventual disappearance of the immigrant cultures into an overall "American culture." As it has turned out, this was not the desire of many
immigrants themselves, and as early as 1818 there were nationality
group petitions soliciting for ethnic communalities. These petitions
were denied because of *"the principle that the formal agencies of American government could not be used to establish territorial ethnic enclaves
throughout the nation.* Whatever ethnic communality was to be achieved
(the special situation of the American Indians excepted) must be
achieved by voluntary action within a legal framework which was
formally cognizant only of individuals" (Gordon, 1964: 133).

Although ethnic communities could therefore not be legally established, actual ethnic societies rapidly developed. Group nationality
settlements were common, and the addition of old friends, relatives,
neighbors, and countrymen meant that in a strange new land ethnic ties
in the form of a familiar language and culture flourished.

> And so came into being the ethnic church, conducting services in the
> native language; the ethnic school for appropriate indoctrination of the
> young, the newspaper published in the native tongue, the mutual aid
> societies, the recreational groups, and beneath the formal structure, the
> informal network of ethnically enclosed cliques and friendship patterns
> which guaranteed both comfortable socializing and the confinement of
> marriage within the ancestral group (Gordon, 1964: 134).

Cultural pluralism was therefore a fact in early America, even though its formulation as a plausible theory is of relatively recent origin. The rise of nationalism, patriotism, and Americanism during World War I sorely tested the model of ethnic enclaves and ethnic cultures, and much of what is written about culture conflict, ethnic self-hatred, and identity is a result of these conflicting ideologies.

Social workers, especially those who worked in the settlement houses and "slums," were the first to recognize the role of an ethnic heritage and its institutions in helping immigrants to adjust to the new society. The effects of rapid Americanization were not always beneficial; there were intergenerational conflicts, with children turning against their immigrant parents, and symptoms of social and family disorganization such as crime, delinquency, and mental illness.

One of the earliest statements of the pluralist viewpoint was by Kallen (1915), who rejected the melting pot as the correct model for American society. Instead, he was impressed by the ability of ethnic groups to adapt to particular regions and to preserve their own language, religion, communal institutions, and ancestral culture. Yet they also learned the English language, communicated with others readily, and participated in the overall economic and political life of the nation. Kallen argued for cultural diversity based on a model of a federation or commonwealth of national cultures. He felt that such a model represented the best of democratic ideals because individuals are implicated in groups, and therefore democracy for the individual must also mean democracy for the group.

Several important themes were presented by Kallen. (1) Since ethnic membership rests on ancestry and family connections, it is involuntary, but it gives the individual that connection which is of special significance for personality satisfactions and development. (2) The pluralistic position harmonizes with American political and social life. The imposition of Anglo-Saxon comformity is a violation of our ideals. Pluralism encourages the right to be different but equal. (3) The nation as a whole benefits from the existence of ethnic cultures. There is a direct ethnic contribution to enrich and broaden the cultural heritage; and the competition, interaction, and creative relationships among the various cultures will continue to stimulate the nation.

The most important of Kallen's themes, from an ethnic perspective, is that of equality—an unequal pluralism, based on the "inferiority" of ethnic groups, is not a good model of cultural pluralism. The stratification system in the United States has prevented many ethnic groups from achieving equality, which in turn has affected their perceptions of the desirability of their own cultures.

Another problem in cultural pluralism is the risk of categorically assigning individuals into groups through birth (although ethnic groups are accustomed to this process). Such roles remain frozen throughout a person's life, severely limiting his freedom of choice. Another unfortunate consequence of labeling individuals is that it has negated many of their human qualities. Ethnic groups have been necessary to majority groups merely as a source of labor. They have been treated as the byproducts of the economic system and once they had outlived their usefulness they were no longer welcome.

The position of the residual ethnics is aptly described in the San Francisco *Chronicle* in 1910:

> Had the Japanese laborer throttled his ambition to progress along the lines of American citizenship and industrial development, he probably would have attracted small attention to the public mind. Japanese ambition is to progress beyond mere servility to the plane of the better class of American workman and to own a home with him. The moment that this position is exercised, the Japanese ceases to be an ideal laborer.

It is within this context that we view the destructiveness of popular ideologies such as Anglo conformity and the melting pot, for such perceptions create subgroups who have no other alternative but to remain residual to the system. They can never be part of the core since the ideology ignores their basic physical attributes.

Other alternatives to the models of Anglo-conformity and the melting pot, such as cultural pluralism, are the most desirable from the ethnic perspective. Several ethnic minorities, especially those from Asia, have had some degree of success in American society through such a development. However, drawing parallels from one culture to another is extremely risky because there are so many dissimilar variables.

For example, to be effective, the pluralistic subculture must have a wide range of individuals and institutions and adequate resources. For racial groups who have lived under discrimination, segregation, and prejudice for a long time, this requirement will be extremely difficult to fulfill. Instead, they may find a large proportion of their population clustered in the lower classes and caught in cultures of "poverty" or "despair"; cultural pluralism would have no demonstrable effect as long as the conditions of life remain on a day-to-day subsistence basis. Unless these conditions are drastically changed, the situation of large numbers of ethnics will remain intolerable.

Major Questions

The questions on race relations in the United States are multiple, complex, and conflicting. There is little consensus even on what the major questions are, but the following are important enough to be included in any discussion.

61

1. What are the goals of American society? Are they Anglo-conformity, the melting pot, cultural pluralism, or what? What are some of the preconditions that must be met before these goals can be realistically assessed by the subordinated minorities?
2. How can we empirically demonstrate and evaluate the effectiveness of some of these goals?
3. How do we prevent today's "solutions" from becoming tomorrow's rigidities and orthodoxies?

BIBLIOGRAPHY

BANTON, MICHAEL (1967). *Race Relations.* London: Tavistock Publications.

BERELSON, BERNARD and G. STEINER (1964). *Human Behavior.* New York: Harcourt Brace Jovanovich.

BLAUNER, ROBERT (1971). "Colonized and Immigrant Minorities." Unpublished study. Personal correspondence.

―――― (1969). "Internal Colonialism and Ghetto Revolt." *Social Problems,* 16 (4): 393–408.

BOGARDUS, EMORY S. (1930). "A Race Relations Cycle." *American Journal of Sociology,* 35 (4): 612–17.

COSER, LEWIS (1965). *George Simmel.* Englewood Cliffs, N.J.: Prentice-Hall, Inc.

DANIELS, ROGER and HARRY H. L. KITANO (1970). *American Racism: Exploration of the Nature of Prejudice.* Englewood Cliffs, N.J.: Prentice-Hall, Inc.

GLAZER, NATHAN (1972). "America's Race Paradox." In Rosen, ed., *Nation of Nations.* New York: Random House, Inc. Pp. 165–80.

GLUCKMAN, MAX (1956). "Analysis of a Social Situation in Modern Zululand." Rhodes-Livingstone Papers No. 28. Manchester: Manchester University Press.

―――― (1955). *Custom and Conflict in Africa.* Oxford: Blackwell.

GORDON, MILTON (1964). *Assimilation in American Life.* New York: Oxford University Press. All excerpts are reprinted by permission of the publisher.

HIGHAM, JOHN (1955). *Strangers in the Land.* New Brunswick, N.J.: Rutgers University Press.

KALLEN, HORACE (1915). "Democracy vs. the Melting Pot." *The Nation* (February 18 and 25).

KENNEDY, RUBY JO REEVES (1944). "Single or Triple Melting Pot? Intermarriage Trends in New Haven, 1870–1940." *American Journal of Sociology,* 49 (4): 331–39.

―――― (1952). "Single or Triple Melting Pot? Intermarriage Trends in New Haven, 1870–1950." *American Journal of Sociology,* 58 (1): 56–59.

MASON, PHILLIP (1970). *Race Relations.* London: Oxford University Press.

PARK, ROBERT E. (1950). *Race and Culture.* New York: The Free Press.

REDFIELD, ROBERT, RALPH LINTON and MELVILLE J. HERSKOVITS (1936). "Memorandum for the Study of Acculturation." *American Anthropologist,* 38 (1).

San Francisco *Chronicle*, 1910.

SHIBUTANI, TAMOTSU and KIAN M. KWAN (1965). *Ethnic Stratification.* New York: The Macmillan Company.

TAYLOR, GEORGE ROGERS, ed. (1949). *The Turner Thesis Concerning the Role of the Frontier in American History.* Boston: D. C. Heath and Company.

TURNER, FREDERICK J. (1963). *The Frontier in American History.* New York: Holt, Rinehart and Winston, Inc.

VAN DEN BERGHE, P. (1967). *Race and Racism.* New York: John Wiley & Sons, Inc.

ZANGWILL, ISRAEL (1909). *The Melting Pot.* New York: The Macmillan Company.

DISCRIMINATION 3

We have described the function, maintenance and pervasiveness of prejudice; it is an attitude that works in many ways: it promotes group unity and identification, supplies cues and scapegoats, serves ethnocentric purposes, and provides needed symbols.

Perhaps the most important task in race relations then is not to eradicate prejudiced attitudes but to prevent them from being acted out (discrimination). As MacIver says, "Wherever the direct attack is feasible —that is, the attack on discrimination itself— it is more promising than the indirect attack—that is, the attack on prejudice itself. It is more effective to challenge conditions than to challenge attitudes and feelings" (MacIver, 1948: 64).

Discrimination leads to inequality and to disadvantage. The limited access to recreational or social facilities, and the denial of basic civil rights and of opportunities for employment, education, and housing place subordinate groups in a weaker position. The problem is exacerbated in a competitive system such as ours where the handicaps of race and discrimination may be too much to overcome for many members of minority groups.

The assumption that prejudice and discrimination are related in a causal sequence and that the former is an attitude and the latter its behavioral component is reasonably clear, even though there is little compelling empirical data to strongly support the relationship.

Blalock (1967) indicates that one of the major problems with the use of the term in ethnic relations is that it must be measured indirectly, thus necessitating a set of theoretical assumptions, many of them untestable. Definitions of discrimination vary, although most carry some notion of intent. Blalock criticizes some of the early definitions such as F. H. Hankins' "unequal treatment of equals." This definition emphasizes the differential treatment on the basis of one characteristic, ethnic group, but may ignore a variety of other qualities. For example, if a nonwhite professor and a white professor are treated differently, this may be an example of racial discrimination. However, they would have to be "equal in all other respects," a condition that seldom occurs. Questions of what schools they attended, their training, their productivity, their personalities, and a variety of other factors may also enter into the "unequal treatment."

There are similar problems in other definitions of discrimination. Williams' definition (1947: 39) is "the differential treatment of individuals considered to belong to a particular social group." Since individuals belong to many groups, the definition lacks precision. Allport (1954) emphasizes that differential treatment based on individual qualities is not discrimination. The critical question is how can one tell whether or not the treatment is based on individual or group traits, since any given individual has many different traits and group memberships. Therefore, discrimination can seldom be measured except by its dependent variables, segregation and inequality. Nevertheless, one can argue that certain independent variables lead to discrimination, which in turn produces inequality, segregation, and disadvantage.

Racial discrimination from our perspective is the "disadvantaged treatment of individuals and groups by racial signs." It is a barrier to prevent minority groups from equal participation in the society.

The clearest examples of discrimination are the legal restrictions based on race. For example, our immigration laws have consistently discriminated against Asians; antimiscegenation laws and restrictions limiting citizenship are barriers based on racist assumptions. A recent legally sanctioned discriminatory action was the wartime evacuation of the Japanese, whereby one criterion, Japanese ancestry, was sufficient to incarcerate over 110,000 individuals.

Segregation

Segregation is a form of discrimination. It is easier to measure than discrimination because it can be directly observed, although its mea- **66** surement is not without its own complications. Segregation means the act, process, or state of being separate or set apart. It is a form of isolation that limits social relations, communication, and contact and may be enforced legally or by common custom. Thus, it is most often observed and measured in housing.

HOUSING

Terms such as the ghetto, the black belt, the barrios, Little Tokyo, or Chinatown are examples of segregated housing. As important as segregation itself are the other interactions controlled by housing. As Allport mentions, housing segregation determines what schools children attend, and the kinds of stores, medical facilities, and churches. Friends and neighbors will tend to come from among the segregated group; and if the housing happens to be overcrowded and poor, as it usually is, segregation becomes synonymous with slum conditions, drug use, and a high rate of crime (Allport, 1954: 269).

Discrimination in housing has affected many people, with color playing an important role in determining who is affected. For although European immigrants such as the Italians, Jews, and Irish have faced housing discrimination, discriminatory practices directed toward them have subsided as their identifiability and cultural differences decrease. The greatest amount of discrimination is directed toward Negroes, and it is decreasing at a rate much slower than for any other minority group (Simpson and Yinger, 1965: 327–28).

Inequalities in housing are perpetuated by the following white beliefs: deteriorating property values, Negro "bad housekeeping" and disorderly behavior, interracial conflict, fear of inundation, fear of loss of status (Grier and Grier, 1959: 27–36). Fear of intimate social interaction is another factor.

The widespread white fears of deteriorating property values with the entrance of nonwhites into a neighborhood has prompted various studies. Laurenti's study (1960) comparing property values between areas where nonwhites have moved into a neighborhood and "control areas," within the same time period, revealed that property values are based on the interaction of many factors: (1) strength of desire of whites to move out and the nonwhites to move in; (2) willingness of whites to purchase property in racially mixed neighborhoods; (3) housing choices open to both groups; (4) purchasing power of the involved groups; (5) trend of values in the area; (6) general state of business.

Laurenti's major finding was that the entrance of blacks into all-white neighborhoods was not necessarily associated with decreasing property values. Instead, prices tended to remain stable or to rise. Overall, the entrance of blacks into previously all-white neighborhoods has raised, lowered, or stabilized prices so that factors other than racial intrusion are also in operation.

Although numerous laws have been passed to prohibit segregation and discrimination in housing, many methods have been employed to **67** skirt these laws. The method cited by the United States Commission on Civil Rights as most effective and widely used is simply the refusal to sell. Another method was the racial restrictive covenant made between two parties stipulating that the purchaser of the property will not sell or rent his property to members of specific minority or religious groups. This method is no longer legal. The National Association of Real Estate Boards adheres to the principle that the property owner has the right to specify certain conditions concerning the sale or rental of his property and that realtors are obligated to comply with these terms. Housing provides one clear example of the conflict between the "right" of the individual to sell to whom he pleases, and the societal "rights" in specifying nondiscriminatory clauses in the sale.

Statements made by mortgage bankers in the Washington, D.C. area to the Commission on Civil Rights suggest that financing is made difficult to minority-group members who wish to locate "in areas that are not recognized as being racially mixed, on the premise that such an investment would not be attractive to institutional lenders." Federal Housing Authority (FHA) loans also used to encourage discriminatory treatment of minorities.

The cost of discrimination in housing has been great. Members of minority groups are not free to obtain housing according to their financial means; and they pay higher prices for lower quality housing than whites would pay. The effects on morale, ambition, and expectation are destructive. The blight of slum areas spreads, urban renewal lags, and racial tension increases.

Segregation intensifies the visibility of the minority group and marks off its boundaries, giving rise to problems of conflict and social control. Ethnic riots often occur along the "boundaries," and social-control problems within segregated areas are usually quite high—policemen, firemen, and other representatives of the larger community are looked upon as intruders and often treated with hostility.

VOLUNTARY AND FORCED SEGREGATION

Segregation can be voluntary or forced. The fundamental difference is simple—voluntary segregation is not based on discrimination, the larger social structure is perceived as more open, and a choice is potentially available. Under forced conditions, however, there is no choice. Historically, ethnic segregation has usually been forced, and it lasts a long time.

Segregation and insulation are convenient for the majority. There is now a place where "that element" lives; both voluntary and accidental confrontation can be minimized. There is also the opportunity to retain and sharpen discriminatory practices. Schools and services in racially segregated areas can be controlled through meager budgets and inferior services. Children of racial minorities are taught by less-experienced teachers, suffer from overcrowded conditions, and generally receive an inferior education. As Daniels and Kitano (1970: 25) illustrate:

> The lower status racial group member seldom meets whites on equal grounds. He is born, reared, and educated under ghetto conditions. Education and job opportunities on the "outside" require a different kind of background and experience. His background limits his opportunities.

Segregation can also be functional for the minority-group member. He may feel more comfortable among his own "kind"—food, services, language, and customs are more attuned to his needs. He can limit his contacts with his "superiors"—he can make friends and participate in life within the segregated, ethnic enclave.

Desegregated housing, on the other hand, has a substantial influence on ethnic attitudes. Deutsch and Collins (1951) and subsequent studies have shown that desegregated housing stimulates friendlier, more cohesive, and cooperative activity, which in turn fosters intergroup friendship and encourages the reduction of prejudice and discrimination. The favorable attitudinal change occurs among blacks as well as whites (Works, 1961).

The Chinese in California are an example of segregation arising from discrimination, described by Berry (1958: 288). Although some of the Chinese fought discriminatory legislation in the courts, and others returned to their homeland, most of them migrated to the larger California cities and proceeded to segregate themselves from the larger society. They withdrew socially, politically, economically, physically, and psychologically. Most took up occupations less competitive with the whites; and in the Chinatowns, they developed their own temples, structures, and institutions and maintained their own styles of life.

HOUSING SOLUTIONS

A change in the pattern of segregated housing should have profound effects on race relations. However, it has remained one of the most difficult areas to change, even though the facts show the high cost of maintaining ghettos to the entire community. Some of the forces behind housing discrimination illustrate the complexity of the issue, even though there is the clear, definable goal of a free and open housing market.

Individual ownership is a basic American value, and this includes the right to dispose of property on an individual basis and the right to make a profit. Fair-housing bills and antidiscrimination clauses attempt to open up housing but up to now have proved to be of minor importance. If segregated ghetto housing is profitable to an individual, then the **69** probability of individual change is lessened. If an individual wishes to sell only to certain groups, he will find a way to circumvent the open-housing laws.

Supporting him are the real estate salesmen, realtors, builders, investors, and bankers. They all have vested interests in maintaining the status quo if it is highly profitable, and will therefore perpetuate segregated housing. The good of the community and the nation is given a lower priority.

Finally, there is the role of the minorities themselves. Most lack the income for better housing; they also have their fears, anxieties, and preferences that help to maintain the patterns of segregation. The interaction of all of these factors make integrated housing a less viable solution, even though the government has officially decreed a racially open market in housing.

The overall effect of these patterns is reflected in a report of the National Urban Coalition (Los Angeles *Times,* 1972). The flight of the whites to the suburbs is dramatically illustrated by 1970 Census data showing that the nonwhite population of the nation's central cities has climbed by 4 million since 1960, while the white population has dropped 600,000 for the same period. Cities such as Detroit, St. Louis, and Baltimore are approaching a 50 percent level of nonwhites.

The rise of ethnic populations in the cities per se is not a problem, but the general neglect that follows the white exodus is. Jobs, services, and other necessities of city living generally drop as nonwhites take over, and there is often a rise in crime and delinquency, as well as increased welfare roles. As Linowitz, former ambassador to the Organization of American States says, "[tax revenues] and better housing are following the migration of affluent whites to the suburbs and leaving the cities in worse shape than before the riots of the mid-1960s" (Los Angeles *Times,* 1972: 6).

DISCRIMINATION IN EMPLOYMENT

The disparity between white and nonwhite is obvious when we analyze the nation's economy. Statistics compiled jointly in 1962 by the Bureau of Labor Statistics and the Bureau of the Census classified approximately one out of three nonwhite families as poor. All ethnic minorities have confronted discriminatory barriers to economic success, but the group most affected by economic discrimination has been the Negroes, whose family income is only 58 percent of white family income (Kain, 1969: 35).

Education, often considered a major determinant of income, can partially explain the disparity between black and white incomes. In 1960 24 percent of Negroes 25 years or older had not finished 5 years or less of schooling as opposed to 7 percent of whites. The Negro is not only handicapped by the quantity but also the quality of education received. Data indicates that education received in black schools is inferior to that of predominantly white schools, which further helps establish unequal conditions.

Residential segregation is another explanatory factor in the income disparity between whites and nonwhites, for it often creates transportation difficulties that prevents blacks from holding jobs outside their area.

Extreme criticism can be directed at the racial discrimination and segregation in labor unions, since they are an important factor in income and control employment to a great extent. Although formal racial discrimination has been denounced by the national federations, (the AFL, the CIO, and the AFL-CIO), many local and national unions continue to use informal means to exclude Negroes (Kain, 1969: 20). The main technique has been to exclude Negroes and other minority-group members from apprenticeship training programs for skilled trade.

The cost of racial discrimination has been great not only to the Negro, but to other nonwhites and to the national economy. After tabulating data from the 1960 Census, and adjusting for differences between white and nonwhites in education, occupational categories, and region of residence, Siegal discovered that "with the single exception of nonwhite farmers in the North, the figures show that at every eduucational level in every occupational group, and in the North as well as the South, minorities have earnings less than most whites." He estimated the differential in income at most occupational and educational levels between white and nonwhite to be as great as $1,000 with the largest difference in the South (Kain, 1969: 61–62).

The 1960 Census was also used by the Council of Economic Advisors in 1965 to estimate the cost of discrimination to the national economy. The Council stated that the personal income of the nation would be $12.8 billion greater if Negroes having education equal to whites were given equal pay; that the gross national product would rise an additional 3.7 percent; and that the entire economy would greatly benefit by granting better education to Negroes and by destroying job discrimination. (Kain, 1969: 59).

There are a number of interrelated factors that complicate simple figures on minority-group employment and income. For example, Japanese employment and income (Kitano, 1969), ranks only second to the majority group. However, with education and training taken into account, the Japanese should have the highest income of all. Employment discrimination is responsible for this.

Occupational improvement is another area where the figures are deceptive. When ethnic groups are measured against their own base line of decades ago, the upward slope is impressive; however, when ethnic progress is measured against the improved patterns of the whites, then the rates may be proportionately less. This relative deprivation, coupled with higher expectations, is hypothesized to be responsible for the great tension and frustration among many minorities.

An analysis of job categories (e.g., professionals) is also enlightening; for minorities are generally among the lowest paid of the professionals, and their self-employment figures probably include a high proportion of "mama and papa" businesses with marginal incomes.

DISCRIMINATION IN THE SCHOOLS

The Supreme Court's landmark decision of May 17, 1954, on public school desegregation marked the beginning of a new educational era. Education, the court declared, was "perhaps the most important function of state and local governments" and "a principal instrument in awakening the child to cultural values, in preparing him for later professional training, and in helping him to adjust to his environment" (Simpson and Yinger, 1965: 419).

The decision reversed the *Plessy and Ferguson* decision of 1896, which was used to justify excluding blacks from the separate white public schools. The Court unanimously agreed to the unconstitutionality of the "separate but equal" doctrine, and concluded that "separate educational facilities are inherently unequal" and have "a detrimental effect upon the colored children." School segregation is "usually interpreted as denoting the inferiority of the Negro group," and this "affects the motivation of the child to learn," and "therefore has a tendency to retard the educational and mental development of Negro children and to deprive them of some of the benefits they would receive in a racially integrated school system" (Marden, 1968: 295).

The Court did not establish deadlines or timetables for the desegregation of public schools, but it did specify that action be taken with all deliberate speed. This exhortation was met with tremendous white resistance, especially in the South. Desegregation of elementary and secondary public schools, colleges, and universities proceeded at a very sluggish pace. A survey taken a decade after the decision by *Southern School News* showed that only 9.2 percent of Negro pupils in 17 Southern and border States, including the District of Columbia, were attending desegregated public schools (Marden, 1968: 296).

A large range of techniques was employed to oppose and inhibit school desegregation. Unruly demonstrations, proceedings to impeach the justices of the Supreme Court, closing of schools, and prohibiting the

NAACP from providing legal aid were some of the methods used. Legislative acts and resolutions were passed, state constitutions were amended, and private schools were established. Negroes who supported desegregation were threatened with physical violence and economic pressures. Token intergration also helped in slowing down progress (Simpson and Yinger, 1965: 421–23).

Segregated housing patterns, aided by the trend of heavier Negro and minority concentration in metropolitan areas and white dispersal to the suburbs, also contributed to school desegregation problems. This factor presents the issue of de jure and de facto segregation, for although school boards of particular districts may be officially desegregated, areas within the district may either be all black or all white. This pattern of de facto public school segregation is nationwide, and as Pettigrew states, "has serious consequences for any attempt to provide equal educational opportunity" for children of this or following generations (1971: 58). His main thesis is that segregation of schools means an inferior education for minority group children.

Pettigrew's interpretation is supported by the 1966 Coleman Report, as well as by other studies that used different methodological techniques and samples. The Coleman Report's basic finding was that children of all social backgrounds tended to perform better in schools with a predominantly middle-class environment, especially in later grades where more direct influence of the peer group commenced. The correlation between the social class of the student body and achievement scores was significant (Pettigrew, 1971: 58). The implications of this finding are clear when one notes that only about one-fourth of American Negroes belong to the middle-class.

However, desegregation alone is not sufficient. An analysis of the Coleman Report by the Civil Rights Commission found that interracial acceptance was the intervening variable that determined whether a school was merely desegregated or truly integrated (Pettigrew, 1971: 64). And since studies indicate that interracial acceptance is achieved through the integration of white and Negro children in early grades for the benefit of both groups, maximum efforts to fully integrate schools are imperative.

Means for Achieving Integrated Schools

There are many ways to integrate schools. Perhaps the most basic, but also the most difficult to achieve, is to desegregate neighborhoods. Local control of neighborhood schools could be maintained, since integrated neighborhoods would lead to integrated schools. But, the major stumbling block is discrimination in housing.

73

Several bussing methods have been tried; one is to bus ghetto children out of their areas, making it essentially a one-way process. This type of bussing has been going on rather quietly in many school districts and has met with minimal resistance. For example, some of the wealthier schools in Los Angeles have bussed in ghetto children for a number of years, and the program has run along very smoothly.

Another method is to totally desegregate the schools by bussing all the children in and out. There has developed a tremendous resistance to this type of bussing among many Americans, including ethnic groups themselves. Some of the reasons behind this resistance are clearly racist; however, there are other factors that are difficult to classify in simplistic, discriminatory terms.

For example, some Chinese parents in San Francisco are actively opposed to bussing. They explain that many Chinatown youngsters are from Hong Kong and have little fluency in English. Schools in Chinatown can provide a more comfortable setting and an understanding background for many of these children; there is no point in sending them to areas scattered throughout the city.

The problem is an illustration of a means-end dilemma. Most Americans profess a desire for equality of opportunity and are willing to state that they are for equality and justice in education. However, the means for achieving this goal, such as school bussing, have met with tremendous resistance.

School Desegregation:
An Example of the Rashomon Phenomenon

Greenwood (1972), writing for the Los Angeles *Times,* presented an overall view of the effects of California school desegregation in 1972. Clear, measurable effects of desegregation on equally clear, measurable goals might have produced a higher consensus, but the absence of such criteria has provided a good example of the Rashomon phenomenon in action. For example, comments by various school personnel concerning desegregation included: "We were expecting the worst and the worst never came"; "Is it worth it?" and "I'm pleased. I'm happy. I think it's working."

Some of the schools were desegregated under court order; others did so voluntarily; some were desegregated quite recently, others had set up bussing and other "means" many years before. Some of the results of desegregation were as follows:

ACHIEVEMENT

Although research results were quite limited, the general impression was that the academic achievement of minority-group youngsters in   74

desegregated schools had not shown a significant, across-the-board rise.
The academic achievement of white youngsters appeared to be unaffected.
However, these results are still so recent that generalizations may have
to wait many more years. In the meantime, individuals with varying
points of view can look at the figures and advocate a number of different
approaches.

BUSSING

Districts that had desegregated or had used bussing for a long time
viewed bussing as an accepted routine. But in more recently desegregated
districts, it was openly resented or accepted grudgingly. Many parents
felt that bussing was the cause of many problems. Generally, even under
two-way bussing, the minority children have done most of the traveling.

COMMUNITY REACTION

While some community members threatened to boycott and demonstrate at the beginning of desegregation, there was no actual violence.
There have been largely unsuccessful attempts to recall school board
members, and support for the program ran generally stronger in the
minority community. In Riverside, three years after desegregation, parents
of elementary school children were asked if they favored the program.
About two-thirds said yes, with the black response the most strongly
affirmative (80 percent), followed by the Mexican Americans and the
whites.

Other Issues

Several other important factors overshadow the more emotional issues
connected with desegregation and bussing. One has been the increased
parental involvement with the schools, especially in the minority community. The entrance of white students into previously neglected ghetto
schools has also resulted in greater attention to those schools. The distribution of minority children to previously solid, middle-class schools
has triggered an evaluation of what constitutes good teaching and a
relevant curriculum. Some districts have reported that desegregation has
brought both white and minority parents together and that social contact
has increased.

DISCIPLINARY BEHAVIOR

There had been conflict with racial overtones especially at the
junior and senior high levels immediately after desegregation. However,
the disciplinary problems seemed to be lessening over time; in one study,
20 percent of the school personnel answered that they were concerned
with such problems, but two years later the figure had dropped to 5   75

percent. The problem has been exacerbated by anxious parents who have read racial overtones into all school incidents.

WHITE FLIGHT

Some whites withdrew from the schools. Most school districts mentioned the declining white attendance, and some proportion of the flight was no doubt caused by desegregation fears. However, because of the rapid mobility of California society, it was difficult to assess this factor with any degree of accuracy.

School desegregation in California has had its successes, failures, and in-betweens. It has stirred up anxieties about a black turnover, has exposed the racist feelings of many teachers and parents, and has lead to confrontations. It has not brought about instant academic success nor a high degree of racial interaction and harmony. Yet, it has brought together people who have never met each other before, and has worked out smoothly in most instances, especially after an initial trial period, and is beginning to create an integrated community of children.

EDUCATIONAL OPPORTUNITY PROGRAMS (EOP)

The Educational Opportunity Programs (EOP) are primarily for minority students at the college and university level. Although there is no nationwide model, and state programs vary widely, the basic idea behind the program is an exciting one. It recognizes the handicaps and barriers facing minority-group students; therefore, it attempts to provide financial, counseling, housing, and other types of assistance to both recruit minorities into four-year institutions and to assist them towards graduation. The programs in California have helped many heretofore unreached minorities; the number continuing towards successful completion of a bachelor's degree has been high; however, they have come about at a time of reduced educational budgets so that the future of the programs remains in doubt (Kitano and Miller, 1970).

The program provides another example of the various perspectives that are used to define the success of a program. In our survey (Kitano and Miller, 1970), we had a large number of college administrators and professors evaluate EOP. The answers ranged from some who felt that the lowering of the standards of the University of California would be such a blow that the university could never hope to recover, to those who felt that the entrance of a large number of minority students with their different life styles was absolutely the best thing that could happen to the university.

Ironically, politicians have been constantly pointing out to the minorities that a college education and degree is necessary for success and accusing them of not recognizing this fact in American life. Now, just as these minorities are beginning to take advantage of the newly available educational opportunities, funding has come to a standstill. In fact, politicians are now hypocritically questioning whether everyone has a "right" to a college education; some are now advocating a much more conservative and elitist view of public education. Too little and too late may again be the story for America's ethnics.

EDUCATION: THE MAGIC PATH?

Although education has been one of the most important means for immigrant groups mobility, it does not necessarily lead to a better life. The depression of the 1930s saw unemployed college graduates and technically qualified people in menial occupations. Many underdeveloped countries also seem to have a surplus of college educated people who subsequently find it difficult to participate in their own societies.

Also, there is a universal bias in our college admittance criteria. Most colleges rely on computerized test scores, past standards, and other such data as the most important factors in college acceptances. The process insures that those ethnics who are most like the dominant groups will get in and survive. It has been difficult to change these practices because most Americans, including the ethnics, identify with universalistic norms and talk about quality education and the importance of standards.

We may be approaching a point where we are saturated with highly educated ethnics in specific areas. Constant addition of newly trained ethnics without a corresponding expansion of opportunities may soon show us that education per se is not enough.

CAUSES OF DISCRIMINATION AND SEGREGATION

Presumably, all of the "causes" that were listed as reasons behind prejudice are also valid for discrimination and segregation. However, there can be discrimination without prejudice and prejudice that does not lead to discrimination.

For example, by using "objective standards" to assess the qualifications of potential applicants (e.g., education, training, background, and standard test scores), a nonprejudiced admission officer in a university may discriminate against minority-group individuals. Conversely, a football coach may personally detest Negroes but provide them with equal opportunity on the playing field.

The interaction among prejudice, discrimination, and segregation is so intimate that the terms are often used interchangeably. We will present three "causes" of discriminatory behavior that will overlap with the hypothesized causes of prejudice. The three variables are: (1) color, (2) nationality, and (3) culture.

COLOR

The variable of visibility is the most powerful single factor in avoidance behavior. Color provides a most convenient excuse to practice discrimination, and white supremacists have developed classificatory schema based on skin pigmentation. For example, one common ranking scheme based on erroneous assumptions of race superiority is the following: (1) Caucasian, (2) Mongolian, (3) American Indian, and (4) Negro. Even within the categories there is a ranking system from light to dark so that blonde, Nordic Caucasian is presumed to be higher in status than a darker-skinned Southern European.

Psychoanalytic writers such as Kovel (1970) have provided the most thorough (but also the most untestable) explanations concerning the relationship between color and discrimination. The roots of racism are nourished by the fantasies that whites have developed about the black man, and as Kovel says,

> Bedeviled is indeed the word. The devil was a construct in Western thought before the Westerner encountered black people. Eventually, black people themselves came to represent this construct. The devil is black; and so . . . were Africans—if not absolutely black at least mightily dark. Blackness was the nuclear fantasy, and joined with its polar cognate, whiteness, the two being symbolic abstractions of a human vision of a world that in reality has no such absolutes (1970: 62).

When Europeans discovered that black people pursued a different way of life, that they did not clothe themselves in the European style, and generally behaved much more freely with their bodies, the fantasy of blackness was intensified. Therefore their blackness, nakedness, and unchristian ways shaped the belief that blacks were damned and a symbol of the devil. Terms such as dirty, soiled, deathlike, sinister, horrible, and wicked were correlated with blackness (Kovel, 1970).

Another stream of though that validated the fantasy came from the Bible. The blacks were descendants of Ham, who had looked upon his father naked and did not cover him as did his more obedient brothers. As a punishment, God willed that Ham's son Chris, or Canaan, and all of his descendants would be black and banished from sight. What is black and banished cannot be seen, and according to Jordan, represents one of the earliest recorded instances of racism (Jordan, 1968).

Frantz Fanon (1967), a powerful voice in black consciousness, also emphasizes that in Europe, the black man is the symbol of evil. Satan is black, the torturer is the black man; and concretely and symbolically, the black man stands for the bad side of the character. As he says, "As long as one cannot understand this fact, one is doomed to talk in circles about the 'black problem.' In the Western-dominated world the Negro is the symbol of sin" (Kovel, 1970: 188).

In psychoanalytic terms, blackness was associated with the id and the unconscious, and various repressed ideas were only realized symbolically through the fantasies of race. The theme of African canabalism, the myth of Negro sexual prowess, and the pathological fear of the rape of white women are variations of the unconscious fantasies associated with blackness.

The problem with many of the tenets of psychoanalytic theory is the difficulty of adequately validating propositions. Nevertheless, the almost universal history of European oppression of people of color may warrant a much deeper analysis of the symbolism, since it would be difficult to understand the brutality of white racism solely on the basis of a difference in skin pigmentation.

There is some evidence that lighter skin color is considered more desirable in cultures other than the European. Many Japanese attempt to avoid the direct rays of the sun in order to remain pale; the initial behavior of the natives of Mexico and parts of South America toward the lighter-skinned European indicates that they also held some preconceived notions about skin color.

NATIONALITY

Discriminatory behavior against ethnic groups has often been determined by the relationships between their homelands and America. Obviously, with fluctuations in international relations, friends may find themselves enemies, and the reverse, in short periods of time. Oddly enough, to have come from an enemy nation is not entirely a disadvantage to the immigrant. For one thing, he probably has come from a nation strong enough to be worth considering inimical, and he may also have the support and protection of his government. The Chinese suffered during their early years in California, partially because they did not have the backing of an international power, while the Japanese immigrant was more protected by his relationship with the stronger Japanese nation during the same period. However, what happened to this group during World War II exemplifies the disadvantage of coming from an enemy nation.

Nationality by itself can be used as a discriminatory device—the treatment of German nationals during World War I stands as an example. However, nationality is generally an invisible factor and is therefore not a powerful predictor of discrimination unless it is linked to the more visible variable of race or color. The previously mentioned wartime evacuation of the Japanese during World War II used the criteria of race and nationality to incarcerate Japanese Americans, while the white Germans and Italians, also related to "enemy nations," were generally left untouched.

CULTURE

Discriminatory behavior against minority groups was often justified because of their "strange and alien ways." There were notions about the unassimilability of certain cultures—the Northern Europeans were considered the most compatible, whereas other cultures were less so. Our immigration laws, especially that of 1924, reflected these discriminatory features so that quotas were distributed on a nation-culture-color basis.

The easiest to categorize cultural aspects are life styles—dress, language, and consumption and communication patterns. Therefore, those styles most distant from Anglo-Saxon culture will tend to evoke prejudicial and discriminatory behavior. For example, those life styles furthest from the ethic of hard work and self-denial will probably raise the hostility of the majority group the quickest. Mention of welfare mothers having color TVs (whether true or untrue) will immediately provoke demands for a public investigation of welfare fraud.

However, even more important than the discrepancy between cultures are those cultural styles that allow for (1) a congruence and a "fit" with the dominant culture, or (2) a symbiotic or adaptive style that in essence will follow majority role prescriptions about how minority groups should behave.

The cultural behavior of the minority group in question is not necessarily the reason behind discrimination. For example, the Japanese in the United States exhibit much of the same life style today that they did several decades ago, and yet in one era they were deemed unassimilable heathens, unfit for any of the rights of American citizenship. Now they are often referred to as a model minority, even though it is our observation that they have not changed that much.

An ideal minority from a racist perspective may be one whose styles will accept discrimination and conform to its restrictions. Conversely, an "obnoxious" style will tend to question discrimination and actively seek to remove such barriers. Such ethnic groups will be accused of not knowing their place in the society.

Finally the culture of the ethnic group can protect it from the shock of discrimination and culture conflict. Ethnic organization and cohesion can play a major role in maintaining the ethnic qualities until the processes of acculturation are able to take over. Conversely, the destruction of the native cultures of Africa through slavery has made the discrimination against the Negro all the more effective.

Visibility is linked with prejudice and discrimination and involves the following hypothesized sequence:

Independent Variable	Intervening Variable	Dependent Variable
visibility (color)	prejudice, culture	discrimination segregation

The experience of certain Indian tribes illustrates the highest level of discriminatory behavior. They were distinctly visible; they were viewed as members of an enemy nation; they were perceived as threats to the existence of small Western settlements; they were thought to be unassimilable because of their strange and alien cultures; their life styles were neither similar, congruent, nor symbiotic to the white man's culture, and they were never powerful enough to be seen as a major retaliatory threat. They were subject to high discriminatory behavior, including strategies leading to decimation and extermination. Therefore it comes as no surprise that the most systematic attempts to eliminate an ethnic group have been against the American Indian.

BIBLIOGRAPHY

ALLPORT, GORDON (1954). *The Nature of Prejudice*. Boston: Beacon Press. Pp. 51–52.

BERRY, BURTON (1958). *Race and Ethnic Relations*. Boston: Houghton Mifflin Company.

BLALOCK, HUBERT M. (1967). *Toward a Theory of Minority Group Relations*. New York: John Wiley & Sons, Inc.

DANIELS, ROGER, and HARRY H. L. KITANO (1970). *American Racism: Exploration of the Nature of Prejudice*. Englewood Cliffs, N.J.: Prentice-Hall, Inc.

DEUTSCH, M., and M. E. COLLINS (1951). *Interracial Housing: A Psychological Evaluation of a Social Experiment*. Minneapolis: University of Minnesota Press.

FANON, FRANTZ (1967). *Black Skin, White Masks*. New York: Grove Press.

GREENWOOD, NOEL (1972). "School Desegregation—Successes, Failures, Surprises." Los Angeles *Times* (May 2, 1972), Section C, p. 1.

GRIER, EUNICE and GEORGE GRIER (1959). *Discrimination in Housing: A Handbook of Fact*. Report of the United States Commission on Civil Rights. New York: Anti-defamation League of Bnai' B'rith.

JORDON, WINTHROP (1968). *White over Black*. Baltimore: Penguin Books, Inc.

KAIN, JOHN, ed. (1969). *Race and Poverty*. Englewood Cliffs, N.J.: Prentice-Hall, Inc.

KITANO, HARRY H. L. (1969). *Japanese Americans: The Evolution of a Subculture*. Englewood Cliffs, N.J.: Prentice-Hall, Inc.

——— and DOROTHY MILLER (1970). *An Assessment of Education Opportunity Programs in California Higher Education*. Sacramento, Cal.: Coordinating Council of Higher Education.

KOVEL, JOEL (1970). *White Racism*. New York: Pantheon Books.

LAURENTI, LUIGI (1965). *Property Values and Race*. Berkeley: University of California Press.

Los Angeles *Times* (1972). "Starting Flight of Whites to Suburbs Noted." June 1, 1972. Part I-B, pp. 6–7.

MACIVER, ROBERT M. (1948). *The More Perfect Union*. New York: The Macmillan Company.

MARDEN, CHARLES and GLADYS MEYER (1968). *Minorities in American Society*. New York: Van Nostrand.

SIMPSON, GEORGE E. and J. M. YINGER (1965). *Racial and Cultural Minorities*. New York: Harper & Row, Publishers.

WILLIAMS, ROBIN JR. (1947). *The Reduction of Intergroup Tensions*. New York: Social Science Research Council. P. 39.

WORKS, E. (1961). "The Prejudice-Interaction Hypothesis from the Point of View of the Negro Minority Group." *American Journal of Sociology*, 67: 47–52.

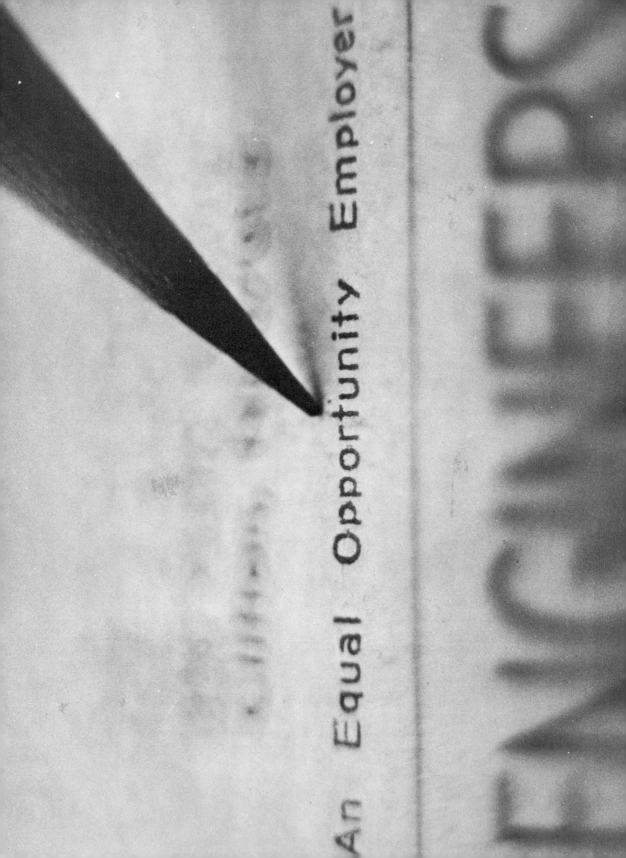

DISCRIMINATION: NUMBERS, COMPETITION, AND POWER 4

Discrimination and segregation are the major variables in maintaining the boundaries between the dominant and the subordinate racial groups; and the visibility variables—color and life style—are critical in the process. However, there are also a number of other variables, hypothesized by Blalock (1967), that are related to discrimination and segregation. These include (1) numbers and proportions, (2) social distance, (3) competition, (4) power threat, (5) competitive and pressure resources, and (6) status. In this chapter we will discuss the relation of each of these variables to discrimination and segregation.

NUMBERS AND PROPORTIONS

Perhaps the simplest cause of discriminatory behavior is the threat of numbers. As shown in Figure 4–1, as the size of the minority increases, discrimination will also increase.

Schermerhorn provides another way of relating minority groups, number, and power.

Dominant groups serve as guardians and sustainers of the controlling   83

Numerical
size

Figure 4–1. 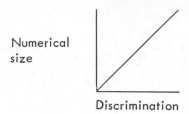 Discrimination

TABLE 4-1
DOMINANT GROUPS

	Size	Power	
Group A	+	+	Majority group
Group B	−	+	Elite group
Subordinate Groups			
Group C	+	−	Mass subjects
Group D	−	−	Minority groups

Source: Schermerhorn (1970: 13).

value system and are in a position to allocate the rewards. Conversely, the subordinate groups are more prone to be the "victims" of the social structure and are powerless to "impose" their ways of living on the dominant groups. The immediate source of dominant-group power is its sheer size, although disorganized groups (the masses) remain powerless even though they are large in number, while those with special resources (the elite), even though small in number do have power.

The threat and power of numbers may be actual or imagined—the effects are similar. For example, in California elaborate geometric charts were devised showing the state being overrun by "yellow hordes" (in reality these hordes almost never exceeded 1 to 2 percent of the population). One typical reaction was that of V. S. McClatchy, the publisher of a major California newspaper chain, who believed that:

> Careful tables of increase of the Japanese population in the United States . . . place the total in the United States . . . in 1923 at 318,000; in 1933 at 542,000; in 1943 at 870,000; in 1963 at 2,000,000; in 2003 at 10,000,000; and in 2063 at 100,000,000 (Daniels and Kitano, 1970: 52).

It is interesting to note that the estimated Japanese population in the United States in 1963 was about 500,000, a figure well below McCatchy's projected 2,000,000. Nevertheless, the specter of hordes of Japanese was one important factor leading to discriminatory legislation

84

against them and other Asians. Racial groups who are perceived to "breed like rabbits" have always been targets for some form of control.

Generally, the smaller the ethnic minority group, the less threatening it is. The one nonwhite family in an all-white community is accepted with friendliness (although it invariably has a low status); and these communities generally congratulate themselves for their racial openness. During the evacuation of World War II, many Japanese Americans experienced much less discrimination in the East Coast and Midwest because their groups were small and scattered. The overall belief is that discrimination rises only if larger numbers of the minority begin to enter the "paradise."

However, numbers themselves are not reliable predictors of discriminatory behavior under most circumstances and may only be relevant when there are actually only one or two visible ethnic minorities in a town or city of some size.

SOCIAL DISTANCE

Another form of relationship between minority-group percentage and discrimination is shown in Figure 4–2. The discrimination curve is a high,

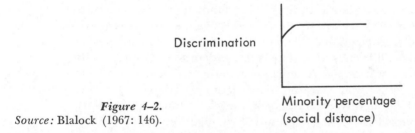

Discrimination

Minority percentage
(social distance)

Figure 4–2.
Source: Blalock (1967: 146).

almost straight line and has little to do with the size of the minority group. Blalock uses the examples of intermarriage and segregated housing. Discrimination remains high whether the minority group is large or small.

Numerous empirical examples are available. Early studies by Bogardus (1930) using the concept of social distance assessed the degrees of social intimacy in relation to specific minorities. The degrees of social intimacy ranged over marriage, club membership, friendships, neighbors, employment, citizenship, and exclusion. Overall there was a predictable pattern: nonwhite groups were kept at a social distance. The one group that appeared consistently at the bottom was the Turks; even among American Negroes, Turks were ranked at the bottom. As we can infer, discrimination against them had little to do with the threat of numbers.

Social distance is maintained through attitudes of liking and dis-

85

liking. In many instances the object of dislike is unknown or heavily stereotyped. For example, Katz and Braly (1933) asked students to list all traits they thought typical of a number of ethnic groups. Negroes were regarded to be superstitious, lazy, happy-go-lucky, ignorant, and musical. Jews were seen to be shrewd, mercenary, industrious, grasping, intelligent, and ambitious.

The important point in the study of stereotypes was how this "fantasy" about other groups, whether phrased positively or not, becomes the "reality" of intergroup relations. Therefore, people feel that they can avoid or discriminate against their fellow citizens through perceived imaginary traits.

COMPETITION

Competition arises from a simple premise—that when two or more individuals are striving for the same scarce resources, the success of one implies the relative failure for the other. Therefore, discriminatory behavior can limit competition. The intensity of the competition is related to several factors, such as the strength of the goals, the number of satisfactory alternatives, and the number and power of the competitors.

The area of economic competition provides examples of how this belief can be translated into a motive for discrimination. For example, many Californians felt that the Chinese laborers of the early twentieth century were unfair competitors: They worked long hours for low wages, used their family and friends for cheap labor, seldom took holidays, and were therefore a threat to the American standard of living. It was felt that the white worker would be the main victim. His loss of job and income lowered his ability to buy goods, which in turn would hurt others. The Chinese laborers and their unfair competition was one of the presumed causes for the high unemployment during the economic depression of the 1870s.

A more logical economic interpretation would reverse the argument: —the more efficient Chinese laborers would force the white workers to cut costs thereby lowering food prices and saving money for housewives, who could then spend more for other products. But as in many racial arguments, emotions took precedence over the facts. The Chinese Exclusion Act of 1882 was one specific attempt to limit competition by prohibiting Chinese immigration to the United States.

Racist thinking limited the competition between poor whites and Negroes in the South. Rather than the lower-class groups of both races uniting to compete against the white rulers, the lower-class whites made their own deprivations more bearable by looking down on the even more deprived Negro. Poor whites were often at the forefront in backing discriminatory legislation against the Negroes, even in cases where they too might suffer (e.g., the poll tax).

Perhaps initially, discrimination may rise as the perceived ethnic competition rises, but after it reaches a certain point, other factors come into play. For example, Japanese gardeners faced initial difficulty in establishing themselves. However, once they became established, in spite of discriminatory behavior, a rise in their numbers did not lead to further discrimination. In fact, gardening is an example where a visible minority was so successful as competitors that they almost completely dominated the field. The curve of discrimination may then actually drop because of their control. The condition may remain as long as the dominant group is not capable of competing.

Professional sports provides a variation of the model of competition. One important factor is the rather unique feedback pattern in athletics. Batting averages, the number of yards gained, or basketball points scored provide a quick quantitative evaluation of an individual's level of performance, and it is difficult to discriminate in the face of overpowering evidence. Therefore the better the feedback in terms of individual performance, the less likelihood of discrimination. High individual performance has its effect on the group. If a minority player can help the team to win, then there is little chance that he will be discriminated against.

Blalock (1967) proposes a number of other correlations between athletic teams (and by implication, other similar groups) and discrimination. If discriminatory barriers are maintained, an individual, and therefore the team, will not be able to perform to its maximum capabilities. Under these conditions discriminatory barriers will be greatly lowered. This is especially true in professional sports, particularly basketball and baseball. It was not too long ago when both of these sports were all white. Now there is a preponderance of black athletes on all-star teams.

POWER THREAT

Perceived minority-group power is related to discrimination. Power threat is intimately related to numbers, average resources, and mobilization. Resources refer to the actual sources of power, or "those properties of the individual or group that provide the power potential or ability to exercise power" (Blalock, 1967: 113). Bierstedt (1950) includes under resources, money, prestige, property, natural and supernatural powers, and such factors as knowledge, competence, deceit, fraud, secrecy, physical strength, voting rights, the ability to bear arms, and membership in organizations such as unions. Power is a multiplicative function of total resources and the degree to which these sources are mobilized.

Groups may gain power through the pooling of resources; political power may be exercised through bloc voting. Even a relatively small number of any group may exercise power if high proportions of other groups are inactive. Both of the power variables—resources and mobilization—depend on motivation. Resources depend primarily on "the motivation and goals of persons over whom power is exercised, whereas mobilization is more largely a function of the goals of the persons exerting the power" (Blalock, 1967: 114).

There are relationships among the possession of resources, goals, and the degree of domination. If an individual possesses those resources necessary for obtaining his most important goals (e.g., financial independence), he becomes less subject to the control of others. Or, if such resources become unavailable, he may gain greater independence by renouncing these goals. For example, if a man no longer desires a college degree, he is less subject to collegiate domination. If a man no longer wants to gamble, the attraction of the poker game will diminish. As he becomes less subject to these desires, his ability to achieve other goals may be increased.

As Blalock says, "Whenever A can limit B's access to a given goal, a certain restriction is placed on B's power over A with respect to other goals. Therefore, although power is always relative to particular goals, power in any one area depends upon the availability of resources for achieving other goals" (Blalock, 1967: 114). Power is also readily generalized so that it can be used to beget additional power.

Generally, the greater the resources, the larger the number of alternative means for goal satisfaction. Individuals (and groups) with a wide variety of alternatives can therefore choose among them and ignore objectives for which resources are more limited. How are these considerations relevant to minority groups?

Individuals and groups with the most alternatives available will be more apt to rely on ideological and other considerations than race alone. For example, a large, efficient manufacturer with high sales can incorporate adequate personnel policies, including nondiscriminatory clauses. But a marginal producer who has to "exploit" his labor in order to survive may have to rely on discriminatory practices, including the deliberate hiring of minority workers at substandard wages.

Similarly, on an individual level, there are those with adequate personal resources to achieve "power" over others but who do not have to use this potential power to dominate others. Conversely, Fromm (1947) describes those who never realize their own potential but who still feel the need to have power over others. This would be possible in a stratification system where skin color allowed one group to achieve instant power over the other.

Tedeschi and his colleagues (1970) present a dyadic theory of power and influence based on a target's compliance to contingent threats and promises. The more believable a threat or promise, the more likely the target will comply with requests or demands from the source. The probabilities of the source punishing noncompliance to threats or rewarding compliance to promises are defined as "threat and promise credi bilities." Attraction, esteem, status, and prestige are all postively related to the believability of promises.

Sources of Power

French and Raven (1959) have classified the sources of power into five types:

1. reward power
2. coercive, or punishment power
3. legitimate power
4. referent power
5. expert power

The first two types of power depend on the possession of resources that permit the holder to either reward or punish. Legitimate power relates to authority, often based on contracts, promises, or commitments made by one individual to another. Referent power relates to the notion of charisma, whereby one individual identifies with and likes another and desires to do as the other requests; love and sexuality may be variants of this. Expert power is based on special knowledge or expertise.

To this list we would add that of morality, which may control some of the more naked uses of power by arousing feelings of guilt. However, discriminatory behavior can be justified by appealing to moral superiority. Invoking the name of God for one's side has often led to some of the highest levels of discrimination.

Many hypotheses are suggested by the French and Raven list. Referent power is one of the historical facts of race relations—certain charismatic majority (as well as ethnic) group leaders have been looked upon as people to trust and to follow, while others, who may be advocating the same programs, are looked upon with hostility and suspicion. Legitimate power based on treaties and promises continues to "explain" our treatment of the American Indian. Appropriately enough, the Indians are also analyzing past treaties in order to exert pressure for more adequate treatment. A more permanent means of maintaining power is for the powerless group to internalize the differential roles. Once internalization occurs, the observable source of power can disappear (e.g., old treaties) but the powerless behavior will continue.

In the case of race relations, the paternalism of the dominant group involves a combination of all five kinds of power. However, questions are now raised concerning the relevance of certain kinds of majority-group resources to maintain power over the minority. White dominance is no longer looked upon as legitimate (3), nor is expert power (5) looked upon as the salvation that the white man can give the minorities. Referent power (4) is no longer a significant source of social control

89

since separatism, pluralism, and ethnic identity have limited the number of nonwhites who identify with and try to please the white man, as well as the number of white men who can evoke feelings of trust and faith among the nonwhites. This leaves only two resources—tangible rewards or punishments as means of power and control, and it is not surprising that current programs are based on these variables. Economic resources, jobs, and training programs provide the "reward" potential, while the growth and power of police forces illustrates the punishment dimension.

COMPETITIVE AND PRESSURE RESOURCES

A minority group also has the resources with which to maintain or possibly even better its position. Blalock refers to competitive and pressure resources, with the former term referring to those qualities, skills, and objects that dominant-group members may desire. Special skills and buying power are examples of competitive resources and are related to "reward power" in the French and Raven model. The major hypotheses concerning competitive resources is that such reward power, which may be real or potential, will quite likely lead to changes in discriminatory behavior by the dominant group much more effectively than "punishment power." Perhaps the picture of millions of ethnics possessing ample down payments, and substantial incomes would change the suburban pattern of segregated housing more quickly than any other single factor.

Pressure resources represent potential punishment power. Political action, boycotts, civil disruptions, heckling, and other forms of coercion are often used to extract certain concessions from the dominant group. Such actions may have only token results, and it is questionable how much permanent progress has been attained.

Both competitive and pressure resources have their limitations. Both depend on observability, although competitive resources are more likely to produce positive attraction and an increase in referent power. Pressure resources are especially dependent on continuous application and therefore necessitate a high degree of minority coordination, as well as the assistance of a wider coalition. Once the pressure is relaxed, there is always the risk of a quick return to the old ways.

Since minorities possess far fewer resources than the dominant group, the pressure must be carefully applied, and the target skillfully selected and defined. The targets themselves must be vulnerable to the specific sanctions. Blalock says, "For example, pressure may be applied on certain 'gatekeepers' of discrimination such as school boards, employers, merchants, realtors, or financial agencies." (Blalock, 1967: 119). Coalitions must be formed so that the limited pressure resources of minorities can be brought to bear on effective issues. The major disadvantages of pressure resources are that they may be too widely diffused and therefore prove to be highly ineffective, or they may invite the use of counter-pressures and thus boomerang on their users.

Many immigrant groups have used "competitive resources" in order to move upward in the American system. Some have used the small-business route; others have become highly educated professionals. These factors have made them more or less desirable to the American economy. However, the very success of minority groups may involve retaliatory action in the form of more discrimination. What may occur is a perpetual minority that occupies a special niche in the system but is always vulnerable to periodic discrimination.

Power and the Mobilization of Resources

A minority group's total resources must be organized to a high degree and with a certain amount of efficiency. Resources always involve proportions and fractions—only a certain proportion of eligible voters vote; only a certain proportion of a group will participate in a boycott; and only a fraction of a minority group's financial resources will be brought to bear on a significant issue. Good coordination and effective leadership on a relevant issue may raise the level of action.

The degree of mobilization is intimately related to motivation, and Atkinson's formulation (1964) is an especially relevant one. He sees motivation as a multiplicative function of three variables: (1) motives m (interval states), (2) expectancies, E (perceived probabilities of achieving objectives), and (3) incentives I (objective rewards or punishments). Each individual has a number of different motives, expectancies, and incentives. Actual behavior is the result of several components, each in the multiplicative form of $m \times E \times I$.

The model applies to minority-majority group relations. Minority mobilization will be close to zero if any of these variables is lacking. However, when minority mobilization is low, there are several alternative explanations: an acceptance of the status quo; resignation (i.e. low perceived probabilities of desired change); or a perceived nonrewarding or punishment situation. However in the multiplicative model, all factors must be present for mobilization to take place.

Power and the Discrimination Curve

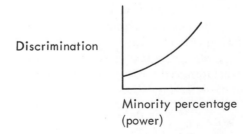

Discrimination

Minority percentage (power)

Figure 4–3.
Source: Blalock (1967: 152).

91

The overall nonlinear relationship between discrimination and power is presented in Figure 4–3. If whites are to maintain a constant power advantage over minorities, then their degree of mobilization and power must rise the same rate as that of the minorities.

The implications of this hypothesis are important in race relations. Unless minority resources are kept at approximately zero under a system such as slavery, the majority group will need to maintain its high dominance and increase its discrimination as the minority group gets larger. Therefore, there is a predicted increase in discrimination because of the power threat as the minority percentage increases. (The competition for limited resources can also exhibit the same nonlinear pattern.) The following three forms of discrimination can be hypothesized as a result of the power threat.

Three General Types of Discrimination and the Power Threat

Blalock illustrates three general areas where power threat and discrimination are closely related. These include: (1) restriction of the minority's political rights, (2) symbolic forms of segregation, and (3) a threat-oriented ideology system.

It is presumed that as the power threat increases, the dominant group will disproportionately emphasize mobilizing its resources through organizational and ideological techniques. As the issue comes to a head, the form of the struggle will become much more conscious and deliberate. If there has already been a relatively high degree of discrimination, the perceived increase in minority-group power should lead to higher stress and instability, since fewer discriminatory weapons will be left to maintain power and social control.

The most relevant examples are the discriminatory practices in the South (high proportion of visible minority) as against the practices in the North (low proportion of visible minority). As the proportions change (i.e., some Northern city proportions of minorities are changing), the discriminatory practices in the area may also change.

POLITICAL RESTRICTION

One of the most obvious steps for the dominant group to take when threatened by the growth of a subordinate group is to restrict voting and other political rights. Discrimination may take a wide variety of forms; a poll tax, literacy tests, and the like may make voting more difficult for the target minority (poor and illiterate whites may also suffer). For a period of time such strategies may suffice, but increased numbers and other pressures (including education and economic advancement) may overcome these barriers. Intimidation and other strategies may be added, **92** but in the long run, discrimination aimed at preventing or restricting the minority group in voting may prove to be ineffectual.

But there remain other levels. Ballots may be miscounted or stuffed; candidates may offer little choice; ethnic candidates (even though they may represent a numerical majority) may not find their names on the ballot or lack adequate funding; and there may be very few influential political appointments of minority individuals.

Generally, discrimination has been the highest in areas where visible minorities were perceived as a threat to dominant-group power. Many of the described practices were in the South; the people of California have often handled their fears of "yellow hordes" through effective political means. The immigrants from Asia were unable to vote or to testify against the white; and California voters have consistently passed laws discriminating against Asians, including the restriction of immigration—a power delegated only to the federal government.

The basic motive behind these behaviors is hypothesized as related to the "fears" of the dominant group that the perceived power of minority numbers may enable them to eventually take over. The power-threat variable may not necessarily be intimately linked to prejudice—basically nonprejudiced people may discriminate to restrict the power of minorities.

SYMBOLIC SEGREGATION

To maintain white dominance, a much more conscious mobilization of forces is needed in the South than in the North. There are certain organized symbolic forms of segregation present in the South—for example, the Jim Crow laws that actively separate the groups. Rest rooms, drinking fountains, and restaurants were not segregated for economic reasons but to prevent social contacts and to symbolize the line demarcating the two groups. As Blalock says, "The Jim Crow laws have, in addition, numerous psychological functions for dominant-group individuals, particularly those whose economic statuses are comparable to the minority. As Van Woodward has carefully documented, the passage of most Jim Crow legislation took place at a time when poor whites were gaining political leverage, while remaining economically little better off than the Negro. The symbolic value of these various forms of segregation should be highest for those whose status claims are otherwise negligible. Mobilization, in the form of organized violent reactions to infringement of rules, can be expected to be most immediate and pronounced among those lower-class elements of the dominant group" (Blalock, 1967: 164–65).

The symbolic functions of segregation create coalition between the white elite and the less economically advantaged white—the voting power of the white masses is channeled into mechanisms that assure them a higher social status than that of the minority.

93

Blalock mentions that these symbols of segregation and inferiority tend to increase minority-group mobilization. For example, whites sitting with blacks at a restaurant may only be a minor problem, but this action holds implications about the social structure and stratification. However, minority-group mobilization may be the most effective way to attack public segregation. In the long run, white maintenance of the symbols of segregation will probably enhance minority-group cohesion, and therefore lead to the eventual eradication of basic barriers.

THREAT-ORIENTED IDEOLOGIES

Belief systems and ideologies serve both individual and group needs. The ever-present threat of a numerically large minority raises the intensity with which certain beliefs are held. The differences between the North and the South can be used as an illustration. The Southerners feel much more threatened because of their numerical inferiority.

For example, some Southerners glorify the "Uncle Toms" and "Mammys" as nostalgic figures and have an intense dread and intensive hatred for the militant "Yankee" Negro. Such contrasting beliefs concerning the minority are rarer in the North and are disappearing even in the South (Blalock, 1967: 166).

Southerners may use a defensive ideology that can be turned on and off according to the perceived threat to white dominance. It is a mixture of nostalgia, fear of change, and a resentment of attacks on Southern mores. A similar belief system is apparently part of the South African ideology, but with the added vision of an ideal future state of complete racial separation (apartheid) in which the numerically powerful native is no longer a threat to white dominance. In the United States, such ideologies are almost nonexistent in the less-threatened North, where people often prefer simply to forget that the Negro exists.

Southern ideology also tends to exaggerate certain threatening aspects of Negro sexuality. The fear of rape and the projection of the oversexed, overaggressive, criminally inclined Negro male prompt severe social controls over the numerically powerful minority. Such fears have also spread to the North, but not to such a great extent.

There is a constant fear that change will bring with it bloodshed and violence, and memories of the past may take on a sacred quality. One way of inhibiting change is to emphasize that "there will be bloodshed." Another process is the quick jump from premise to conclusion so that "if we let them eat together, the next thing you know they'll be sleeping together." Such beliefs serve to arouse reactions to even minor changes.

Finally, there is a pronounced hostility towards potential allies of the minority. The term "nigger-lover" is a common epithet in the South just as "Jap-lover" was in the West. The dominant group is sensitive to any perceived "defections" from their ranks, which should be closed when confronted with the fearsome ideology of race.

STATUS CONSCIOUSNESS

Status plays an important part in the lives of most Americans, and the role of minority group is strongly influenced by this consideration. As Blalock says, "One of the most pervasive and subtle forms of minority discrimination is that of avoidance, particularly in situations implying social equality or involving potential intimacy" (1967: 51).

Minority groups occupy a generally low status in American society. Therefore, status-conscious whites avoid lower-status individuals, especially of color, and thus strengthen prejudicial perceptions. Even professions are stigmatized if they involve working with low-status groups, the prestige of professions often being related to their client group. For example, professions who work with the poor are generally of lower status, and even within a profession, the Beverly Hills doctor is given higher status than his colleague who works with the poor.

Although not all avoidance behavior is motivated by status considerations (e.g. there may be differences based on values, interests, personalities, or styles of life), much of the avoidance of minorities is. The mixture of ethnicity and status is often difficult to unravel—the junior executive avoids all close contact with the janitor both because the janitor is of low status and because he is black.

Equal-status contact between dominant- and subordinate-group members can be threatening and uncomfortable for both sides. The white individual may be irritated at the familiarity of the "uppity" minority-group member, and the ethnic individual may be sensitive to any sign of condescension from his white peer. Therefore, ritualistic, or "gaming" behaviors are often used to mask the conflict.

Status in the past has often resulted in predictable reciprocal behavior. Whereas dominant-group styles encouraged the avoidance of lower-status ethnic groups, lower-status groups prided themselves on their friendships with dominant-group members. Ethnic groups could gauge the rise in their status by the number of whites who could be expected to attend a social gathering. However, the things that go to make up status and "fashionability," the styles and the people associated with them, can shift dramatically as they have in the past. Therefore, if interracial gatherings become fashionable, the status-oriented individual may go out of his way to attend them.

Ethnicity, social position, and status provide some interesting topics for research. For example, for a white person, does associating with an Asian, a Chicano, or a black provide more status? What if the Asian were a gardener, the Chicano a lawyer, and the black a doctor? **95**

Blalock (1967: 67–69) makes several propositions concerning status loss and various situational factors.

1. The greater the status gap between two individuals involved in a highly visible equal-status contact, the greater the expected status loss to the individual having the higher status.

2. The lower the average status of the minority group, the greater the status loss to dominant-group members engaging in visible equal-status contacts with the minority.

3. The more visible an equal-status contact situation is to other members of the dominant group, the greater the status loss to the dominant-group individual having such contacts with the minority.

4. In situations where there is a high degree of anonymity, equal-status contacts with highly visible minorities (e.g., racial minorities) will bring about a greater loss in status than will contacts with less-visible minorities (e.g., ethnic or religious minorities) having the same average status.

5. The greater the degree to which social contacts within the community affect one's overall status or chances for upward mobility, the greater the status loss to dominant-group members engaging in equal-status contacts with low-status minorities.

6. The more "liberal" the norms of one's occupation in permitting equal-status contacts with minorities, the less the status loss resulting from such contacts. The college professor may be rewarded for his interracial contacts, whereas the president of the chamber of commerce may find such "crossing" more difficult.

7. The greater the general prejudice level within a community, the greater the status loss resulting from equal-status contacts. Beyond a certain point, the status loss may be so great that virtually no contact takes place, regardless of status consciousness.

8. The larger and more heterogeneous the community, the less important are one's social contacts as determinants of overall status, and the more important are such impersonal factors as income, occupation, and education.

Where there is a strong linkage between prejudice and discrimination—such as in race and color—change may be much more difficult than when discrimination is linked to other conditions, provided that those conditions are changeable. However, where there is such a linkage, a direct attack may be the most appropriate, since the attitude and the behavior are so intimately linked.

Other areas, such as power threats and housing segregation, call for different tactics. One major problem has been the fleeing of the whites out of an area as nonwhites move in so that housing segregation continues. How can one set up a system whereby such movement does not constantly occur? If a minority can provide competitive resources to demonstrate that it is an asset rather than a liability, such fleeing might be discouraged. Under present conditions, such an apeal might be disastrous. By providing minorities with more alternatives (i.e., more spendable income and better housing) some of the pressure could be eased; conversely by making white alternatives (i.e., suburban living) more available to the nonwhite, the motive for fleeing might also be controlled.

In other areas, such as the threat of numbers and status concerns, discrimination is less direct, therefore the focus should be on other levels. Equalizing the status differential will lessen discriminatory behavior; demonstrating that a black mayor really is as effective (or ineffective) as a white mayor may change the climate of political restrictions.

Prejudice, discrimination, and segregation isolates a minority group and puts it in a disadvantaged position in the social system. In a competitive society, poor housing, poor education, and legal restrictions place additional barriers on groups who often begin their struggle from an already handicapped position.

BIBLIOGRAPHY

ATKINSON, JOHN W. (1964). *An Introduction to Motivation.* New York: Van Nostrand Reinhold.

BIERSTEDT, ROBERT (1950). "An Analysis of Social Power." *American Sociological Review,* 15: 730–38.

BLALOCK, HUBERT M. (1967). *Toward a Theory of Minority Group Relations.* New York: John Wiley & Sons, Inc.

BOGARDUS, E. S. (1930). "A Race Relations Cycle." *American Journal of Sociology,* 35 (4): 612–17.

DANIELS, ROGER and HARRY H. L. KITANO (1970). *American Racism.* Englewood Cliffs, N.J.: Prentice-Hall, Inc.

FRENCH, JOHN R. and BERTRAM RAVEN (1959). "The Bases of Social Power." In Cartwright, ed., *Studies in Social Power.* Ann Arbor: University of Michigan Press. Chapter 9.

FROMM, ERICH (1947). *Man for Himself.* New York: Holt, Rinehart and Winston, Inc.

KATZ, D. and K. BRABEY (1933). "Racial Stereotypes in One Hundred College Students." *Journal of Abnormal Social Psychology,* 28: 280–90.

PETTIGREW, THOMAS (1971). *Racially Separate or Together.* New York: McGraw-Hill Book Company.

SCHERMERHORN, R. A. (1970). *Comparative Ethnic Relations.* New York: Random House, Inc.

TEDESCHI, JAMES T., THOMAS V. BONOMA, BARRY R. SCHLENKER, and SVENN LINDSKOLD (1970). "Power, Influence, and Behavioral Compliance." *Law and Society Review,* 4 (4): 521–44.

UNITED STATES DEPARTMENT OF LABOR, Bureau of Labor Statistics (1966). *The Negro in the United States: Their Economic and Social Situation.* Bulletin 1511, Table A-2.

CONSEQUENCES OF PREJUDICE, DISCRIMINATION, AND SEGREGATION 5

Perhaps the most value-laden topic in ethnic relations concerns minority-group responses to prejudice, discrimination, and segregation. Terms such as "good," "healthy," "dysfunctional," "problem," and "conflict" are widely used to describe the interaction between groups. Therefore it is extremely important to identify the users of these terms and why they perceive the interaction in this fashion.

One of the more dramatic examples of the adaptability of human beings to given conditions and situations has been the past accommodation of many subordinate groups to their less-than-equal status with minimal signs of overt conflict. Racially oppressed groups, whether in the United States or in other parts of the world, have seldom challenged the inequities. As Berry states:

> It is an amazing fact . . . that some human beings have an infinite capacity to endure injustice without retaliation, and apparently without resentment against their oppressors. Instances . . . are numerous, and they come from every part of the world where one group dominates another. Militant leaders of protest movements have been driven to despair by the apathy. . . . Members of dominant groups have often commented on the cheerfulness and loyalty . . . among those who would seem to have no reason for such sentiments (1958: 479).

The ability of the oppressed to mask their resentment and hostility, and the inability of the majority to perceive beyond their stereotypes have combined to prolong some of the more common sayings of the past such as "Our Negroes are always happy"; "The Japanese are content behind barbed wire"; "Indians enjoy reservation life"; and "The Chinese like it in Chinatown."

This chapter will review some of the consequences of our racial stratification system and focus on the adaptation of the minorities to their subordinate position in society.

CONFLICT

One important question concerning intergroup relations concerns conflict. Does conflict always follow the meeting of diverse groups? There does appear to be some type of conflict in almost all interethnic contacts, as Berry writes:

> . . . even before the dawn of history, primitive bands were moving over the face of the earth, encountering strange peoples, and trespassing upon their lands. Archaeologists suspect that these prehistoric contacts resulted in wars and bloodshed, and in the destruction and displacement of one group by another. Historic evidence supports such guesses, and indicates that conflict of some sort is a common occurrence when unlike peoples meet (1958: 411).

But as we have indicated in Chapter Two, there are a variety of outcomes when different people meet. A "conflict-free" adaptation seems to be difficult to achieve, although not always, as the following example shows.

The Tungus and the Cossacks

Lindgren (1938) published a report in 1932 about two racially and culturally different groups, the Tungus and the Cossacks, who resided as neighbors without any apparent conflict. The Tungus were Mongolian nomads who lived off the reindeer and hunting for their sustenance. The Cossacks were Caucasoid descendants of the Russians who invaded Asia at an earlier time. They were Christian village-dwellers who relied primarily on agriculture and stock-raising for their livelihood. Hypothesized reasons for the lack of apparent conflict between these groups included the following:

1. The numbers of both groups were small (less than 1,000), and of approximately equal size.
2. There was little competition for land and resources. There was ample

100

room for both groups to practice their own different ways of making a living.

3. The outside influences were of a nature that drew the groups together. For example, in 1908, the Chinese government imposed taxes upon the fur trade of the Cossacks, which affected the Tungus too. Therefore, both groups viewed themselves as being oppressed by an outside force.

4. The two cultures established a supplementary and complementary relationship, rather than one based on antagonism and competition.

5. Neither group thought itself racially superior. They respected each other's attitudes, values, and cultural practices such as marriage, use of land and property.

If these factors are the key to peaceful intergroup neighborliness, this kind of harmony will be difficult to duplicate in today's world. Size has become virtually uncontrollable, and numerical equality is almost never a reality; perhaps even more important, power relationships between groups are usually unbalanced. Technology, specialization, and urbanization have created increased competition for space, housing, employment, and shrinking resources; and our economic system values competition over cooperation. Race and color are divisive symbols, and the feeling of white superiority and the development of a stratification system built upon color has limited any dreams of racial equality and harmony.

There is a great need for systematic research to explore those variables that affect race relationships. For example, it is possible to predict the consequences of change by using the Tungus and Cossacks as a model. What would be the effect of competition for scarcer resources? How would urbanization and a change in the economic system change race relations? Would a change in numbers or the balance lead to increased conflict? What would happen if one group began to feel superior? Since the social scientist cannot bring large groups into a laboratory to test his hypotheses, he must rely on field studies and sophisticated observations for his information.

Also, any analysis of intergroup relations can be misleading if the research covers only a narrow period of time. Even the most conflicting relationships, whether in marriage, international relations, or interracial contacts, will have periods of relative tranquility. Therefore the assumption that the Tungus and Cossacks are a "conflict-free" example may be erroneous. Finally, some forms of conflict are difficult to assess because they are not obvious. Groups may internalize conflict and give only intangible evidence of it.

Conflict as a Value Question?

There is another subtle factor concerning conflict and the values of the researcher. Horton (1971) refers to the biases between "order" and

101

"conflict" theorists and makes the point that many sociologists are apparently unaware of their own values. For example, Freudian terminology arises from an upper bourgeois patriarchal group with a strong sexual and individualistic orientation; American sociologists' analyses of social problems before 1940 reflect a small, rural town bias; and much current contemporary analysis reflects the researchers' experiences under bureaucratic and administrative organizations.

The area of race relations is particularly sensitive to the values of the researcher. Conflict theory emphasizes that "social problems and social change arise from the exploitive and alienating practices of dominant groups; they are responses to the discrepancy between what is and what is in the process of becoming. Social problems, therefore, reflect not the administrative problems of the social system, nor the failure of individuals to perform their system roles as in the order explanation, but the adaptive failure of society to meet changing individual needs" (Horton, 1971: 20).

Order theories imply consensus and use terms like "adjustment," "conformity," and "deviation." "The standards for defining health are the legitimate values of the social system and its requisites for goal attainment and maintenance. Deviation is the opposite of social conformity and means the failure of individuals to perform their legitimate social roles; deviants are out of adjustment" (Horton, 1971: 19).

Explanation of ethnic problems invariably involve the writer's values, ideology, and perspectives. "Terms like 'moral dilemma,' 'pluralism,' 'assimilation,' and 'integration' describe motives for desirable action: they are definitions placed on human action, not the action independent of social values" (Horton, 1971: 31). The basic error is not that the scientist thinks in these terms, but that he is not aware of it. The comfort of "objectivity" is an untenable myth. Therefore, the idea of a "conflict-free" adaptation between ethnic groups may in reality only reflect the values of the researcher himself, rather than any "outside" phenomenon.

Since there are two viewpoints from which to assess conflict, it is interesting to note which position is chosen. Those who choose the majority perspective often see minority groups as deviant, disorganized, in high conflict, and as examples of social problem behavior. Others, writing from a minority perspective, see the conflict as noble, militant, and having high moral justification.

ADAPTIVE RESPONSES

Simpson and Yinger (1965) suggest three basic responses to conflict: acceptance, aggression, and avoidance. These responses are related to the types of social interaction employed in sociological analysis: association (acceptance), dissociation (aggression), and the absence of communication (avoidance).

Merton (1957) suggested that there is a relationship between societal structures and individual responses. Merton's theory was designed to discover how some "social structures exert a definite pressure upon certain persons in the society to engage in nonconforming rather than conforming conduct" (Merton, 1957: 132). Merton's theory consists of several elements, including culturally defined goals, acceptable modes of reaching those goals, anomie, and types of adaptation. It attempts to demonstrate the importance of sociological variables in creating deviant behavior.

For example, success (the goal) in American terms may mean acquiring material wealth. If the pressures towards this goal are exceptionally strong, then considerations of how to attain the goal (the means) may become less important. When the technically most effective procedure takes precedence over culturally approved values or institutionally prescribed conduct, the society becomes unstable, or to use Durkheim's term, it is in a state of "anomie" or normlessness.

Examples are numerous. In competitive athletics the strain towards winning might include deliberate attempts to injure a "star" opponent or subsidizing and recruiting athletes by bending rules and redefining the game so that sheer winning, no matter what the costs, becomes more important than participation. The athletes who show faint twinges of conscience and protest their inocence when caught in illegal acts demonstrate that they are familiar with the institutional rules of the game but have deliberately ignored them in order to win.

Although Merton's model applied to deviant behavior, many of his insights are appropriate for ethnic groups. Minorities strive for the same success goals as other groups in American society, but the barriers of racism limit their access by legitimate means. The resultant strain may lead to high levels of anomic behavior, including retreatism, rebellion, and overconformity.

Class and ethnic stratification systems are not the critical factors in creating strain; rather, strain results more from the defeat and disappointment of heightened expectations. Presumably under slavery where an individual did not expect to become "successful" in general societal terms, there was less stress than under the current conditions, which create an obvious incongruence.

Minorities react to prejudice and discrimination through acceptance, aggression, and avoidance. No ethnic group has ever chosen and retained any of these patterns exclusively, yet certain adaptive styles are associated with specific ethnic groups. However, ethnic-group adaptation is a *response* to prejudice, discrimination, and segregation; and therefore it is the dependent, rather than the independent variable of the series.

Perhaps the most common adaptive pattern of ethnic minorities has been their seeming acceptance of subordinate status. The power relationships may leave them almost no alternative; and even if many minorities may not really believe in the superiority of the white man, most often they act as if they do.

It is necessary to hypothesize several motivations to explain this pattern. Perhaps the most important is the desire to be like the majority group; conformity to dominant-group role prescriptions is a primary goal. Another important factor is that most minorities prefer the "means" of the American system—law and order, conformity, conflict-free adaptation, and a "don't rock the boat" attitude; no matter what the provocation, an ethnic individual's response is primarily acceptance. It would be considered poor form to do otherwise.

Certain subcultural values that lead to acceptance are another factor. The "fate orientation," expressed by the Japanese as *shikataganai* ("it can't be helped") or by Latin Americans as *que sera, sera* ("what will be, will be"), encourages this type of adjustment. There is also the belief in some cultures that hardship and suffering are important ingredients in character-building; and the stoic, accepting response is a test of one's nature.

Forms of acceptance vary; ritualistic behavior, superpatriotism, and the internalization of stress are three of them.

RITUALISTIC ADAPTATION

Ritualistic adaptation involves scaling down or abandoning high cultural goals and retaining the moralistic prescriptions of the society. Therefore, a person in this situation lowers his level of aspiration—"he is playing safe," "he's not sticking his neck out," and "he's not shooting for the stars." He will conform to the mandates of the larger society and will socialize his children accordingly. Merton hypothesizes that ritualism may be most appropriate for the lower middle class; the person who always goes by the rules and the bureaucratic mind are examples of ritualistic adaptation. It also appears as one of the dominant adaptations for ethnic minorities.

By ritualism, minority groups retain a faith that some of the means and norms in the system will guarantee their acceptability. For example, many ethnics vote faithfully with the expectation that their participation in this procedure will be meaningful. Voting, however, does not basically change the system, unless the minority has achieved power through political and organizational maneuvers. Then, of course, it is no longer a minority in a political sense.

The ballot has been used by the majority group as a tool for discrimination. Californians of previous eras voted to restrict the im- **104** migration of Chinese; voted alien land laws to deny the ownership of land to the Japanese, and present day referendums, often deceptively worded, attempt to foster through the ballot, racist practices. The problem of the popular ballot is that it is a two-edged sword, and if one group has numerical superiority, their power can be used to strengthen their position at the expense of the minority.

SUPERPATRIOTISM

Another means of adapting to the problems of isolation from a system is to overidentify with it. The rituals of belonging—learning the anthems and slogans, copying the slang, adopting the dress and the styles—play an important part in the acculturation of nonwhite groups.

The dynamics of ritualism often involve incongruous actions. For example, many Japanese who were placed in the wartime "relocation" centers maintained a strict loyalty to the United States. The Pledge of Allegiance, "The Star-Spangled Banner," and the American flag became extremely important to them and many purchased war bonds and donated quantities of blood. Others even volunteered for the army and eventually gave their lives for "democracy" while their parents, brothers, and sisters were still behind barbed wire. They practiced these rituals believing that these actions would prove to the larger world that they too were Americans.

INTERNALIZATION OF STRESS

Another form of acceptance is the internalization of stress. To grit one's teeth and accept reality is considered to be mature in some cultures. From a psychoanalytic perspective, the internalization and repression may have dysfunctional effects upon the individual. For example, in the Japanese population, there is a high incidence of internal disorders such as stomach ulcers and bowel problems. (My father used to relate how when walking in San Francisco, he would be deliberately shoved off the sidewalk by white bullies. Rather than venting his anger, he would internalize his feelings through gritting his teeth and using the Japanese concept of "ga-man"—accepting whatever one is dealt. It was considered more mature to draw in one's breath and not cry, complain, or strike back.)

The major decisions on acceptance lie with the majority—they can prescribe the conditions by which ethnic members have to live and to react, and they can make those stringent and arbitrary conditions that strain the level of acceptance to the breaking point. History shows how difficult it is for groups in command to understand that their use of power is the most important factor in the survival of their system. The old adage tying power and corruption remains an insightful one.

Aggression generally involves some kind of retaliation. Aggression takes many forms—it may be a direct retaliation to the dominant group; it may mean striking out at more vulnerable groups, or it may be masked so as to be barely detectable.

At an earlier time, the lack of overt aggression was often taken as a sign of contentment, especially among slaves. However, more recent interpretations of slave adjustment have revealed the indirect and hidden ways in which less powerful groups often show their hostility and resentment against their plight. For example, Powdermaker (1943) coins the term "aggressive meekness" to illustrate a style of adapation that masks the true thoughts and feelings of slaves in their overtly meek and submissive public role.

Aggression can be classified into four kinds: direct, indirect, displaced, and a change of goals.

Direct Aggression

Direct aggression grows out of acute despair. The power arrangements are such that most ethnics see little hope of gaining much through this approach. The resources of the dominant group are truly impressive, especially when compared to those of the minorities. Money, numbers, firepower, legal justification, and institutional resources are so clearly under the control of the majority that only under unusual circumstances will minorities direct their aggression clearly at the dominators.

INSURRECTIONS

An insurrection involves the use of armed force against the established order. The main differences among insurrections, rebellions, and revolutions are those of purpose, size, and scope.

Racial insurrections have been frequent in the history in the United States. Contrary to some interpretations of American history that emphasize the contentment of the slaves, there were constant plots, which though never seriously threatening the institution of slavery, caused much concern to the white population (Aptheker, 1943; Carroll, 1938; Franklin, 1948).

DENMARK VESEY

Denmark Vesey purchased his freedom in 1800. He established himself as a carpenter in Charleston, South Carolina, and for twenty years lived as a respectable "free Negro" and enjoyed a relatively comfortable existence. He was, however, a sensitive person, and he was unhappy over his own freedom and success while others of his race were in slavery. He therefore set about to plot a revolt. His plans were carefully laid, and his associates were chosen with utmost scrutiny. Over a period of years they collected **106** their weapons—daggers, bayonets, and pike heads. The second Sunday in July, 1822, was set as the date for the revolt. The whites, however, were informed, and Vesey hastily moved the date ahead one month. His assistants, scattered as they were for miles around Charleston, did not all get the word, and the insurrection was readily quashed. Estimates of the number of Negroes involved in the plot ran as high as 9,000. About 139 were arrested, 47 of whom were condemned. Four white men were imprisoned and fined for implication in the plot and for encouraging the Negroes (Berry, 1958: 133).

NAT TURNER

Nat Turner was a slave who belonged to a Virginia planter, Joseph Travis. He was a mystic who felt a divine call to free his people. The solar eclipse of February, 1831, convinced him that the time had come for him to deliver the Negroes from bondage. The date was to be the Fourth of July; but Turner became ill, and he postponed the date until he should see another divine sign. On August 13, 1831, it seemed to him that the sun turned "a peculiar greenish blue," and he therefore chose August 21 as the date for the revolt. He and his followers began by killing their master and his family, and then roamed the countryside destroying other whites. Within twenty-four hours a total of sixty whites had been killed. State and federal troops were called, and the Negroes were speedily overwhelmed. More than a hundred slaves were killed in the encounter, and thirteen slaves and three free Negroes were immediately hanged. Turner himself was captured two months later and was promptly executed (Berry, 1958: 133).

Novelist William Styron's fictionalized account of Nat Turner's rebellion was an immediate success; it was reviewed in major publications and was a Book-of-the-Month-Club selection. However, the most dramatic adverse reaction came from members of the black intellectual community; most felt that Styron's Nat Turner bore little resemblance to the real man and instead saw a racist caricature of a black slave, motivated by lust for white women.

As Hamilton says:

We will not permit Styron's "meditation" to leave unchallenged an image of Nat Turner as a fanatical black man who dreams of going to bed with white women, who holds nothing but contempt for his fellow blacks, and who understands, somewhat, the basic human desire to be free but still believes in the basic humanity of some slaveholders.

We will not permit Styron to picture unchallenged Nat Turner as a leader who did not understand that the military defeat should not be confused with the ideological victory: i.e., a blow for freedom. The rebellion of 1831, led by Nat Turner, is important today for blacks to understand and for whites to accept precisely because its lesson is that there will be leaders who *will* rise up—against all odds—to strike blows for freedom against an oppressive, inhumane system. And there can be no refuge in the thought that Turner felt himself divinely inspired or waited for signs from heaven, etc. The important thing is that the desire for human freedom resides in the black breast as well as in any other. No

107

amount of explicating about the harshness of slavery or the gentleness of slavery, about the docility of the masses of slaves, etc. can keep that desire from exploding. Man—black or white or yellow or red—moves to maximize his freedom: THAT is the lesson of Nat Turner that Styron did not deal with (Hamilton, 1968: 74).

RACE RIOTS

Rioting is as old as history. It is a temporary outbreak, mostly spontaneous, of mass disorder. Racial antagonisms are not necessarily the sole occasions for riots. Rioting, often involving more than one side, is more of an urban phenomenon and is different from insurrections, rebellions, or revolutions in that there is no overt intention of overthrowing the existing political order.

The history of the United States is dotted with race riots. In 1837, over 15,000 Bostonians participated in an Irish riot; black-white riots were constant from three decades before the Civil War to the present. Longres, Roberts, and Shinn (1966) analyze race riots in the twentieth century and include some of the more prominent: Springfield, Illinois, 1908; East St. Louis, 1917; Washington, D.C., 1919; Chicago, 1919; Los Angeles, 1943; Detroit, 1943; Harlem, 1943; New York, 1964; Rochester, 1964; and Los Angeles, 1965. One interesting pattern emerged—the earlier riots were generally characterized by the whites being the aggressors with reversal of roles over time. However, most of the injured and arrested were black.

WATTS (LOS ANGELES, 1965)

The Watts riots of August 11–17, 1965, probably mark a watershed in recent race relations. As Daniels and Kitano say:

Watts was not the first riot—there had been serious disturbances in seven Eastern cities the summer before—but it was the first that appeared to have the character of a rebellion. Perhaps the most surprising thing about it was that it happened in Los Angeles, which, only the year previous, had been ranked by the National Urban League as most favorable to Negroes of sixty-eight American cities examined. Although the riots have been widely studied, there is no consensus among its students, but the basic facts are reasonably clear.

On the evening of August 11, 1965, the Negro ghetto of Los Angeles erupted into a flurry of outbreaks of mob violence, at first centered near (but not in) a small area known as Watts; it soon spread over much of the vast ghetto. It was set off by a seemingly routine arrest of a drunken driver; it produced 144 hours of anarchic looting, arson, assault, and homicide. This happened in an area that supposedly had exemplary race relations. More than half the Negro population of the state lived in Los Angeles County (461,000 as enumerated by the 1960 Census), most of them in the overcrowded South Los Angeles ghetto that sprawled over some fifty square miles. The housing there was (and remains) substandard. It consists of one- and two-story single and multifamily structures, most of which have at least the hint of a lawn. About half were built before World War II, which is very old for Los Angeles housing. Many of these units, however, are sound and well maintained. These atypical ghetto conditions made it possible for civic leaders (including some Negro leaders) to insist that the city had no real race-relations problem, a kind of dream state peculiarly appropriate to a region that boasts Hollywood and Disneyland. Similar wishful thinking prevailed in the same quarters during much of the Great Depression, when local leaders tried to maintain that Los Angeles was the economic "white spot" of the nation. Reality finally punctured both illusions; both however, like most illusions, had some basis in reality. As bad as conditions were for the white emigrés of the 1930s—think of Steinbeck's Joads—and are for the Negro newcomers now, they are distinctly better than the conditions they left behind. But in all too many instances these conditions have not lived up to the expectations of the new arrivals, and it is these partially thwarted expectations that have made California, and other Northern and Western "promised lands," sociological and political powder kegs, with a markedly lower flash point than the objective conditions within them might suggest.

If the Watts riots seem similar to earlier ethnic violence, that similarity is largely superficial. The most obvious difference is that the earlier violence had been that of a majority directed against a particular minority. The Watts riots (and similar events in other cities) saw a minority—really a small minority within a minority—lash out blindly against the society which, it seemed to them, was oppressing them intolerably. (Historically it would probably be more accurate to suggest that society was not easing its restrictions as fast as expectations were rising.) Another difference is that these riots were largely directed against property, and quite often Negro-owned and occupied property. The aggressors were almost all Negroes, and so, ironically, were most of the victims.

The ingredients for the Watts and other riots—apart from mimesis after Watts—were simple: an alienated group squeezed into a small ghetto. Within that group there are growing numbers (almost all the estimates are too small) of undereducated, underskilled, and therefore unemployed youths in a nation with the greatest educational system in the world. In Los Angeles the ghetto is not an area of abject poverty—about 60 percent of the population get some kind of welfare, and California standards are relatively high—but of apathy, resentment, and hopelessness. These ingredients were detonated, in Los Angeles, by a casual incident which resulted in an opportunity for some to lash back at society in general and the police in particular, and gave many, many more a chance for vicarious pleasure in watching them do it.

That this widespread alienation exists so noticeably at a time when Negroes seem to be making such great strides, has puzzled and perplexed many, but it should be quite clear that although the social revolution that John Kenneth Galbraith has dubbed "affluence" has affected the American Negro, North and South, not nearly enough of it has trickled down. But within the same society that sees many Negroes achieving upward social mobility and a few grasping political and economic power, there are within most Negro communities large numbers of socially alienated young men and women, children of the welfare state at its worst, who have neither known extreme economic deprivation nor ever experience a "normal" family life. They have not even been able to indulge in the humblest aspect of the American Dream, *the reasonable expectation that their children would have a chance to better themselves*. It was these people who made and enjoyed the Los Angeles riots, and the many similar incidents that have followed (Daniels and Kitano, 1970: 82–84).

109

Strikes and boycotts are more often associated with economic conflict and labor disputes rather than racial interaction. Nevertheless, these forms have also been used and vary in their effectiveness.

One of the most effective boycotts in recent history was that involving Martin Luther King and the Montgomery, Alabama, bus system. The incident started on December 1, 1965, when a Negro seamstress, Mrs. Rosa Parks, refused to give up her seat and move to the back of the bus when ordered to do so by the bus driver. By the time the Negroes called off the boycott approximately one year later, Negro patronage of the bus lines had dropped as much as 90 percent; Dr. King was found guilty of an illegal boycott, and was fined and sentenced to jail. The case was moved up to the Supreme Court. On November 13, 1966, the United States Supreme Court declared that the Alabama law requiring the segregation of buses was unconstitutional.

Boycotts and strikes have been used on both sides and in a variety of different ways. Early Californians were urged to boycott "Jap" businesses; often Chinese and Japanese laborers were used as strike breakers, and the Japanese were known to band together to boycott certain white establishments who were known to be antioriental.

AIR HIGHJACKING

A newer form of aggression has been the threat to blow up or to kidnap airplanes in order to effect change. It is based on the old principle of ransom and blackmail, whereby one group attempts to extract concessions from another group by holding something of value.

The motivations for highjacking vary—personal profit, the release of political prisoners, the dramatization of the plight of a pariah group, or a change in a dominant group's policy. The tactics are usually a desperate attempt by a powerless group to equalize the power differential, if only temporarily, and its effectiveness to bring about long-term change is open to question. However, the precautions instituted by air lines as a response to the threat of bombing and highjacking indicate the vulnerability of more powerful groups to such acts.

Indirect Aggression

A more typical method of handling aggressive feelings is through indirect actions. Much indirect aggression must be inferred and therefore suffers the limitations of interpretation. Nevertheless, it is an important adaptation since it may invite less retaliation than a direct act.

FINE ARTS AND LITERATURE

Writers, poets, painters, musicians, and actors often deal with oppression and interracial relationships in their unique fashion. Black **110** writers such as Richard Wright, LeRoi Jones, and James Baldwin were able to convey their message of conflict and suffering to much larger audiences. As Berry says:

> This practice of utilizing the fine arts as weapons of protest is not, of course, limited to the American Negro. Perhaps all oppressed peoples do so, as well as the dominant races who employ their arts in supporting the status quo. Even the preliterate peoples of the earth have sought, through their arts, to deliver a blow to those who dominated and exploited them (1958: 41).

STAGES IN ETHNIC HUMOR

Ethnic humor has been another important way of dealing with conflict. The "put on," the "bad mouth," and ethnic jokes are all attempts to find a more socially acceptable way of dealing with basic conflict and aggression. The number of jokes about the Jews, Negroes, Italians, Irish, Chinese, Japanese, Poles, and Mexicans and their continued popularity can be viewed as symptomatic of the use of "humor" to handle aggression.

There is a hypothesized pattern to ethnic humor that is related to the cohesion, identity, and perceived acceptance of a group. The pattern takes two different forms.

The first form deals with humor directed against the "oppressor." The first stage is so disguised that only in-group members perceive the butt of the jokes. As the group feels more comfortable, the humor becomes much more overt—the disguise is replaced by euphemisms, then eventually by direct references. The final stage occurs when the humor is not limited to ethnic-group audiences but is shared with the oppressor.

The second form deals with humor by the ethnic group about itself. The first stage is private and confined to the membership; this is followed by a more public display, but still within a localized group. As the group gains acceptance, a fellow ethnic member may feel comfortable enough to carry the humor outside the group. The final stage in this pattern is when the ethnic group is able to tolerate a nonethnic member telling ethnic jokes.

This series may help to explain the sensitivities of various ethnic groups to jokes and stereotypes—not all groups are at the same stage, and what is considered appropriate for one group may be offensive to another.

Passive Resistance

Another means of forestalling overt conflict is passive resistance. The origins of passive resistance are probably as old as man himself, and phrases such as "turn the other cheek" or Martin Luther King's exhortation to his followers, "Face violence if necessary, but refuse to return violence" indicate its philosophical underpinnings.

The name most intimately linked to passive resistance is Mohandas K. Gandhi, and more recent followers such as Reverend King acknowledge Gandhi's influence. There is a strong oriental aspect to passive resistance as well as elements of stoicism and internalization, rather than direct action in the face of obstacles.

JOB SLOWDOWNS, TURNOVER, INEFFICIENCY, TARDINESS

Simpson and Yinger (1965) mention several variations of aggression that are forms of passive resistance. One is the job slowdown whereby ethnic members may work extremely slowly; another is "carelessness" whereby objects are accidentally dropped and broken. Irresponsibility, shoddy work, and inefficiency are also ways in which minorities can react against the dominant system. Dominant group reactions provide an interesting commentary on the dominant group's perceptions. Instead of linking some of these actions to aggression, there is a tendency to characterize and stereotype the minority culture as careless, or sloppy or accident prone. Some even advance a genetic inferiority explanation.

Another technique of indirect aggression is high labor turnover, tardiness, and unreliability. Suddenly walking off a job, or coming in late and then leaving early, fall into this category. A practice that makes "bookers" and coordinators of programs uncontrollably angry is when ethnics agree to participate in a program, then cancel at the last minute, or do not show up at all; or if he does show up, he may make a number of outrageous demands as the price of his participation.

ROLE CHANGES

Another indirect means of handling aggression is to either withdraw or to change the forms of racial roles. For example, an ethnic individual may suddenly change his deferential pattern in a social situation and ask to be served first, or he may publically challenge the opinions of majority-group members at unusual times. Or he may exaggerate his ethnic role in a manner calculated to embarrass a majority-group member. Cohen (1958) provides an example of how a form of military etiquette, the hand salute, can mask aggressive feelings. By overconforming one can strain the system; ten enlisted men saluting separately can force ten response salutes from a single passing officer.

Behavioral patterns at variance with expected roles can also be a means of indirect aggression. The stereotype of the welfare mother with a Cadillac and a color TV (if there are such people) is an example of an aggressive response through behavior that is not normally expected of individuals in this category. The outraged reactions of society to this stereotype indicates the reciprocal feelings held by many against those who do not follow prescribed norms for "poor" people.

112

Some ethnic groups handle aggression through high achievement and competitive excellence. Instead of carelessness, indifference, and inefficiency, they may handle their aggression by sublimating their drives.

DISPLACED AGGRESSION

The displacement of aggression is similar to scapegoating (see Chapter 4). Displacement may occur within a group, making fellow ethnic members targets for much hostility and aggresion. Often without realizing that discrimination, segregation, and prejudice are the major problems, minorities consider each other to be the "cause" of their frustrations. Other minorities can also be targets of displaced aggression, such as in squabbles over the funding of poverty programs.

CHANGE OF GOALS

Perhaps the most revolutionary and rebellious action of the ethnic minorities has been to change their goals. The narrow goal of "being white" and its variations including integration (conforming to white standards) no longer have the almost universal support that they once had. The unrealistic goal of becoming white, with its subsequent strains and anomie, has been replaced by newer goals. Many of these goals are still not clearly articulated, but major variations include pluralism and separatism.

Much of the action has come in the form of organized protests. There has developed a wide variety of social movements—from highly emotional, religious, and nationalistic movements to those that use sophisticated legal, political, and economic weapons. In the Negro group alone are such diverse groups as the NAACP, the Urban League, CORE, the Black Panthers, and the Black Muslims. Some movements are dedicated to changing the goals, and others strive to open the American system to include more people of color; but they all arose from the stresses caused by the barriers that limit the participation of ethnics in American democracy.

Avoidance

Because of the difficulty in abolishing racial barriers as well as the penalties of active aggression, many ethnics adapt by avoiding the problem altogether. Avoidance covers two broad types of adaptation: withdrawing from most forms of interracial contact; and assimilating, denying, or retreating from the intolerable situation.

For example, ethnics may avoid situations where they may face prejudice in housing by not applying in certain areas; they may walk across the street rather than face even the simplest communication with someone from the majority group. They may use certain lotions or cosmetics that enable them to "pass"; or they resort to drugs or withdraw into mental illness.

According to Simpson and Yinger (1965: 159), the most complete form of avoidance is withdrawing entirely from the minority group. "Passing," however is quite difficult for most ethnics because of the color line. By changing their names and accents, and altering their physiological features, some ethnics hope to pass into the larger community. Although there is always the fear of discovery, this is perhaps the most decisive way to avoid the penalties of ethnic status.

Some groups try to "seal off" contact. Sealing off can occur on different levels—the upper class of an ethnic group might voluntarily seclude itself from both lower-class members of their own ethnic group and members of the dominant group; other ethnic classes might form purposely segregated communities to limit contact with the majority. However, this type of adaptation is often insufficient since members remain primarily dependent on the majority community for economic and other needs. Finally, some try to insulate themselves by remaining constantly mobile. This moving around may help limit interaction in some ways, but in the long run, it leads to greater exposure and higher intergroup contact.

RETREATISM AND WITHDRAWAL

Retreatism involves the rejection of the cultural goals and the institutional means. People who retreat have "dropped out"; they may be in the society but are not part of it. They adapt to the problem through defeatism and resignation. Mental patients, pariahs, outcasts, vagabonds, tramps, chronic alcoholics, drug addicts, and hippies are examples of individuals and groups who have adopted a retreatist posture, because of their continued failure to reach a goal by legitimate means or by illegitimate means, due to internalized and societal prohibitions. It is most often a private, rather than a group adaptation.

A large percentage of all school drop-outs, mental patients, and drug addicts are ethnic children. Drug-taking, of course, is one of the oldest ways to "escape from reality" and avoid conflict. But the ultimate retreat is mental illness—the flight into a world of dreams and fantasy. Schizophrenia and suicide represent the most extreme examples of avoidance.

Not all forms of adaptation and aggression discussed in this chapter are a direct result of prejudice, discrimination, and segregation. Hostility, aggressiveness, and conflict are present wherever there is human interaction; even without racism, these behaviors would continue to exist. However, the range of coping behaviors used by individuals and groups is very wide; racism exacts a greater toll in ruined lives and potentials than is realized by those who consider it only morally unjustified or economically expensive.

APTHEKER, HERBERT (1943). *American Negro Slave Revolts*. New York: Columbia University Press.

ATKINSON, J. W. (1964). *An Introduction to Motivation*. New York: Van Nostrand Reinhold.

BERRY, BREWTON (1958). *Race and Ethnic Relations*. Boston: Houghton, Mifflin Company. All excerpts are reprinted by permission of the publisher.

CARROLL, JOSEPH C. (1938). *Slave Insurrections in the United States, 1800–1860*. Boston: Chapman and Grimes.

COHEN, JEHUDI (1958). "Some Aspects of Ritualized Behavior in Interpersonal Situations." *Human Relations*, 2: 195–215.

DANIELS, ROGER and HARRY H. L. KITANO (1970). *American Racism: Exploration of the Nature of Prejudice*. Englewood Cliffs, N.J.: Prentice-Hall, Inc. All excerpts are reprinted by permission of the publisher.

FRANKLIN, JOHN HOPE (1948). *From Slavery to Freedom*. New York: Alfred A. Knopf, Inc.

HAMILTON, CHARLES (1968). "Our Nat Turner and William Styron's Creation." In Clarke, ed., *William Styron's Nat Turner: Ten Black Writers Respond*. Boston: Beacon Press. Pp. 73–78.

HORTON, JOHN (1971). "Order and Conflict Theories of Social Problems as Competing Ideologies." In Yetman and Steele, eds., *Majority and Minority*. Boston: Allyn and Bacon. Pp. 15–31.

LINDGREN, ETHEL JOHN (1938). "An Example of Culture Contact Without Conflict." *American Anthropologist*, 40 (4): 605–621.

LONGRES, JOHN, CARL ROBERTS, and KENNETH SHINN (1966). *Some Similarities and Differences in Northern-Urban Race Riots Involving Negroes During the 20th Century*. Unpublished MSW Thesis. Los Angeles: University of California.

MERTON, ROBERT (1957). *Social Theory and Social Structure*, rev. ed. New York: The Free Press. Pp. 131–194.

POWDERMAKER, HORTENSE (1943). "The Channeling of Negro Aggression by the Cultural Process." *American Journal of Sociology*, 5 (48): 750–58.

SIMPSON, GEORGE EATON and J. MILTON YINGER (1965). *Racial and Cultural Minorities: An Analysis of Prejudice and Discrimination*. New York: Harper & Row, Publishers.

Black Men Helped Build America

IDENTITY 6

Minority-group behavior is primarily the reaction of subordinated, less powerful populations to their position in the social structure, group position being an important determinant of ethnic behavior. Therefore, if racism makes the subordinated group feel "inferior," it will tend to make the dominant group feel "superior," at least temporarily. It may engender such attitudes as "noblesse oblige," paternalism, and blindness and complacency; it leads to such beliefs as "it's their own fault." Racial differences have been explained by theories of biological and cultural inferiority, and subordinated groups are exploited economically and sexually. Some members of the dominant group react with guilt and even revulsion at the specter of a racial stratification system in a "democratic society," while others fear the possible violent consequences of maintaining the strict barriers between the privileged and unprivileged.

Some point to the economic and social costs of racism and the loss of talent and productivity, the high rate of crime and delinquency, and the loss of national honor through condoning practices that are at variance with national goals and rhetoric.

All of these points of view, ranging from the moral and the ideological to the very pragmatic, illustrate the main thesis that racism affects all members of the system, but in different ways. Therefore, any simple proposition for understanding and eliminating racism gravely misrepresents the complexity of the problem because racism means so many different things to so many different people, both in the majority and minority populations.

One of the most important effects of racism is its impact on the "self" and "identity"—how the ethnic individual sees and feels about himself and his world. If discrimination, prejudice, segregation, and racism had no effect on the development of individuals, whether of the minority or the majority, there would be no point in discussing them. However, it can be demonstrated that racism raises formidable barriers to personal fulfillment and maturity.

IDENTITY

A newspaper article appearing in the Washington, D.C., *Evening Star* (1972) points up a relatively common story of interracial contact.

> *Lagos, Nigeria* (AP). Thirteen years in Britain, with education at Eton College, has left a Nigerian youth facing a cruel dilemma that many African blacks suffer when they go abroad. It is the problem of lost identity. "Who do I really belong to?" the youth asked in an article he wrote for a Nigerian newspaper. "I am virtually ashamed of my race and color. I have no desire to be white; but my mind is a hundred percent white. As a result, my parents and I do not speak the same language. I cannot picture the day when I will, if ever, return home to settle. . . . When people have amicably asked my name, I have no name. I have often actually replied: My friend, I have no name. My fellow blacks call me Uncle Tom. In America they call me nigger, and in England they call me immigrant. . . ."

Although drawn from a different setting, this situation is similar to that of ethnic groups in the United States. The concept of an ethnic identity—the "who am I?"—is compounded by the essentially negative connotations saddled upon the questioner if he happens to have identifiable racial features at variance with what is considered "desirable" in the United States.

The problem of an overall identity, not just ethnic identity, is critical in modern society. The problem of identity is minor in more traditional cultures where populations have remained relatively homogeneous and stable, and family names, villages, and neighborhoods have continued unchanged. But immigrants to the United States have been required to discard their ancestral and national identities and adopt newer ones based on the image of the self-made man. In addition, the highly mobile social system with heterogeneous populations and ever-changing life

118

styles has made the problem of establishing one's identity very difficult in America. Some of the hypothesized correlates of the lack of identity include: rootlessness, alienation, anomie, and confused self-concept.

Psychoanalyst Erik Erikson (1950) sees identity as the product of the interaction between self and the social environment. The internal organization of the self provides the framework from which the individual views the world; the environment provides the surrounds, the stimulus, and the "input." The self goes through a number of developmental stages, (e.g., oral, anal, genital) and the successful integration of each stage is important in achieving maturity.

Dai (1961) provides a perspective similar to Erikson's. The parents' love and security form the base from which the individual is socialized into the culture through an ever widening perspective. Diverse group membership during adolescence provides exposure to various roles and role conflict; later stages include intimate sexual relationships and a sense of productivity through occupational accomplishment. The full personality is a result of the successful integration of the various stages.

The sociologist Gordon (1964) has also been concerned with problems of identity. The following diagram illustrating the various "layers" is from Gordon and comprises the core of an "American identity."

Figure 6–1 Identity of an American.
Source: Gordon (1964: 24).

The American identity includes race, religion, and national origin. The term "ethnic group" is used as the key to social psychological identity, and the individual's ability to come to grips with his race, religion, and nationality provides him with the tools for dealing with his identity.

119

Self theory, from an interactionist perspective, emphasizes that "self" is derived and defined through acts stemming from the roles and statuses that the individual occupies and with which he is identified. An individual's reference group plays an important part in this process. The attitudes that one has about self are the best indices to one's plan of action, as well as to the action itself, in that they serve as the anchoring points from which self and other evaluations are made. These attitudes may be even more important in relatively unfamiliar situations since previous role recipes may provide inadequate information and lead to a higher dependence on stereotypes.

For example, many ethnics avoid long, extended trips that necessitate stopping at many motels and private facilities, because from their past interactions with the majority, they know there is a great potential for embarrassing situations. It may be more comfortable to know that one is unwelcome, rather than to face the doubt and anxiety of unfamiliar situations.

RACE (COLOR)

The most important part of the ethnic identity is color and visibility. The easy identification of the ethnic leads to an instant categorization which shapes much of the initial interactions in a color-conscious society. The unsuccessful integration of this variable can lead to repression, denial, avoidance, and to gross distortions of identity. Shame of self and one's own background are detriments when dealing with the larger society. Attempts to alter one's image through operations (e.g. eye or hair straightening) are desperate attempts to alter the negative view of self.

Other variables making up an ethnic identity such as cultural styles, national origin, and religion have been discussed in previous chapters and although important, are not nearly as critical as race.

Ethnic identity is made up of the following components:

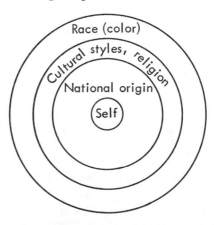

Figure 6-2 Ethnic identity.

There is an interaction among all social variables, race being the major independent variable. Most of our models concerning the development of self and identity ignore or give minor importance to this variable, whereas it is the single most important factor differentiating between majority-group and ethnic-group development. Ethnic identity develops in three major stages.[1]

STAGES IN ETHNIC IDENTITY

Stage 1

Racism in our society is the environment from which both the larger society and the ethnic individual begin to pick up the cues and role signs that shape majority and minority-group interaction. Stage I consists of the following hypothesized five steps:

STEP 1

Ideas about white superiority and racism arise from diverse sources. They include all of the "causes" of prejudice and discrimination discussed in Chapters One, Two, and Three. Removing all these causes will not necessarily have an immediate effect on race relations because of the racial attitudes that have become a part of our culture. The search for a cause or causes is not the most important step because of the impossibility of ever isolating such phenomena. But it is important to understand the background of American racism.

STEP 2

Relative to the number of overt and professed racists in the United States, the number of unverbalized and therefore "unknown" racists is extremely high. Kovel (1970) discusses three "ideal" types of racists and illustrates how historical changes have affected their styles:

The overt racist. This type openly professes his racism and is active in keeping nonwhites down. Kovel uses the term "dominative racist," and the descriptions are familiar. The studies in *The Authoritarian Personality* (1950) have described the "little man," whose life begins to revolve around external power and his hate relationship to people of color. He is apt to come from the lower middle class and both envies and hates those whites who are above him.[2]

When Negroes were under slavery, the overt racist was better able to act out his dominative strategy, but he finds it much more difficult

---

[1] The stages are adapted from processes hypothesized by Thomas Scheff (1968: 8–22) in the development of mental illness.
[2] The popular TV show "All in the Family" depicts Archie Bunker as a prototype of the overt racist. See also *The Authoritarian Personality*.

under modern conditions. The prototype of the overt racist was Dennis Kearney (see Chapter Nine); today he would be a member of the Ku Klux Klan. However, times have changed, and the actual number of overt, professed racists is probably not too large. There is little to gain from directly dominating another group, even if it were possible; the "aversive" racist is a truer representative of today's problem.

The aversive racist. The aversive racist is much more responsive to the demands of the modern culture than the overt bigot. The aversive racist may behave in exceedingly constructive and principled ways; he may give money and support civil rights causes, and will more often than not be on the "right" side of racial issues. But, the aversive racist always maintains a distance between himself and people of color. Whereas the dominative type desires a personal tie with his victim, the aversive type turns away and walls himself off.

Kovel mentions the early Quakers as one historical example of this type. Although they were among the first to attack slavery and attend to the welfare of the black man, they also retained their sense of aversion. Their cemeteries had separate sections for Negroes, and no significant number of Negroes participated in the Society.

President Woodrow Wilson is another example. As Kovel says:

> Wilson stated in 1912 that he wished to see "justice . . . to the colored people." Yet [he] equated white virtue with power. He did not hesitate to apply that power . . . despite [his previous] fine ideals. Wilson put the coup de grace to the misfortunes of black Americans by issuing an executive order which racially segregated the eating and toilet facilities of federal civil workers (1970: 31).

He also gave Southern officials the right to discharge black employees on any ground they saw fit, and he unhesitatingly dismissed black criticism of his position.

The aversive racist is often highly educated—he may be a man of intelligence, style, and class. But when a minority gets too close, he is apt to flee to the suburbs and worry excessively that "his daughter might marry one"; under extreme stress, he may regress into open bigotry.

Kovel feels that most Americans are either dominative or aversive racists, although there is an obviously broad overlap. There are racists who wish to oppress minorities either directly through domination or indirectly through avoidance. One is "hot," and generally comes from the South, the other is "cool" and comes from the North. When the "hot" one is provoked, he may resort to violence; when the "cool" one is faced with a problem, he tends to turn away, or hide behind a wall of restrictions and laws. An aversive racist may even fear ethnic groups he has never or ever will meet, and his behavior will almost always ensure it. The number of Americans who fall into this category must be very high. **122**

The institutional racist. Some of the previous forms of racism have become obsolete. Racism, which began as the direct domination of one person over another, has evolved into a much more complex phenomenon. The term "institutional racism," or "metaracism" (Kovel, 1970), reflects this more subtle problem. The individuals who participate in it may not be particularly racist themselves, but they reinforce and strengthen the problem through their acquiescence in the racism of the larger cultural order.

Because of its subtlety, it is one of the more difficult types of racism to identify or combat. The prototype of metaracism according to Kovel is the modern United States Army. This immensely powerful system has incorporated and elevated many minorities, but its top echelons remain almost all white. However, this racism takes a much more subtle form than leadership structure. It is the irony of the plight of the minority in this equal-opportunity setting: "Isn't [the army] simply the mechanized— indeed the robotized—reduction of humanity to selfless tools of the will of culture, the grinding of both black and white into gray? Nowhere in our culture is there less freedom, less autonomy, less originality, joy and affirmation; nowhere is there more cold calculation, more mindless regimentation, more dullness, more banality—and *more racial equality"* (Kovel, 1970: 217). And nowhere can one find the seeds of the destruction of our own culture more clearly symbolized than in our armed forces.

Institutional racism exists in large corporations, unions, and bureaucracies. The need for token numbers of minorities often results in decent employment for a few; there is little direct oppression, and certain real gains can be observed. But, in the long run, the metaracist structures may be the most frightening. The state, bureaucracy, or corporation that functions with computerized efficiency makes demands that in themselves are destructive. For in our culture, the worship of output and production leads to some degree of equal treatment for minorities; but the great bureaucracies and corporations need deadened and abstracted beings in order to operate and therefore must police and control their own populations.

Today's urban minorities experience all three types of racism just described. The urban slum dweller, "suffers dominative racism at the hands of the police, aversive racism at the hands of white employers, unions, and shopkeepers, and metaracism at the hands of . . . dehumanized welfare agencies" (Kovel, 1970: 223).

STEP 3

Most racist actions and thoughts are denied or are transistory and therefore may not be an integral part of the personality of the average American.

This is a corollary of Step 2. Many Americans make bigoted remarks and racial slurs are a common part of our social system, but they **123** may not necessarily be that deeply ingrained in the minds of many Americans. The notion that racial prejudice is "bad" and something to be denied indicates that the "norms towards conformity" may be working to the benefit of race relations. But one should also be aware that racism is taking on more "modern and subtler forms."

Several other factors may serve to lessen racial divisions. There are alternate classification systems that dilute pure racial hostility, such as religion and social class. There is also the change of American goals to include variations of pluralism that may prove more tolerant of differences. Multiple minority groups can also serve to deflect attacks.

STEP 4

Nevertheless, racist thoughts and actions are still sufficiently widespread to maintain discriminatory restrictions. Aversive and institutional racism reflect the current barriers. The quest for equality by minority groups is blocked primarily by institutions and organizations. Major current research emphasis should be on these newer and more powerful racial barriers. The one optimistic sign (even though there are also regressive signs) is that federal legislation endorses "opening up" the system to ethnic groups.

STEP 5

The formal and legal restrictions constitute one portion of the barrier; the informal network of social and fraternal organizations which reinforce racism represent another, but almost impregnable barrier. Issues such as local and community control, public and private facilities, and school bussing often include strong racial overtones. Social and fraternal organizations will be difficult to change under the present environment. For example, Bradshaw (1972) conducted a survey of private social clubs for the Los Angeles *Times*. Membership in these exclusive clubs provided many benefits such as a second home, a sense of status, a wide range of athletic activities, and important business, social, and political contacts. One of the overriding characteristics of these clubs was the racism that systematically excluded blacks, Chicanos, Asians, and Jews. The Los Angeles Country Club, located on one of the most valuable pieces of undeveloped real estate in the United States, was composed primarily of elderly Anglo-Saxon whites who paid up to $25,000 to get in. One member suggested that show-business people were excluded because if actors were to join, then their bosses, the Jewish studio heads, might also gain a foothold. The possibility of any non-white minorities becoming members remained very remote and unlikely.

The five steps provide the major "input" from the majority, and the message comes to the minority group member from the mass media; the educational system; the political, legal, judicial, and economic systems; and even from members of his own group. Even though there are strong

124

minority voices standing up for the integrity of the "self" and a positive identity for the ethnic individual, these voices are often drowned out by the volume from those who repeat, "you are inferior; you are less than a whole American."

Stage II

The first five steps under Stage I present the climate of racism; Stage II hypothesizes how the process "takes," so that the actors on both sides of the stratification system begin to behave in accordance with some of the prescriptions. Relatively stable racial roles begin to develop through the power of the majority and the deference of the minority. The individual's identity is built upon the continuity of his experiences, his expectations, his performance in social interaction, and his ability to read the cues for his interaction. Entry into the role is complete when the role becomes a part of the individual's expectations, and these expectations are reaffirmed and validated in social interaction.

STEP 6

Stereotyped minority-group behavior is learned in early childhood. The ability to differentiate between the "white man" (and power) and one's own ethnic people is constantly learned and relearned. Conversely, the white man learns about his "superiority" and fulfills the role of validating the inferiority of the ethnic. His role is constantly reinforced by his social and organizational interaction.

The ethnic child learns much from urban areas and types of residence; the less desirable areas and shabbier houses are linked to ethnics, while the dominant group lives in the better sections. Mass media, the school system, cultural heroes, and other models reinforce the image of a superior and desirable group that is distinct from the rest.

If these "surrounds" were not sufficient, childhood socialization in ethnic families is also geared towards the "realities of life." Richard Wright (1937) writes how his mother taught him to live under Jim Crow, after he had been severely beaten by some white boys.

> When night fell my mother came from the white folks' kitchen. I raced down the street to meet her. I could just feel in my bones that she would understand. I knew she would tell me exactly what to do next time. I grabbed her hand and babbled out the whole story. She examined my wound, then slapped me.
> "How come yuh didn't hide?" she asked me. "How come yuh always fightin'?"
> I was outraged, and bawled. Between sobs I told her that I didn't have any trees or hedges to hide behind. There wasn't a thing I could have used as a trench. And you couldn't throw very far when you were behind the brick pillars of a house. She grabbed a barrel stave, dragged me home, whipped me naked, and beat me till I had a fever of one hundred and two.

She would smack my rump with the stave and, while the skin was still smarting, impart to me gems of Jim Crow wisdom. I was never to throw cinders any more. I was never to fight any more wars. I was never, never, under any conditions, to fight white folks again. And they were absolutely right in clouting me with the broken milk bottle. Didn't I know she was working hard every day in the hot kitchens of the white folks to make money to take care of me? When was I ever going to learn to be a good boy? She couldn't be bothered with my fights. She finished by telling me that I ought to be thankful to God as long as I lived that they didn't kill me (Wright, 1937).

The realization that the warm, loving parent perceives ethnics and "white folks" differently is often difficult for the ethnic child to handle. But the realities of the power differential are such that most ethnic parents socialize their children to recognize the color and the power differences. In most instances, such a pattern is deemed necessary for survival.

It may be easier in terms of continuity to learn the realities of race from early childhood. The jolt of finding out that one is different and therefore less acceptable is always difficult, and this realization at a later age without previous preparation can be a severe trauma. For example, we have met many Asians who had grown up on the East Coast "with little overt prejudice and discrimination" until they reached the age of serious dating and marriage. They then discovered that they were undesirable, and many of them moved to Los Angeles and thoroughly immersed themselves in the ethnic community, isolating themselves from the white world.

STEP 7

The stereotype of one's ethnic group is continually reaffirmed, especially in schools and on the job. As was pointed out earlier, the stereotypes often become the reality. Concepts such as the self-fulfilling prophecy, Skinner's operant conditioning, and other precepts of learning theory are all applicable—what minorities do and do not do in school, on the job, in their homes, and in their social interaction is shaped by the expectations and reinforcements of the more powerful group.

The mass media play an extremely important part in the process. Labelling and stereotyping are reinforced by discriminatory laws, prejudices, habits, and customs; with the cooperation of individuals, organizations and institutions shape the behavior of both the minority and majority according to the stereotype.

STEP 8

Minority-group socialization has another dimension—socialization into one's own ethnic group. Very little research evidence is available in this area, but the duality of the socialization—behaving in one way in white society, and in another way with one's own group—is a part of all minority growing up. Perhaps, the freer, more exploratory type of self that develops with one's peers provides part of the buffer that enables many minority-group individuals to grow up with an adequate view of self. Most members of the majority group never see this side of the minority group.

For example, the stereotype of the quiet, conforming, hard-working, highly motivated Japanese-American student is quite widespread. And if one limits his observations to the public schools, the observation appears valid. However, the behavior of many Japanese-American students in ethnic language schools cancels the image. The Japanese language school the author attended after the regular school day was often pure chaos. Shouting, profanity, book-throwing, cheating, rowdiness, and disorder were all widespread. The students often bragged about how many Japanese teachers they had been able to drive out of the profession. Interviews with current Japanese-American students indicate that some of this behavior still persists in ethnic schools.

Ethnics are forced to employ multiple identities and roles. Not only do they have to adjust to the normal societal roles in their families and in their jobs, they also have to come to terms with their subordinate ethnic status. Ethnics must be careful about going to certain places, filling certain positions, performing out of the generally prescribed roles: they must remain wary in social situations.

Conversely, majority-group members are more able to develop a single, universal identity. The dominant-group member does not have to be as careful since his position allows him to perform in a consistent manner. Others generally have to adapt to him. He defines the situation and is in control of the interaction. He therefore can travel throughout the world secure in his status and can interact with others on a fairly predictable basis. The picture of the domineering, aggressive American ("the ugly American") who "comes on strong" no matter where, is an example of an individual who is generally used to having his way.

Clues as to feelings about ethnicity, self, and the treatment accorded to majority-group members can be deduced from the following interview with an articulate Japanese woman:

> The way my family treats my white husband as something special really stands out. The rest of my sisters are married to Nisei [Japanese] men; they are all good citizens and nobody makes a fuss. But the special niche given to the white man—bowing, scraping, deferring, and the attempts to please him—should give you some idea of the role differences, even today.

Stage III

The final stage of the ethnic identity is confirmed when the individual begins to accept the roles prescribed by the majority society. Roles become stabilized under the following hypothesized conditions.

STEP 9

The labelled minority is rewarded for playing the stereotyped role.

STEP 10

The labelled minority is punished if it attempts to play a less conventional role.

The propositions apply to the great majority of the ethnics; there are individual exceptions, the talented few, but it is more comfortable for most to play out the role. Some of the roles may even be well paid and include a rise in status; nevertheless, they are stereotypes and are always pointed out to demonstrate the openness of the system. Once a person is placed in such a status, he is rewarded for conformity and punished for deviant behavior.

Overt punishment is not the only barrier. There is no opportunity to play other roles (e.g., ethnics are restricted to a few roles in movies and television); thus the range of choices is narrowed, and the ethnic stereotype is reinforced.

STEP 11

In times of crisis involving the minority group, options are greatly reduced, and the stereotyped role may be the only feasible alternative. An ethnic-group individual is constantly reminded of his vulnerability. During World War II, the Japanese American survived by playing the role of a patriot. During race riots in Watts, the normal activities of those ethnics not even remotely involved were also restricted; Negro respondents reported that many white colleagues were constantly suspicious ("are you one of them?").

STEP 12

The final stage of the ethnic identity is achieved when the ethnic individual internalizes the stereotyped roles preferred by the majority. He may even believe that his role is the best of all possible roles and that those who wish to change the ethnic stratification system are crackpots, "commies," or worse. He may even believe that he is not an ethnic at all and overidentify with the majority group.

This hypothesized identity process appears to be "normal" under present social conditions. But is it normal for ethnics to internalize the prescriptions of the larger system and act according to the stereotypes? Is the internalization that takes place in Step 12 desirable? This process can be very destructive to the ethnic individual in American society.

These stages are part and parcel of the American system. They are predicated on the assumption that the dominant community will retain its power and will prescribe the criteria for being "American." The de- **128** velopment of a more pluralistic system based on ethnic pride should have a profound effect on ethnic identity.

INSTANT IDENTITY

One of the interesting facets of self and identity has been the arrival of "instant" ethnic identity; colors previously associated with negative qualities—black, yellow, brown, and red—have quickly become respectable. If we analyze the phenomenon more closely, there are perceptible gradations. Initially, white was "right"; with the rise of ethnic pride, however, terms such as "oreo," "banana," "coconut," and "apple" became popular metaphors to describe individuals who held basically white attitudes, despite their outer coloring.

The pride in blackness, yellowness, redness, and brownness has often been accompanied by a flow of high rhetoric. Now, however, rhetoric does not suffice, and ethnic university students expect a basic education that will enable them to cope with the world.

The emergence of an instant identity opens to question the developmental models of a healthy self and personality integration. Under a racist system with dominant group control, it is impossible for ethnics to arrive at a healthy concept of self. They are initially surrounded by a negative atmosphere that challenges their worth; they are socialized into a second-class citizenship by lowering their expectations and teaching them circumscribed roles—a process which is validated through outside experience. The eventual internalization and integration of these realities means the acceptance of a pariah status.

We see many healthy ethnics, including those who do not accept their second-class status and those who accommodate; future models of personality development must take into account the processes that ethnics and minorities go through. The dynamics of an instant identity should also be explored.

BIBLIOGRAPHY

ADORNO, THEODOR et al. (1950). *The Authoritarian Personality*. New York: Harper & Row, Publishers.

BRADSHAW, JON (1972). "Any Number Can't Play," *Los Angeles Times*, pp. 7, 9, 10, 12.

DAI, MASUOKA JITSUICHI and PRESTON VALIEN (1961). *Race Relations: Problems and Theory*. Chapel Hill: University of North Carolina Press.

ERIKSON, ERIK (1950). *Childhood and Society*. New York: W. W. Norton & Co.

GORDON, MILTON (1964). *Assimilation in American Life*. New York: Oxford University Press.

KOVEL, JOEL (1970). *White Racism*. New York: Pantheon Books.

SCHEFF, THOMAS (1968). "The Role of the Mentally Ill and the Dynamics of Mental Disorder." In Spitzer and Denzin, eds., *The Mental Patient*. New York: McGraw-Hill Book Company. Pp. 8–22.

Washington, D.C. *Evening Star* (1972). January 12. P. B-11.

WRIGHT, RICHARD (1937). "The Ethics of Living Jim Crow." *Uncle Tom's Children*. New York: Harper & Row, Publishers.

SUMMARY
OF
PART ONE

Although racism as a form of social stratification is a relatively recent
phenomenon, prejudice, discrimination, and segregation have long been
a part of history. Because increased mobility among different races will
be accompanied by more frequent interracial interaction, factors that
"cause" racism must be better understood if better race relations are to
be achieved.

Racism, as with most of our social phenomena, is not simply linked
in a linear fashion to prejudice, discrimination, and segregation. It is
intertwined with many other variables. Therefore a direct attack on its
"cause" (e.g., fear of strangers) may meet with limited success. For example, some of the hypothesized reasons for discrimination include fear
of economic, social, and occupational loss, loss of status, racial inundation,
intermarriage, and loss of power. Others view racism as the product of a
competitive, capitalistic system or as a manifestation of man's subconscious. Racism is also closely related to goals. If Anglo conformity
remains as the primary model of American society, then large numbers
of our citizenry will remain alienated; on the other hand, a more pluralistic schema may encourage the diversity that will allow wider participation by minorities.

One of the consequences of a stratification system that assigns non-white groups to the bottom social status levels is their isolation and separation from the rest of society. Under extreme circumstances there have been instances of concentration camps, extermination, and genocide.

Although on the surface it appears that groups assigned to a pariah status have adapted to their circumstances quietly, a closer analysis indicates that the apparent docility may be deceptive. There have been racial revolts and riots, strikes and boycotts, the use of ethnic humor, job slowdowns, role changes, changes in goals, avoidance, and retreat. Even those who have seemingly accepted their lot may mask their resentment through indirect aggression.

One of the most serious consequences of racism is its possible effect on an individual's identity. An ethnic identity may include lower self-perceptions, lower feelings of worth, lower expectations, and the internalization of the role of a second-class citizen. However, such a development may be avoidable with the current redefinitions of positive ethnic identities and greater self-awareness.

THE MAJOR ETHNIC GROUPS II

The second section will discuss how selected minority groups have adapted to life in the United States. Although one could analyze each ethnic group as if it lived in a vacuum, one cannot ignore the most important factor—its *interaction* with the majority culture.

Minorities have often been forced into positions where sheer survival has been a primary task. Subordinated groups have little power to impose their "culture" on others, in contrast to dominant groups. Yet much writing ignores the critical factor in the relationship between dominant and subordinated groups. Minority groups have been viewed as isolated entities, and their adaptations have been given various labels by the majority group. The general implication is that minorities have created their own problems by maintaining their cultural traditions, and they would become more acceptable and successful if only they could get rid of them.

Much scholarly writing in the past has been racist—even the "scientific" writing reeks of paternalism at best and outright racism at worst. The one universal standard has been white Anglo-Saxon Protestantism, and "success" and "failure" has had to be evaluated from this norm. Those groups closest to WASP norms in values, life styles, family patterns and culture have been deemed the most successful. Ethnic groups from distant cultures have been considered disadvantaged, and the inference has been that they must be changed, isolated, or destroyed.

In a power sense the interpretations may be correct: dominant groups do what they think is right, and develop and maintain organizations that reinforce their system. Those groups that do not adjust are considered deviant and become primary targets for "assistance."

GROUPS TO BE STUDIED

We expect the reader to view the interaction between ethnic groups and the white majority in a nonmoralistic way—that is, to avoid the use of labels such as "good" or "bad" when looking at the phenomenon. We include the following groups: American Indians; blacks; Asian Americans, including the Chinese, Japanese, and the Filipinos; Mexican Americans; and the Puerto Ricans. Ideally, we would have preferred to use the same framework for dealing with each ethnic group. However, the available material was often uneven and dissimilar; therefore, although a common theme is applied to each group, the framework is not identical. The reader should consult the original material whenever possible.

Historical Background

The following is a short summary of the important concepts and the people who have shaped our ideas about race.

EARLY RACE RELATIONS IN THE UNITED STATES

The United States has been considered a racist society only recently. Many Americans in the past have been cognizant of our racial problems, but they still strongly believed the basic tenets of "liberty and equality for all." Yet, in studying the beginnings of our country it is impossible to escape some aspects of racial differentiation, discrimination, and stratification. The first immigrants were Europeans, bringing with them European perceptions, experiences, and the basic attitude of European superiority. But even among Europeans there were differences. Southern Europeans with darker skins defined "whiteness" much more broadly. In the 1500s, Southern Europeans considered Asians to be white; after 1800 Northern Europeans considered them to be "colored." Native Africans were universally thought to be black.

EUROPEAN AND "WHITE" RACISM

From most social science and historical data, it is impossible to cite a date, incident, or occurrence that pinpoints the beginning of European, or "white," racism. Daniels and Kitano (1970) indicate that "white racism" is a product of the expansion of Europe, of the technological superiority which, from its beginning in the late fifteenth century, allowed **136**

Europeans to dominate the entire world. Europeans came to associate their technological success with the belief in their innate superiority, a belief that was further strengthened by their ability to establish control over many non-European people. European culture, civilization, and people were presumed to be superior to all other races of mankind.

The attitude of white superiority is, from a historical perspective, a recent phenomenon. *The Adventures of Marco Polo* in the thirteenth century was written from the point of view of a member of a relatively undeveloped European nation who confronted a superior Asian culture. The Indian historian, K. M. Pannikar (1959) calls the period between 1498 and 1945 the "Vasco da Gama epoch," the only period in Asian history in which that continent's destiny was controlled by non-Asians. However, "by the end of the seventeenth century, the European assumption of superiority was fully established. Whatever national and parochial loyalties might divide Europeans at home, in the frontier areas, which they were exploiting, they began to view white men as a distinct class. This was true wherever Europeans came into contact with men of color: in Asia, in the Antipodes, in Africa, and in North and South America" (Daniels and Kitano, 1970).

SOCIAL DARWINISM

The rational, scientific-minded Western world has often tried to validate its racist thought with scholarly and academic sources. Therefore, the theories of Charles Darwin, introduced in 1859 with the publication of *On the Origin of Species by Means of Natural Selection,* were quickly seized and translated into laws of social development pertinent to societies, nations, and races. The "survival of the fittest," the most advanced, and the most civilized was nature's way of producing superior men, nations, and races. The inferior races were those unable to compete with the white world, and phrases such as "the struggle for existence," and "superior and inferior races" became common. Racist ideas were not new to historical writings before social Darwinism, but the theory reinforced the existing racist philosophies.

The most influential social Darwinist in America and the outstanding spokesman for the concept of a biologically determined society was William Graham Sumner. Sumner tried to temper the optimistic, humanitarian, democratic social thought of eighteenth century America with the pessimism of Ricardo and Malthus and the prestige of Darwin. He tried to convince his contemporaries of the realities of social struggle and the natural forces to which they had to succumb. He preached that social order was predestined and that the survival of the fittest was the salvation of the economically elect. American middle-class virtues and the conservative traditon were fully evident in Sumner, who believed man's relation to nature to be hard and demanding, and labor, self- 137 denial, and suffering to be necessary and inevitable. Personal character developed through economic activity, which rewarded those men of good character who devoted their lives to hard work and punished those who were "negligent, shiftless, inefficient, silly, and imprudent" (Hofstadter, 1968: 11).

The Darwinian influence was also evident in the naturalism of contemporary novelists such as Jack London, a racist and socialist who placed great emphasis on pride of race. His heroes were always of the appropriate ancestry, and his inferior beings were either Jews or half-breeds. Socialism, he proclaimed "is devised so as to give more strength to these certain kindred favoured races so that they may survive and inherit the earth to the extinction of the lesser, weaker races" (Banton, 1967: 42).

The social Darwinist's belief in the inevitability of evolutionary processes affected many political arguments in the 1900s. Herbert Spencer denied the efficacy of remedial legislation as a device for social progress, which he believed came about through the natural laws of development. His argument has a familiar ring: there are scholars today who feel that "inferior" races will not benefit from academic training.

The growth of imperialism was strongly influenced and justified by evolutionary teaching. Competition and struggle were looked upon as a natural process in which survival was the ultimate goal. Success at subjugating colonial peoples was proof in itself that the colonizers were by nature superior and more fit and therefore destined by the inevitable course of events to control the lands of the colored races. Success served to justify any kind of action; the means by which it was achieved remained unimportant. Humanitarian policies only upset or delayed the natural course of events, and the slogan "Blessed are the strong, for they shall prey upon the weak" characterized the whole movement.

American expansion into Indian territories—the theft of their land and genocide of their people—was believed by many to be the Will of God. Ignorance of the white man's god was often proof in itself that the Indian was inferior. Because the Indian was capable of only a "savage" stage of civilization, he was expected not to stand in the way of natural progress of the superior white civilization.

IMMIGRATION ACT OF 1924

Legislation in 1924 restricting immigration and establishing a quota system aimed at preserving the existing balance between national groups, reflected the racist fear of the general population. One of the leading spokesmen of the times was H. F. Osborn. There were also the lawyer, Lothrop Stoddard, and Madison Grant, author of *The Passing of the Great Race* (1916). Grant claimed that "the result of the mixture of two races, in the long run, gives us a race reverting to the more ancient, generalized and lower type. The cross between a white man and a Negro is a Negro; the cross between a white man and a Hindu is a Hindu; and the cross between any of the three European races and a Jew is a Jew" (Gossett, 1963: 353). Fear of general racial deterioration due to assimilation of poor immigrant stock actively preyed on the minds of many Americans.

After World War I, scientific racism seemed to falter when anthropologists such as Bronislaw Malinowski and Franz Boas raised new questions about race. Boas asked one simple question: what proof is there that race determines mentality and temperment? (Gossett, 1963: 429). Much of the racial folklore that exists today was the science of a century ago. Will the same relationship obtain between today's science and tomorrow's?

BIBLIOGRAPHY

BANTON, MICHAEL (1967). *Race Relations*. London: Tavistock Publications.

BODMER, WALTER F. and LUIGI L. CAVALLI-SFORZA (1970). "Intelligence and Race." *Scientific American,* 223 (4): 19–29.

CRAMB, J. A. (1915). *The Origins and Destiny of Imperial Britain*. London: John Murray.

DANIELS, ROGER and HARRY H. L. KITANO (1970). *American Racism: Exploration of the Nature of Prejudice*. Englewood Cliffs, N.J.: Prentice-Hall, Inc.

GOSSETT, THOMAS F. (1963). *Race: The History of an Idea in America*. Dallas: SMU Press.

HOFSTADTER, RICHARD (1968). *Social Darwinism in American Thought*. Boston: Beacon Press.

JENSEN, ARTHUR R. (1969). "How Much Can We Boost IQ and Scholastic Achievement?" *Harvard Functional Review,* 39 (1): 1–123.

JORDAN, WINTHROP D. (1968). *White over Black*. Baltimore: Penguin Books, Inc.

KOVEL, JOEL (1970). *White Racism*. New York: Pantheon Books.

PANNIKAR, KAVALAM M. (1959). *Asia and Western Dominance: A Survey of the Vasco Da Gama Epoch of Asian History, 1498–1945*. New York: Humanities Press.

TAYLOR, E. G. R., ed. (1935). *The Original Writings and Correspondence of the Two Richard Hakluyts*. Second series, LXXVI. London: Hakluyt Society Publications.

THE AMERICAN INDIANS 7

The word "Indian" elicits images of tom-toms, war whoops, horses, loin-cloths, and scalps. Decades of Hollywood epics depicting the Indian as "savage" have established the stereotype as the Indian reality. Perhaps at one time the image might have been laid mercifully to rest, but the insatiable needs of television have resurrected the Indian in all of his clichéd grandeur. Therefore the popular mind conceives of an American Indian who talks in monosyllables ("ugh"); who runs around almost totally naked (except for a few feathers); who is stoic and expressionless (the cigar store Indian); and who can follow a trail over granite mountains.

There is also the popular dichotomy between the "good" Indian—faithful, loyal, but inferior to the white man (Tonto)—and the "bad" one—tricky, treacherous, sly, and resistant to the white man's ways (Geronimo). As with most stereotypes, these perceptions contain elements of truth, but the basic error is the error of all caricatures—the Indian does not emerge as a human being with qualities that elicit empathy, understanding, and identification.

However, even more damaging to the Indian are some of the beliefs held by the more sophisticated, who blame the Indians' "culture" for their plight: the high rates of alcoholism, early school dropouts, and poverty. Simplified deductions can then be drawn: The Indian culture should be destroyed and the Indians acculturated to American ways, even if many die in the process. If acculturation does not work, then isolation in reservations is a partial solution, with the requirement that "we" teach "them" how to live, survive, and raise their children.

But as we have indicated, it is not the "fault" of the Indians' culture that they are not successful in American terms, any more than the cultures of the blacks, Chicanos, Asians, and Puerto Ricans are the main causes of their problems. We are instead observing the *interaction* between cultures and ethnic groups—what happens when one culture encounters another. And the problem is intensified when one group, the whites, establishes a superordinate-subordinate relationship based on skin color and erects boundaries that limit mobility from one category to another. The question faced by all pariah groups is how to adapt to their own location within a racist social system.

BRIEF BACKGROUND AND HISTORY[1]

Perhaps the European view of the Indians is best exemplified by the name "Indian," which was given to the natives of North and South America by explorers such as Columbus who were actually seeking a direct route to the East "Indies" in Southeast Asia. For the term "Indian," which has stuck up to the present day, covers a widely disparate group of peoples with different languages, cultures, political divisions, and levels of civilization and organization. Rather than indicating these differences, the term conceals them and automatically demotes all Indians to the lower level of the ethnic stratification system. The most important ignored fact about the Indians is their diversity. There was, and still is, no one kind of Indian nor one tribe nor one nation. Rather, the American Indians represent as much variety as the peoples living on the Eureasian land mass. Their linguistic resources include at least a dozen distinct stocks, and within each stock are languages as disparate as English and Russian.

Indian technology and culture also reflect this diversity. The Mayas, Aztecs, and Incas developed complex social organizations and a sophisticated technology, while tribes such as the Paiute had a much simpler social system.

---

[1] Much of the material in this section is drawn from the book, *Indian Americans* by Murray Wax (Englewood Cliffs, N.J.: Prentice-Hall, Inc., 1971).

The earliest European contact with the Yaquis took place in 1553 along the coast of the Gulf of California. Early Spaniards quickly found the Yaquis to be brave and dangerous fighters; they were stubborn, independent, and extremely courageous in their willingness to fight for their own way of life. They were also highly curious about the culture of the Europeans.

Wax writes:

> The Jesuits found the Yaqui a highly receptive people. Their population of about 30,000 had been dispersed in some 80 rancherias; it was now baptized and concentrated in eight new towns. Agricultural cultivation was improved and intensified, and soon the fertile river bottoms were producing sufficiently for a considerable surplus to be exported. However, in time, the area of Spanish settlement crept close to the Yaqui border, and civil authorities began pressing to divide the Yaqui lands (which were held in common), to require payment of tribute and taxation, and to open the area for settlement. In 1740 the Yaqui "revolted" and killed or chased away all Spaniards other than "their" Jesuits. When, in 1767, the Jesuits were expelled from New Spain, leadership devolved upon the Yaquis themselves, and although they had continually to defend themselves against Spanish and Mexican attempts at conquest and absorption, they remained fundamentally autonomous communities for over another century (Wax, 1971: 11).

The Yaquis learned much from the Spaniards. They developed agricultural patterns and worked in mining and the fishing industry. However, the most interesting development was in their religion. The Yaquis developed their own cult of the Virgin and were guided by the belief that Jesus had been born in one of their eight towns, Belém (Bethlehem). The Yaqui belief included a story that Jesus had traveled in their own country, curing the sick and fighting evil.

Integration

In 1828 after Mexico became an independent nation, three idealistic laws were passed designed to integrate the Indians into the new state. It was felt that the Spanish distinctions of race and birth had perpetuated a caste system that had led to the divisive Indian struggles. Therefore by declaring that *all* people would be Mexican citizens entitled to land and titles, the new government hoped that a truly integrated Mexico would emerge.

However, the Yaquis and their neighbors had visualized an independent Indian nation, rather than beng integrated into the new Mexican republic. The stage was set for continuous conflict and battles, and massacres and cruelty were common. The capture and execution of

143

the Yaqui leader, Cajeme, in 1887 signaled the end of organized resistance; but guerrilla warfare continued, and as late as 1926, Mexican
military campaigns were mounted against Yaquis.

The Yaquis' resistance was based on a number of factors. Probably
the most important was their communal orientation, which meant that
such "progressive" programs as the redistribution of lands and integration would destroy their own economic and spiritual communal base.

Their effectiveness in resisting the government was aided by their
cohesion and organization. They had developed an autonomous system,
including a military arm that was closely tied in with their spiritual
existence. Yaqui "pluralism" was not narrow and parochial, but instead
included many who were fluent in Spanish and had participated in the
wider world.

After the collapse of organized resistance in the late nineteenth
century, the Mexican government instituted a dispersal policy that forced
the Yaquis to move away from their homes while inducing outsiders to
colonize Yaqui land. The Yaquis soon spread throughout Mexico and
the southwestern United States, although many tried to return to their
own lands when possible. In 1939 the less fertile bank of the Yaqui River
was reserved exclusively for the Yaquis, and they were able to resettle
where three of their original towns had been. Yaqui communities have
also been established recently in the United States. In the 1960s several
thousand Yaquis were residing on the outskirts of Tucson.

The Yaquis have resisted their encounters with different "white"
cultures; they maintain a pluralistic style and insist on group solidarity.

THE CALIFORNIA INDIAN [2]

The California Indians met two major invaders—the immigrants who
came north from Mexico and west from the states. According to Daniels
and Kitano:

> Each group brought with it a common contempt for the native Indian,
> but a contempt shaped by the quite different values of Ibero- and Anglo-
> America. Each group subjugated and suppressed the Indian in the quite
> different ways suggested by its own culture and its own experience in
> white-Indian relations. Each ran roughshod over the natives and neither
> considered, in any way, their wishes. Each group regarded the Indian as
> subhuman; neither accorded him any real say about his own destiny,
> except perhaps, giving him a choice of how he wanted to die—in hopeless
> battle or in an even more hopeless existence. California racism, then, dates
> back to the eighteenth century, back to the earliest settlement by Euro-
> peans and their descendents (1970: 29).

---

[2] Much of this material is found in Roger Daniels and Harry Kitano, *American
Racism: Exploration of the Nature of Prejudice* (Englewood Cliffs, N.J.: Prentice-
Hall, Inc., 1970).

In the late eighteenth century when the Spanish-Mexican settlement began, there were fewer than 250,000 Indians in all of California (the great anthropologist A. L. Kroeber thought perhaps only 133,000). Although this is a miniscule number by modern standards, it was a much denser aboriginal population than existed in most of North America. The California Indians, existing in a relatively benign environment, were not particularly warlike. Their martial characteristics were much less developed than those of the Indians of the plains or the eastern forests. They fished, hunted, and gathered acorns.

Starting in 1769, the advance guard of European civilization began to push northward from Mexico. These Spanish-Mexican intruders did not come in large numbers; by the end of the Mexican period in the 1840s, there were fewer than 10,000 persons of European ancestry in the province.

Although Ibero-Indian relations in California were punctuated by the usual murders and massacres typical of the rest of the continent, the classic relationship was that of an allegedly benevolent despotism in which the Indians were forced into a quasifeudal mold and taught the virtues of agricultural labor and Christian worship. No one can doubt that the Franciscan Fathers (who became the self-appointed spiritual and temporal overlords of those Indians whom they could corral and domesticate) were motivated by the concepts of Christian charity and duty—as Father Juan Crespi put it, "for the greater glory of God through the conversion of souls." But the whole Christian-heathen dichotomy in which the brown-robed priests viewed the inhabitants effectively prevented them from seeing the Indians as men with human rights. Apart from their immortal souls they were children to be protected, trained, and punished. Those Indians who became attached to the missions had no economic problems: food, clothing, and shelter were relatively abundant, certainly more than they had been before the Europeans came. Nineteenth-century writers liked to speak of the "white man's burden" of training these "new-caught, sullen peoples, half-devil and half-child"; however anthropologists and psychologists have questioned the utility of these enforced values. Missionization established the Indian as an inferior adjunct to an essentially pastoral-agricultural economy; more important, perhaps, it aimed at eradicating almost every trace of Indian culture. Some authorities feel that, in the final analysis, this systematic destruction of the nonmaterial aspects of the California Indian's culture left him defenseless in what the nineteenth century like to call the "struggle for existence," a struggle which the overwhelming majority of California Indians lost.

But missionization, however destructive of the nonmaterial culture of the California Indians, did provide the mission "neophytes" with the means for existence, and for some, the hope of a better life to come. After the dissolution of the mission communities, in both the Mexican (1822–1847) and American periods, much of the little that had been allowed the Indian was taken away. In the Mexican period, the missions were secularized and the Indians attached to the missions were transformed into pastoral and agricultural workers on the various rancheros; shortly after the American annexation following the Mexican War, the American system of reservations was instituted. Following what was already standard American practice, the Indians were almost invariably relocated on land the white man did not want. In March, 1851, one of the first Indian agents in California wrote Washington, D.C., that he had just concluded a treaty with six Northern California tribes which gave the Indians "all the land they demanded since this land was not of a character to be useful to whites." Just a year later, however, a more astute agent, recognizing that the great influx of Americans from the "states" promised to take up "every habitable foot of ground in California," started the first California reservation.

The reservation system provided for only a tiny minority of California's dwindling Indian population. After two decades of American occupation, the number of Indians had fallen drastically to an estimated 21,000; only 3,000 of these were under government protection on reservations. E. E. Dale, an eminent historian of the American Indian, has observed that, under the reservation policy "the aggressive and warlike received consideration because they were dangerous, while the peaceful and inoffensive were neglected and furnished scant protection against unscrupulous whites." Most of the decline in the population of the California Indian can be blamed on the "peaceful" attrition by European civilization and its attendant diseases. Apart from the few on the squalid reservations, most California Indians were poor, landless, and nomadic, sometimes wandering over a fairly broad expanse of territory, sometimes over a very restricted area. The Indian had no civil rights under American law; he was prohibited from giving evidence against white men; if arrested for "vagrancy," he could be farmed out to the highest bidder for a period which the law limited to four months, but which in practice was often longer; even children were often kidnapped and put into service that was close to slavery. But to these dehumanizing and gradually decimating conditions—by 1900 the state's Indian population was down to about 10,000—was added an occasional period of "warfare" which, for the tribe or group involved was sometimes, quite literally, genocide.

This decimation, this near extermination of California's Indian population, was a relatively slow and largely undramatic process. Most California Indians were not slaughtered; they just died, quietly and obscurely. An occasional protest—like Helen Hunt Jackson's *A Century of Dishonor* (1881)—was made (or is being made) to alleviate the distress of the survivors. We really know very little about California Indian life and practically nothing about individual Indians.

One California Indian is known, and his story, as written by Theodora Kroeber, will have to stand as proxy for an otherwise unknown people. Whether Ishi, as he was called, was "representative," is, of course, a question that cannot be answered. There is no doubt about the quality of his story; it is one of almost unsurpassed horror. By a historical "accident," he was perhaps the last "wild" Indian—the sole survivor, by a few years, of the Yahi tribe.

The Yahi were a tiny "tribelet" of perhaps 2,000 souls occupying a few dozen square miles of territory north of Sacramento. In the space of one bloody year, 1864, when Ishi was a small boy, all but a few dozen of his people were hunted down and destroyed by organized and legally sanctioned parties of armed whites. The survivors of this bloody year, perhaps fifty in all, were further harassed and hunted and killed for the next few years. Then, the surviving handful, a remnant of a remnant, went into what Mrs. Kroeber calls "the long concealment," which lasted about four decades. When, on August 29, 1911, an exhausted, middle-aged male Yahi Indian was captured near Oroville, California, the "tribelet" was down to a lone survivor, Ishi. He lived four and half more years in the friendly "custody" of anthropologists at the University of California. When he died, of natural causes, on March 25, 1916, a minor variety of *homo sapiens* ceased to exist; the Yahi had become, in the words of our pioneer ancestors, "good Indians."

The fate of the Yahi, symbolically at least, can stand for both the majority of California's Indians and as a polar example of the way whites have treated nonwhites. But thousands of Indians did survive; some merged into the general population; the vast majority of ethnically identifiable Indians continue to exist on the fringes of American life, technically within our society, but actually almost wholly apart from it. Those surviving, less dramatic casualties of what one writer has called the "transit of civilization" from the Old World to the New, also represent a kind of extreme example of white-nonwhite relations in America; physical and legal separation—what we would call apartheid in another land.

THE IROQUOIS[3]

Whereas the Spanish had sought precious metals and had been zealous missionaries, the English, French, and Dutch had been primarily interested in furs. The exchange of animal pelts for guns, ammunition, and other manufactured goods established a trade relationship between the Europeans and the Indians in the Northeast.

The name of "Iroquois" was given to the League of Five Nations,

---

[3] Much of this material is found in Murray Wax, *American Indians* (Englewood Cliffs, N.J.: Prentice-Hall, Inc., 1971).

consisting of the Seneca, Onondaga, Cayuga, Oneida, and Mohawk. Later a sixth tribe, the Tuscaroras from North Carolina, was added. As Wax says:

> Its peoples had been living in settled villages near streambeds where the women could plant their gardens of maize, beans and squash. In addition to serving as warriors, the men contributed fish and game to the diet. The machinery of their League was primarily an arrangement for maintaining peace and harmony among the member tribes, and except for issues of conflict among tribes, affairs were largely in the hands of the separate tribes and villages (1971: 13–14).

By the middle of the seventeenth century, the Iroquois had exhausted the furs (especially beaver) in their own territory. Therefore, they began to look for new lands and became an expansionist nation. They eventually came into conflict with tribes of the northern confederacy such as the Huron who were active in the French trade. By forming a much more aggressive military and commercial alliance, the League was able to achieve large-scale military victories and to expand their hegemony. It appeared for a time that the Iroquois would extend their power over the entire Eastern seaboard, but the Creek confederacies in the South were too powerful, and the Canadian tribes remained more closely allied to the French.

The League fought with the British in the French and Indian Wars so that by the 1700s:

> The Iroquois were becoming both powerful and acculturated: eleven Indian nations were living with the Seneca, numerous whites were intermarrying and a distinctive blend of cultures was emerging. . . . (Wax, 1971: 14–15).

But many white colonists were not pleased by the success of the Iroquois. Nevertheless, the British Crown perceived the Indians as powerful allies against the French: the Royal Order of 1763 sealed off the western lands from white settlers and recognized Indian ownership. Wax states:

> The Order was not received well among the colonists, and was one of the grievances that was to lead to the Revolutionary War. During the conflict, the League, following its successful system of neutrality in the wars of the whites, tried at first to hold itself aloof (1971: 15).

The peace treaty, following the end of the Revolutionary War, made no provision for the Indian allies of the British. Settlers and land speculators seized the opportunity to invade Indian lands. Maltreatment and conflict led to the decimation of the Iroquois. The national government preferred the friendship of the Indian allies, but they could not control the actions of the settlers and speculators, who often threatened to organize new border states and to secede; eventually the Iroquois were forced to flee to their English friends in Canada.

THE DAKOTA HORSE NOMADS

Wax gives the name "horse nomads" to those Indian tribes who developed elegant skills on horseback and who adopted a nomadic existence of following the buffalo. These tribes developed skin tepees and other features of light travel that enabled them to carry on their nomadic activities. In the process, they developed competitive and aggressive warriors who could travel long distances swiftly and quietly, constantly in search of horses, buffalo, scalps, loot, and fame.

Among the tribes who took up this style of existence (early Spanish colonists had brought the horses to the Rio Grande Valley in 1598) were the Blackfoot, Arapaho, Cheyenne, Comanche, and the Crow.

The Tetons, one of the tribes making up the Sioux, were among the earliest to take to the Plains. Wax says:

> The Teton became the scourge of the northern Plains, acquiring a reputation for irascibility, impetuosity and stealthy ferocity. The settled agriculturalist tribes, which had built a rich ceremonial existence and complex societal organization, could not cope with the Dakota raids, even though they themselves acquired the horse and some of the traits of the horse nomads. The Teton harassed the traders who attempted to utilize the Missouri River; later they continued the sport with the wagon trains crossing the Plains. Peaceable contact with the whites was mainly via French traders who established their posts along the riverine routes and took Indian women to wife (1971: 18–19).

The development of the rapid-fire revolver and the introduction of cattle spelled the end of the horse nomad. With the advent of barbed wire, the Homestead Act, cattle ranches, and the railroad, the Plains Indians came to be seen as a menace to law and order. Although pitched battles were generally won by the white man, the most effective means of gaining control over the Indians was by paper and pencil—the treaty. These documents, of which there were many, provided certain conditions that both sides promised to live up to in order to guarantee a more peaceful coexistence. Relationships under various treaties were periodically strained. In 1874, the dscovery of gold in the Black Hills brought a flood of new white settlers. Many of them complained about harassment from the Sioux and demanded that they return to their reservation; this conflict ended with the defeat and annihilation of General Custer at Little Big Horn in 1876. However, the Indian victory was only temporary, and in the long run, they were the losers. Reservation life, dependency on congressional appropriations, white opportunism, and swindling left most Indians half-starved and diseased.

Perhaps the symbolic end to overt Indian resistance was the massacre at Wounded Knee, South Dakota, in 1890. The "battle" was the culmination of the army's attempt to disarm and herd the Indians under Chief Big Foot into a cavalry camp. By the end of the massacre, an estimated 300 (out of 350) Indian men, women, and children had been gunned down (Brown, 1970).

The army had been aroused to panic by a pan-Indian movement centered around the Ghost Dance. In 1890, Kicking Bear related that a voice had commanded him to go forth and meet the ghosts of Indians who were to return and inhabit the earth. He had had visions of a Messiah, a crucifixion, and the return of great herds of buffalo and wild horses. The Indians who danced the Ghost Dance would be suspended in the air to await the coming of a new earth, inhabited only by Indians. The Ghost Dance spread rapidly, and white agents were empowered to stop it (Brown, 1970: 434–35). The Ghost Dance caused rumors of potential Indian unity and was one factor leading to the massacre at Wounded Knee. From this time on, the Indians became a part of the various bureaucracies, created to "help" them. Wax concludes,

> Wounded Knee was not the only massacre by whites of defenseless Indians, nor was Custer's Last Stand the only defeat by Indians of an Army unit; however, both involved a flamboyant and heroic people, and so have been remembered by Americans and added to their folklore. Both events were also to be the last of their kind, not only for the Sioux, but for the Plains Indians; thereafter, the history of the peoples becomes a matter of reservation life under the aegis of the Indian service (1971: 21–22).

CURRENT PICTURE

As was pointed out before, if the whites could not acculturate the Indians, they either exterminated them or isolated them on reservations. Recent Indian migration to urban areas has changed the picture somewhat, but segregated living in ghettoes and other lower-class areas has continued to limit equal-status interaction with the white community. Many Indians who "relocated" in the urban areas have returned to the reservations.

Of all the ethnic groups, the Indian is in the best position to question "law and order," "justice," and the credibility of the white man. Deloria (1973) traces the logic of white men in their quest for Indian lands and territory. Although much of the land was conquered by simple armed force, the more powerful weapon was the concept of the Doctrine of Discovery. This doctrine had been used by Christian nations and the Church to establish hegemony over large portions of the earth by simply declaring them "discovered." By a few simple statements ("I plant this flag in the name of my King"), aboriginal lands came under Christian mandate.

WHO IS AN INDIAN?

The Indian has been an extremely successful "integrator," and there is a problem of identifying just who is an Indian. In the past, white soldiers, vagabonds, trappers, hunters, and traders—primarily adult, single men— invaded Indian lands and mated with Indian women. Of course, there were strong taboos againt half-breed offspring, but the number of Americans with some percentage of Indian blood must run in the millions.

At the time of European settlement, the number of Indians in the United States had been estimated as low as one million and as high as ten million. By 1800, the native population was about 600,000, and by 1850 it had shrunk to about 250,000; malnutrition and disease (with extermination and genocide thrown in) were the primary causes. The 1960 Census showed a total of 523,591 Indians; the 1970 figures are 792,730.[4] The question of who is to be counted as an Indian is extremely complex. The U.S. Census Bureau procedures allow much leeway to the census-taker and the self-report. Since there have been social, psychological, and political disabilities connected with being classified as an Indian, many Indians with an incentive to "pass" have become non-Indians. But it may soon be in vogue to be Indian again, and the Census statistics may rise.

The Bureau of Indian Affairs (BIA) regards any person who qualifies as an heir to reservation land an Indian, and the definition arises from their legal responsibilities. When awards and benefits are given to Indian tribes as plaintiffs, individuals who are marginal in terms of Indian social life, traits, and identification may become Indian. Finally, there are many who have adopted an Indian life style, some permanently, others on weekends or on festive occasions, and yet may not have a drop of Indian blood. Depending on the criteria, they may all qualify as "Indians."

INDIAN PROBLEMS AND SURVIVAL

The Family and the Band

The ethnocentric ideal of white America is the nuclear family—husband, wife, and two children. Therefore, one of the targets for many reformers

---

[4] The major areas of Indian settlement include Oklahoma with 98,468; followed by Arizona with 95,812; California with 91,108; and New Mexico with 72,788.

151

was the Indian "band," composed of kinsmen "who recognized obligations to each other, including the sharing of certain kinds of property, and the joint organization of rituals and festivals" (Wax, 1971: 75). Bands were most common to reservation life; decisions and actions emerged from group discussion and consensus rather than from a leader.

Bands were quite egalitarian and served as mutual assistance societies. There was much sharing, and there might be a massive redistribution of property when someone died. Therefore, there was little opportunity for one man or one family to accumulate and maintain vast amounts of property for any length of time. Band organization limited the opportunities for individual Indians to become wealthy; but it also prevented others from being ignored or left to starve.

Another characteristic of the band was its particularistic pattern. Members of one band network were not obligated to share with those outside their own network. This "ignoring" of outsiders has caused much white misunderstanding.

There is no single Indian nation per se. There are instead many more local units such as bands of kith and kin. But white administrators have been used to dealing with units such as countries and nations or with smaller units such as the family. They frown upon band interdependence, especially when there appears to be much freeloading. There is no incentive to gather, hoard, and save, because those Indians who have accumulated some food or cash are descended upon by their band members until the surplus is exhausted. The band culture conflicts with the American values of individual achievement, accumulation of wealth, saving for the future, and individual industry.

Wax, however, although recognizing some of the problems caused by the band, feels that it is the strength of the band organization—its vitality, tenacity, and flexibility—which has enabled Indian communities to survive at all. The patterns of sharing, voluntary cooperation, equality, and solidarity have sustained the Indian under the most severe conditions of hardship, whereas other forms of organization (such as the individual family) probably would have led to the total destruction of the group.

Money

The acculturated and urbanized Indians use money in the same manner as the majority culture. However, money takes on a different aspect for those on reservations, where there is little opportunity for agricultural or industrial employment and low cash incomes.

The Indian is able to survive on little money because of the band organization with its mutual assistance, sharing, and pooling. This unit goes far beyond the nuclear family and the extended family, and includes a complex of families living close together. There are also many "free" services. Surplus foods and health care are provided; wood and water are available; and while they are not grand, there are cabins. Since everyone lives under similar circumstances, the competitive strains of the American social system (e.g., having a bigger house, keeping up with the Joneses) are lacking.

Under these circumstances, the Indians use the money for specialties and luxuries. Cash is paid out for sweets, clothes, and trips to relatives, which appalls the "sensible" welfare workers who have nuclear families and live on fixed, scheduled incomes. They accuse the Indians of being irresponsible, haphazard, and ignorant of the value of money; they try to deprive the Indians of their cash, and instead provide the goods and services they think are necessary.

A similar situation exists in some colleges and universities that are granted large amounts of money to teach and train Indians. As Wax says:

> In a sense, the universities have inherited the social role played in the nineteenth century by missionary groups who came to control the reservations because the federal operations could not be kept free of the taint of political corruption. But, just as the missionaries, the universities are insulated from the influence of local Indian communities, and organize their programs according to ideologies, professional codes, and bureaucratic procedures that exclude any control by the relatively uneducated Indians. As the universities build staffs and operate programs, they become increasingly dependent upon these monies, and constitute a vested interest of some potency in maintaining reservations in a subordinated state (1971: 82).

Education

Immigrant groups have always believed education to be the major route to "success"; they think education will allow them to be assimilated into the American way of life. But many of them give up their ethnic "ways" only to find their entrance into the American system blocked. This leaves them in the category of "part white ethnics" with its subsequent problems of identity, alienation, and marginality. The Indian child who does extremely well in school may be looked upon as "marginal" or deviant if the vast majority of his peers adopt other norms.

The interaction between Indians and white society's schools is often painful. There is a gulf between the parents and the school system, especially on the reservations, and the cultural separateness of the children and their teachers is another barrier. The outsider (the teacher) vainly tries to impose unfamiliar and even dysfunctional styles on the lives of the insiders (the Indian children). There may be much confusion, inattention, and little actual learning, even though by the middle grades there may be a semblance of order and quietness. Predictably, scholastic achievement test scores reveal a steady decline with advancemnt in grade. Wax feels that the failure of educators to recognize and integrate the Indian peer society in educational tasks is at the root of the difficulty. Other explanations include the alienation of the children from both schools and parents; the inadequate curriculum of the schools (English as a second language); the simple lack of linguistic facility, and the question of motivation, identification, and confidence. One could also question the meaning of an American education for the Indian.

Wax cites some typical conflicts that occur in the schools when teachers are unaware of the peer society. Indian pupils hesitate to perform individually before the class not only because they do not want to be exposed as inadequate but also because they do not want to demonstrate their individual superiority and thereby the inferiority of their peers. However, if competition is based on a peer-group basis (such as on athletic teams), they can become excellent participants.

The Cherokees have an ethic of "harmony." Gulick (1960) emphasizes that the self-assertive, aggressive individual destroys this harmony, and yet many teachers promote "self," aggressiveness, and assertiveness as student ideals. For the tribal Cherokee, this individuated interaction is morally very troublesome. Individual victory, achievement, and exposure—desirable norms in the larger society—are met with uncomfortable and passive resistance by the minority. Wax claims that a blindfolded man could discern the sharp differences between the Oklahomans of white and Cherokee background. The timbre and loudness of the voices and the frantic attempts to get the attention of the teacher clearly differentiate the whites from the Indians.

The error of many teachers, is their desire to disrupt the peer society for individual reward and effort. It is the peer society that provides the Indian with his sense of identity and self; the destruction of this tie is to deprive the individual with one of his most important sources of security and worth.

Reforms in the educational process for Indians have proved to be as difficult to carry out as reforms in any other area of Indian-white relationships. More and more Indians are moving into urban areas, and federal monies set aside for their special education are probably absorbed into the general fund. The BIA schools continue to have their problems and tend to reflect the interests of the local pressure groups. There are few Indians in colleges and universities; education has not been the "ladder to success" for most Indians.

ALCOHOLISM

The vulnerability of the Indian to alcohol has become a legend. However, the Indian style of drinking does not consist in demure cocktails before dinner or "holding one's liquor like a gentleman"—rather, it is what Wax calls "binge drinking." This drinking takes place in peer groups, usually of young males and is often associated with driving at high speeds and encounters with the police, with the promise of danger and possible disaster.

Some have argued that the relative newness of liquor in Indian life has led to some of the current problems, and that the Indian has not yet had time to work out a culturally acceptable way of drinking (at least from majority norms). The problem is compounded by the fact that many Indians value states of trance and euphoria and the all-important warrior rituals that are recreated under the influence of alcohol. The conflict between being an Indian warrior or a "failure" in Western terms can be partially forgotten when one is inebriated.

Whatever the reason, liquor has often gotten Indians into trouble with law-enforcement agencies. In 1960, the rate of Indian arrests for crimes related to alcohol was twelve times the national average and five times that of the Negroes. And drunkenness seems to rise as the Indian migrates to urban areas.

Statistics also show a high proportion of Indians in penal institutions. For example, in South Dakota where the Indians represent about 5 percent of the total state population, they constitute over 33 percent of the prison population. As with most "official" statistics, the reasons behind the incarceration may be questioned; nevertheless, it provides one indication of a continuing social problem.

DEPENDENCY

The United States dealings with the Indian have encouraged a dependency and irresponsibility especially in relationship to inheritance laws. Instead of considering rights, duties, privileges, and responsibilities in the complex net of Indan social relationships, the United States views the membership of each person as a case of heirship to a piece of property (Wax, 1971). This encourages the individual to think solely in terms of rights, privileges, and rewards, and not in terms of duties, responsibilities, and obligations. For example, anyone who can show Indian blood may be eligible for various federal benefits (in health, education, employment) regardless of whether he participates in an Indian community or contributes to its existence. Similar Anglo-Saxon inheritance logic is applied to voting on tribal matters, the sale of property, and other proceedings, with the result that the functioning Indian tribal society is constantly disrupted by those whose only bond with the group is that of blood.

155

Of relatively recent origin has been the rise of young Indian militancy. A true Indianism is espoused, and the roles of the sell-out (the "white-noser"), the pseudo-Indian, the "yes" man ("Uncle Tomahawk"), the bureaucracy, and the goals of Anglo-conformism are decried.

In 1973, Indians reoccupied Wounded Knee as a symbolic gesture of their unresolved problems. The motives of the participants and the reactions of the government varied, but the reminder of broken treaties, unkept promises, and continued second-class treatment was difficult to ignore.

Indian Personality

Spindler and Spindler (1957) have examined empirical studies, observations, writings, and impressions in order to ascertain if there are psychological characteristics that may be considered universal among North American Indian tribes. Although there are numerous exceptions, the following were among the more widely shared psychological characteristics: nondemonstrative emotionality and reserve; a high degree of social control over interpersonal in-group aggression; generosity used as a social device; autonomy of the individual; ability to endure pain, hardship, hunger, and frustration without external evidence of discomfort; highly aggressive and daring behavior in military exploits; a generalized fear that the world is a dangerous place; a fear of witchcraft; a fondness for practical jokes; attention to the concrete realities of the present; practicality in contrast to abstract integration of long-term goals; dependence upon the supernatural; and an orientation more toward fate than to personal "will." These characteristics are, of course, not fixed, and variations and change do occur. As with all personality variables, they reflect the needs of the individual.

There is evidence that some of the psychological traits are quite deep-rooted and resistant to change. A study by Wallace (1951) indicates that the Tuscarora Iroquois are not as afraid of heights as most American males. Therefore, many high-construction laborers in certain parts of the country are Tuscaroras; but in their savings and consumption habits, they remain more "Indian" than "American." Despite 150 years of white example, often accompanied by persuasion and punishment, they do not compulsively maintain their cars and equipment like most Americans. They do not save money regularly, are not punctual for appointments, and do not maintain their houses in a white middle class manner despite the protestations of the larger community.

The problem with most cross-cultural psychological tests is the assumption that white standards are "normality." Most of the descriptions of the Indian personality and behavior are firmly rooted in this tradition; **156**

Indian behavior is not seen as a reaction to the white world and as a defense against problems.

NATIVE TYPE

Spindler describes various Indian psychological types which have been generated by their interaction with the contemporary American culture. These represent various kinds of personal and social adaptation to cultural change. The "native" type was raised as an Indian and has had only peripheral and marginal contact with the white man. He represents the modal, aboriginal personality of whatever tribal group he is a member. For example, Spindler indicates that if he were a Menominee, he would accept the dictates of fate, would retain his equanimity under stress, and would be high on self-control. His fantasies include men and animals transforming themselves into one another, and his dreams provide a source of inspiration. His personality functions well under a traditional setting, but he is unequipped, psychologically and technologically, for the competitive American world. He is aware of this and is nostalgic for the old days, but realizes that there is no return. By definition, he is aged, and the ancient Indian culture will probably die with the passing away of his generation.

REAFFIRMATIVE NATIVE TYPE

This type is generally represented by younger men who were raised as Indians, frequently by grandparents. But they have been exposed to the white culture through boarding schools and part-time work outside the reservation. Either because they were not motivated to become "American" or because they were blocked in doing so, they have "returned" to the tradition-oriented group on the reservation. However, although they have returned, their position is much more ambivalent than the native type; they often have reservations about their traditional culture. They also are ambivalent about the white and may feel personally inadequate in their identifications with either Indians or whites. Spindler indicates that this type probably constitutes the largest number of native-oriented groups existing on reservations today.

TRANSITIONAL TYPES

All Indians are in a transitional stage and are caught in a marginal position. There is no one transitional type, but the term can be used to describe those whose basic psychological structures are still Indian but have had this structure eroded, most often by regressive breakdowns. For example, they may lose their self-control; their rich fantasy life may become depleted; or they may develop marked anxiety with outbursts of overt and sometimes destructive hostility. They may also be remarkably

generous and dangerously hostile, especially when drunk. The transitionals are the unknown quotient in tribal decision-making because they
change their positions so abruptly. Spindler feels that the unpredictable,
aggressive types constitute a sizeable proportion of most tribes.

A SPECIAL TYPE

In many Indian communities, there exists various religious groups
such as the Native American Church. They represent another solution to
the problems of culture conflict and self-doubt brought about by the
impact of the white culture. They often serve as a stabilizing point for
the free-floating, marginal Indians. They also provide a coherent rationalization of the culture conflict itself since in their religious observ-
ances, white and Indian patterns of belief and behavior are intermingled.

For example, the Peyotists among the Menominee are concerned
with their past lives, preoccupied with sins and salvation and with the
meanings of the Peyote ritual and rationale. They are people who are
somewhat more organized than the ungrouped transitionals, and are
sufficiently reality-centered to earn a living and to lead more ordered
lives.

The use of peyote as a religious experience has met with white
opposition. But the current dreams for a pluralistic society have encouraged a revival of an Indian religious heritage independent of white
religious practices. Indians stress that their religion and culture are so
deeply intertwined that they cannot be conveniently separated.

ACCULTURATED TYPES

There are many kinds of acculturated types, depending on local
circumstances and contact. Generally, the acculturated type does not
display the stoic emotional control characteristic of the native type,
nor does he exhibit the anxiety and unpredictable hostility of the
transitional type, nor the self-involvement and search for resolution of
personal and cultural conflict of the Peyotists. Instead, emotions and
aggressions are channeled directly toward success through economic and
occupational advancement. He controls and integrates his anxiety through
goal orientations—he becomes a middle-class, achievement-oriented
American. This type is not usually found on reservations, for he is
generally apt to leave and become assimilated into the American social
structure.

All of these types represent hypothesized adaptations of subordinated
populations to the realities of life in a racist society. No one adaptation
is necessarily superior to the other, although certain styles may be preferred according to the values of the observer. As with many of our
ethnic groups, a newer type is also emerging; this type tries to establish

an Indian identity that cuts across tribal and other localized affiliations.
He may become militant and attempt to build upon "red power"; he considers the white man and his legal machinery to be the major barriers toward a better Indian life.

INDIAN WOMEN

Spindler indicates that because of the greater continuity of the Indian woman's vote, she exhibits consistent overall differences in her adaptation to culture change. Indian women tend to be less anxious and tense; they react more quickly solving problems, exhibit more emotional control, and are more limited in their intellectual interests and experiences than the males. However, the samples of the study were small, and the variations from tribe to tribe and area by area are wide.

For example, the derogatory term "squaw" was drawn from white perceptions about ideal male-female relationships. But in reality a woman's place in the social order of an Indian society was often better than a white woman's. Indian women generally enjoyed a good deal more independence and autonomy than their white counterparts, and in times of widowhood and financial need, they could turn to their tribe, while white women were often left to the care of the almshouse. Women could be leaders in some tribes and "squaws" in others, and only the biased eyes of an observer representing a "superior" culture could transform this incredible diversity into simplistic categories.

Poverty

After all that has been said and done to the Indian, the biggest problem is poverty. The Indian is the poorest of the poor, and his struggle for existence overrides all other concerns. For example, his average yearly income is about $1,500; and 40 to 45 percent of employable Indians are unemployed (New York *Times,* 1967). To a considerable extent, poverty is responsible for his lack of education, especially at the college level, his unemployment, and his lack of skills.

Poverty is also related to his powerlessness. As Deloria (1970) indicates, Indian children were "kidnapped" and taken away to government boarding schools, often thousands of miles away. They were whipped if they used their native language. Indian ceremonies were banned even on their own reservations. "People thought that by banning everything Indian, they could bring the individual Indians from the Stone Age to the Electric Age in one generation" (Deloria, 1970: 109).

The tragedy of the Indians' plight is in a sense the irony of America. In his rage for progress, the white man has not only threatened the Indian with extinction, he has also plundered the land, decimated its

natural resources, brought about overcrowdedness, pollution and destroyed much of the natural richness of the country. One national magazine put it this way:

> From its Indian citizens, the United States may yet learn some lessons
> about restoring the balance between man and his surroundings. The In-
> dian has always been a partner of nature, not a destroyer of it. In the
> legends he wrote about mountains, trees, lakes and canyons, in his under-
> standing of the spiritual force of nature, he has maintained a vision of
> coherence and beauty: the land and the men upon it must exist in harmony
> (*Life* magazine, 1971: 38).

TABLE 7–1
INDIAN POPULATION OF THE
UNITED STATES FOR SPECIFIED YEARS *

1890	248,253
1920	244,437
1940	333,369
1950	357,499
1960	523,591
1970	792,730

* Many students of Indian affairs feel that the Census reports are underestimated.

Source: U.S. Bureau of the Census. General population, 1970. U.S. Department of
Commerce.

BIBLIOGRAPHY

BROWN, DEE (1970). *Bury My Heart at Wounded Knee.* New York: Holt,
Rinehart & Winston, Inc.

CAHN, EDGAR, ed. (1969). *Our Brother's Keeper: The Indian in White
America.* New York: New Community Press.

DELORIA, VINE JR. (1972). "An Indian's Plea to the Churches." Los Angeles
Times, February 6, Section G. Pp. 1–2.

——— (1973). "Bury our Hopes at Wounded Knee." Los Angeles *Times,*
April 1. P. 1.

——— (1970). *We Talk, You Listen.* New York: The Macmillan Company.

GULICK, JOHN (1960). *Cherokees at the Crossroads.* Chapel Hill: University
of North Carolina, Institute for Research in Social Science.

KROEBER, THEODORA (1964). *Ishii.* Berkeley, Calif.: Parnassus Press.

Life Magazine (1971). "Our Indian Heritage." July 2. Pp. 38–67.

McSWAIN, ROMOLA MAE (1965). *The Role of Wives in the Urban Adjustment of Navaho Migrant Families to Denver, Colorado.* Master of Arts
Thesis. Honolulu: University of Hawaii, Department of Anthropolgy.

NASH, GARY (1970). "Red, White and Black: The Origins of Racism in
Colonial America." In Nash and Weiss, eds., *The Great Fear.* New
York: Holt, Rinehart & Winston, Inc. Pp. 1–26.

New York *Times* (1967). February 19. P. 33.

SPINDLER and SPINDLER (1957). In Murray, *Indian Americans*. Engle - wood Cliffs, N.J.: Prentice-Hall, Inc.

WALLACE, ANTHONY F. C. (1951). *Some Psychological Determinants of Culture Change in an Iroquoian Community*. Washington, D.C.: U.S. Bureau of Ethnology, Bulletin, No. 149. Pp. 59–76.

WAX, MURRAY (1971). *Indian Americans*. Englewood Cliffs, N.J.: Prentice-Hall, Inc. All excerpts are reprinted by permission of the publisher.

THE
AFRO-AMERICANS 8

The Afro-Americans have been the prime movers in bringing about changes in ethnic relations, for of the ethnic groups, they have been in the United States the longest (except for the Indians). Several factors have interacted to place blacks at the forefront of social change. Most important, they have become American, including an identity and expectations that are a part of the system; and in the process, the blacks have raised the fundamental question, can people of color truly share in the American dream? Some immigrant groups have not had to face the question as concretely as the blacks because of a nationality or religious identity that could serve as a substitute. The blacks are numerically the largest non-white minority; but as with most ethnic groups, much of their early adaptation was characterized by periods of acceptance and accommodation.

The very process of incorporating the American ideals, and the high expectations that go with them, have created what Festinger labels a cognitive discrepancy that appears to have been resolved through a push for social change. (The discrepancy refers to a gap between what is expected and what can be realistically achieved.) Perhaps as we look back, we might wonder why it took so long.

The first African arrivals in the United States were twenty slaves who were sold to Virginia settlers in 1619, one year before the coming of the *Mayflower*. Studies by Donnan (1935) and Herskovits (1941) indicate that the vast majority of slaves imported to the American colonies came from an area not more than two hundred miles inland along the coast of West Africa. The black migrants represented many different African cultures that ranged from sophisticated empires to isolated groups; but once in America, they were mistreated alike. Slaves were sold and scattered throughout the new country, and systematic efforts were made to stamp out their native cultures. Although some of the African culture has survived in language, folktales, and music, it was generally impossible for the slave to maintain the old ways.

Several conditions were responsible for this state. First, the slave was generally a younger person and was less attuned to his native culture. Upon arrival, he was thrown in with Africans from all different groups; then finally, his socialization was geared toward the slave system. The two categories—white–nonwhite, superior–inferior—were beginning to form.

Initially, the status of the black man was not clearly defined; in the seventeenth century, he was an indentured servant with rights to freedom after fulfilling contractual obligations. However, because of his color and the ease of identification, a racial caste system evolved; white indentured servants on the other hand were not faced with the prospect of being permanent pariahs.

The transformation from laborer to slave was a complicated process, and it can never be accurately traced, according to Jordan (1968); however it must have been due in part to the Englishmen's view of the Negro's blackness, religion, different styles of life, animality, and sexuality. Further, slaves became social and economic necessities because conditions in America called for a permanent, subservient, and controllable labor force.

The need for laborers was one major reason behind the constant search for new groups to migrate to the United States; there were certain specifications—they had to be good workers of an amply replenishable supply, and they had to somehow adapt to the caste system by lowering their expectations, since such dreams were reserved for their racial "superiors." The steady importation of fresh laborers reinforced the early color barrier.

The development of the color barrier and of two distinct categories is a major cause of our present racial difficulties. There are no white indentured servants now—they were absorbed and integrated into the mainstream, and no doubt, many of their descendants now refer proudly to their early, pioneer stock.

There were also "free" blacks. However, "free" is a comparative term; on one hand, they were freer than slaves, but on the other hand, they were surrounded by the restrictions created by the white society. The boundary restrictions of the two-category system were already in effect—occupations were closed; voting was difficult; and property rights were limited. Laws, customs, and power were lined up against the free blacks; and if the regular means of maintaining social control seemed insufficient, race riots, burnings, and killings kept the Negroes in their place. Finally, they were under the constant threat of being relegated back to slaves.

SLAVERY

The single most important experience for the black man in the United States has been living under the conditions of slavery. It has stamped both slave and slave-owner with an indelible mark that has been difficult to erase even though the Emancipation Proclamation is well over 100 years old, and today no one can claim to have lived under slavery. Yet the system that classifies people into human–subhuman, master–servant, adult–child, owner–owned, and the techniques of maintaining this disparity have survived in both overt and subtle forms. The apartheid system of South Africa (see pp. 47–48) is a current "ideal" model of a two-category system. The United States slave system, however, was also a brutal model.

As with most institutions, slavery evolved variously, depending on the locale. Different owners took different tacks, and there were instances of humane treatment. The picture of the contented, loyal black slave beside his kind white master was quite real in a number of cases. Nevertheless, slavery always meant the degradation of a human being to the status of property.

The Notion of Property

The notion that slaves were property was central to their treatment. Therefore, since they were defined as subhuman they could be completely dominated by their master and used in whatever way he chose. They were bought, sold, given away, or eliminated. The master, for his part, provided room and board, medical care, and any other treatment he saw fit.

Because they were regarded as property, slave women were used sexually or for breeding purposes. The great disadvantage from the owner's perspective was the constant problem of socialization and social control. Discipline was important; the slave had to be trained for a subservient but productive role. Submission and loyalty were included by making slaves fearful and dependent.

165

The slave "culture" could not be maintained by a single family or community alone. There was a host of supporting organizations that served its needs.

Because they were property, slaves enjoyed no family life, civil rights, nor could they enter into legally binding relationships such as marriage. Husbands, wives, and children could be separated at any time; a stable family system was nonexistent. The father was not the head of the family; parents had little say or power in running their family; and the child's status was determined to a great extent by his relationship with his mother (Stampp, 1956). Slavery was also a permanent state. Once a slave, always a slave; there was no reasonable hope of passing on higher expectations to a new generation.

The adverse conditions of slavery can best be left to the imagination. Morbidity and mortality rates were high. Illness, filth, disorder, and disruption were common conditions. Slaves were desired for their labor, and equal social interaction with whites was nonexistent. Education and other means of self-advancement and upward mobility were restricted.

One might well ask how slavery lasted for so long. The numerically inferior white man was able to dominate most of the world for several hundred years. His superior technology, better organization, missionary idealism (both spiritual and economic) and his ability to capitalize on the divisiveness of conquered peoples helped him to maintain power and control.

Indians as Slaves?

The same logic that led to the use of Africans as slaves could have been applied to the American Indians. As Jordan (1968) indicates, the Indian was also different from the Englishman in complexion, religion, nationality, "savagery," and "bestiality." In short, he was closer to the Negro than the white man; he was treated similarly, yet he was not considered to be as desirable a slave as the black.

Jordan mentions certain factors that contributed to the difference. First, in the initial confrontation, the Englishman was more interested in "converting" and "civilizing" the Indians than the Negroes. Second, the "culture" of the Indians made them less enslavable. They were not used to settled agriculture, and their life styles (although there were so many different Indian life styles that some of them might have fit readily into the pattern of slavery) were generally not suited for slavery.

But the most important single difference was related to power. The Indians had land the white man wanted, and they were able to retaliate and to mount reprisals in a way that the Negroes never could. The Indians were also dealt with diplomatically, which meant a degree of equal-status conduct. Then there were "friendly" Indian tribes and nations, and there had to be some discriminatory standard.

Finally, Indians had to be treated as nations, and this created social distance, detachment, and even respect since Englishmen admired independent, fighting nations, even if they were antagonists. Conversely, the Negroes did not represent a nation; and since their labor was so necessary, intimate daily contact was established under less than equal conditions.

As Jordan indicates, the Indian, rather than the Negro, became symbolic of America—the profile of the Indian and the buffalo, not the Negro, graced the famous five-cent piece.

The Civil War

The problem of slavery was one of the critical factors leading to the Civil War. However, neither side really conceived of the black as an equal. For example, the Northern armies rejected early Negro enlistees for a variety of reasons, most of them overtly racist, and having to do with Negro inferiority and cowardice.

However, "as the war developed . . . army commanders were permitted to use their own discretion about utilizing Negroes. Some commanders insisted on returning runaway slaves to their owner, and others permitted them to fight. . . . When they were finally permitted to enlist . . . Negroes did so enthusiastically. By the end of the Civil War, approximately 186,000 black troops had been enrolled. These troops took part in 198 battles and suffered 68,000 casualties" (Pinkney: 1969, 19). Even more took part in the overall war effort as servants, laborers, and spies; but a familiar racist pattern was in evidence—blacks served in segregated units under white officers.

The Confederate armies were less successful in enlisting black soldiers. The South was limited by one basic fear—that armed blacks might turn against their former masters. Late in the war, the Confederates drafted a conscription bill, but most blacks fled rather than be drafted into the Southern army.

The role of the black soldier in the Civil War has been underplayed and devalued in the past, but more recent research suggests the important role they played in the Union victory.[1]

The Postwar Period

The Emancipation Proclamation, signed January 1, 1863, while the war was still in progress, brought a formal end to the institution of slavery. In retrospect, although the bill was a dramatic political gesture, it created

---

[1] In subsequent wars—World Wars I and II, Korea, and Vietnam—black soldiers fought in great numbers on the side of democracy and equality overseas while facing discriminatory barriers at home.

vast problems for most slaves. There had been very little planning for active black citizen participation, a necessary step since Negroes had lived under the bonds of slavery, illiteracy, and dependence for so many years. The president also made it clear that the primary purpose of the Proclamation was to preserve the Union, rather than to abolish slavery.

The South was a defeated and devastated country following the end of the Civil War. Reconstruction of the area seemed far more important than civil rights and the living conditions of the "newly emancipated." Moreover, the defeated Southerners still maintained their feelings about the inferiority of their former slaves, and violence, both legal and illegal, was a common solution to racial problems.

For example, DuBois (1935) writes that Southerners tried to re-institute slavery through a series of legalisms that would recreate the institution in everything but name. The Black Codes specified conditions of work, property rights, rights to public assembly, ownership of firearms, and other aspects of Negro life. Blacks could be arrested by any white man—suggesting apartheid: "Every Negro freedman who shall be found on the streets . . . after ten o'clock at night without a written pass or permit . . . shall be imprisoned . . . or pay a fine" (DuBois: 1935, 177). Although the Black Codes were suspended by the Freedman's Bureau before they became fully effective, most Southerners actively opposed granting equality to their former slaves. Rather, a return to the two-category system, whether called slavery or another name, was their choice.

Reconstruction

For a short time after the Civil War, blacks actively participated in the political arenas in the South. A series of Reconstruction acts and the passage of the Fifteenth Amendment (1870) guaranteed Negroes the right to vote. The Civil Rights Act of 1866 gave blacks the rights of American citizenship, and the Fourteenth Amendment prohibited states from depriving any person of life, liberty, or property without due process of law and also guaranteed equal protection. According to Pinkney, "During the period of Radical Reconstruction black people participated in politics to a greater extent than in any other period in American history. . . . They often held important offices, but there was never a Negro governor. There were two lieutenant-governors, and several Negroes represented their states in the United States Congress" (1969: 25).

However, violence against blacks was a constant problem. The disputed election of Republican President Hays, which resulted in the Compromise of 1877, was a turning point for the freed slaves. Rather than advancing toward equality, they moved back to the pre-Civil War era. Federal troops were withdrawn from the South, and the old Southern leadership rapidly returned.

The years from 1877 to 1954 could be labelled the "dark ages" for the Negroes in the United States. The Civil War had been fought and "won"; the Emancipation Proclamation abolished formal slavery; there was the opportunity for a newer relationship, but the clock did not move forward. The conditions under which Negroes were forced to live belied any free status. The boundaries of the two-category stratification system—prejudice, discrimination, and segregation—became stronger than ever. The Negroes were, for all intents and purposes, relegated to a caste position based on color, and no black man could expect equal treatment. Informal, "spontaneous" methods of maintaining the boundaries and keeping the blacks in their place were frequently used. Lynchings were one of the most popular.

Lynchings

Lynching has long been a part of interracial history. Although the origin of the lynch law is somewhat clouded, there is an association with Charles Lynch, a Virginia Quaker who was born near the present city of Lynchburg, Virginia in 1736 (Shay, 1938). Although Lynch was sympathetic to the colonies, during the revolution, he did not actively participate in the rebellion. However, when the existing laws and courts of justice were unable to cope with some Tories who were stealing horses for the British armies, Lynch and several companions decided to take the law into their own hands. They caught the thieves, held court, brought witnesses, then meted out punishment to those who they felt were guilty. The first "lynchings" were whippings and lashings, not hangings.

Lynching was one means of handling conflict, usually with only a semblance of a trial, through extralegal means, against individuals who were suspected, accused, or convicted of a violation of laws, customs, or mores. At this early stage, blacks were seldom the victims; instead, they were horse thieves, wife beaters, gamblers, and murderers. Execution was an added "refinement."

Blacks became the primary targets in the decades preceding the Civil War, and increasingly so after the war. As Berry says:

> Finally, the period of the Civil War and the Reconstruction saw the pattern of lynching firmly established: courts of law, though in full operation are circumvented; no effort is made to determine the guilt of the accused; punishment is invariably death, often accompanied by torture; and the victim is usually a Negro (1958: 125).

As with much "official data" in the social sciences, secondary sources must be relied upon to ascertain the number of lynchings, and they often **169** furnish unreliable statistics. One source estimates the number of lynchings since 1882 to be more than 5,000 (Shay, 1938: 7). However, lynching has declined in popularity over time. It reached its height in 1892, when there were 235 recorded lynchings; by the 1920s the average number had dropped to 31.2 per year, and since the 1920s, there have been only scattered reports.

The following generalizations can be made about lynchings (Berry, 1958).

1. There is a relationship between sex and lynching; the presumed violation of a white woman was a major incentive to mob action.
2. There were a surprising number of trivial causes for lynching, such as insulting a white man, circulating radical literature, and drunkenness.
3. The character of lynching has changed over time—from floggings to executions—and so have the victims—from white to black.
4. Indians, Mexicans, Japanese, Chinese, and Filipinos have also been victims. On other occasions, Italians, Swiss, Jewish, and Bohemians have been lynched.
5. The causes of lynching lie much deeper than the triggering event. Attitudes toward the law, complex economic and social conditions, the frontier heritage in American culture, and racism are responsible for many of the actions.
6. Lynching as a form of boundary maintenance has been replaced by more sophisticated forms of control.

Although lynching served primarily as a symbolic device to keep the black man "in his place," it was symptomatic of the racial barriers. Any form of behavior that threatened the ego of the white Southerner could be punished violently.

As could be expected under these negative conditions, there was an exodus of blacks from the South to the Northern urban areas. There was the promise of more jobs and better social opportunities. However, the blacks discovered that racism was not confined to the South, and that Northern white behavior was less than "Christian." A number of laws, customs, standards, and rationalizations brought about barriers and the creation of segregated areas often as severe as those in the South. A newer feature, mob violence in the form of race riots, was added to the already impressive list of techniques to maintain white superiority. Step'n Fetchit was the only acceptable black model of the times.

CURRENT SCENE

Of all the ethnic groups, the history of the Negro is probably the most important to understand because he has suffered the greatest degradation, and his treatment has been the least humane. The "culture" of other groups may have been different, and life in the old country was often under nonequalitarian systems, but the closed system of slavery has no parallel in recent history.

Negroes are the largest and most visible minority group; they are in the process of evolving a community and family system, and some of their problems can be assessed through an analysis of official statistics.

Numbers

The sheer number of blacks presents the greatest threat to white supremacy. In 1965, they numbered over 21 million, or 10.8 percent of the population; and by 1970, they numbered 22,580,289, or 11.1 percent.

Pinkney states that at the time of the first U.S. Census in 1790, blacks represented an even higher percentage. They constituted 19.3

TABLE 8–1
THE NEGRO POPULATION OF THE UNITED STATES, 1790–1965

Year	Total U.S. Population	Total Negro Population	Percent Negro
1970	203,211,926	22,580,289	11.1
1965	193,818,000	20,944,000	10.8
1960	179,323,175	18,874,831	10.5
1950	150,697,361	15,042,286	10.0
1940	131,669,275	12,865,518	9.8
1930	122,775,046	11,891,143	9.7
1920	105,710,620	10,463,131	9.9
1910	91,972,266	9,797,763	10.7
1900	75,944,575	8,833,994	11.6
1890	62,974,714	7,488,676	11.9
1880	50,155,783	6,580,973	13.1
1870	39,818,449	5,392,172	13.5
1860	31,443,321	4,441,830	14.1
1850	23,191,876	3,638,808	15.7
1840	17,069,453	2,873,648	16.8
1830	12,866,020	2,328,642	18.1
1820	9,638,453	1,771,656	18.4
1810	7,239,881	1,377,808	19.0
1800	5,308,483	1,002,037	18.9
1790	3,929,214	757,208	19.3

Source: Computed from data from the following U.S. Bureau of the Census publications: *Historical Statistics of the United States, Colonial Times to 1957*, Series A 59–70, p. 9, and Series A 17–21, p. 8; *1960 Census of Population, Characteristics of Population, U.S. Summary*, Vol. 1, Part 1, Table 44; *Statistical Abstract of the United States, 1966*, Table 9, p. 11. The 1965 data represent estimates published in *Current Population Reports*, Series P-20, No. 155, "Negro Population: March, 1965," p. 1. The data on the Negro population for 1870 have been adjusted by the Bureau of the Census to account for underenumeration in Southern states.

percent (750,000) of that early population; their growth has been steady ever since.[2]

The general life expectancy of blacks (and other nonwhites) is lower than for whites (Table 8–2). Possible causes include generally poorer health care, inadequate nourishment, and impoverished living conditions.

TABLE 8–2
LIFE EXPECTANCY IN PRIME WORKING YEARS: 1960 AND 1968
(ADDITIONAL YEARS OF LIFE EXPECTED)

| | 1960 | | | 1968 | | |
Age	Negro and other races	White	Difference	Negro and other races	White	Difference
25	43.1	48.3	−5.2	42.6	48.6	−6.0
35	34.3	38.8	−4.5	34.0	39.1	−5.1
45	26.2	29.7	−3.5	26.2	30.0	−3.8
55	19.3	21.5	−2.2	19.2	21.8	−2.6

Source: U.S. Department of Commerce (1970: 97). United States Census Special Studies: The Social and Economic Status of the Negroes in the United States. Bureau of Labor Statistics Report.

The Community

The black migration from the rural South to the urban North has been understandable. They have tried to escape low rural incomes ($1,750 median in 1964) and a life of poverty, landlessness, dependency, and second-class status. Southern black rural communities are readily identifiable with their unpaved streets, slum housing, inadequate plumbing, and a general shabby ambience.

Southern community life generally reflects the malaise of rural Southern communities. The stratification of black and white minimizes social interaction and whatever relationships between the races occur in the economic realm. Virtually all of the land is held by whites so that for the rural black man, a life of hard work, low income, poor education, and poor treatment continue to be realistic expectations.

The segregated church and school remain as the dominant community institutions. Baptist congregations are the largest, and one of the functions of the church is to provide emotional relief and an outlet for

---

[2] One interesting fact about the population, which is also a commentary on the effects of racism, concerns the male-female ratio. According to the 1970 Census, black sex ratios are relatively equal through the age of fourteen, but from fifteen years on there were almost ten black females for every nine black males (Jackson, 1972). Jackson hypothesizes that black males generally die earlier than black females from heart and lung disease, alcoholism and drugs, automobile and industrial accidents, homicide, and suicide.

a life of extreme hardship. Significantly, individual clergymen such as the late Reverend Martin Luther King, Jr. have played an important part in the civil rights movement.

The Urban Community

In 1960, 73 percent of all blacks lived in the urban areas; in the North and West, they were almost exclusively (95 percent) urbanites.

> In 1970, four out of every ten Negroes in the United States were living in the 30 cities with the largest Negro population. This percent of the total Negro population of the United States residing in the 30 selected cities has shown a steady increase since 1950.
>
> Among these 30 cities, New York and Chicago have maintained their first and second rank, respectively, over the last three decades. Detroit, in 1970, has displaced Philadelphia as the third ranking place and Washington, D.C. has remained fifth (U.S. Department of Commerce: 1970: 17).

However, life in the North may not be that much of an improvement over life in the rural South. The Negro is likely to live in the most blighted and decayed section of the city. The housing is older, more dilapidated, segregated, and overcrowded; as Pinkney states:

> Chief among the characteristics of the urban black community are its powerlessness and its dependence on the frequently hostile white community which surrounds it. These enclaves are kept powerless by powerful individuals and institutions in the white community. The dwellings of the urban black community are usually owned by absentee white landlords and institutions, and no attempt is made to maintain the buildings or to provide the customary services to their inhabitants. Residential buildings, for which the occupants are charged high rents, frequently do not provide safe and adequate shelter. Often they are owned by wealthy and politically prominent suburban residents. Community services, such as garbage collection and street cleaning, are provided less frequently than in the white community (Pinkney, 1969: 61).

In many ways the black community is like a colonial possession: it is economically and politically dependent upon the white world. It is there to serve the larger community with its supply of cheap labor. The community does not make the important decisions—the decisions are made by white Americans. In periods of disorder the ethnic enclaves are sealed off, and specially trained police and military forces with riot equipment are rushed into emergency positions. The root causes of the disruptions are seldom touched; when conditions are restored to "normality," the armed forces are withdrawn, but remain alert for other calls.

TABLE 8–3
NEGRO POPULATION, 1970, 1960, AND 1950, FOR 30 CITIES WITH THE LARGEST NEGRO POPULATION (RANK ACCORDING TO 1970 NEGRO POPULATION. NUMBERS IN THOUSANDS)

Rank			1970		1960		1950	
Total population	Negro population	City and State	Number	Percent Negro	Number	Percent Negro	Number	Percent Negro
		United States, total	22,578	11	18,872	11	15,042	10
		30 selected cities, total	9,217	29	6,837	22	4,501	15
		Percent of U.S.	41	(X)	36	(X)	30	(X)
1	1	New York, N.Y.	1,667	21	1,088	14	749	10
2	2	Chicago, Ill.	1,103	33	813	23	493	14
5	3	Detroit, Mich.	660	44	482	29	299	16
4	4	Philadelphia, Pa.	654	34	529	26	376	18
9	5	Washington, D.C.	538	71	412	54	280	35
3	6	Los Angeles, Calif.	504	18	335	14	171	9
7	7	Baltimore, Md.	420	46	326	35	224	24
6	8	Houston, Tex.	317	26	215	23	125	21
10	9	Cleveland, Ohio	288	38	251	29	148	16
19	10	New Orleans, La.	267	45	234	37	181	32
27	11	Atlanta, Ga.	255	51	186	38	121	37
18	12	St. Louis, Mo.	254	41	214	29	153	18
17	13	Memphis, Tenn.	243	39	184	37	147	37
8	14	Dallas, Tex.	210	25	129	19	58	13
36	15	Newark, N.J.	207	54	138	34	75	17
11	16	Indianapolis, Ind.	134	18	98	21	64	15
48	17	Birmingham, Ala.	126	42	135	40	130	40
29	18	Cincinnati, Ohio	125	28	109	22	78	16
38	19	Oakland, Calif.	125	35	84	23	48	12
23	20	Jacksonville, Fla.	118	22	106[1]	23[1]	82[1]	27[1]
26	21	Kansas City, Mo.	112	22	83	18	56	12
12	22	Milwaukee, Wis.	105	15	62	8	22	3
24	23	Pittsburgh, Pa.	105	20	101	17	82	12
57	24	Richmond, Va.	105	42	92	42	73	32
16	25	Boston, Mass.	105	16	63	9	40	5
21	26	Columbus, Ohio	100	19	77	16	45	12
13	27	San Francisco, Calif.	96	13	74	10	43	6
28	28	Buffalo, N.Y.	94	20	71	13	37	6
75	29	Gary, Ind.	93	53	69	39	39	29
30	30	Nashville-Davidson, Tenn.	88	20	76[1]	19[1]	64[1]	20[1]

X Not applicable.

[1] 1960 and 1950 populations revised in accordance with 1970 boundaries.

Source: U.S. Department of Commerce, Bureau of the Census (1970: 17).

Most of the status distinctions within the ethnic community parallel those of the white community. Variables such as income, occupation, education, and family background are common measures of status in most cultures. Other indications of social status include property ownership, organizational affiliation, leadership ability, charisma, and life style. Life style is an especially interesting variable and will be discussed more fully later.

Certain distinctions in social status such as white ancestry, skin color, speech accent, and cultural similarities to the whites used to be important to the black subculture. The growth of black identity and changed views on color and white ancestry have led to a reevaluation of these variables.

The Upper Classes

A relatively visible class structure appears in the Negro community. Drake and Cayton (1945) described a small upper class, made up of persons with the most money, education, political power, and the "best" family backgrounds. Most of them were doctors, lawyers, newspaper editors, civic leaders, and politicians. More stress was placed on education, professional status, and life style than on income.

Billingsley (1968) comments on the differences between the old and new upper classes. The group described by Drake and Cayton was primarily the old upper class. They were men and women whose parents belonged to the upper or middle classes. Their privileged status extended back to the slave days, when they were given inheritances and more education. Many have done remarkably well—men such as Senator Edward Brooke and Justice Thurgood Marshall are exceptional by any standard. But Billingsley adds that it would be an error to think that these men pulled themselves up by the bootstraps. They came from families who had already given them a head start, and they were able to build upon the many opportunities available to upper-class people.

The most common characteristic of the new upper class is that their mobility has been achieved in one generation. The primary attributes have been talent and luck. Many have gained wealth and prestige by becoming athletic and show business celebrities. Another small group receives an upper-class income by means of the "shadier" occupations— gambling, racketeering, and hustling; through their own abilities they are able to wield a considerable amount of influence in the Negro community (Billingsley, 1968). Finally, there is a small group of newly elected government officials such as mayors (ex-mayors Stokes of Cleveland, Hatcher of Gary) who have risen from humble origins to become attorneys and then to gain high political office.

175

The upper class as a group generally supports civil rights activities through the NAACP or the Urban League; they are usually Protestants and are active in social clubs such as fraternities and sororities (Pinkney, 1969). They usually entertain at home, and their guests are of equal status.

However, the "black elite" in the Los Angeles Community has changed (Los Angeles *Times,* 1972). An upper class has not been established, and there appears to be a rapprochement between the social classes around the issue of black identity. Leadership positions have not gone automatically to the financially successful.

The Middle Classes

There is a growing black middle class. The occupational categories cover a wide range—professionals, independent businessmen, clerical and service workers, and laborers. There are many civil service workers, public school teachers, ministers, and social workers.

Like the white middle class, black middle-class families are small, stable, and "planned;" they want to own their own homes and are concerned about the quality of public schools. They usually belong to a number of organizations and social clubs and have perceptions and values similar to their white counterparts.

But there are several important differences. Billingsley refers to the precarious economic situation of most Negroes; they do not enjoy the same measure of financial security as do the whites. Therefore, they tend to make up for this insecurity by highly visible spending and consumption patterns: the familiar stereotypes of Cadillacs, sharp clothes, and traveling first class that have nothing to do with income. Life style becomes extremely important.

Frazier (1957) uses the term "black bourgeoisie" for members of the middle class. He sees many living in a fantasy world and emulating white values and culture. The world of fraternities and sororities is a way of escaping the stigma of color and traditional black culture; the building up of an American life style without the corresponding economic basis lies at the root of the fantasy. They are concerned about respectability and desire to maintain certain standards of living, often without adequate economic means, and this creates high stress.

The Lower Classes

The lower-class blacks lie at the bottom of the community class structure. Most blacks fall into this category—Pinkney (1969) estimates that as many as two-thirds of the urban blacks belong to the lower class. But they do not belong to the simple, stereotyped group of welfare recipients. As Billingsley says:

Most Negro families are composed of ordinary people. They do not get their names in the paper as outstanding representatives of the Negro race, and they do not show up on the welfare rolls or in the crime statistics. They are headed by men and women who work and support their families, manage to keep their families together and out of trouble most of the time. They are not what might be generally conceived of as "achieving families." They are likely to be overlooked when the white community goes looking for a Negro to sit on an interracial committee, or take a job where Negroes have not been hired before. For they have not gone to college and they are not part of that middle- and upper-class group most likely to come into intimate, daily contact with the white world. At the same time, they are likely to be overlooked by the poverty program and other efforts to uplift the poor and disadvantaged. They often do not qualify to take part in these programs because they are not on welfare. They are, in a word, just folks. . . . And yet, these ordinary Negro families are often the backbone of the Negro community. They are virtually unknown to white people, particularly white people who depend on books and other mass media for their knowledge of life in the most important ethnic subsociety in America today (1968: 137).

Billingsley divides the lower class into three distinct groupings: the working nonpoor, the working poor, and the nonworking poor. The working nonpoor are semiskilled but often well-paid men in industrial jobs: truck drivers, construction workers, and auto mechanics; if it were not for the color of their skins, they would comprise a majority of some labor unions and possess modest homes in the suburbs. But only a relatively small elite constitutes the hard-hat lower class among the blacks.

The working poor comprise the majority of poor blacks. They live "in nuclear families headed by men who work hard every day, and are still unable to earn enough to pull their families out of poverty" (Billingsley, 1968: 139). These families are self-supporting and include the unskilled laborers, service workers, domestics, janitors, and porters. Many of the values that we associate with working-class people—hard work, frugality, a college education, and wanting a better life for their children—are part of their culture. But this group remains invisible and is likely to be ignored when individuals representing the black community are selected.

The bottom rung of the lower-class ladder holds the nonworking poor, sometimes referred to as the "underclass." Pinkney (1969) estimates that as many as two-thirds of the urban blacks fall into this category. They include the chronically unemployed, the welfare recipient, and the newcomer from the South. Family disorganization runs high and they are only brought to the attention of the larger public by means of violent acts or political slogans. They become the stereotype of the urban, disorganized black; they are readily available scapegoats for absorbing some of the frustrations of the taxpayer. Their interaction with the larger society consists primarily in being "clients" to social workers, teachers, and other professionals, or in being "problems" to policemen; needless to say, they are "nothings" to the majority who ignore and forget their existence.

The overriding characteristic of lower-class blacks is alienation. They are powerless; they have very little hope for a better future; and they lack the education and organization to help alleviate their despair and suffering. They tend to belong to fundamentalist churches and are rejected by blacks of higher status. One of the more damaging factors affecting the status of all blacks is that the lower-class black man serves as the stereotype for those who want to maintain the boundaries between races.

THE FAMILY

It is impossible to talk about the black family without discussing the influence of the surrounding communities, both black and white. It is shortsighted to assume that the family exists in isolation and is therefore the "independent" variable which "causes" problems. From this perspective "family disorganization" becomes the "cause," and social problems such as crime, delinquency, and mental illness become the "effects" of the family pattern. But the family itself can be thought of as a response or adaptation to the pressures of survival, and its structure and function is a reflection of a host of other variables.

The distortions are even more pronounced when the white family is used as the standard of excellence. For many members of ethnic groups, there is nothing magical about the white family structure with its ever-increasing rates of separation and divorce. The Moynihan report views with alarm statistics that show nearly one-quarter of all Negro families in 1960 to be headed by females and, therefore, falling apart. Moynihan says, "At the heart of the deterioration of the fabric of Negro society is the deterioration of the Negro family. It is the fundamental source of the weakness of the Negro community at the present time" (Moynihan, 1965: 1). Black writers like Billingsley have questioned the Moynihan report's emphasis—"nearly one-quarter"—which leaves over three-quarters of Negro families with a normal structure. As Bernard says,

> Many readers . . . will be surprised to learn that the "typical" (in the sense of commonest) type of family among Negroes is one in which both husband and wife are living together in their first marriage (Bernard, 1966: Preface).

However, disorganization in many black communities extends far beyond the family itself. Racism, boundary-maintenance mechanisms, and pariah-group status are but a few of the variables that have created pressures on all black institutions, including the family. For example, **178** adequate income alone would help greatly in making black families independent. The lack of income forces an interdependence with the surrounding community. If jobs are scarce and the Negro father is unemployed, the nuclear family will break down (as would any family), especially when the presence of a male in the home makes the family ineligible for public welfare. Conversely, as job security and income are assured, stable, middle-class family patterns will no doubt emerge.[3]

Family Structures

There is a wide range of black families, and they have many variations. Billingsley (1968) presents the various structures (Table 8–4).

TABLE 8–4
NEGRO FAMILY STRUCTURE

Types of Family	Household Head		Other Household Members		
	Husband and Wife	*Single Parent*	*Children*	*Other Relatives*	*Non-relatives*
Nuclear Families					
I: Incipient Nuclear Family	X				
II: Simple Nuclear Family	X		X		
III: Attenuated Nuclear Family		X	X		
Extended Families					
IV: Incipient Extended Family	X			X	
V: Simple Extended Family	X		X	X	
VI: Attenuated Extended Family		X	X	X	
Augmented Families					
VII: Incipient Augmented Family	X				X
VIII: Incipient Extended Augmented Family	X			X	X
IX: Nuclear Augmented Family	X		X		X
X: Nuclear Extended Augmented Family	X		X	X	X
XI: Attenuated Augmented Family		X	X		X
XII: Attenuated Extended Augmented Family		X	X	X	X

Source: Billingsley (1968: 17).

[3] Billingsley (1968) has shown that the black family in Africa was strong and central to African civilization. Generally, it was male-dominated and had various patterns of marriage, lineage, kinship ties, rights, and obligations. Slavery broke up these patterns and did not permit black families to assimilate American culture.

179

Each structure represents a different constellation of members and is a response to certain needs and circumstances; each fulfills certain functions. Given such complex structures, it would be quite false to say that the black family is a "tangle of pathology;" rather, the families are legitimate subsystems of the larger society and represent groups adapting to the needs of their membership.

Since 1950, there has been a gradual decline in the number of black (and other nonwhite) husband–wife type families (a decrease of 77.7 percent to 67.4 percent), and a corresponding rise in the female-headed household (Table 8–5). It is difficult to pinpoint any one reason for this change.

TABLE 8–5
PERCENT DISTRIBUTION OF FAMILIES BY TYPE: 1950, 1955, 1960, AND 1966 TO 1971

Year	Husband-wife		Other male head		Female head [1]	
	Negro and other races	*White*	*Negro and other races*	*White*	*Negro and other races*	*White*
1950	77.7	88.0	4.7	3.5	17.6	8.5
1955	75.3	87.9	4.0	3.0	20.7	9.0
1960	73.6	88.7	4.0	2.6	22.4	8.7
1966	72.7	88.8	3.7	2.3	23.7	8.9
1967	72.6	88.7	3.9	2.1	23.6	9.1
1968	69.1	88.9	4.5	2.2	26.4	8.9
1969	68.7	88.8	3.9	2.3	27.3	8.9
1970	69.7	88.7	3.5	2.3	26.8	9.1
1971	67.4	88.3	3.7	2.3	28.9	9.4

Most of the tables in this section show data on families for the year 1970. Figures on families from the March 1971 Current Population Survey, which recently became available, have been included only in this table in this section.
[1] Female heads of families include widowed and single women, women whose husbands are in the armed services or otherwise away from home involuntarily, as well as those separated from their husbands through divorce or marital discord.
Source: U.S. Department of Commerce, Bureau of the Census (1970: 107).

Low Income

The dramatic problem for the black family is low income. As Pinkney states, "Although black families were larger, they earned significantly less than white families. In 1964, the median income for black families was $3,700" (1969: 94) while the white family median income was $6,900.

In 1969, the median black (and other nonwhite) family income was $6,191 while that of a white family was $9,794. Although there has been a rise in the black income, the dollar gap discrepancy between the races has actually increased from $2,500 in 1947 to about $3,600 in 1969 (Table 8–6).

TABLE 8–6
DISTRIBUTION OF FAMILIES BY INCOME IN 1947, 1960, AND 1969
(ADJUSTED FOR PRICE CHANGES, IN 1969 DOLLARS)

Income	Negro and other races			White		
	1947	1960	1969	1947	1960	1969
Number of families (thousands)	3,117	4,333	5,215	34,120	41,123	46,022
Percent	100	100	100	100	100	100
Under $3,000	57	38	20	21	14	8
$3,000 to $4,999	25	22	19	26	14	10
$5,000 to $6,999	9	16	17	24	19	12
$7,000 to $9,999	6	14	20	17	26	22
$10,000 to $14,999	3	7	16	12	18	28
$15,000 and over		2	8		9	21
Median income	$2,660	$4,001	$6,191	$5,194	$7,252	$9,794

Source: U.S. Department of Commerce, Bureau of the Census (1970: 26).

Other Problems

The stereotype of the black family—many children fathered by separate males, desertion, dependence on welfare, and matriarchal structure—more accurately describes the underclass. The lower the income, the less goods, services, and opportunities. The stress of living for the poor is therefore extremely high; and when the duration and intensity of poverty is taken into consideration, the high rate of "problem" behavior comes as no surprise. Statistics indicate that the rate of illegitimacy for black Americans is eight times the rate for whites (and that a disproportionately high percentage of black children grow up in broken homes (Pinkney, 1969: 96). Crime, delinquency, mental illness, drug addiction, and other signs of a troubled population are all present. Official data on social problems are difficult to interpret because they are subject to a large number of biases. Nevertheless, these high rates continue because of tremendously negative environmental conditions, rigid boundary maintenance mechanisms that "keep them in their place," overall lack of opportunities, and the racist attitudes of most Americans.

In other areas, statistics [4] show that 17 percent of blacks (including

[4] For complete statistics see the U.S. Department of Commerce, Bureau of the Census (1970: 42, 48, 77).

other nonwhite races) are on welfare, as opposed to 4 percent of whites. (It is interesting to note, however, that the total number of whites receiving public assistance is several million higher than the total nonwhite group.) Likewise, the unemployment rate for blacks remains disproportionately high. In 1970, it was almost two times the white unemployment rate. This has been relatively constant over the years. School dropouts also show a disproportionate number of black youths. At age nineteen, 44 percent of black males were not completing high school as compared to 12.9 percent of white males.

THE RACIAL STRATIFICATION SYSTEM AND THE BLACKS

The racial stratification system with the white-black category saw its full effectiveness under the institution of slavery. Those factors which were used to maintain the separation are still very much in evidence today, although the great change has been from a completely closed system to one that is a little more open.

Status

Evidence that the two-category system of racial stratification is not a completely closed one can be inferred from the status of individual blacks. The two most prominent fields for the breakthrough have been athletics and the entertainment industry. Willie Mays and Henry Aaron have become household names, heroes, and idols to thousands of youngsters of all ethnic backgrounds, and entertainers such as Bill Cosby, Flip Wilson, Nancy Wilson, Mahalia Jackson, the late Louis Armstrong, and Duke Ellington have won universal acclaim. Recognition has come relatively late for many—the breaking down of the color barrier in baseball by Jackie Robinson seems ages ago, but measured in historical terms, occurred only yesterday.

There has been an increase in the number of blacks serving in Congress, in state legislatures, as mayors, and as other elected officials (Table 8–7). Public office will be one popular method for black mobility and representation, primarily because of their numerical power.

But the acceptance and success of individual "stars" does little to alter the status of the great majority of blacks. The two-category system, although not a completely closed one, is still impenetrable to most. Some have referred to it as a net or a sieve, whereby the vast majority are trapped by certain boundaries and cannot get any further, while a few manage to slip through. It appears to be an accurate analogy to the experiences of the black population in the United States.

The black man remains the most visible in a color-conscious society. As we have indicated, color has taken on symbolic tones since it is difficult

TABLE 8–7
NEGRO LEGISLATORS AND NEGROES ELECTED TO
OTHER PUBLIC OFFICE: 1962, 1964, 1966, 1968, AND 1970

Subject	1962	1964	1966	1968	1970 [1]
U.S. Senate					
United States	—	—	1	1	1
South	—	—	—	—	—
U.S. House of Representatives					
United States	4	5	6	9	13
South	—	—	—	—	2
State Legislatures					
United States	52	94	148	172	198
South	6	16	37	53	70
Mayors					
United States	(NA)	(NA)	(NA)	29	81
South	(NA)	(NA)	(NA)	17	47
Other elected officials					
United States	(NA)	(NA)	(NA)	914	1,567
South	(NA)	(NA)	(NA)	468	763

Figures for each year shown represent the total number of elected blacks holding office at that time, not just those elected in that year.
— Represents zero. NA Not available.
[1] Figures are current as of March 1971.
Source: U.S. Department of Commerce, Bureau of the Census (1970: 142).

to explain the aversion to blackness strictly on pigmentation alone. It remains the cornerstone to white racism: the identifiability, the ease of classification, and the development of a response set to blacks in general (rather than as individual human beings), remains deeply ingrained in American society.

Perhaps the most dramatic change in recent times has been that of the positive identification with color. Whereas at one time to be white was desirable, the change to "black is beautiful" has redefined the meaning of color. Other ethnic groups have also been going through such a process —former pejoratives such as yellow and brown have changed in meaning. Since color is an attribute that is impossible to change, the shift toward a positive identity in relation to pigmentation can only be a healthy phenomenon. For the alternative is to deny a reality and to practice a wishful expectation that can never be fulfilled.

Segregation has been so successful that the black ghettos in urban areas have developed a considerable amount of localized numerical voting power. In fact blacks already constitute a majority in Washington, D.C., and are close to a majority in several other large cities. If the whites continue to flee to the suburbs as blacks move into the inner city, the blacks will be able to hold great political power in some areas. Politicians cannot ignore the power of a large number of voters. But the power of numbers has only limited uses. It may be responsive to the political realities, but it needs to develop from a broader base. The blacks must become equal in education and income before they can participate with some degree of equality in the present American system.

The Black Revolt

The year 1955 saw the beginning of a changed social movement among the blacks (Geschwender, 1971: 3). Previously there had been revolts, insurrections, runaways, the Niagara movement, and Marcus Garvey's "Back-to-Africa" drive that signaled the desire for social change among many blacks. But generally, these acts were isolated, uncoordinated, and lacked continuity over time, although the last two were more ambitious. There have also been organizations—the underground railroad, the abolitionist movement, the NAACP, and the Urban League aimed at amelioration and change, but they have all been under white control.

Several important factors lie behind the historical development of these social movements. World Wars I and II provided a major impetus for social change: (1) they opened up job opportunities previously unavailable to many Negroes; (2) they provided new experiences and new exposure, especially to those who were sent overseas; and (3) they raised the level of black expectations and standards of living so that during the postwar readjustment periods, many blacks were unwilling to settle for less.

Blacks began to feel acutely deprived and dissatisfied when they compared their situation to the rapid progress of the whites. Whites had made impressive gains in jobs, income, and education but the blacks lagged far behind. Even so, between 1940 and 1960, blacks began to enter the universities at an accelerated rate. Rather than feeling alienated from their background, these educated blacks felt a responsibility toward their communities and reestablished ties with them. Thus arose a collective sense of deprivation, an awareness of common grievances, a view of the white man as the maintainer of the barriers, and the beginning of black solidarity.

184

The civil rights movement in the early 1950s was dominated by middle-class blacks and college students. As late as 1962, the middle-class black was at the forefront (Orbell, 1967); but by 1964, differences in class background began to diminish (Orum and Orum, 1968). As the movement shifted from black middle-class domination, its tactics also became more militant. Leaders also changed rapidly (Killian and Smith, 1960; McWorter and Crain, 1967) as the moods and responses of the movement evolved and strategies shifted. Newer organizations came into being—a wider spectrum of tactics replaced the accommodationist strategies of the previous era. Terms such as "direct action," "confrontation," and "non-negotiable demands" reflected this newer response.

The Supreme Court Decision of 1954

The 1954 Supreme Court decision prohibiting racial segregation in public education was another important milestone in race relations. But as with most landmarks, it was not an isolated, accidental occurrence; rather the decision itself was both the culmination and the beginning of a series of actions affecting the two most important features of boundary mainte-nance—legal discrimination and legal segregation.

There was a corresponding change in the Afro-Americans. Many no longer accept the status quo of the two-category stratification system; the past has given way to a new series of strategies. Whiteness and white role prescriptions are no longer the desired norms; blackness in the forms of black militancy, black power, black identity, and black autonomy have come to the fore. Similar movements in former colonized African areas add an additional impetus, and have led some whites to suspect a world-wide conspiracy. Other members of the dominant majority are now aware that their ideas of democracy and the "melting pot" were based on ethnocentric and racist assumptions. They recognize adaptation, adjust-ment, and acculturation has been a one-way flow—from people of color to that of one color: white.

But the stresses created by newer goals, strategies, and techniques have led to conflict, often of a tragic nature. Violence has been used to maintain the boundaries, and violence has been used to change them. The rhetoric has flowed on and on while newer leaders replace new leaders.

Black Power

The "black power" slogan emerged during a nonviolent march through Mississippi led by William Meredith in 1966. A shot fired by a white hit Meredith and turned a relatively small demonstration into a major one. Stokely Carmichael became the chief advocate of black power, defining it as "the ability of black people to politically get together and organize themselves so that they can speak from a position of strength rather than a position of weakness" (Ladner, 1967: 202). However, since that time there have been so many definitions and applications of this phrase that its original meaning has been misunderstood (Franklin, 1969).

Generally, the black power movement has sought to redistribute the power in society by any means possible. The black power ideology is mainly socialistic and sees capitalism as the major problem because of its exploitative nature. The overthrow of capitalism would eradicate the exploitation; black autonomy, community control of the ghettos, and economic self-sufficiency are viewed as means by which power can be established to oppose all forms of capitalism.

Another branch of its ideology sees power in the hands of a few whites. Blacks, as well as poor whites, are exploited by this select few. Black power contains the possibility of an alliance between blacks and exploited whites.

Black Separatism

Black separatism hopes to create an independent black nation. This may be a temporary goal in order to integrate the blacks and build a power base from which they can attain full equality. Though the advocates of black power and black separatism may differ in rhetoric and tactics, their goals are essentially the same (Gerschwender, 1971).

The two major variations within the black separatist movement are tactical separatism and ultimate separatism (Gerschwender, 1971: 434). Tactical separatism views separation as a means of gaining control over one's own destiny and achieving self-determination by driving out the white colonists who own or control the ghetto industries and schools. Ultimate separatism sees separation as an end in itself rather than as a means to gain power, and desires a strictly black state.

Among the first avowedly separatist movements after World War II was the Nation of Islam (Black Muslim) which espoused ultimate separatism (Howard, 1966). It preached that white men were devils created by a black scientist named Yakub. The whites were considered mentally, physically, and morally inferior to the blacks, who were the first to populate the earth. Yakub's work was met with anger by Allah, who ordained that the white race shall rule for a fixed amount of time over the blacks. In the process the blacks will suffer, but they will gain a greater appreciation of their spiritual worth by comparing themselves to the whites. The Black Muslims desired to free blacks from all white influence and secure land for themselves within the continental United States. Further, their goal was to make the black men aware of their special role and future destiny as black men and to educate them to their past history.

186

Though the Black Muslim movement has split since its inception and its actual membership has never been fully ascertained, it proved to be a threat to the white establishment. The Muslims became the targets of police harassment and negative publicity.

All these changes in strategies threatened white domination. Predictably, in some instances whites mounted a counterreaction out of fear and hostility (Franklin and Starr, 1967), which in turn triggered the formation of black protective and defense organizations.

Increasing Violence and Urban Riots

One of the results of the changes in tactics and strategies has been the increase in violent interaction. The period from 1964 to 1968 was characterized by urban riots and slogans such as "Burn, baby, burn," and "Kill the pigs." Expectations had risen through a series of advances in civil rights. For example, the Civil Rights Acts of 1964 and 1965 desegregated public facilities, ensured voting rights, and addressed the problem of job discrimination. However the effect of these changes on black lives was very slow; there were numerous instances of white intransigence and violence—bombings, intimidation, and the ever-present charges of police brutality (Lieberson and Silverman, 1965). It did not help when most of these charges went unheeded.

Only small percentages of the total Negro population actually participated in outbursts in any given city; most of the urban riots were spontaneous (Meier and Rudwick, 1969) and loosely organized, if at all (Downes, 1968). The participants tended to be younger Negroes between the ages of fifteen and twenty-four, better educated, with incomes comparable to nonparticipants, although the former possessed a slight increase in unemployment. They were motivated by a sense of relative deprivation, which gave the groups a feeling of solidarity. White-owned property was the primary target of violence (Downes, 1968; Meier and Rudwick, 1969).

Government and industry responded to the outbursts with jobs and promises of better conditions. But as the riots of 1967 continued into 1968, many blacks began to question their cost in black lives in cities such as Newark and Detroit. The riots were seen to be counterproductive, and potentially violent outbursts, were "de-fused." Ghetto riots diminished and virtually disappeared in the early 1970s, but they were replaced by a series of shoot-outs between black militants and police (Knopf, 1969).

It is impossible to comfortably predict what course black-white relationships will take. However, they will probably be governed by much more realistic appraisals of the differential power relationships between the groups. Wider coalitions, possibly with the "third world," may be formed; disruptive guerilla tactics may also be used. But there will probably also be an increasing reliance on the legal and political systems to arbitrate race relations, although blacks will become seriously disillusioned with the legal and political system if the decisions are slow to be translated into tangible actions that lead to a better life for the ethnics. However, as we have constantly emphasized, the primary power for shaping the change remains with the white world.

The premature closure of opportunities and the subsequent feelings of hopelessness can only exacerbate desperate actions. We may begin to see a rise in "crazy" behavior, if individuals and small groups feel that the risk of death is preferable to a painful day by day existence. A society itself must be partially sick if it denies even the opportunity to dream of a better life.

SUMMARY

The situation of the blacks provides an illustration of the Rashomon phenomenon. One view is that black progress has been impressive. There has been a sharp rise in black enrollment in colleges and universities; many more black officials have been elected to public offices; incomes have increased; and there is much more acceptance in mass communications media. Compared to decades ago, there is cause for optimism.

But another perspective questions this progress. The black "rise" is negligible when compared to white progress. Black unemployment and school dropout rates continue to be as high as ever. Further, society cannot meet their rising expectations, and continued racial tensions have tended to polarize the hostile attitudes of many whites. The problem has been exacerbated by the unwillingness of organizations and institutions (Type II and III racism as described in Chapter 6) to deal with the problem except on a token basis. Therefore, in relative terms, the blacks are as far from their goals of equality and justice as they were years ago.

We feel that although there has been progress, the lot of the blacks has remained unchanged. The discontent that was manifested in Watts stirred the country into action, but as Newsweek (1973) indicates, almost a decade after the incident the problems remain as large as ever. Furthermore, it seems that the points of view of Jensen and Shockley have become the operating models of the society.

It should be remembered that Jensen (1969), after studying the results of IQ tests, concluded that there was a genetic inferiority in the IQ of a black. This was not a new interpretation since Spencer also presented similar views many years earlier. From this assumption Jensen argued that compensatory programs were useless (e.g., head start) and that a different type of career would be wiser for those races with this inbred inferiority. **188**

Although the scientific community strongly questioned these studies, its concerns were misdirected. While the scientists argued among themselves, the more powerful politicians effectively put into practice many of Jensen's ideas. Federal programs aimed at aiding the minorities have been cut; there is more support for the idea that college is not for everyone and that there is dignity in even the most monotonous and unrewarding work. It is not a paranoid reaction when blacks feel that the message of a closed system is aimed primarily at them.

BIBLIOGRAPHY

BERNARD, JESSIE (1966). *Marriage and Family Among Negroes*. Englewood Cliffs, N. J.: Prentice-Hall, Inc.

BERRY, BREWTON (1951). *Race Relations*. Cambridge, Mass.: The Riverside Press.

BILLINGSLEY, ANDREW (1968). *Black Families in White America*. Englewood Cliffs, N. J.; Prentice-Hall, Inc.

DOHRENWEND, BARBARA S. and BRUCE DOHRENWEND (1970). "Class and Race as Status-related Sources of Stress." In Levine and Scotch, eds., Social Stress. Chicago: Aldine Press. Pp. 111–40.

DONNAN, E. (1935). "Documents Illustrative of the History of the Slave Trade to America." *Carnegie Institute Publications*, 4 (409).

DOWNES, BRYAN T. (1968). "Social and Political Characteristics of Riot Cities: A Comparitive Study." *Social Science Quarterly*, 49. 504–20.

DRAKE, ST. CLAIR and HORACE CAYTON (1945). *Black Metropolis*. New York: Harcourt, Brace and World.

DuBOIS, W. E. B. (1935). *Black Reconstruction*. New York: Harcourt, Brace and World.

FRANKLIN, RAYMOND S. (1969). "The Political Economy of Black Power." *Social Problems*, 16: 286–301.

FRANKLIN, JOHN HOPE and ISIDORE STARR, eds. (1967). *The Negro in 20th Century America*. New York: Random House, Inc. Pp. 185–258.

FRAZIER, E. FRANKLIN (1957). *Black Bourgeoisie*. Glencoe: Illinois Free Press.

——— (1957). *The Negro in the United States*. New York: The Macmillan Company.

GERSCHWENDER, JAMES A., ed. (1971). *The Black Revolt*. Englewood Cliffs, N. J.: Prentice-Hall, Inc.

HERSKOVITS, M. J. (1930). *The Anthropometry of the American Negro*. New York: Columbia University Press.

——— (1941). *The Myth of the Negro Past*. New York: Harper & Row, Publishers.

HOWARD, JOHN R. (1966). "The Making of a Black Muslim." *Trans-Action*, 4: 15–21.

JACKSON, JACQUELYNE (1972). "Where Are the Black Men?" *Ebony*, March: 99–104.

JENSEN, ARTHUR R. (1969). "How Much Can We Boost IQ and Scholastic Achievement?" *Harvard Educational Review,* 5 (39): 1–123.

JORDAN, WINTHROP D. (1968). *White over Black.* Baltimore: Penguin Books.

KILLIAN, LEWIS M. and CHARLES U. SMITH (1960). "Negro Protest Leaders in a Southern Community." *Social Forces* 38: 253–57.

KOCH, SHARON FAY (1972). "Changing Attitudes of Los Angeles' Black Elite." Los Angeles *Times* (April 16), Section I, p. 1.

KNOPF, TERRY ANN (1969). "Sniping—A New Pattern of Violence?" *Trans-Action,* 47: 22–29.

LADNER, JOYCE (1967). "What 'Black Power' Means to Negroes in Mississippi." *Trans-Action* 5: 7–15.

LIEBERSON, STANLEY and ARNOLD R. SILVERMAN (1965). "The Precipitants and Underlying Conditions of Race Riots." *American Sociological Review* 30: 887–98.

LOMAX, LOUIS (1962). "Negro Revolt" In Gerschwender, ed., *The Black Revolt.* New York: Harper & Row, Publishers. Pp. 92–111, 133–43.

McWORTER, GERALD A. and ROBERT L. CRAIN (1967). "Subcommunity Gladiatorial Competition: Civil Rights Leadership as a Competitive Process." *Social Forces,* 46: 8–32.

MEIER, AUGUST and ELLIOTT RUDWICK (1969). "Black Violence in the 20th Century: A Study in Rhetoric and Retaliation." In Graham and Gurr, eds., *Violence in America: Historical and Comparative Perspectives. A Report to the National Commission on the Causes and Prevention of Violence.*

MOYNIHAN, DANIEL P. (1965). *The Negro Family: The Case for National Action.* Washington, D.C.: United States Department of Labor, Office of Planning and Research.

NELSON, HAROLD A. (1967). "The Defenders: A Case Study of an Informal Police Organization." *Social Problems,* 15: 127–47.

Newsweek (1973). "Black America Now." February 19. Pp. 25–31. (Overseas edition.)

ORBELL, JOHN M. (1967). "Protest Participation Among Southern Negro College Students." *The American Political Science Review,* 61: 446–56.

ORUM, ANTHONY M. and AMY M. ORUM (1968). "The Class and Status Bases of Negro Student Protest." *Social Science Quarterly,* 49: 521–33.

PINKNEY, ALPHONSO (1969). *Black Americans.* Englewood Cliffs, N.J.: Prentice-Hall, Inc.

PLOSKI, HARRY (1971). *The Negro Almanac.* New York: The Bellwether Company.

SEARS, DAVID O. and T. M. TOMLINSON (1968). "Riot Ideology in Los Angeles: A Study of Negro Attitudes." *Social Science Quarterly,* 49: 485–503.

SHAY, FRANK (1938). *Judge Lynch: His First Hundred Years.* New York: Ives Washburn, Inc.

STAMPP, KENNETH (1956). *The Peculiar Institution.* New York: Alfred A. Knopf, Inc.

WOODWARD, C. VANN (1951). *Renuion and Reaction.* Boston: Little, Brown & Co.

UNITED STATES DEPARTMENT OF COMMERCE, BUREAU OF THE CENSUS (1970).
   *Special Studies: The Social and Economic Status of Negroes in the
   United States.* Bureau of Labor Statistics Report.

UNITED STATES DEPARTMENT OF LABOR, BUREAU OF LABOR STATISTICS
   (1966). *The Negroes in the United States: Their Economic and
   Social Situation.* Washington, D. C.: U.S. Government Printing Office.
   P. 141.

THE
CHINESE
AMERICANS 9

The Asian Americans [1] are one of the smallest ethnic minorities. The 1970 Census established the following figures: Chinese, 435,062; Filipinos, 343,060; and Japanese, 591,290. Together the three major Asian groups total 1,369,412 in a country of 203,211,926. The low figures are somewhat ironic, for it was not too long ago that white Americans feared the "yellow peril" and envisioned the United States being overrun by hordes of little yellow men. It is also a commentary on the rapidity of racial change, for the "yellow peril" is now the "model minority" (Kitano and Sue, 1973). The Asians are often cited as an example of good race relations in the United States, but a more cynical view is that they are compared with the "unruly" minorities who are adapting with much less quietness and conformity.

Although white America has continually looked upon the Asians as a homogeneous group, nothing could be further from the truth. They represent different nationalities and cultures, and even within their own cultures there are wide disparities. One of the distortions of racism is to lump diverse groups into one category, or at best, into a few stereotypes:

---

[1] Much of the historical material on the Asian Americans is drawn from Daniels and Kitano (1970).

the Chinese laundryman, the Japanese gardener, and the Filipino gambler.

If we look at the group more closely, we see problems that have hitherto been hidden by the stereotypes. The problems of unrest, the elderly (Kalish and Moriwaki, 1973), and the mentally ill (Berk and Hirata, 1973), are partially obscured because of the general adaptive style used by the Asian minorities in their quest for survival and acceptance in the white man's world. It would have been sheer folly for most Asians to challenge the power of the dominant culture; the small, scattered Asian communities could not hope to survive by confronting and inviting the retaliation of the more powerful Americans. But even when they attempted to acculturate through invisibility, they were objects of attack. This is partly because racism sees anything but white faces as different and therefore, inferior, and partly because of American's peculiar relationship with the countries that make up the Far East. Americans have so strongly associated Asian Americans with their home nations that even today, Asians three and four generations removed from the homeland of their forebearers are expected to be experts on China, Japan, and the Philippines. (This book will concentrate on these three groups—the Chinese, the Japanese, and the Filipino.[2])

The Chinese were the first Asian immigrants to enter the United States in significant numbers. They came to the West Coast in the 1840s because of economic reverses, local rebellions, and social discontent in China (Purcell, 1965).

The Chinese have not been a very mobile people. They have generally preferred to stay in China, and fears of them overrunning the earth have little basis in historical fact. China has never been an expansionist nation, especially when compared to the Western countries that have established and maintained far-flung empires and spheres of influence over the past several hundred years. And yet the European nations and the United States have constantly feared Chinese expansionism.

Most Chinese immigrants came from two Southern provinces, Fukien and Kwangtung—or more specifically, two villages in Kwangtung Province, Chung Shan (formerly Hsiang Shan) and Ssu Yi. (The Kwangtung area had had considerable contact with the Western world.)

EARLY YEARS[3]

At first the Chinese immigrants were well received in California. They were regarded as objects of curiosity, and because they were willing to

---

[2] Unfortunately, there is very little published data on the Koreans, Vietnamese, and other groups. Therefore, they will not be included.

[3] Much of the historical material is from Roger Daniels and Harry H. L. Kitano, *American Racism: Exploration of the Nature of Prejudice* (Englewood Cliffs, N.J.: Prentice-Hall, Inc., 1970).

provide supplementary rather than competing economic services, there was little or no objection to them. In fact in August, 1850, when Chinese, on two occasions, participated in San Francisco civic ceremonies, their colorful costumes, according to a local chronicler, made "a fine and pleasing appearance." This warm reception can be better understood if the fantastic inflation that the gold rush produced in California is taken into account. In San Francisco, in 1850, a common laborer received a dollar an hour; on the East Coast he would have received a dollar a day. A loaf of bread, priced at about a nickel elsewhere, cost fifty cents. Laundry rates were astronomical: prices as high as $20 per dozen items have been reported. Some Californians actually sent their dirty clothes to Honolulu and Canton. This inflation was a result of the gold strikes and the extreme shortage of women; those women who were in the labor force worked at more glamorous occupations than domestic service. The Chinese (and later, the Japanese) quickly filled the jobs that were generally regarded as women's work.

But most Chinese, like other forty-niners, eventually made their way into the diggings, and it was in the lawless mining regions that anti-Chinese feeling first broke out. By 1852, hostility toward the Chinese was already well developed and showed that curious mixture of class and race antagonism that was to be one of its hallmarks. One writer reports the following resolution passed by a miner's meeting:

> Be it resolved: That it is the duty of the miners to take the matter into their own hands . . . to erect such barriers as shall be sufficient to check this Asiatic inundation. . . . That the Capitalists, ship-owners and merchants and others who are encouraging or engaged in the importation of these burlesques on humanity would crowd their ships with the long-tailed, horned, and cloven-hoofed inhabitants of the infernal regions (if they could make a profit on it).

> Resolved: That no Asiatic or South Sea Islander be permitted to mine in this district either for himself or for others, and that these resolutions shall be a part and parcel of our mining laws (Daniels and Kitano, 1970: 36).

Despite such resolutions, the Chinese population of California continued to grow: in 1852 there were perhaps 25,000 in the state; a decade later there were more than 50,000. Almost all were adult males; among the Chinese migrants males outnumbered females by at least 15 to 1; among contemporary European immigrants the figure was about 2½ to 1. Throughout the 1850s, '60s, and '70s, Chinese accounted for 10 percent or more of the California population. Despite virulent opposition, the economic oportunities for Chinese in California were so great that they continued to come for three decades. The hostility was more than verbal; first in the mining districts and then in the cities, Chinese were robbed, beaten, and murdered. These crimes were rarely punished due to the notorious laxity of law enforcement in California at the time. Whatever chance a Chinese might have had to obtain justice vanished because of a ruling that no Chinese could testify against a white man. An 1849 law had provided that "no Black, or mulatto person, or Indian, shall be allowed to give evidence in favor of, or against a white man." Five years later, the Chief Justice of the California Supreme Court, himself a member of the anti-immigrant "Know Nothing," or American Party, ruled that Chinese were included within the scope of the prohibition because:

> The anomalous spectacle of a distinct people, living in our community, recognizing no laws of this State except through necessity, bringing with them their prejudices and national feuds, in which they indulge in open violation of the law; whose mendacity is proverbial; a race of people whom nature has marked as inferior, and who are incapable of progress or intellectual development beyond a certain point, as their history has shown; differing in language, opinion, color, and physical conformation; between whom and ourselves nature has placed an impassable difference, is now presented and for them is claimed, not only the right to swear away the life of a citizen, but the further privilege of participating with us in administering the affairs of our Government (Daniels and Kitano, 1970: 37).

The Chief Justice was perhaps the first Californian to speculate publicly upon the possibility of an Oriental inundation, a fantasy which would later grip the Western imagination under the rubric of the "Yellow Peril."

By the 1860s, anti-Chinese sentiment had developed to the point where it was political suicide for anyone to take their side. The presence of the Chinese promoted all white men to a superior status. It also blurred differences within the white majority and solidified it to the extent that Jews and Catholics, who were usually scapegoats elsewhere, were more readily accepted in places like San Francisco and Los Angeles. Chinese competition also forced white workingmen to band together.

The Chinese issue smoldered in California during the late 1850s and early '60s; at the end of the 1860s, it burst into flame. The Census of 1870, which probably underestimated their number, showed that a fourth of the state's 50,000 Chinese lived in San Francisco, which had become the undisputed center of anti-Chinese agitation. The situation in San Francisco had been exacerbated by the constant influx of new immigrants (some 15,000 had arrived between 1870 and 1871), the continued expulsion of Chinese from the mining districts, and perhaps most crucial, the arrival of 10,000 Chinese laborers after the completion of the Central Pacific Railroad. The increase in Chinese population, together with a severe economic depression, produced an explosive situation throughout the state. In the sleepy village of Los Angeles, for example, some twenty Chinese were killed by gunfire and hanging on October 24, 1871—an outrage that must have involved, in one way or another, most of the adult male inhabitants. But it was in San Francisco, in 1870, that the anti-Chinese movement came to a head.

The Chinese throughout California lived in distinct communities, **196** of the country, were able to put into practice overt discriminatory laws. The American labor movement gave its support, but it is clear that political expediency rather than principles was responsible for a majority of the congressional votes. Within the state, the old demand that the "Chinese Must Go!" quickly lost most of its force. Within a few decades most Californians, faced with a new threat of "yellow inundation" from the Japanese, were already remembering the then diminishing Chinese with a trace of nostalgia that would have shocked both the Kearneyites and their hapless targets.

The anti-Chinese movement of the 1860s and '70s must be counted "successful," for it not only achieved an immediate goal, Chinese exclusion, but helped to shape a restrictive pattern to which our immigration laws adhered for almost a century. Some historians have judged this democratic "antidemocratic" manifestation as an aberration in our popular heritage. Professor Charles A. Barker, for example, in his monumental biography of Henry George, tells us that his subject's "Californian attitude toward Chinese immigration" was an exception to his "Jeffersonian and Jacksonian principles." This is a basic misunderstanding of the period, and of the relationship between popular feeling and race. Jefferson and Jackson shared and perpetuated the racist prejudices of their own times, and those who have followed in their tradition have usually done the same. In ethnic, if not in economic matters, enlightenment has been more prevalent among the upper than the lower classes (Daniels and Kitano, 1970).

And it is not surprising that this is so. In late nineteenth-century California, anti-Chinese attitudes were part and parcel of the struggle for the rights of labor. One can be repelled by the racist views expressed by George and other spokesmen for the workingman and still realize that within the context of their times they could hardly be otherwise. Since with the close of the frontier (and the California frontier, in the Turnerian sense, closed in the 1860s), free and unlimited immigration had become primarily a source of cheap industrial labor; therefore, some kind of immigration restriction was almost a foregone conclusion, if organized labor was to grow and prosper. Few today can "approve" the racist and discriminatory forms that it took; but considering the times, it was only to be expected. Federal immigration restriction legislation, which first discriminated against Asians, was soon directed against Southern and Eastern Europeans, the "new" immigrants who began to dominate the national immigration statistics from the 1880s on. Had the frontier—whose disappearance is traditionally dated at 1890—been exhausted while the "old" immigration was still dominant, a more equitable restrictive law might have ensued. Immigration restriction was originally fostered by forces that are usually labelled progressive; by the 1920s, when it became law, it had attracted broad support from the most reactionary elements in our national life. Liberal historians (and most historians are now liberals) have been reluctant to come to grips with this essential paradox of American life: movements for economic democracy have usually been violently opposed to a throughgoing ethnic democracy. Nowhere can this strain of American racism be seen more clearly than in the anti-Chinese movement.

One other fact should be remembered about the Chinese experience in the United States. In the late 1930s and during World War II, the Chinese became our friends and allies, although the general tone of the friendship was condescending (the Filipinos did not escape it either, and were referred to as our "little brown brothers"). Their peace-loving nature was emphasized; they had fought valiantly against the "sly, tricky Jap"; they were different from their more aggressive neighbor; and they were honest, hard-working, gentle, and compliant. In many ways, this praise deflected from the everyday humiliation, harassment, and deprivation faced by many Chinese, even with the relatively favorable attitude toward all Orientals (except the Japanese) at this time (Daniels and Kitano, 1970).

CURRENT SCENE

The Chinese in the United States represent a compact, urbanized population with large clusters in Hawaii, San Francisco, Los Angeles, and New York. In these "Chinatowns" one can experience all the sights, sounds, and smells of China. Chinatowns present a diverse, or "exotic" facade. One can hear different languages and music (from atonal Chinese classics to modern rock); one can taste rare foods, investigate small shops, choose from a staggering number of restaurants, and behold natives, newcomers, old and young intermingling with the tourists (especially on weekends) and the odors of barbecued pork, ginger, and soy sauce. Other streets have the quiet, residential air of a typical middle-class community. Yet the temptation to stereotype this diversity is so strong that mention of the word "Chinese" usually elicits images of: "opium dens, Tong wars, coolie labor, the yellow peril, highbinders, hatchetmen, laundries, waiters, houseboys, slave wages, unassimilable aliens, and so on" (Sung, 1967: 1–2).

These stereotypes survive because there has been no adequate information. As Sung says, "From 1909 when Professor Mary Coolidge's book, *Chinese Immigration,* was published, to 1960, when Professor Rose Hum Lee's book, *The Chinese in the United States of America,* was imported from Hong Kong, no serious work about this neglected minority appeared in the United States" (1967: 2). The void was filled by Hollywood movies, newspaper articles, and novels that up until World War II portrayed the Chinese as variations of Fu Manchu and the Dragon Lady.

We will present a broad picture of the Chinese family, although there is no "typical Chinese family," just as there is no typical American family. The variations within a culture may be as wide as between cultures, but generalizations based upon family patterns are possible.

The changes in the structure and style of the Chinese family life that the immigrant brought with him developed from acculturation, exposure to newer models, and challenges in the new country. Like the Japanese family (Kitano and Manning, 1973), it is the interaction of the power, the culture, and the visibility of the ethnic community with the American culture that explains the development of the Asian family style in the United States.

The Chinese family is a cohesive and extended family structure that has survived many generations (Hsu, 1971). It is a model that includes ancestor worship, duty and obligation, filial piety, and importance of .he family name. Love and romance are not important. Roles are clearly defined with father and eldest son playing the most prominent roles. The primary role of the woman is to please her husband and in-laws, and to produce sons to carry on the family line. Since there is no legal age at which children become independent, there is continued dependence on the family throughout life.

There is a continuity in family control and discipline. Obedience to parents is central: ideally, children are to obey parental wishes, stay by them, and provide a source of pride and comfort. In this fashion they are permanently tied to their parents, and are entrusted not to perform any actions that would bring shame and dishonor to the family.

There are clear reciprocal obligations: in exchange for being good and dutiful children, parents are responsible for educating and supporting their children and arranging for suitable marriages. The family unit is the central theme; custom even indicates that parents can not freely dispose of their property because it also belongs to their sons (Hsu, 1971).

Relatives play an important part of this family system. The widespread combining of families can be seen by the relatively small number of Chinese surnames (Hsu estimates a core of about 400 to 500) which provide the bulk of Chinese names.[4]

Ethnocentric biases are clearly observable when discussing various family systems. Westerners put a high priority on individual freedom and mobility and to tend to think of systems that have a large kinship network as unhappy, confining, and backward—and there are many dramatic instances where this is true.

---

4 The usual Chinese surname consists of three characters: the first, the surname; the second, indicating the man's generation in the clan; and the last, his own character.

But as Hsu (1971) points out, there are advantages to the extended kinship system as well. The Chinese way gives individuals a greater sense of security and a means of dealing with the world. Unattractive women do not have to become lonely old maids; men with less ability or motivation do not have to strive constantly for an individual identity; old people do not live in fear of being thrown out of the home as their productive years decline to face their last years in a home for the aged. (There are risks and consequences in any type of family or kinship system, and preferring one over the other is essentially a matter of values.)

Most of the studies describe upper-class Chinese families, and one is left to conjecture on the family life of the peasants. For example, Tom (1971) views the Chinese-American heritage in terms different from those of most traditional writers. Rather than discussing the scholar-official class, which did not immigrate to the United States in any significant numbers, he focuses on the powerless peasant and considers him to be major figure in Chinese immigration. The peasant was dominated by the psychology of survival; he minded his own business and took care of his own problems, expecting to be left alone. The peasant had little power to define culture, to control relationships, or to develop a vigorous individual identity; rather his best chance for survival was to be ignored by those who were more powerful. Those were the conditions for most peasants in China, and the similarity of their treatment under California racism shaped a similar adaptation.

Changes in the United States

The "ideal" family structure of China could never be duplicated in the United States. First, there were very few Chinese women, as was pointed out before. Most able-bodied young immigrants had a "sojourner mentality"; they intended to return to China rather than send for their wives and children. And finally, the old family system was more suited to an agricultural society, and probably would never have survived in the rapidly changing, urbanized, and technology-oriented United States.

These conditions often led to what Sung calls the "mutilated family"—a family united in bond, such as marriage, but separated physically. "In other words, the Chinese men in the United States were [often] family men without the presence of family members, which explains why there were four times as many married men as married women in the census of 1930" (Sung, 1967: 155). Chinese tradition was certainly one bar to these families getting together; another was the discriminatory features of the Immigration Act of 1924, which made it practically impossible for a married Chinese man to send for his wife and family. The mutilated family was the predominant form of family life among the Chinese in the

United States until more liberal legislation was passed after the end of World War II (Sung, 1967: 156).

The mutilated marriage refers to cases where men married in China before immigrating and left China without bringing their wives. After many years of separation, (for some as long as 30 years) there was the chance to rejoin their spouses again. These reunions tested the old phrase, "absence makes the heart grow fonder." The husband and wife were each brought up in a different culture under completely different circumstances. Sung (1967) describes a number of marital failures arising from clashing expectations; Rose Hum Lee (1957) cites a divorce rate of 8.5 among the Chinese in San Francisco.

There was also another way of marrying. Although many of the Chinese immigrants remained bachelors during most of their lives in the United States, the liberalization of immigration laws after World War II enabled many to go to Hong Kong in search of wives. The courtship was instantaneous and complete strangers often found themselves married to each other. In many cases, older men, accustomed to a life of hardship in the United States, married younger, more "modernized" Chinese women. After marriage, they returned to the crowded, dilapidated quarters of the urban Chinatowns on the West Coast and it is probable that many became seriously disillusioned.

But, as Sung writes: "In spite of the stresses and strains borne by both husband and wife in the transition, the Chinese family usually remains intact. Discord and unhappiness are generally turned inward toward the self and are reflected in a higher suicide rate rather than divorce statistics" (1967: 161–62). Suicide has been one form of protest for Chinese women caught in unbearable matrimonial situations.

Today, family patterns reflect age and class differences. The wide kinship patterns of old China are uncommon; Sung writes that the husband generally occupies a stronger position than the wife in the Chinese-American family. Unless the woman is an aristocrat, highly educated, or quite modern, she will tend to stay in the background.

Parents born in China tend to have more children than those born in America (Sung, 1967: 165); "discipline is strict and punishment immediate in the Chinese household" (168). Deviant behavior is not a personal matter between an individual and his conscience, but encompasses a wider net, including his family and loved ones upon whom dishonor and shame could fall.

Although there is much handling, hugging, and kissing when young, as the child grows older these overt expressions are often withdrawn. The child is shoved "firmly towards independence and maturity. Emulation of adult behavior is encouraged. The mother does not invite confidences nor direct talks and discussions. She commands and decides what is best for the children, and the children are expected to obey. Disobedience is not tolerated and corporal punishment is freely meted out" (Sung, 1967: 169). The father plays a distant role in the family proceedings. He is the authority, and maintains his superior position by means of a certain emotional distance.

Changes in China

The picture of Chinese family life that we have presented is based on pre-World War II principles, and it is interesting to contrast that style of life with the view of Mao Tse Tung. We quote from selected articles of the marriage law of the people's republic, promulgated by the Central People's Government on May 1, 1950 (Yang, 1959).

> *Article 1.* The arbitrary and compulsory feudal marriage system, which is based on the superiority of man over woman and which ignores the children's interest is abolished.
>
> *Article 2.* Polygamy, concubinage, child betrothal, interference with the remarriage of widows and the exaction of money or gifts in connection with marriage shall be prohibited.
>
> *Article 7.* Husband and wife are companions living together and shall enjoy equal status in the home.
>
> *Article 8.* Husband and wife are duty bound to love, respect, assist and look after each other, to live in harmony, to engage in production, to care for the children and to strive jointly for the welfare of the family and for the building up of a new society.
>
> *Articles 9, 10, 11, 12.* Both husband and wife shall have the rights to free choices of occupations and free participation in work or in social activities . . . equal rights in the possession and management of family property . . . right to use his or her own family name . . . right to inherit each other's property.
>
> *Article 15.* Children born out of wedlock shall enjoy the same rights as children born in lawful wedlock.
>
> *Articles 17–18.* Divorce shall be granted when both the husband and wife desire it.

As can be seen, the new marriage laws in China are quite different from the marriage customs in "old China." The extremeness of the old norms, as seen by Mao, was one important factor in bringing about the changes.

School Experiences

Most teachers comment upon the delightful qualities of Chinese children. Liu (1950) compared teacher's perceptions of Caucasian and Chinese children and found that teachers remarked on the better behavior, obedience, and self-reliance of Chinese-American youngsters. The Chinese, like their Asian counterparts, the Japanese, have done very well in the American educational system and rank as one of the highest educated of the minority groups.

Conflict may arise when Chinese youngsters perceive the different styles of their Caucasian peers. They see the informal and casual relationships that Americans strike up with their parents, and are often apt to wonder whether the American model is more desirable. And as with most children of immigrant parents, they see their own hard-working but poor parents; their restricted life styles; the frugality and the limited English in the home. The comparison may cause them to be ashamed of their parents, family, and ethnic group.

SOCIAL PROBLEMS

Rates of problem behavior such as crime and delinquency have historically been low (Beach, 1932), although there is current concern about the rise in delinquency. Part of the explanation for these low rates can be attributed to strong family controls, as well as modal life styles that encourage the individual to internalize his problems, and a cohesive community that prefers to handle problems in its own way. Much deviant behavior may remain hidden from official sources. However, there has been a recent influx of many young immigrants with minimal English skills from Hong Kong. The lack of opportunity for absorption into the Anglo and ethnic communities can be hypothesized as one source of high potential strain that might lead to a rise in social problem behavior.

Official rates of mental illness (with their limitations) indicate that the Chinese currently have a high rate (Kitano, 1969; Berk and Hirota, 1973). Berk and Hirota, tracing mental illness historically among the Chinese in California, indicate that the high increase in mental hospital commitments cannot be attributed solely to the demographic composition (e.g., old, single males) of the population. They hypothesize that the rise may be due to a reduction in the cohesion of the Chinese community, the loss of alternative institutions to cope with increasing problem behavior, and the source of social control moving from the ethnic to the larger community. In any instance, the Chinese are beginning to become much more visible to the institutions of social control and prevention.

CHINESE ORGANIZATIONS IN AMERICA

Since emigration generally meant leaving kinship ties at home, there developed in the United States groupings along several lines. They included family name associations along the old kinship models, and locality organizations based on previous village ties. Hsu (1971) comments on the relative fluidity of such organizations, thereby making it difficult to accurately assess their size. Kinship and locality ties tend to be highly binding.

One important factor is that older Chinese organizations are highly specific, limited in scope and membership, and conservative. Recruitment and socialization techniques are predicated upon concrete relationships. These organizations seldom have links with other organizations, nor are they apt to be "cause" oriented. Very few old organizations are involved in charitable causes or focus upon social welfare activities. It is just not their style.

Organizations, such as the Six Companies in San Francisco, gained an inordinate amount of power through a variety of factors. The restricted opportunities in a racist structure limited the alternatives for most Chinese; the clan and kinship systems ensured a solid membership loyalty. Under these conditions, the Chinese could exploit members of their own group, especially new immigrants with no English or vocational skills, who were highly dependent on ethnic organizations.

New organizations are more apt to reflect the American pattern. Golf clubs and service organizations, such as the Chinese Lions Clubs, are symptomatic of the influences of acculturation, although their membership is limited to a select group. In spite of these changes Hsu (1971) feels that the kinship and locality organizations will persist for a very long time; that the American-born Chinese will be slow in initiating or joining cause-oriented organizations, especially of an abstract nature; and finally, in the long run, newer associations will tend to reflect social and professional interests, although the type, extent, and ethnicity of their membership will be highly dependent on the area of residence and the opportunities available in the dominant culture.

RELIGION

The Chinese attitudes toward religion reflect the spirit of the culture. Since the Chinese have been nonexpansionist and nondenominational, they have neither sent their missionaries forth to proselytize the world nor have they been divided by conflicts between sects and denominations. Instead, they have kept a relaxed and polite distance; they have incorporated foreign gods and respected all varieties of supernatural belief. Organized religion, ritualistic attendance, and loyalty to one church has not been the pattern; there are few membership drives, and selective membership, tithing, and the like are not common. Relationships with family and kin tend to have a higher priority than those with gods and temples.

Hsu feels that among the Chinese in Hawaii roughly one third are Christian. But their Christianity includes many Chinese ways. For example, except for direct church-sponsored events, very few meetings open or close with a prayer. There is a tendency to reduce rather than increase the influence of the church.

OTHER PATTERNS IN THE CHINESE COMMUNITY

Friendship patterns in the Chinese community are often secondary to family and kin relationships. Therefore, the Chinese individual is unable to move about as freely as his American counterpart. He is a part of a much larger human network and has less need to go outside it. He does try to bring outsiders into the network; and in this sense, friendships could be labelled "additive," whereas American patterns could be called "replacements."

Several consequences can be deduced from this type of friendship, kinship, and locality network. Helping others within the network is common and includes what could be looked upon as intrusion and intervention concerning family disputes. (Most Americans would be disturbed over this kind of "meddling.") Friendships also tend to be of long duration and are not like the shortlived, "brittle" American kind. Even business relationships, so sacred to the American system, are secondary to the other links; charges of nepotism and reverse discrimination are often hurled at Chinese establishments. However, acculturation has changed some Chinese patterns. Many have taken the American business model to heart and give high priority to economic matters; but in their social dealings, they may still retain the ethnic network.

PERSONALITY

A study by Sue and Kirk (in press) on Chinese-American students at the University of California, Berkeley, tested personality differences between Chinese students and those of other ethnic backgrounds. The test results indicated the following: (1) Chinese students score higher on quantitative and lower on verbal sections of ability tests; (2) they are more interested in physical sciences, applied technical fields, and business occupations and less interested in social sciences, aesthetic and cultural fields, and verbal and linguistic vocations; (3) they prefer more concrete and tangible approaches to life, and are more conforming and less socially extroverted compared to other students.

Sue and Kirk offer several cultural explanations for Chinese-American students' lower verbal and higher quantitative scores. First is their bilingual background with an insufficient knowledge of English. Second, Chinese-American families restrain strong feelings, which inhibits communication. Third, higher quantitative scores could indicate compensatory means of expression. Fourth, quantitative activity by nature emphasizes a "structured, impersonal, and logical approach"—attributes **207** found most desirable to Chinese-American students. Finally, early immigrants may have encouraged their children to enter vocations that would maximize economic and social mobility; vocations in the physical sciences instead of the social sciences seemed most conducive to this goal, since the latter required skills in written and oral communication and an understanding of Western culture.

Analysis of the family structure provides further explanations for differences in test results. For example, family emphasis on tradition, set rules for behavior, conformity, respect for authority, and submergence of individuality help explain the discomforts of Chinese-American students in new situations, and also their tendency to show greater anxiety and less tolerance for ambiguity. Their great emphasis on family loyalty and their distrust of those outside the family contribute to the impression of their lack of concern for the welfare of others. The Chinese tend to "control" their behavior through guilt and shame; they worry over the conflict between their culture and the dominant one; and they feel acute discomfort when communicating outside the family. All these factors result in greater emotional distress.

Sue and Kirk warn that their results may be exaggerated because many Chinese Americans are leaving their families and subculture for the first time; to be independent in a new social setting requires a greater degree of adjustment for people who are used to prolonged family dependency and obligation. They conclude that "care must be taken in cultural interpretations of traits in terms of values." For example, Westerners consider being "inhibited" undesirable because they favor "spontaneity." But the Chinese consider the former characteristic to be a sign of self-control and maturity and the latter to be an indication of bad manners. However, Tom (1971) cites a number of limitations in using psychological tests and models on Chinese Americans. He feels that it is a mistake to judge Chinese Americans by white Anglo-Saxon personality typologies.

Confrontation in Chinatown

The image of the docile, conforming, shuffling "Chinaman," bowing to his master, was shattered by recent events in various Chinatowns. It was inevitable that mounting unemployment, perpetual overcrowded conditions, segregation, and discrimination would eventually lead to some type of outbreak, and a series of incidents, as described by Tom Wolfe in *Esquire* (December, 1969), is particularly colorful.

The confrontation began on February 14, 1969. Members of the "Free University of Chinatown Kids, Unincorporated," other student militants from Berkeley and San Francisco State, and a coalition of gangs, gathered outside the San Francisco Unified School District administration building carrying picket signs protesting: "DON'T TEACH US TO BE WHITE."

The time for confrontation is ripe. The beginnings of street revolution actually began last year during the Lunar New Year when the Wah Ching—"Chinese Youth"—Chinatown's largest and fiercest gang of approximately 300 Hong Kong born youth, angry and desperate, threatened to burn down Chinatown in protest to the non-availability of jobs and education. Even the Chinese and Japanese intellectuals who before ignored Chinatown as uncultivated and backward, began focusing their attention on the abject conditions of Chinatown and formed the Asian American Political Alliance and for the first time recognized "the People" as the force behind the revolution, rather than the usual establishment spokesmen.

The demonstrators outside the San Francisco School District administration building move into the school administration's main hall, Nourse Auditorium, where the foundation for the second confrontation is grounded. Two weeks later Dr. Robert Jenkins, Superintendent of Schools for San Francisco and five other administrators of the San Francisco Unified School District hold a public forum in the auditorium of the Commodore Stockton Elementary School to discuss the educational needs of Chinatown.

As Dr. Jenkins presented statistics about the school budget, federal moneys, teacher-pupil ratio, and bad linkage with the State Labor Department, tension mounted and finally pandemonium broke loose. Cherry bombs were hurled at the speakers; cries of "Bullshit!" "Right On!" "Off the Pigs!" resounded. Dr. Jenkins and his colleagues fled as the police enveloped the auditorium.

That there is trouble in Chinatown is now clear; fantasies of a Chinatown in harmony with its own community members and with those outside the community, are now dispelled. Change is imminent as the forces of American culture capture the Chinese community, separating them further away from the traditional ways of the older generation.

OTHER PROBLEMS

Overcrowded Chinatowns are not conducive to good health. The tuberculosis rate in San Francisco among Chinese was 104 per 100,000 compared to 49.6 among the whites. Tuberculosis is often equated with poverty, poor diets and unsanitary, overcrowded facilities (Chin, 1965).

Housing for many Chinese is old and poor; crime on the increase and employment under "sweat shop" conditions are not unusual. The Chinese garment shops in San Francisco are notorious for long hours and meager compensation, and upward mobility into supervisorial and administrative positions remains difficult (Chin, 1965).

Overt, blatant discrimination and hostility are not the major problems for most Chinese. But as with many ethnic groups, past experiences have led to a lowering of expectations. There remains the social distance with the majority group, as well as unresolved tensions with some of the other major ethnic groups.

A major problem for many Chinese is bicultural adaptation. The Chinese must choose between assimilating and acculturating. A bicultural individual is one who "acculturates" to a certain extent and sees the value of learning the "American way," especially in the systems of higher education. But he does not wish to "assimilate" because he sees the value of retaining much of his ethnic heritage and culture, especially its language and life styles. Yet he cannot be completely satisfied in being only "ethnic."

The problem of bicultural adaptation is relatively new, and there appear to be no previous models from which to make an evaluation. Immigrants have always had this problem, but it has somehow been given minor attention as a viable model. One generation deems it "schizophrenic," and another deems it "un-American" or "Uncle Tom." Language is one of the more prominent features of bicultural adaptation; it also involves a selective preference for social and cultural relationships from both cultures. There is no blind allegiance to one culture or the other.

Bicultural adaptation is unquestionably functional. Most of the writer's Asian acquaintances have adopted a bicultural style appropriate to life in the United States. But the current emphasis on ethnic identity and solidarity may force a further modification of this model.

SUMMARY

The Chinese in the United States are just beginning to be known to the rest of the country. As more information becomes available, the tremendous diversity among the people of this country is gradually revealed. The most visible and the best known Chinese (the highly educated intellectuals) comprise only one small part of this group, as do the stereotyped coolies.

New situations expose further diversity: In the early 1970s, when the San Francisco schools began to integrate with bussing, the Chinese formed a major opposition group. They mounted a boycott and started their own freedom schools. Yet other Chinese actively worked with the school system in its integration plans. The Chinese had many reasons to resist bussing. There was undoubtedly a degree of racism; they also wanted local autonomy and control; they felt that many Chinese who were less skilled in the English language faced unfair competition.

The stressful conditions faced by many members of this group—overcrowded quarters in cramped Chinatowns, the constant flow of new immigrants, and the lack of opportunities—cannot be ignored much longer. To assume that "all Asians have made it" will only add to the discontent. Unless some attention is paid to their needs and problems, another group will face *the discrepancy* between American ideals and the racial realities.

BIBLIOGRAPHY

BEACH, W. C. (1932). *Oriental Crime in California*. Stanford: Stanford University Press.

BERK, BERNARD and LUCIE HIROTA (1973). "Mental Illness Among the Chinese: Myth or Reality?" *Journal of Social Issues* (in press).

CHIN, JAMES WILBUR (1965). *Problems of Assimilation and Cultural Pluralism Among Chinese Americans in San Francisco: An Exploratory Study*. Masters of Art Thesis. Stockton, Calif.: University of the Pacific, Dept. of Sociology.

DANIELS, ROGER and HARRY H. L. KITANO (1970). *American Racism: Exploration of the Nature of Prejudice*. Englewood Cliffs, N.J.: Prentice-Hall, Inc.

HSU, FRANCIS L. K. (1971). *The Challenge of the American Dream: The Chinese in the United States*. Belmont, Calif.: Wadsworth Publishing Company, Inc.

KALISH, RICHARD and SHARON MORIWAKI (1973). "The World of the Elderly Asian American." *Journal of Social Issues* (in press).

KITANO, HARRY H. L. (1969). "Japanese-American Mental Illness." In Plog and Edgerton, eds., *Changing Perspectives on Mental Illness*. New York: Holt, Rinehart and Winston, Inc. Pp. 256–84.

———— and AKEMI K. MANNING (1973). "The Japanese-American Family." (In process.)

———— and STANLEY SUE (1973). "The Model Minorities." *Journal of Social Issues* (in press).

LEE, ROSE HUM (1957). "Established Chinese Families in the San Francisco Bay Area." *Midwest Sociologist*, 19–26.

LEVINE, GENE and DARREL MONTERO (1973). "Socioeconomic Mobility Among Three Generations of Japanese Americans." *Journal of Social Issues* (in press).

LIU, CHING HO (1950). *The Influence of Cultural Background on the Moral Judgment of Children*. Ph.D. Thesis. New York: Columbia University.

PURCELL, VICTOR (1965). *The Chinese in Southeast Asia*, 2nd ed. London: Oxford University Press. Chapter 2.

SUE, STANLEY and HARRY H. L. KITANO (1973). "Stereotypes as a Measure of Success." *Journal of Social Issues* (in press).

SUNG, BETTY LEE (1967). *Mountain of Gold*. New York: The Macmillan Company.

TOM, BEN (1971). "The Ghetto of the Mind: Notes on the Historical Psychology of Chinese America." *Amerasia Journal*, 1 (3): 1–31.

WOLFE, TOM (1969). "The New Yellow Peril." *Esquire Magazine*, December. Pp. 190–200.

YANG, C. K. (1959). *The Chinese Family in the Communist Revolution*. Cambridge: The Technology Press, Massachusetts Institute of Technology.

THE
JAPANESE
AMERICANS 10

In many ways, the history of the Japanese Americans is similar to that of the Chinese, except that they arrived later.[1] The initial group was made up primarily of young males, many of whom intended to return to Japan; they were imported for their labor; they faced many of the barriers and restrictions that were erected for the Chinese, they looked alike ("can you tell them apart?") at least to the majority; and most important, they quickly became primary targets for racism in California and the West Coast.

But the Japanese and Chinese are different, not only on the gross levels of nationality and culture, but also on a number of others. For example, Lyman (n.d.) contrasts the community organizations of the two groups and describes how each represents different needs. The Japanese came from a developing industrial nation; the Chinese from a primarily agricultural one; the Japanese used their embassy and consular officials as resources, whereas the Chinese depended on informal organizations. Many Japanese brought their wives with them and started families almost

---

[1] Much of the material in this chapter has been drawn from Roger Daniels and Harry H. L. Kitano, *American Racism: Exploration of the Nature of Prejudice* (Englewood Cliffs, N.J.: Prentice-Hall, Inc., 1970).

immediately, whereas the Chinese often left their wives back in China. Therefore, there were important differences in sexual and recreational patterns.

Because their children were born in America, the Japanese were immediately concerned about acculturation, whereas this stage was delayed among the first Chinese immigrants since they had so few children. Each of these factors is important in explaining some of the patterns of differential adaptation, and only under the incredible stereotyping of racism do the Chinese and the Japanese appear identical. And as with all of our ethnic groups, the individual differences within the group are so wide that any generalizations have to be carefully limited.

The first-generation immigrants, known as the *Issei,* were relatively homogeneous: most of them were young and had had four to six years of schooling; most were male; and most had come from rural Japan. The Issei came primarily from Southern Japan, particularly the prefectures of Hiroshima, Fukuoka, Kumamoto, Wakayama, and Yamaguchi. They found employment as agricultural laborers, in small business, or as service workers, often working with or for other Japanese; they also established small shops of their own. Japanese tend to be interdependent, and segregated housing patterns served to reinforce the existing ethnic network.

Some Issei returned to Japan in these early days, considering themselves "successful" and hoping to lead a more leisurely life in the home country; others returned as "failures." Those who remained in the United States sent "calls" to Japan for women in order to marry and raise children; this practice made their communities in the U.S. more permanent. Men and women were brought together through an exchange of photos, and many young women were called "picture brides."

The children of the Issei, or *Nisei,* were generally born between 1910 and 1940, and by the 1970s were in their middle years. Although they were influenced by their parents, they became acculturated to America much more than the Issei. Discrimination and prejudice caused many Nisei to lower their expectations and life styles in order to make a living in the United States. One writer has called them the "quiet generation" (Hosokawa, 1969); and although there was a minor furor in the ethnic community over the title, it is a reasonable description.

The *Sansei,* or third generation, were born after World War II; and by the 1970s were in high school, college, and in the work force. The differences within this group are perhaps the greatest and reflect the vast changes and stratifications of the youngest generations of American society. For example, older Sansei may still retain the values and styles of their Nisei parents, but the younger groups are often radical and militant.[2]

---

2 There are also other Japanese groups that should be mentioned; the *Kibei* were born in the United States of Issei parents but were sent back to Japan

The background of the Japanese American therefore provides a set of convenient categories for analysis. One is age-generation, with relatively homogeneous age-groupings that arose primarily from the discriminatory immigration laws. An unforeseen, beneficial effect of this legislation was to organize the Japanese so that they were able to pool their resources and create and maintain an ethnic network without the continuous introduction of new migrants to complicate the picture.

The other category is historical; the wartime evacuation of the Japanese (1942–45) clearly separates the prewar and postwar conditions. In this chapter we will briefly describe the wartime evacuation, then concentrate on the current situation.

THE WARTIME EVACUATION

Japanese Americans came into a negative prominence during World War II. The evacuation has been variously termed as America's "greatest wartime mistake" and "America's day of infamy." It is the main subject of recent books by Daniels (1971); Girdner and Loftis (1969), Myer (1971), Bosworth (1967), Fisher (1965), Spicer (1969), and Zeller (1969). Previous books were by Eaton (1952), Grodzins (1949), Leighton (1945), Okubo (1946), Thomas, Kikuchi, and Sakoda (1952), Thomas and Nishimoto (1946), and Tenbroek et al. (1954). There were also many government documents and articles, and most books on Japanese Americans discuss the subject.

However, the evacuation has remained relatively obscure to most Americans; practically every non-Japanese the author has ever met has been ignorant of this event, but sympathetic when told about it. "If we only knew," is the usual reply with its brave, but futile implication that things would have been different. But empirical evidence from the wartime years does not present a reassuring picture. For example, Bloom and Riemer (1945) surveyed various student campuses in 1943; 63 percent of the West Coast and 73 percent in the Midwest felt that the handling of the Japanese during this period was correct. A more recent survey in conjunction with the Japanese American Research Project at UCLA in 1969 (approximately twenty-five years after the evacuation) indicated that over 48 percent of California respondents surveyed felt that the evacuation was justified.

---

for much of their upbringing—primarily in the 1930s; Japanese businessmen have constantly visited this country, except for the interrupt of World War II; there were an estimated 25,000 war brides by 1960; there is an uncounted number from Hawaii; and new immigrants began to arrive from Japan from 1954 on and represent a new Issei.

The necessary conditions for placing groups behind barbed wire (or for more severe actions, such as extermination and genocide) are shaped by prior events, especially by prejudice, discrimination, and segregation (Daniels and Kitano, 1970). Prejudice, usually maintained by stereotyping, leads to the avoidance of a group; discrimination and segregation, maintained by laws, customs, and norms fosters disadvantage and isolation. For a group so cut off, stereotypes become the operating reality since there is no way of effectively correcting the biased information. If certain "incidents" crystallize the already negative sentiments, more permanent solutions (concentration camps, exile, isolation, and extermination) may be instituted.

For example, prior to 1954, the Issei could not become U.S. citizens; therefore certain basic civil rights had never been a part of their expectations: they were the targets of stereotyping and legal harassment. Issei could neither vote nor freely own land; nuisance laws prevented them from employing white girls and the prices of their California state fishing licenses were set deliberately high. Antimiscegenation laws discouraged the Issei from believing that they were equal to the white man. Stereotyped as less than human, and placed at a competitive disadvantage by laws and customs, they were limited in their opportunities for any kind of equal status contact.

The Nisei had been segregated into Little Tokyos and Osakas, usually in the older and less desirable areas of the cities. These Japanese communities were able to maintain effective social control over their members, and there were none of the usual signs of social disorganization such as high rates of crime and delinquency.

However, segregated ethnic groups lack any equal-access contact and are subject to ethnic stereotypes on the part of the dominant group. The problem is not solely with dominant group perceptions; other minorities may see the stereotypes as the reality, and even members of the target group may turn on each other—those with the "desired" qualities (e.g., who are more acculturated) may reject their peers. As a consequence, target minorities often find themselves stereotyped, isolated, avoided, and fighting among themselves. The Japanese in the United States at the time of Pearl Harbor were victims of all of the boundary-maintenance mechanisms; the Filipinos, Chinese, and Koreans had turned against them; most of the majority group thought in terms of the stereotype of the "sly, sneaky, tricky, Jap"; and politicians and journalists played upon popular anti-Japanese sentiments. The group itself was divided by generation (Issei, Nisei, Kibei) and by American and Japanese loyalties. Therefore, they were ripe for the events that followed the attack on Pearl Harbor.

216

Action against the Japanese was triggered by the attack on Pearl Harbor. But plans for the "final" solution were never clear. Instead it was the momentum established by a series of actions: the cumulative effect of many decisions; past feelings and actions of prejudice, discrimination, and segregation; panic, racism, and the wartime atmosphere all combined to shape the eventual decision to evacuate and incarcerate the entire Japanese population along the West Coast, whether citizen or alien.

Immediately after December 7, 1941, the FBI rounded up selected enemy aliens, including 2,192 Japanese. Even this roundup, which was logical enough at the time, had its ludicrous moments. The arrested were those who had contributed money to Japan, who had achieved some degree of prominence, or who belonged to certain organizations. (My father was taken away initially on the charge of possessing illegal contraband—which turned out to be several flashlights and a knife.)

Pressure Grows

The incarceration of only selected aliens did not satisfy the Hearst press. The cry, "Japs Must Go," was echoed by the syndicated Hearst columnist Henry McLemore when he wrote on January 29, 1942:

> I am for the immediate removal of every Japanese on the West Coast to a point deep in the interior . . ., let 'em be pinched, hurt, and hungry. Personally, I hate Japanese. And that goes for all of them.

Those advocating the removal of the Japanese included individuals such as then California Attorney General Earl Warren, "liberal" columnist Walter Lippman, and civil-rights fighter Carey McWilliams; the usual patriotic and right-wing organizations; farm and labor groups; the press; local and national magazines and newspapers. Most organizations usually alert to cases of blatant discrimination remained silent.

In chronological sequence, the following events occurred: On January 29, 1942, United States Attorney General Francis Biddle established security areas along the Pacific Coast from which all enemy aliens were to be removed. On February 19, 1942, President Roosevelt signed Executive Order 9066, which designated restricted military areas and authorized the building of "relocation camps." The ten camps were scattered over California, Arizona, Idaho, Wyoming, Colorado, Utah, and Arkansas.

In March 1942, the evacuation of persons of Japanese ancestry, defined as anyone with as little as ⅛ Japanese blood, began; and by November, more than 110,000 West Coast Japanese, most of them American citizens, were behind barbed wire. The rapid, smooth, and efficient evacuation was aided by the cooperation of the Japanese people themselves. They responded to posted notices to register, voluntarily assembled

217

at designated points, and marched willingly to the trains and busses sent to haul them to the camps.

But beneath this accommodating facade lay the disruption of years of effort. Homes and possessions were abandoned; personal treasures were sold for a fraction of their value, or were stolen; farms and gardens were ruined; families disintegrated. None of the Japanese seemed to expect fair play or justice. The evacuation was done "for the good of the Japanese themselves." (It is this kind of thinking that encouraged the United States to bomb villages and hamlets in Southeast Asia "for the good of the inhabitants.")

Although there were riots (Kitano, 1969: 34), draft-dodging (Daniels, 1971), and other acts of resistance, most Japanese accepted it, or were resigned to it (*shi-kata-ga-nai*). Several individual cases were brought to the Supreme Court (Kitano, 1696: 39–40); and although there was no direct ruling on the evacuation, the decisions supported the legality of the action. Therefore, in all of its phases, the forced evacuation and incarceration of the Japanese, whether citizens or aliens, was legally sanctioned.

The evacuation ended in 1944 as it started, on a legal note, when the Supreme Court ruling on the Endo case revoked the West Coast exclusion orders. Effective January 2, 1945, the Japanese were no longer under forcible detention (Kitano, 1969: 40).

Although there were problems in getting some Japanese to leave, by June 1946 the concentration camps were closed. There were incidents of vandalism and terrorism against the Japanese when they returned to their homes on the West Coast but these soon ended. Some Japanese moved to the Midwest and to the East Coast, but many returned to California and by 1970, the majority were again on the West Coast.

Racism

The most reasonable conclusion is that racism was the primary factor in the removal of the Japanese. The definition of who was Japanese was based on "blood," and the presumption of guilt by ancestry condemned the entire "race" to incarceration. As Daniels and Kitano (1970) indicate, the actions of Germans was attributed to evil and sick individuals, but the actions of the Japanese were attributed to an evil race.

If the Japanese were a menace to the West Coast, then they should have been even more of a menace to Hawaii. But there was no mass jailing of Japanese on the much more vulnerable islands, and this fact supports the belief that West Coast racism was primarily responsible for the concentration camps. Although Hawaii was not free of racial prejudice and discrimination, it was a racial paradise compared to California. Further, the Japanese were vital to Hawaii's economy (resource power); there were many more Japanese in Hawaii (numerical power); and the commander of the area was a much more enlightened man (knowledge power) than his counterpart on the West Coast.

Was there a possibility that the Japanese Americans could have suffered the same treatment in America as the Jews did in Germany? Could the Japanese have been placed in death ovens? Were they ever faced with the danger of extermination? Before answering these questions, a series of other events bearing on this issue will be described.

Daniels (1971) reports that when the decision to move the Japanese into the interior was planned, the Army called a special meeting of governors of Western States in Salt Lake City on April 7, 1942. Milton Eisenhower was asked to present information to the select group, and one of the basic questions was what would happen to the "Japs" after the war. The United States administration wanted to handle the evacuees with some degree of restraint; there were ideas of homesteading and the like, but the hostility of the Western governors soon quelled any liberal approach. Cries that no state should be a "dumping ground for California's problems" were typical, and there was almost no alternative but to build settlements on the model of concentration camps with barbed-wire fences and armed guards. The paranoia and fear caused by the Japanese stereotype was powerful indeed.

A government that could herd a race of people into concentration camps could probably also exterminate them. For example, if the Japanese had invaded Hawaii and were threatening the West Coast, passions could have run even higher. Or, if the Japanese had been actually dropping bombs on United States cities, the administration might have used the ultimate retaliation against the Japanese Americans behind barbed wire. The extermination of a group, of course, does not necessarily mean overt violence. Inadequate diets, the separation of sexes, and sterilization were all mentioned as "solutions" for the Japanese at one time by members of the United States Congress. The important point is that the momentum acquired through prejudice, stereotyping, discrimination, segregation, and the neutralization of the human qualities of the target group ("tricky, sneaky yellow dogs") sets the stage for more dramatic solutions. Other processes then take over. Organizational roles ("I was just doing my duty") can assume such high priority that placing innocent people behind barbed wire is simple. The colonel who was in charge of putting the Japanese into the camps received high commendation for the effectiveness of his operation. There is little question that if the orders were for more drastic solutions, they would have been dispatched with the efficiency and speed of a people proud of their organizational ability and their reputation for following through on "orders."

THE PRESENT

Numbers

The 1970 Census reported 591,290 Japanese in the United States. The two most populous states for the Japanese are Hawaii (217,307) and

California (213,280). Nationally, the Japanese represent but .02 percent of the United States total of over 203 million. Although there are Japanese scattered throughout the United States, they remain primarily in the Coast states. In Hawaii they represent one of the largest ethnic units (36.7 percent) and have achieved a degree of political power.

Visibility

The Japanese are a physically visible population, although their Asian features are similar to the Chinese and the Korean, at least to the white majority. Their life styles are less visible; they live quiet lives and their dress and their consumption patterns do not stand out. Like their Asian neighbors, they do not quite fit into the black or white categories. In South Africa for business purposes they may be classified as "white," but not on a social level. In the South during World War II they were considered white, and therefore the color classification of the Japanese is not an absolute. However, their distinctive oriental features, including their smaller, slanted eyes, their shorter physical stature, and straight, black hair make them easily identifiable ethnics.

One of the techniques adopted by many Japanese was to become less visible. The life styles of most Japanese did not reflect their social class position. They consistently lived "below" the average non-Japanese individual of a similar class position.[3] Actions that might bring attention to them, especially of a negative nature, were discouraged. Loud talking, loud clothes, big cars, and fancy houses were thought to present a negative image and so were generally discouraged as popular models. To be quiet, to conform, to be modest and to refrain from actions of a deviant nature were strong role prescriptions.

Conversely, visibility in terms of clean and conservative clothes, getting good grades, and belonging to "good" organizations (e.g., YMCA, Scouts) was strongly encouraged. Some attempted to "pass" by having eye operations and adopting Anglo names [4] but the proportion has been extremely low. Perhaps the model choice for handling the problem of visibility has been "psychological passing": identifying and acquiring the American culture at such a rapid rate that they have been termed as America's model minority.

Social Class

Whatever power the Japanese Americans have achieved is probably due to social status. They are one of the highest educated groups in the

---

[3] This is still true of many Japanese Americans today although many Sansei of our acquaintance are beginning to react to the conservative style of their parents. They want the most expensive things from the most prestigious stores; they dress to draw attention; and they constantly clash with their parents over consumption patterns.

[4] A common compromise in terms of names is for a very Anglicized first name with the ethnic surname.

United States, and their school achievement remains consistently high. Their incomes are among the highest of all ethnic groups; many have become professionals; their housing pattern reflects a middle-class status, and very few would be considered "poor" (Kitano, 1969). Although the first Issei group started on a relatively homogeneous lower-class level, by the 1970s there has been sufficient differentiation to support a wider class structure. There are millionaires (usually land investors); there are many professionals such as doctors, lawyers, dentists, optometrists, and pharmacists; there are many teachers, nurses, and engineers; there are the familiar gardeners; and there are a great many farmers. Many also are federal civil service employees.

Occupational mobility and educational achievement are closely related. Levine and Montero (1973), in a study analyzing three generations of Japanese report that the higher the education level of the Issei, the more likely that their sons were in high status occupations. They also report that a high proportion of the Nisei (71 percent) were in white collar jobs and that the higher status Nisei differed from the blue collar Nisei in that they (1) tended to live in primarily white neighborhoods; (2) were less adamant about their children marrying within the ethnic group; (3) were less involved in the ethnic community, including the Buddhist church; (4) were less likely to speak or read Japanese as fluently or as well. It is interesting to note that 15 percent of the blue collar workers had incomes of $10,000 per year or more (this reflects the income of the independent Japanese gardener).

The Levine and Montero findings can be questioned as to their sample. It was a three-generational study with the original sample chosen from Issei lists, compiled primarily from Japanese community organization rosters. Therefore, as the authors emphasize, there is a bias against the peripheral and unaffiliated Issei, and the bias may have been compounded by restricting the subsequent interviews to the progeny of the original sample. However, in spite of the biases, the movement toward college and professionalization is strong and is supported by independent observation.

Acculturation

Analyzing the culture of the Japanese will add to our understanding of their acculturation to the United States and help identify some of the variables that may have slowed this process. The power of the ethnic community and ethnic visibility are variables that help explain differential rates of acculturation. For example, the Japanese in Hawaii are much more apt to retain elements of the Japanese culture than Japanese families living in Connecticut (Kitano and Manning, 1973).

Another important factor is the Japanese work ethic. It is such an integral part of their system that one Japanese professor writes, "Japanese work as if they were addicted to it" (Japan *Times*, 1973: 3). The roots of the work orientation can be traced as far back as the teachings of Confucius and Buddha; the familiar Protestant work ethic is a recent borrowing by Europeans of something that has existed in Asia for many centuries (Kitano and Manning, 1973).

The Issei immigrants brought their work ethic to the United States. For many, hard work and effort were desirable goals in themselves. We know of surviving Issei who remain uncomfortable with many of the modern work-saving appliances because they entail so little time, effort, and expenditure of energy.

Although there are difficulties in assessing the culture that the Japanese brought to the United States, Nakane (1965, 1972) presents a framework that is helpful in understanding the Japanese family in Japan. She stresses the importance of situational membership and the role of the "ie" or traditional family unit in socializing family members and in providing the major reference group. Marriages were between "ies" (rather than individuals) and "good ies" trained their men and women for appropriate roles in the Japanese social system. Group power and group control were paramount in shaping the attitudes and behaviors of individuals. The group was of higher priority than individual needs and desires. Relationships within the ethnic community were primarily noncontractual and socialization was toward a narrow living range and dependency.

In general, we now see the Japanese-American family as follows:

1. It has remained an intact family unit with low rates of separation and divorce, although there are changes towards a more American model. The low past rates of divorce (1.3 percent) (Kitano, 1969) are probably rising.

2. The structure of the family was initially vertical, with father and males on top. It could be likened to a traditional family model, in contrast to the modern urban American family. Entertainment and recreation often took place in the family and extended family units. Families were larger; problems were often handled within the unit and the use of outside professionals was a last resort.

3. The "ie" unit was adopted in America to include larger units, including village, "ken," and even the entire Japanese community. It served as an effective social control device; it provided socialization opportunities through ethnic language schools, cultural, and recreational opportunities. The Japanese community became a reference group; the functions were similar to those of an "ie."

4. Socialization and child rearing took into account minority group position, power, and the carrying on of the Japanese culture. Those values, norms, and behaviors most likely to persist were those of the Japanese culture that interacted with the power position of the Japanese in the United States and their visibility in a race-conscious society. Many of these behaviors have also been reinforced by the majority group so that they have become stereotypes of the Japanese. These include quietness, conformity, loyalty, diligence, maximum effort, good citizenship, high school achievement, and group orientation.

5. The situational orientation has been an important part of Japanese-American behavior. Learning how to behave to those above, below, and equal has meant learning appropriate styles. As Kitano states:

> There are elements of a "schizophrenic adaptation" on the part of the Japanese to life in the United States. But most physically identifiable group are also faced with the same problem—the how-to-behave problem when interacting with the majority and the behaviors when with one's own group. Therefore, within one individual there is often the many personalities—the "Uncle Tom" to the white man, deferential and humble; the "good son" to his parents, dutiful and obedient; and the "swinger" to his peers, wise-cracking, loud, and irreverent. And all of these behaviors are real so that none can be said to give a truer picture except in terms of time, place, and situation (1969: 106–7).

The situational approach is intimately related to power. The less powerful have to learn many adaptations; those with power can afford to use one style. Americans expect others to adapt to them and with their power, can often command or buy this recognition. Americans even assume that there are social science universals—"the personality" and "the truth"—whereas the search may be more a reflection of a power position than a social scientific reality.

6. Acculturation has been the most powerful single influence on Japanese behavior. But it has not been a simple linear movement; the variables of power and visibility have shaped differential styles so that Japanese Americans in Hawaii will be different in many instances from their peers along the Pacific and Atlantic seaboards. There is a current reawakening of an ethnic identity and a militancy among the Sansei (Kitano, 1972; Maykovich, 1972) that may slow the trend toward acculturation.

One of the most influential events hastening acculturation was the evacuation of the Japanese during World War II. It broke up the power of the Issei and the ethnic ghettoes; altered family life; scattered Japanese throughout the United States through resettlement; sent many males into the armed forces and overseas; and made many renounce everything Japanese (Kitano, 1969).

7. The Japanese child-rearing techniques involved less direct confrontation than the American techniques. They attempted to provide outside stimuli, divert a child's attention, elicit cooperation, and shape a child's behavior through the force of "others." The fear of being ridiculed, being made to look foolish, and bringing shame on the family were primary sanctions in obtaining desired behavior.

Similar behavior characterized the husband-wife interaction with much more indirect communication, inferences, and unstated feelings, and less of the direct interaction (e.g., loud arguments) that seems more American.

It is our interpretation that Japanese normalize interaction through acknowledgment of differing power positions. As Nakane (1965) indicates, the Japanese social system can be likened to a series of parallels. Each individual is in a set position and has to learn how to interact with those above and those below; escape from the structure is extremely limited. It would therefore be difficult to continually collide head on with those within the system, and various techniques have been developed to handle power, dependence, and potential disruptive conflict.

8. Social class has always been a factor in the Japanese culture but it is difficult to transcribe into the American scene. The "ies" tried to make appropriate matches and "good" families were class conscious. Although most of the immigrants started at the bottom of American class structure, they did not identify with the life styles of the lower classes. Rather, they brought with them many of the values associated with the middle-class: high educational expectations for their children, respect for those in authority (including the police), desire to own property, emphasis on banking and savings, and a future orientation (Kitano, 1969). They seldom fully adopted a lower-class style, even though their incomes and housing were clearly in the ghetto areas.

However, there is an increasing heterogeneity in the Japanese-American community and the development of a more formal social class system (e.g., debutantes, professional organizations). With continued differences in education and income, the system may soon become much more crystallized.

Finally, it is important to emphasize that there is no one American culture, just as there is no one Japanese or Japanese-American culture. Therefore, acculturation means different things to different families and these will be reflected in their attitudes and behaviors. Perhaps the most appropriate generalization is that the Japanese families in the United States were different to begin with and that length of time in the United States has been just one of the many influences leading to further change. But in spite of these differences there appears to be enough of a thread so that it is still possible to talk of a Japanese-American subculture (Kitano and Manning, 1973).

The Community

The old ghetto communities have undergone vast changes. Although there are still recognizable Japanese clusters ("J"-towns), they may be much smaller than before and are usually business centers. The acculturated have moved into better housing; however, the predicted demise of the ethnic community has not taken place. Instead, there are continuing attempts to rebuild and uplift the old Japanese communities, often with capital from Japan, as well as with federal funds.

There are several hypothesized reasons for this rebirth. Part of the motivation comes from business—J-towns are centrally located, are tourist attractions, and do a thriving business. Furthermore, there has been a constant flow of new Japanese immigrants over the past decade, and many of these newcomers feel comfortable in an ethnic community. Then there is the ever-increasing group of businessmen from "wealthy" Japan, as well as Japanese tourists who also enjoy the ethnic communities. Finally, there are many older Issei, especially of limited economic means, who prefer to spend their last years among their ethnic group.

The Japanese business structure was an important factor in building the Japanese community. Both the Chinese (hui) and the Japanese (tanomoshi) used a rotating credit system which makes a pool of money available for investment and credit purposes (Light, 1972). The system also aided community cohesion.

Further, as Light indicates, membership in Oriental organizations, being ascriptive, provided group identity, enforced ethnic honor and pride, and motivated members toward achievement that they would probably not have sought otherwise. In contrast, Light argues that black organizations draw on a culturally undifferentiated mass which includes a high proportion of poor people who do not tend to participate in voluntary organizations. Because there is often a "what's in it for me?" attitude, the organizational elites are forced to spend much of their time working for popular support.

About the Japanese communities, one could generally say:

1. It is much more scattered and dispersed than in earlier times. Business rather than residential centers are more common.
2. Many organizations serve the ethnic community and are modeled after American patterns (i.e., Boy and Girl Scouts, the Y's, the Lions, and other service clubs), but they reflect a structural pluralism.
3. Many ethnic professionals (i.e., doctors, lawyers, pharmacists) are available to the community.
4. The use of majority social service and psychiatric facilities has, until recently, been low due to the availability of ethnic resources within the Japanese community. However, as the ethnic community changes and can no longer provide adequate resources for itself, more Japanese Americans will be dependent on larger community services; or, alternatively, larger community (including federal) financing may be necessary to support ethnic institutions.
5. The ethnic family is still more or less dependent on the community. The Japanese are able to rely on themselves in solving most of their problems, but not all.[5]
6. Japanese communities are not problem-free, contrary to the popular stereotype. Aside from problems common to any community, such as communications, economic well-being, and the like, there are acute problems of the aged; parent-child relationships, and drugs.

PERSONALITY AND CULTURE

Personality measures, based primarily on white norms, provide quite consistent findings. Studies by Arkoff (1959) and Meredith (1965) among others generally indicate that the Japanese are less aggressive, exuberant, and dominating than Caucasians. They are also more deferent, conscientious, and reserved. Everyday observations generally support these findings. However, there are two ways of looking at the phenomenon. The most common explanation is that these traits are part of Japanese socialization and are therefore a part of the Japanese culture; others would say that they are a result of American racism and its power to shape ethnic minorities into "desirable" types. The humble, passive, obedient, deferential, demasculinized male is much less threatening to the dominating group than the virile, aggressive, manipulating, insolent samurai.

Choices Affecting Japanese Behavior

The following four cases indicate the pressures of the dominant culture on immigrant groups, and help explain the influence of broader variables such as race, color and nationality on personality.

Two Hawaiian Issei in the 1920s—Fred Makino, the editor of a newspaper, *Hawaiian Hochi,* and Takie Okumura, a Christian missionary —are described by Jacobs and Landau (1971); both were sincerely interested in their ethnic group but each used quite divergent strategies in his adaptation to the new country.

FRED MAKINO

Fred Makino was a model for those Issei who actively retained their ethnic identity.[6] He came to Hawaii from Japan in 1899, and soon began to perceive some of the problems that faced his ethnic group. He saw the Japanese being exploited by white Hawaiian plantation owners, whereupon he helped the Japanese workers to organize their own unions. He started lawsuits against discriminatory practices and was willing to go to jail for his convictions. He felt that the best protection for a relatively small, powerless minority group was to organize and *actively* fight to protect their own interests, rather than to fade quietly into the background.

Makino's primary emphases were heightening ethnic awareness, promoting ethnic identity, and to fostering group cohesion. Consequently, one of the main tenets in his program was to open and maintain Japanese language schools. Here the Issei and their children could learn their native language, understand their own culture, and resist the attempts of the Americans to "rob" them of their native heritage. He felt it was important that the Japanese build up pride in their ethnicity, that Japanese values (of the Meiji era) be held superior to those of the American culture, and that Japanese institutions and styles were pre-

---

[5] For example, there has been a rise in adolescent drug use among the Japanese in Los Angeles. The ethnic community was tapped for funds and raised enough to start a self-help drug center. However, the continuing rise in drug use may force the Japanese to seek help from the larger community.

[6] We have taken some liberties with Makino's life in order to formulate a model for this category (Kitano, 1972).

ferred and maintained. He advocated political organization—"bloc" power—and felt that pressure was the most effective means of dealing with the white man.

TAKIE OKUMURA

Another Issei, living in Hawaii at the same time as Makino, was Takie Okumura. He perceived the problems of the ethnic community differently and advocated an active, acculturative position—i.e., Japanese should acquire American culture. Okumura felt that the maintenance of Japanese culture was one of the major barriers towards acceptance by the white group. He felt that ethnic living conditions, manners, habits, and customs should be discarded: smelly foods, noisy festivals, loud conversation in Japanese, and prominent Japanese architecture. Any behavior (especially in public) that offended Americans should be controlled or eliminated.

Okumura thought of the Japanese as "visitors," or "guests," in the United States, and felt that they should conduct themselves accordingly. They should do nothing to alienate their hosts: they should go to American schools and be taught and trained as Americans; they should avoid such unpopular acts as labor strikes and slowdowns and should continue to work loyally for their employers, no matter what the provocation.

Okumura felt that if Japanese expected to be Americans, then they must be American in every way. They must associate with them, learn their language, and go to their schools; the only way for a small minority to become successful is to merge with the host culture. Okumura's advice to the Japanese colony was, "above everything else remember that you are guests of this land and be very careful in everything you do" (Jacobs and Landau, 1971: 213).

PRESIDENT S. I. HAYAKAWA

There is little question that the appointment of Dr. S. I. Hayakawa to the presidency of San Francisco State College would have been greeted with unanimous acclaim by the ethnic community during the prewar days, for he epitomizes the idea of integration; he holds a Ph.D., is married to a Caucasian wife, and has just retired as the president of a large educational institution.

Even today he is probably a hero to the majority of the Japanese— but it is not quite unanimous. In Disneyland in April, 1969, a large group of Japanese assembled to pay him honor. Inside the auditorium over 500 people greeted him with a standing ovation. But while the older Nisei were applauding, a smaller, younger group gathered outside waving signs such as "Hayakawa Is a Banana—Yellow Skin but White Inside" or "Hayakawa Is Not Our Spokesman." Such overt expressions would have been rare several years previous, and impossible decades before.

Hayakawa's position illustrates the changes in the ethnic community. At one time being ethnic would have been sufficient to unite and "lead" the Japanese (at least in a public, visible manner); now, there are the larger issues of political stance and ideology. In the long run, these differences are healthy manifestations in any ethnic group.

DR. THOMAS NOGUCHI

The case of Dr. Noguchi, County Coroner of Los Angeles, also occurred in 1969. Dr. Noguchi was dismissed from his position by the Los Angeles County Board of Supervisors on numerous charges that ranged from drug-taking to mental illness to incompetence. In a previous era, he would have quietly resigned and accepted an alternate position. The ethnic community would have been embarrassed by the whole affair and would have preferred the physician to remain quiet and to accept the "demotion."

But instead, Noguchi chose to challenge his dismissal. Even more important, the ethnic community supported him. They quickly raised over $40,000 for the defense fund. The large number of small contributors indicates that many Japanese felt that they had been ignored or passed over in their own job situations. Dr. Noguchi was eventually reinstated as county coroner. The Japanese were exhibiting atypical "Japanese behavior"; rather than accepting and accommodating, they were challenging and confronting. Noguchi's support came from *all* generations and from *all* models.

Overt Dissent

Why, after decades of acceptance, accommodation, assimilation, and inward aggression did overt dissent appear in the Japanese community in the latter 1960s, especially when things were going so well?

First, there are several social-psychological explanations. One relatively consistent social science finding is that periods of dissent, strain, and rebellious behavior often occur when social conditions are improving, whereas extreme deprivation is usually associated with apathy. Concerns for sheer survival take precedence under completely depressed conditions, and are accompanied by low expectations and a feeling of hopelessness. Conversely, as opportunities increase, expectations develop more quickly than actual improvements in social conditions, which in turn sets up strain and dissatisfaction. For example, the Women's Liberation Movement is the strongest in the United States, where women are perhaps more "liberated" than in most other countries; the Watts riots occurred in Los Angeles, where the treatment of the blacks has been presumably "milder" than in other sections of the country.

Another reason is that new generations have formed, and with them, newer ways of being "Asian." For example, by the end of the 1960s, groups with titles such as the Asian-American Political Alliance, the Council of Oriental Organizations, the Yellow Brotherhood, the Third World Liberation Front, and the Red Guards were emerging from the Asian communities. The Asian-American Political Alliance stated: "The crucial question facing us today is not that of integration. Now there is the more compelling question. . . . What is this society which we have sought, too often with ludicrous fever, to become integrated into [sic]?" (*Gidra*, 1969).

Racism and discrimination are central concerns to most of these newer groups who have shifted away from an accomodationist-acceptance mode toward ethnic identity and autonomy. A newspaper titled *Gidra*, produced by Sansei of the college-age generation, challenged the local Japanese, Chinese, and other Asian establishments by advocating stands on such "controversial" issues as student demonstrations, yellow identity, and yellow power.

Coalitions are beginning to be established among all Asian groups, whereas in the past, nationality differences prevented an overall Asian identity. It is difficult to ascertain the number, representation, and power of these groups, but perhaps the differences among Asian groups are disappearing in the push toward pan-Asian identity. There is little question that previous generations of Chinese, Japanese, Koreans, and Filipinos would have been greatly disturbed by this effort.

Another major reason for the increased conflict has been the change in goals. Becoming 100 percent American is no longer the ultimate desire for a great many; and once this drive is modified, previous patterns of accommodation, ritualism, and retreat will have to change.

Generational Change

Perhaps the greatest change can be labeled as generational since it is the Sansei and Yonsei (third and fourth generations) who are at the forefront of the new movement. Given the unequal power relationships, previous generations developed the "indirect styles" as a reasonable strategy. Many Sansei prefer direct confrontation and are impatient with the older Japanese-American ways.

One of the most drastic changes has been interracial marriage. Levine and Montero (1973) indicate that only 8 percent of the Nisei in their study were interracially married, whereas about 33 percent of the Sansei married out of the group. A more comprehensive study by Manning and Kitano (1973) indicates that in 1971 and 1972 the Japanese-American rates of interracial marriage were near 50 percent. This is true in areas as diverse as San Francisco, Fresno, Los Angeles, and Hawaii, and is primarily a Sansei phenomenon since interracial marriages in these areas over a decade ago were below the 20 percent level.

This move toward the "melting pot" is occurring at the same time that others are advocating a strong ethnic identity and pluralism. It may presage an interesting pattern of multiple Japanese-American adjustments which is perhaps the healthiest state since it indicates that both the ethnic and the dominant communities are no longer as "closed" as they once used to be.

The Japanese Americans have come a long way since the evacuation of World War II. Their record of low rates of crime, delinquency, and mental illness, and their high achievement patterns are impressive. However, the plight of the Japanese American who is not a high achiever in school is an especially difficult problem. The school dropout and the new immigrant face problems that are easily ignored because of the relative success of the majority.

But the basic issue is that the Japanese still remain stereotyped, even though the majority feelings are more positive. The labels may change—he is no longer a "Jap," he is a Japanese (Ogawa, 1971)—but he is still less than human. The "successful" label has made it difficult to probe for the many problems that lie within this ethnic group. And because there remains a stereotype that associates the Japanese in America with the Japanese in Japan, many Japanese Americans fear they may once again become targets of American aggression should relations between America and Japan become strained.

BIBLIOGRAPHY

ARKOFF, ABE (1959). "Need Patterns in Two Generations of Japanese Americans in Hawaii." *The Journal of Social Psychology*, 50: 75–79.

BLOOM, LEONARD and RUTH RIEMER (1945). "Attitudes of College Students Toward Japanese Americans." *Sociometry*, 8 (2).

BOSWORTH, ALLAN P. (1967). *America's Concentration Camps*. New York: W. W. Norton & Co., Inc.

DANIELS, ROGER (1971). *Concentration Camps U.S.A.: Japanese Americans and World War II*. New York: Holt, Rinehart and Winston, Inc.

—— and HARRY H. L. KITANO (1970). *American Racism: Exploration of the Nature of Prejudice*. Englewood Cliffs, N.J.: Prentice-Hall, Inc.

EATON, ALLEN H. (1952). *Beauty Behind Barbed Wire: The Arts of the Japanese in Our War Relocation Camps*. New York: Harper & Row, Publishers.

FISHER, A. R. (1965), *Exile of a Race*. Seattle: Ford T. Publishers.

Gidra (newspaper), 1 (5): August 1969.

GIRDNER, AUDRIE and ANNE LOFTIS (1969). *The Great Betrayal*. New York: The Macmillan Company.

GRODZINS, M. (1949). *Americans Betrayed*. Chicago: University of Chicago Press.

HOSOKAWA, WILLIAM (1969). *Nisei: The Quiet Americans*. New York: William Morrow and Co., Inc.

JACOBS, PAUL and SAUL LANDAU (1971). *To Serve the Devil*. New York: Vintage Books. Pp. 166–270.

Japan *Times* (1973). P. 3.

KITANO, HARRY H. L. (1972). "Japanese American Dissent." In Rosenstone and Boskin, eds., *Seasons of Rebellion*. New York: Holt, Rinehart and Winston, Inc.

——— (1969). *Japanese Americans: The Evolution of a Subculture*. Englewood Cliffs, N.J.: Prentice-Hall, Inc.

——— and AKEMI K. MANNING (1973). "The Japanese-American Family." (In process.)

LEIGHTON, ALEXANDER (1945). *The Governing of Men*. Princeton, N.J.: Princeton University Press. P. 344.

LEVINE, GENE and DARREL M. MONTERO (1973)."Socioeconomic Mobility Among Three Generations of Japanese Americans." *Journal of Social Issues* (in press).

LIGHT, IVAN (1972). *Ethnic Enterprise in American Business and Welfare Among Chinese, Japanese, and Blacks*. Berkeley and Los Angeles: University of California Press.

LYMAN, STANFORD (n.d.). "Contrasts in the Community Organization of Chinese and Japanese in North America." Unpublished paper. Sonoma, Calif.: Sonoma State College.

MANNING, AKEMI K. and HARRY H. L. KITANO (1973). "Interracial Marriage: A Picture of the Japanese Americans." *Journal of Social Issues* (in press).

MEREDITH, GERALD M. (1965). "Observations on the Acculturation of Sansei Japanese Americans in Hawaii." *Psychologia*, 8 (1 and 2).

MYER, DILLON (1971). *Uprooted Americans*. Tuscon: University of Arizona Press.

NAKANE, CHIE (1972). *Japanese Society*. Berkeley and Los Angeles: University of California Press.

——— (1965). "Towards a Theory of Japanese Social Structure." *The Economic Weekly*.

OGAWA, DENNIS (1971). From Japs to Japanese. Berkeley, Calif.: McCutchan Publishing Co.

OKUBO, MINE (1946). *Citizen 13660*. New York: Columbia University Press.

PETERSEN, WILLIAM (1971). *Japanese Americans*. New York: Random House, Inc.

SPICER, EDWARD H., ASAEL T. HANSEN, KATHERINE LUOMALA, and MARVIN K. OPLER (1969). *Impounded People*. Tuscon: University of Arizona Press.

TENBROEK, JACOBUS, EDWARD N. BARNHART, and FLOYD W. MATSON (1970). *Prejudice, War and the Constitution*. Berkeley and Los Angeles: University of California Press. (Original printing, 1954.)

THOMAS, DOROTHY S., CHARLES KIKUCHI, and JAMES SAKODA (1952). *The Salvage*. Berkeley and Los Angeles: University of California Press.

THOMAS, DOROTHY S. and RICHARD NISHIMOTO (1946). *The Spoilage*. Berkeley and Los Angeles: University of California Press.

TINKER, JOHN (n.d.). "Intermarriage and Ethnic Boundaries." Unpublished study. Fresno, Calif.: Fresno State College.

ZELLER, WILLIAM D. (1969). *An Educational Drama*. New York: The American Press.

THE
FILIPINOS 11

The Filipino followed the Chinese and Japanese immigration to America.[1] It was a largely male immigration, and the young men who came essentially filled the niche in the labor force that had been occupied by the Japanese, who by the 1920s were no longer available in significant numbers to work for Caucasian growers. Had Japanese immigration not been cut off, it is probable that the Filipino migration would not have been as large as it was. The Filipino, however, thanks to American imperialism, enjoyed a different status than did other Asians. Like other Asians, Filipinos were not eligible for naturalization; but since the United States owned the Philippines they were not aliens, but nationals. As such, they traveled under United States passports and could not be excluded from the United States. Congress eventually rectified this by passing, in 1935, the Tydings-McDuffie Act, which granted a deferred independence to the Philippines but imposed immediately a rigid quota of fifty a year, thus ending, for all practical purposes, Filipino immigration. Ironically, some of the leading anti-Filipino nativists in California were among the chief advocates of Philippine independence, since independence—or to be

---

1 Much of the historical material is drawn from Daniels and Kitano (1970).

precise, the promise of independence was the *sine qua non* of exclusion.

The major thrust of Filipino immigration lasted about ten years. In 1920 there had been only 5,000 Filipinos in the whole country (3,000 in California); by the next Census the figures had risen to 45,000 nationwide, with about 30,000 in California. Yet this tiny minority raised the hackles of the California exclusionists, who saw the Filipinos as yet another Asian horde about to overwhelm Caucasian California. A Sacramento exclusionist informed a national magazine audience that since all American Negroes were descended from a small slave nucleus, even this tiny group represented a danger. Ignoring the fact that very few women came from the Philippines, he insisted, with that mindless arithmetic that California exclusionists delighted in, that "Filipinos do not hesitate to have nine children . . . [which means] 729 great-grandchildren as against the white parents' twenty-seven."

But the explosive nature of the Filipino problem was caused not by Filipino reproduction, but by Filipino sex. The sex bugaboo, the ravishing of pure white women by lascivious oriental men, had always lurked in the background of the anti-oriental movements in California. It had never become, overtly at least, a major factor for the simple reason that sex relations between oriental men and occidental women had been all but nonexistent. (Intercourse between males of the majority race and females of the minority races aroused little opposition; Chinese and Japanese prostitutes had been a titillating feature of West Coast brothels since gold-rush days.) With the Filipinos, however, the sex issue became tangible. The Filipinos enjoyed and sought the companionship of Caucasian girls; and soon, in every major center of Filipino population in the state, special dance halls sprung up which catered exclusively to the Filipino trade, and a lucrative trade it was. The basic charge was ten cents a minute and the places did a thriving business.

This kind of "free enterprise" was just too much for most Californians. The conservative Los Angeles *Times* railed against two such dance halls located just a few blocks from the newspaper's headquarters. One set of headlines read:

Taxi-Dance Girls Start Filipinos on Wrong Foot

Lonely Islanders' Quest for Woman Companionship Brings Problems of Grave Nation Moment

Mercenary Women Influence Brown Man's Ego

Minds Made Ripe for Work of Red Organizers

Exclusionists suffered a further shock when the courts ruled that the state's miscegenation statute—which forbade marriages of white persons with Negroes, Mongolians, or mulattoes—did not apply to the Filipinos, who were adjudged Malayans. The California legislature quickly amended the law to extend the ban to "members of the Malay race." In the meantime the alleged sexual aggressiveness of the Filipinos had set off a good deal of mob violence. (It could be argued that the Filipinos were merely conforming to the "melting pot" ideal, and thus were more Americanized than other orientals, but this never occurred to California exclusionists.) In addition, the Filipinos, who were often, they felt, exploited by Japanese and Chinese businessmen in the United States, were much more prone to join unions and participate in strikes than earlier Asian immigrants had been, a propensity that caused them to be viewed with alarm in the America of Harding, Coolidge, and Hoover. Despite their willingness to be organized, the California trade-union hierarchy wanted little to do with them, and participated almost as eagerly in the anti-Filipino movement as it had in previous anti-oriental crusades.

Bogardus (1929), in studying early Caucasian attitudes towards the Filipino, found that whites favored their educational ambition, willingness to do menial tasks, and courtesy and politeness while working in hotels and restaurants. But Caucasians feared their economic competition, their inability to engage in heavy farm work; their propensity to strike and quarrel; and their forwardness with white girls. Filipinos were welcome if they remained in their place. Job discrimination sent Filipinos to the bottom of the economic scale, and housing discrimination segregated them into slums. It was inevitable that overt clashes would result. Melendy writes:

> California's first serious riot occurred at a carnival in Exeter on October 24, 1929, when a Filipino stabbed a white man. Prior to the incident, Filipinos had been abused in town, shoved off sidewalks, and molested by white transient workers. At the carnival, whites threw objects at Filipinos, particularly those in the company of white girls. This led to the stabbing (Melendy, 1967: 7).

The most explosive riot occurred in the Watsonville agricultural area in 1930. Anti-Filipino attitudes were set in motion by the chamber of commerce, which passed resolutions harassing Filipinos. The mobs followed suit, and for several days armed white hunting parties roamed the streets looking for Filipinos and invaded dance halls. The violence reached a climax with the killing of a Filipino, numerous assaults, and the burning of Filipino dwellings.

By World War II, attitudes towards Filipinos had changed. The "brave little brown brothers" who fought and died alongside the whites at Bataan and Corregidor became the new stereotype. However, Filipinos were considered to be an invisible minority group that ranked very low in most ethnic classification schemes.

Although they are most often classified as Mongolian and are therefore considered "yellow," Filipinos are of Malayan stock. They also often have Spanish surnames and can be mistaken quite easily for Puerto Ricans or Latin Americans. The 1970 Census listed 343,060 Filipinos in the United States, primarily on the West Coast, with 138,859 in California and 93,915 in Hawaii.

The Filipinos by far are the most disadvantaged Asian group. Their income is lower than that of the Chinese or Japanese; and in California, their annual income in 1965 was the lowest of any ethnic group. They were also the lowest group in number of school years completed.

The Filipinos, or Pinoys, can be divided into four main groups:

1. The first generation, which is composed primarily of males who immigrated in the 1920s. Most went into agricultural labor and retained their native Philippine dialect. Acculturation for them has been slow.
2. The second and third generations, who were born in America and who have very little contact with their native land, language, or culture.
3. The post-World War II arrivals, many of whom are veterans and war victims.
4. The new immigrants, which include many professionals who have come under the liberalized immigration laws of 1965.

The various groupings provide a background for some of the problems facing the Filipinos. For example, the old first-generation immigrants, mostly male, less educated, but hard working, has now grown old. Most of them have remained single and have no family ties. Long arduous lives as fruit pickers or laborers have not netted them much capital. Their isolation and poverty make them extremely vulnerable to changing conditions, especially as their earning power declines. Their last years are usually spent in dingy hotel rooms in California valley towns such as Stockton or in the blighted areas of San Francisco. The irony of their plight can be appreciated if we recall the one guiding ethic of their life: hard work.

Racist barriers discouraged intermarriage for first-generation males, but many were able to find mates from both majority group and other minority-group females. There is almost no empirical data on the number of these intermarriages. However, we would predict a relatively high proportion of separation and divorce, especially when compared to the rates for the other Asian populations. These higher rates of separation and divorce may be attributed to job discrimination, social isolation, subordinate status, as well as to cultural differences such as language and life styles.

The second generation and their children face many problems. In common with most racial minorities they share such problems as lack of social acceptance, low income, low educational achievement, and negative self-image. A special problem has been the lack of education, and some of the difficulties are listed in an unpublished Filipino-American position paper (Cordova et al. (n.d.) : p. 14).

1. There is an obvious lack of encouragement either in the home or in the high schools to go to college and succeed.
2. There is a noticeable absence of proper counseling to help young Filipinos choose between college or training school.
3. Many counselors lack the knowledge, experience, and rapport to adequately deal with Filipino-Americans.
4. Neither the colleges nor the high schools provide any courses in Filipino culture or history.
5. The future plans of many young Filipinos extend no further than the next day, the next month, or the next year.
6. The cost of education is beyond the reach of most Filipino families.

Predictably, there are very few Filipino college graduates. Only five Filipino-Americans graduated from the three major colleges in the Seattle area in 1971.

As with many of their peers in other ethnic communities, the second and third generation youngsters are also unfamiliar with their native country. They generally know nothing of Philippine culture, except through the reminiscences of some older Filipinos with whom they might occasionally be in contact.

The Post-World War II Veteran

A number of veterans came to the United States after World War II. Many of them had been in the Filipino Scouts; some brought their families; and others came by themselves with the idea of sending for their families after finding jobs. The author remembers working with a large group of these veterans who emigrated to San Francisco in the 1950s—many of them were middle-aged, generally unskilled (although they brought with them diplomas from unknown technical and vocational colleges in the Philippines) and quite thoroughly army disciplined. They brought with them a mixture of patriotism, a naive belief of the wonders of the United States, and a hard-work ethic.

Although life was extremely difficult during the early months, the need for unskilled laborers was high, and most of them did make an adaptation to the new country. On occasional meetings in the Asian community, the war veteran can still be spotted by his military bearing and his reminiscences of Bataan and Corregidor.

THE NEWLY ARRIVED

The immigration legislation of 1965 has contributed to a new and large Filipino migration. Prior to the passage of the law, Filipino immigration in 1965 was 2,545, whereas 25,417 entered the country in 1970. They are the fastest growing minority in cities such as San Francisco. There is also a corresponding increase in businesses catering to them; there are now many Filipino restaurants, grocery stores, and movie houses.

There are several reasons for the large current migration: unstable economic and political situation in the native country; the expectation of better opportunities in the United States; and favorable immigration legislation.

The new immigrants are far different from the old-timers of many decades ago. There are many doctors, lawyers, engineers, teachers, and nurses, reflecting the policy of the new immigration legislation of bringing highly skilled and professional people to the United States. Most are well educated and speak English. However, "despite their professional education in the Philippines, [they] are finding difficulty in getting jobs that suit their occupational and educational levels. So Filipino lawyers work as clerks; teachers as secretaries; dentists as aides; engineers as mechanics; and many professionals work also as laborers and janitors" (Cordova et al., p. 12). However, a low-status job in the United States often pays better than a high-status job in the Philippines.

Perhaps it would be best to let Carlos Bulosan, himself a Filipino immigrant and trade-union organizer, have the last word on the subject. In his moving autobiography, *America Is in the Heart,* he describes what it felt like to be a Filipino in California in the 1920s:

> . . . in many ways it was a crime to be a Filipino in California. I came to know that the public streets were not free to my people; we were stopped each time . . . patrolmen saw us a driving a car. We were suspect each time we were seen with a white woman. And perhaps it was this narrowing of our life into an island, into a filthy segment of American society, that had driven [many] Filipinos inward, hating everyone and despising all positive urgencies toward freedom.

BIBLIOGRAPHY

BOGARDUS, EMORY S. (1929). "American Attitudes Towards Filipinos." *Sociology and Social Research,* 14: 59–69.

CORDOVA, FREDERIC, PETER JAMERO, BARRETTO OGILVIE, ROBERT SANTOS,
SILVISTRE TANGALAN, ANDRES TANGALIN, and DALE TIFFANY (n.d.).
Filipino-American Position Paper. Unpublished paper. Seattle, Washington.

DANIELS, ROGER and HARRY H. L. KITANO (1970). *American Racism: Exploration of the Nature of Prejudice*. Englewood Cliffs, N.J.: Prentice-Hall, Inc.

MELENDY, H. BRETT (1967). "California's Discrimination against Filipinos." In *The Filipino Exclusion Movement, 1927–1935*. Occasional Papers No. 1. Quezon City, Philippines: Institute of Asian Studies, University of the Philippines. Pp. 3, 10.

SANIEL, JOSEF, ed. (1967). *The Filipino Exclusion Movement, 1927–1935*. Occasional Papers No. 1. Quezon City, Philippines: Institute of Asian Studies, University of the Philippines.

THE
MEXICAN
AMERICANS 12

The Mexican Americans are one of the most diverse ethnic groups. On one hand, they were an indigenous people who were overpowered by white settlers and are therefore one of the oldest minorities; on the other, their continuing immigration from Mexico to the United States also makes them one of the newest and largest immigrant groups. Some are fully integrated and assimilated into the U.S. and have a high rate of intermarriage, and some live almost exclusively within their ethnic enclaves. Some are aristocrats and millionaires, but most are desperately poor. All of these groups face the problem of adapting to the dominant white culture. Some retain strong ties to Mexico and return there frequently while others prefer a more militant posture and remain in the U.S. There are also those who partially integrate without assimilating but whose lives do not center exclusively within the ethnic enclave.

It is a large and complex ethnic group, yet in spite of this diversity, the Mexican has become stereotyped as a lazy, stoic, and ignorant peasant, or a ruthless, cunning, and untrustworthy "bandito." A more realistic picture of this group is long overdue.

The interaction of the Mexican native with the Europeans started with the Spanish invasion of Mexico during the sixteenth century. The translated chronicles of Diaz (1963) illustrate several factors that are relevant not only for an understanding of Mexico but also provide an insight into race relations. First, the Mexicans were extremely active in defending their lands, and the natives would probably not have been overwhelmed so easily except for the in-fighting among themselves. The use of dissident tribes as allies was a critical factor in the Spanish success. Second, the natives thought Cortes was a god, with his white face and the strange creatures he brought with him—horses. The superiority of European technology and weaponry proved decisive in combat. Finally, the Spanish were strongly motivated by their religious and imperialistic zeal.

The United States became involved with Mexico several centuries later. The Battle of San Jacinto and the "Fall of the Alamo" occurred in 1836. The Gadsden Purchase enabled the United States to acquire Texas, New Mexico, and parts of Colorado, Arizona, Utah, Nevada, and California in 1853. The actual number of Mexicans in these new territories was relatively small, and they were quickly engulfed by the more restless and ambitious white settlers. All Mexicans, whether they were "pure" Spanish and landed or "half-breed" laborers, were perceived by the whites to be inferior. By 1900 they were already a subordinated population, having lost the titles to their land because they could not supply proof of ownership. The white settler made no distinction between the original mexican inhabitants—the "old-timers"—and the immigrant newcomers; they were all consigned to the same low status. Only in New Mexico where the Mexicans retained a numerical superiority, did they retain a degree of political power.

From 1900 on, the Mexicans were influenced by the same general forces that affected Americans in the Southwest. World War I increased the trend toward urbanization and decreased the dependence on agriculture; the Great Depression struck the already vulnerable population with extreme force.

Sleepy Lagoon

Although Mexicans generally shared in the increased opportunities of the World War II years, there were several incidents in California that revealed the extent of white prejudice. The antagonism can be seen in two discrete incidents in Los Angeles in 1942 and 1943: the "Sleepy Lagoon" murder case and the "Zoot-suit" riots.

The "Sleepy Lagon" murder (the press invented the romantic title   **242**

—the scene of the crime was actually an abandoned gravel pit) took place on the night of August 1–2, 1942 (Daniels and Kitano, 1970: 74). The victim was a young Mexican American, José Diaz, apparently slain as the result of intraethnic gang rivalry. Throughout that summer, an artificial "crime wave" had been fabricated by the press and local police and attributed to Mexican-Americans. When the press made a sensation of Diaz's murder (not ordinarily considered newsworthy), the police followed suit with a mass roundup of suspects. Some twenty-four youths were arrested for the murder, and seventeen of them were actually indicted. There was no tangible evidence against any of them, but nevertheless the local authorities embarked on the largest mass trial for murder ever held in the United States. The defendants were beaten by police, were forced to appear in court with unkempt appearances (for a time they were not even allowed to have their hair cut), and eventually, after a long trial, nine were convicted of second-degree murder and the other eight found guilty of lesser crimes. More than two years after the crime, which remains unsolved, the California District Court of Appeals unanimously overturned all of the convictions.

What made this homicide significant was the illegal behavior of local law-enforcement officers, the reaction of the Mexican community to this incident, and the overt message of prejudice directed at the Mexican community.

The hostility of the local police to the Mexican-American population is hard to overstate and was of long duration. Innumerable instances of prejudice could be cited, but perhaps most illuminating are the following excerpts from a report given to the Los Angeles County Grand Jury by the sheriff's "expert" on Mexican-American behavior, Captain E. Duran Ayres. After presenting rather fanciful statistics on ethnicity and crime—the official taxonomy was black, yellow, and red for Negro, Oriental, and Mexican respectively—Captain Ayres embarked on a historio-sociological account of the Mexican in California. "Mexicans," he reported accurately enough,

> are restricted in the main only to certain kinds of labor, and that being the lowest paid. It must be admitted that they are discriminated against and have been heretofore practically barred from learning trades. . . . This has been very much in evidence in our defense plants, in spite of President Roosevelt's instructions to the contrary. . . . Discrimination and segregation . . . in certain restaurants, public swimming plunges, public parks, theaters, and even in schools, cause resentment among the Mexican people. . . . There are certain parks in the state in which a Mexican may not appear, or else only on a certain day of the week. There are certain plunges where they are not allowed to swim, or else only on one day of the week [and that invariably just prior to cleaning and draining], and it is made evident by signs reading . . . "Tuesdays reserved for Negroes and Mexicans." . . . All of this [and much more] applies to both the foreign and American-born Mexicans.

But Ayres followed this narrative with a blatantly racist explanation for Mexican-American crime and delinquency, an explanation
apparently accepted by the grand jury and most of the press and probably
most of the population.

> The Caucasian [and] especially the Anglo-Saxon, when engaged in fighting
> . . . resort[s] to fisticuffs . . .; but this Mexican element considers [good
> sportsmanship] to be a sign of weakness, and all he knows and feels is a
> desire to use a knife or some other lethal weapon. In other words, his
> desire is to kill, or at least let blood. That is why it is difficult for the
> Anglo-Saxon to understand the psychology of the Indian or even the Latin,
> and it is just as difficult for the Indian or Latin to understand the
> psychology of the Anglo-Saxon or those from northern Europe. When
> there is added to this inborn characteristic that has come down through the
> ages, the use of liquor, then we certainly have crimes of violence.

The Zoot-suit Riots

These riots, in the late spring of 1943, have been largely ignored by
historians, but when they are discussed, it is usually made to appear that
the young Mexican-Americans were the aggressors (Daniels and Kitano,
1970: 76). For instance, A. A. Hoehling, in *Home Front, U.S.A.* (1966)
writes:

> . . . the zoot-suiters of Los Angeles . . . were predominantly Mexican
> youths with some Negro disciples, between the ages of sixteen and twenty.
> They wore absurdly long coats with padded shoulders, porkpie hats
> completed by a feather in the back, watch chains so long they almost
> touched the ground, and peg-top trousers tapering to narrow cuffs. . . .
> At best, as one pundit observed, they were "not characterized primarily by
> intellect." They formed themselves into bands with flamboyant names:
> the "Mateo Bombers," "Main Street Zooters," "The Califa," "Sleepy
> Lagooners," "The Black Legion," and many more. Their targets for
> physical harm were members of the armed forces, with a special predilec-
> tion for sailors. The latter fought back with devastating effect. The situa-
> tion quickly deteriorated to the point that the Navy declared Los Angeles
> out of bounds. The city council outlawed the wearing of zoot suits for the
> duration and the city simmered down.

This account, more fantasy than fact, faithfully summarizes what
Hoehling read in the newspapers. The facts of the matter are that after
certain clashes between sailors on pass or leave (not generally the most
decorous group in the population) and civilian teenagers, the sailors,
with the tacit approval of both the naval authorities and the police, made
organized assaults not just on zoot suiters who were a tiny fraction of
Mexican-American youth, but upon any Mexican they could catch. Carey
McWilliams, in *North from Mexico,* describes one organized foray in
which "about two hundred sailors" hired "a fleet of twenty taxicabs" and
cruised around town beating up Mexicans in ones and twos. After

receiving accolades from the press—"Sailor Task Force Hits L.A. Zooters" —the "heroic" servicemen came out in even greater force the next night; the police, although forewarned, did little if anything to inhibit the violence against Mexicans, although they did arrest twenty-seven Mexican youths. For several nights the streets of Los Angeles were turned over to informal "posses" of servicemen who proceeded to beat, strip, and otherwise humiliate every Mexican-American (and some Negroes) they could find. Bars were wrecked, movie theaters invaded, all with the same kind of impunity once granted to vigilantes in San Francisco. Thoroughout it all, the press made it appear that the Mexican-American youths were the aggressors rather than the victims, with headlines like:

44 Zooters Jailed in Attacks on Sailors

Zoot Suit Chiefs Girding for War on Navy

Zoot Suiters Learn Lesson in Fight with Servicemen

An exception to this biased coverage was a small community paper, *The Eastside Journal,* which published eyewitness accounts by reporter Al Waxman. He describes coming upon

> a band of servicemen making a systematic tour of East First Street [in the heart of the main Mexican quarter]. They had just come out of a cocktail bar where four men were nursing bruises. Three autos loaded with Los Angeles policemen were on the scene but the soldiers were not molested. Farther down the street the men stopped a streetcar, forcing the motorman to open the door and proceeded to inspect the clothing of the male passengers. . . .

When Waxman pleaded with local police to put a stop to these activities, they answered that it was a matter for the military police. But the local police themselves contributed positively to the disorder. Waxman continues:

> Four boys came out of a pool hall. They were wearing the zoot suits that have become the symbol of a fighting flag. Police ordered them into arrest cars. One refused. He asked, "Why am I being arrested?" The police officer answered with three swift blows of the night-stick across the boy's head and he went down. As he sprawled, he was kicked in the face. . . . At the next corner, a Mexican mother cried out, "Don't take my boy, he did nothing. He's only fifteen years old. Don't take him." She was struck across the jaw and almost dropped [her] baby.

If they had not already known, Sleepy Lagoon and the Zoot-suit riots made it clear to California's Mexican population just how second class their citizenship was. At the same time that the community's elder sons were dying on foreign battlefields, some of the younger ones were casualties in their own neighborhoods. Before these wartime incidents, a paternalistic myth somewhat obscured the real relationships between the Mexicans and their "Anglo" neighbors; from that time until the present day, that relationship has been more and more resented. Both the Sleepy Lagoon murder case and the Zoot-suit riots were important realities to be faced by the Mexicans. Perhaps the most dramatic was the realization that racism could be turned in a violent manner towards any nonwhite group. Further, "officialdom" in the form of consuls and Mexican establishment "leaders" was not as influential as previously supposed. Finally, the riots were aided by the racist attitudes of many officials, such as the police and those in city hall who were supposed to protect, rather than to persecute the victims.

World War II exposed many Mexicans to a broader world. A large number saw military service and were transported to different parts of the globe. New ideas, new perceptions, and newer styles were being tried and as with most people who benefited from these new exposures, things were never the same again.

IMMIGRATION

Proximity to Mexico

Several factors make the relationship between the United States and Mexico unique. Most of them are related to the proximity of the countries and the disparity of wealth and power between them. Given this disparity, it would be logical to predict the direction of migration and flow, for in the United States even low-level jobs were often better paying than high-level jobs in Mexico. Therefore, the attractiveness of the United States as a place to work provided a tremendous pull that has remained a constant stress between the countries. One attempt to handle this problem has been the "bracero."

The Bracero

The slaves, the Chinese, the Japanese, and the Filipinos were all desired for their ability to work at hard and tedious jobs that most white Americans did not want. They became problems when they desired things that were reserved primarily for white Americans—marriage, a family, civil rights, decent housing, a good education, equal oportunities, and ultimate peer status as Americans. The "bracero" provided an ideal solution. He was brought across the border for a specific purpose, and he could be returned when his services were no longer required. Therefore, after the harvest, he did not have to go on welfare, nor did his children have to be educated at the expense of the American taxpayer. However, by 1964, the general reaction against the use of contract labor had hardened, and the bracero program came to a halt.

A group that has had a pronounced impact on the Mexican-American community has been the illegal alien, or "wetback," an epithet invented by the Anglo community. The ease of crossing the border has created a continuous, unresolved problem between the United States and Mexico. This situation has led to complicated, legal entanglements governing immigration, citizenship rights, and deportation between the two countries. It has also generated great animosity between Mexicans and law-enforcement agencies. Since there is no immediate way of differentiating between citizens and aliens, anyone who looks like a Mexican is halted, searched, identified, and sometimes arrested by immigration and naturalization officers at the border. U.S. citizens of Mexican origin have often been deported because they could not immediately produce the proper documents.

Halt of Unrestricted Immigration

Up until 1965 there was unrestricted immigration between the United States and Mexico. There was no official quota limiting the entrance of Mexicans, but in 1965 Congress imposed a ceiling of 120,000 immigrants from all Western Hemisphere countries, which took effect in 1968. Although there has been no formal evaluation of the effects of this legislation, it is anticipated that the imposing of quotas will simply increase the traffic on the "illegal" immigration routes.

The history of Mexican immigration can be capsulized by the following statements (Moore, 1970):

1. Mexican immigration has never been regulated by formal quotas; therefore, records of early immigration are useless.
2. Immigration has been continuous, but the greatest numbers have migrated in recent times.
3. The various types of immigration have resulted in complicated legal definitions. There are permanently legal and permanently illegal immigrants. There are those who contract on a seasonal basis; others commute daily across the border. Then there is the two-way flow of businessmen, tourists, and students to add to the complexity and confusion.
4. It is still easy for Mexicans to enter the United States by rail, car, and bus.
5. No other minority has ever been deported in such large numbers as the Mexicans. Massive roundups of illegal aliens such as "Operation Wetback" have been regular procedures. Moore (1970) reports that in five years Operation Wetback had rounded up the astonishing total of 3.8 million illegal Mexican immigrants. Most of them were simply expelled without formal proceedings.
6. As long as the discrepancy of wealth and opportunities remain between the two countries, there will continue to be problems of immigration. 247

Most recent Mexican immigrants come from the central area of Mexico, where there is great poverty. Most of them are young, unskilled males with little education (Moore, 1970: 45). They face a difficult time in the United States. Earlier, the United States could have absorbed them into its economy; but opportunities, especially in the less industrialized Southwest, are limited. The additional barrier of the racist stereotype—that Mexicans are lazy, slow, uneducable, and ignorant—will continue to block their mobility for a long time to come.

NONCITIZEN STATUS

Many Mexican immigrants have not become United States citizens. Part of the problem is related to the confusions resulting from dual citizenship. Children born of contract laborers or illegal immigrants in the United States are presumably citizens, but many Mexicans are not aware of the duality. Some Mexicans have lost their United States citizenship by participating in Mexican elections or serving in the Mexican army.

Moore hypothesizes that the low rate of citizenship is consistent with the social isolation of the group. Other reasons for the low rate include their distrust of United States authorities, their expectation of returning to Mexico, bad socioeconomic conditions, and a high rate of illiteracy, as well as the language barrier. There are the additional difficulties of the written examination on United States history that they must pass, and the anxiety raised by the excessive paperwork and bureaucracy. Grebler (1966) indicates that between 1959 and 1966, less than 5 percent of eligible Mexicans became citizens, whereas other immigrant groups were becoming naturalized at rates over 23 percent.

NUMBERS

The Mexican population in the United States in 1970 has been estimated to be just over 5,000,000. Because of their high concentration in several states—Texas, California and New Mexico—they represent a significant minority.

In cities, Mexican Americans are usually found in "barrios" (akin to ghettos). Barrios have been formed from an original Mexican population; these people did not necessarily move there from somewhere else. It is a young population: the overall median age is 19.6 years, and the median age of the third generation is only 13 years. The typical family

size is 4.8 persons in comparison to the 3.4 persons among Southwestern
Anglo groups (Moore, 1970: 57).

The large number of young children implies rapid population
growth, at a time when growth curves for many other groups have declined. The increased pressure of a young, growing population confronting a relatively rigid, racially restrictive opportunity structure may lead
to high conflict unless there are significant changes in race relations.

THE OCCUPATIONAL PICTURE

Although there are differences from state to state, in general, the Mexican
Americans have had little job mobility, and their chances of earning a
livable wage remain low. For example, in 1960 Mexican Americans earned
only $.47 for every dollar that Anglos made. Fully 35 percent of Spanish
surname families fall below the poverty line of $3,000 annual income,
although they comprised less than 10 percent of all families in the
Southwest (Moore, 1970: 60).

Generally, the Mexicans hold the low-paying, less desirable jobs in
most occupational areas. Those in the managerial category are usually
self-employed in marginal occupations. They are excluded, except in
token numbers, from civil service jobs such as in fire and police depart-
ments, and are not found in large numbers in higher-paying unionized
jobs (Moore, 1970: 62).

Other discriminatory trends indicate that even in similar kinds of
work Mexicans are paid less than whites. Unrealistic standards (i.e., the
high school diploma requirement for unskilled jobs) keep the unemployment figures high.

The Problem of Poverty

As can be inferred from the occupational picture, the most pressing
problem for the Mexican family is poverty. They are consistently at the
bottom of the economic ladder, and as a population they remain vastly
overrepresented in the lowest income categories (Mittelbach, 1966).

The relationship between poverty and other variables is well documented. Generally, the poor receive the worst in health care, housing,
and education; they are looked upon with high disfavor by the police,
teachers, and other representatives of the dominant culture; and there is
a high correlation between poverty and crime, delinquency, drug usage,
and mental illness. For the Mexican, as well as for most ethnic minorities,
poverty compounds the prejudice and discrimination that is already
present because of race and nationality.

Up to now, education has not provided Mexican Americans with a ladder to success. Segregation, isolation, inappropriate curriculums, and poor teaching are all partially responsible for this state of affairs. The incidence of functional illiteracy (0 to 4 years of elementary school) is seven times that of the Anglo population and nearly twice that of nonwhites (Moore, 1970: 65).

High dropout rates and low achievement are the major problems. Educators have blamed bilingualism as the major cause, implying that the Spanish language is a major handicap and therefore should be abolished. Others blame their lack of motivation, apathy, and noncompetitive outlook.

The ethnic community blames the irrelevance of the school curriculum and Anglo teachers' prejudiced, stereotyped responses to Mexican children. For example, community members feel that Mexican students are often arbitrarily advised to take nonacademic courses; sometimes they are placed in classes for the mentally retarded (the language handicap may be an important factor in this placement). Whatever the reason, the American educational system is not meeting the Mexicans' needs. For example, a report by the U.S. Civil Rights Commission, reported in the Los Angeles *Times* (McCurdy, 1971), shows the consistent lag in the reading level of Mexican-American children.

TABLE 12–1
PERCENTAGE OF MEXICAN-AMERICAN STUDENTS BELOW AVERAGE READING LEVEL IN VARIOUS LOCALITIES BY SELECTED GRADE

	4th grade	8th grade	12th grade
Los Angeles	57	60	75
California	52	57	62
Texas	52	73	64
Arizona	43	65	75
New Mexico	48	58	53
Colorado	56	55	59

Source: McCurdy (1971).

The results are frightening and support the claim that Mexican Americans are receiving an inferior education. There must be concerted effort to understand the reasons for this lag; a completely new educational approach will probably be necessary.

The Roman Catholic Church has always been presumed to have a strong influence on Mexican Americans ever since the days of the Spanish conquistadors, who arrived with the sword in one hand and the cross in the other. But it is difficult to assess the influence of the Church in modern Mexican-American life. Generalizations differ by area. There certainly is an overall lessening of religious influence on most facets of American life, and it is occurring within this ethnic group as well. But there is also some indication that the Catholic Church had lost its place as an instrument of relevance and social change at an earlier time. Rather than serving as a vehicle for understanding some of the unique problems faced by a disadavantaged, ethnic community and providing some leadership in effecting social change, the Church, dominated by white leadership, has instead adopted a much more conservative, status quo position. But there have been changes: pastoral concerns have been modified in the past to answer the needs of "Americanization," and current appeals for social justice may accelerate the process of making the Church more responsive (Moore, 1970: 97).

Grebler (1970: 449) states that two factors conditioned the relationship between the Church and Mexican Americans. One was the clergy's point of view that Mexicans were uninstructed in their faith and deficient in their adherence to the norms of Church practice. Therefore, much of the clergy's time and energy was spent in ministering to the religious needs of the group, rather than providing a place where the immigrants could find support and comfort in a new and strange land. The other factor was the general poverty of the Catholic Church in the Southwest. The constant shortage of funds and priests made it difficult to plan and expand programs beyond narrow ministerial functions.

This is not to say that the Church has had no influence. Values, rules of conduct, and other standards have been an integral part of the Church program. Parochial schools have played a part in the educational experience of many Mexican Americans. But the Church, with a few exceptions, has not provided the leadership in addressing the primary problems facing the Mexican American—discrimination, poor education, lack of economic opportunities, and poverty.

OTHER INSTITUTIONAL CONTACTS

Law Enforcement

We have already mentioned the strain between the Mexicans and the Bureau of Immigration. Part of this state of affairs can be traced back to 251 the Texas Rangers, who have been dramatized in movies and novels as an elite law enforcement corps. They were founded in 1835 to deal with the Mexican "problem." Needless to say, most Mexicans do not view them the way fiction writers do. The Western tradition of vigilante law enforcement has subjected Mexicans to "law and order" as defined by Arizona mine-owners, Texas ranchers, and California fruit-growers. Much current friction has arisen from encounters between Mexicans and local officials. Mexicans feel they have been the victims of much unnecessary brutality and overzealous law enforcement. The "accidental" shooting of Los Angeles *Times* newspaperman Rueben Salazar in 1970 by a law-enforcement official, and the subsequent lack of a conviction, are typical examples of police relationships.

Social Welfare and Other Public Agencies

Poverty has forced many Mexican Americans to depend on the public welfare system. The problem of public welfare is a recurring one that goes far beyond its implications to one ethnic minority. Upward economic and social mobility is extremely difficult for any ethnic group that finds significant proportions of its members on public welfare, especially, when occupational opportunities are limited.

Relations between Mexicans and the American social welfare establishment were especially strained during the Great Deperession. The need for Mexican labor quickly vanished as jobs became scarce; there was a great push to deport both citizens and aliens by a variety of strategies. Voluntary repatriation was encouraged, and subsistence money was cut off. A bureau was set up for Mexicans applying for relief; it served as a deporting agency and waived questions of constitutionality, justice, and morality in order to save the taxpayers' dollars—it was cheaper simply to transport large groups of Mexicans back to Mexico.

At present, Mexican Americans are very reluctant to use the larger community services available to them. The number of Mexican clientele at health, psychiatric, and counseling clinics is so low that they are often referred to as the "hard to reach." They tend to visit hospitals, child-guidance clinics, family service agencies, and psychiatric facilities only as a last resort. There are very few Mexican Americans in California mental institutions, and hospitalization records indicate that their official mental illness rates are the lowest of any ethnic group (Kitano, 1969). Cultural misunderstanding is the major reason for this state of affairs; modern medicine, with its appointments, impersonal attitudes, and treatment by complete strangers does not appeal to them as a way of handling stress and sickness. So some Mexicans prefer to use local healers (*curandera*) who know their language and the customs. There are also the factors of distance and cost (most professional facilities in a city like Los Angeles are virtually inaccessible except by private car). This is a very serious situation; many Mexican Americans arrive at a hospital near death, when they could have been helped by earlier treatment.

THE FAMILY AND COMMUNITY

The critical aspects of the Mexican family cannot be covered by any easy generalization, but some broad statements on social class and the urban-rural factor can be made.

For example, the low-class rural family generally follows an extended family structure. Relatives on both sides provide emotional and economic support as well as a reference group for accomplishment. Male and female roles tend to be clearly proscribed; masculinity (*machismo*) is of great importance, even outside marriage. The family remains the most important unit; close relationships outside the family are mostly with age peers. Godparents (*compadrazgo*) provide another linkage.

The family patterns in the city are varied. Increasing numbers are moving out of the barrios—some to the periphery and others to the suburbs. Generally, there are differences in life style between those families remaining in the barrio and those surrounded by white neighbors. The rates of assimilation, integration, and change are closely related to the housing patterns. The traditional family is arranged hierarchically: the father occupies the top and is followed by the sons; together they shelter and protect the wife and daughters. The women are expected to cook, raise the children, and serve the needs of the men.

The middle-class family patterns are generally similar, but their more adequate income gives them more freedom of choice. For example, the middle-class Mexican may go to a physician rather than the *curandera*, the attorney rather than the priest; and his children may go to college. Nevertheless, most Mexican families remain quite isolated from the Anglo world since they prefer to associate with their own relatives and the ethnic community.

In urban areas, poverty has shifted the burden of family financial responsibility to the public services and public welfare agencies. It offers an option to many who heretofore had no recourse but to depend on relatives; now they may choose to be more independent of the kinship system. Such a breaking away will have both positive and negative consequences, although the underlying factors of poverty and dependence remain untouched.

Urbanization and acculturation are changing family roles, especially that of the Mexican male. He now helps care for the children and shares family decisions with his wife. The input of the mass media showing models at variance with the traditional roles is important, especially in cities like Los Angeles. The extended family system is also being modified.   253

But much is hidden from majority eyes because of the highly segregated living conditions and the constant flow of new immigrants.

SOCIAL CLASS

Most Mexican-American families are very poor. However, other groups "above" them are constantly changing and evolving away from the older traditions.

Before the American annexation, the upper class was reserved for the "Spanish," and when the United States acquired the territories, most retained this status, the "half-breeds" (*mestizos*) and the native Indians filling the lower positions. The upwardly mobile wanted to be identified as "Spanish"—the purer the better—and traces of this point of view remain.

The mobility pattern for Mexican Americans takes several broad forms. As income and other related circumstances rise, the individual may begin to lead a more comfortable life within the ethnic community. But his contacts and interactions are confined to his ethnic group; and although there may be strong resemblances to the Anglo middle-class, both the middle-class Mexicans and Anglos are generally ignorant of each other, especially since the Anglo stereotype usually does not include a middle-class Mexican (Moore, 1970).

Another type of mobility leads away from the ethnic community. Education, income, and other marks of status result in increased majority-group contacts and perhaps a conscious decision to leave the barrio. The success of this pattern depends on the accessibility of the Anglo world; if it is perceived as open, there may be a permanent move into the larger community. However, the individual choosing this path takes serious risks. Even if he has tried to think and behave like an Anglo, he may find his new world inhospitable, and he may alienate his old friends in the ethnic community.

The third type is bilingual and bicultural, most often a college student, who partially integrates without assimilating. He learns the Anglo system very well but retains many of his ethnic contacts; his life does not center exclusively either in the ethnic enclaves or in the academic world. As his numbers grow, he may develop a subcommunity of ethnic intellectuals.

College students, especially those recruited from the barrios, are often subject to serious conflicts. Much of the initial impetus for going to school came from community members who wanted to be proud of the fact that some of their own could enter a university. However, ethnic students' interests change, and their former friendships in the barrio become strained. Some college students report being called "sell-outs" by those who have remained in the community.

Mexican middle-class norms—the dominant ideal for most Mexicans—are congruent with Anglo prescriptions. There is an emphasis on respect and deference to elders, on getting along with people, and getting ahead in the world. Mexican-American leaders state that as they prepare for their first school experience, most Mexican-American children are willing to learn and to respect, obey, and please the teacher.

However, many consider the Mexicans' values to be the cause of their problems. The literature of the social sciences abounds with comparisons of Mexican and American values, and cultural explanations for the low collective achievements of the Mexican. Perhaps the most widely disseminated study was that of Kluckhohn (1961) which reinforced the impression that Mexican Americans were distinct from Anglos. Subsequent interpretations and generalizations from her study ignored two major points that she made: (1) that the Mexican-American sample was from a remote village in New Mexico, and (2) that basic changes were predicted even in this isolated village. Therefore the "scientific" generalization that the Mexicans were "fate-oriented" and focused on the present rather than the future, became rather widely accepted in social science circles.

Current information indicates that the range of responses of urban Mexican residents is "generally within the range of American cultural values in such critical arenas of life as family, neighbors, and social class" (Grebler, 1970: 423). Most Mexicans were no different from most Americans—the stereotyped Mexican peasant could not survive in an urban environment without some change. Most Mexican Americans, like other Americans, want to get ahead in their work; they want job satisfaction, security, and a higher income. They direct their young toward the professions, and on the whole, "Mexican Americans are not notably more passive, nor do they value integration with relatives more than most populations on which data are available" (Grebler, 1970: 439).

The most distinct feature of Mexican-American culture is the Spanish language. Yet the great majority of Americans are prone to rely more on the stereotypes and their own interpretations of what constitutes Mexican "culture"—the fate orientation, the *mañana* attitude, the passivity, the lack of individualism, and the "Jose Jimenez" image.

Those Anglos who do have some interaction with the Mexican select information that supports their prejudices. For example, interethnic contact between middle-class Anglos and Mexicans most often takes place under institutionalized auspices—professionals such as social workers, nurses, teachers, probation and other law enforcement officers generally see only the Mexicans who are in trouble. Their contacts are generally limited to those Mexicans exhibiting social problems, and their observations become the inferred norm for all Mexicans.

The predictable outcome of these perceptions, therefore, has been   255 the tendency to "blame" the Mexican "culture" for the lack of progress. As we have and will continue to emphasize, ethnic groups do not live in a vacuum; the problem lies in the *interaction* between the majority and the minority, not in the "culture" of the minority.

It is also our impression that the Mexican American belongs to the ethnic group that has the widest spread of political views and ideologies. It is not unusual to see spokesmen advocating both extremely liberal and extremely conservative points of view, whereas it is often difficult to find many right-wing spokesmen in the other ethnic groups.

VISIBILITY

Mexican Americans exhibit a wide range of skin colors—from light Caucasian to dark Indian, and all shades in between. Color was an important stratification variable within the group even before contact with the United States.

Spanish surnames provide another index for identification, although they are not infallible guides. South Americans, Puerto Ricans, Cubans, and Filipinos share many of the same surnames. Dress, food, and music reflect other highly visible cultural styles. But because most Mexicans remain isolated, such visibility is confined to typical tourist havens such as Olvera Street in Los Angeles.

One conspicuous Mexican-American style in the urban areas is the gang. The gang phenomenon, especially as an adolescent socialization force (which may continue through adulthood), is especially intriguing. One common stereotype, even before the zoot-suit riots, was that Mexican-American youngsters generally belonged to gangs and that there was continuous fighting among them. It is an area that has been much observed but underresearched.

THE NEWER MEXICAN

The current term, "Chicano," has been adopted to reflect the needs and concerns of the newer Mexican American. Like those of other groups, these range from developing their own scientists with Chicano perspectives and interpretations to questions of self-identity.

For example, Hernandez (1970) sets forth the following assumptions for Chicanos: (a) that they should maintain their ethnic identity, (b) that they should change and strengthen their socioeconomic status in the larger system, (c) that they should attain a degree of collective independence within the larger social system, and (d) that they should organize and unite the yet unassimilated segments of their community into a larger heterogeneous body in order to achieve their ends.

Perhaps the most powerful Mexican American public figure has been Caesar Chavez. His farm-workers' union, formerly independent but now affiliated with the AFL-CIO, has managed to unite two previously hostile ethnic groups, the Mexicans, who comprise the majority of the union, and the Filipinos. Chavez skillfully combines the techniques of the modern trade-union leader (he has a flair for publicity and has managed to fight off a teamster raid) with that of an early Mexican religious revolutionary (to surmount one union crisis he endured a lengthy fast). Yet even now by all the measurable indices, group consciousness among the Spanish-speaking minority in this country is far below that of the black community.

POLITICAL POWER

Mexican Americans, with their relatively large and concentrated populations, have not yet made an effective impact on the American political system. Social action groups include the Orden Hijos de America (Sons of America) organized in 1921 in San Antonio; the League of United Latin American Citizens (LULACS) established in 1929; the Mexican Congress of 1938; the Coordinating Council for Mexican Youth in 1942; the Community Service Organization (CSO) founded in Los Angeles in 1947 by a small group of Mexican-American war veterans and factory workers; the GI Forum, especially active in the 1950s; and the Mexican-American Political Association (MAPA), California based and organized in 1958 (Tirado: 1970).

It is to be expected that the group will become more active and therefore more powerful politically since segregated residential patterns can lead to localized political power. However, the number of effective Mexican-American leaders remains small; part of the problem is related to the lack of cohesion, organization, and unity within the group.

THREE TYPES

The following three types are representative of a larger proportion of Chicanos in the United States. Ramirez (1971) illustrates the three broad types of adjustment made by Mexican American children to a bicultural world.

Type One

Paul represents the Anglicized Mexican American.

> I don't want to be known as a Mexican-American, but only as American. I was born in this country and raised among Americans. I think like an Anglo, I talk like one, and I dress like one. It's true I don't look like an

257

Anglo and sometimes I am rejected by them, but it would be worse if I
spoke Spanish or said that I was of Mexican descent. I am sorry I do not
get along well with my parents, but their views are old-fashioned. They
still see themselves as Mexican, and they do not understand me. Often
we have arguments, but I ignore them. In fact, I had to move away from
my home because of our disagreements. I wish those people who are always
making noise about being Mexican-Americans would be quiet. We would
all be better off if they would accept things as they are. I just want a good
education. I don't want to be poor. I don't want to be discriminated
against.

Type Two

Roberto represents the Mexican American who is proud of his ethnic
identity.

I am proud of being a Mexican American. We have a rich heritage.
Mexico is a great country that is progressing fast. It has a wonderful history
and culture. My family is the most important thing in the world for me.
I owe my parents everything and I will never complain when they need
me. I don't want to be like the "Paddys" because they don't care about
their families; they just care about themselves and making money. They
don't like anybody who is different. At school, the teachers ignored you
if they knew you weren't going to college, and most of us Mexicans couldn't
afford to go. The things I learned at school were against what my parents
had taught me. I had to choose my parents, because they are old and they
need my help and understanding. Most people, even some Mexican
Americans, look down on us because we are Mexicans, and I hate them.
It is unhealthy and unnatural to want to be something you are not.

Type Three

Then there is Rosa, who has apparently integrated a bicultural perspective.

I am happy to be an American of Mexican descent. Because I am a
Mexican I learned to be close to my family, and they have been a source of
strength and support for me. If things ever got too bad on the outside I
could always come to them for comfort and understanding. My Spanish
also helped me a lot in my education and will also open a lot of doors for
me when I look for a job. As an American I am happy to live in a great
progressive country where we have the freedom to achieve anything we
want. I feel all that I have achieved I owe to the help of my parents, the
encouragement of my teachers, and the chance to live in this country. I
feel very rich and fortunate because I have two cultures rather than just
one.

Rosa views both the Anglo and Mexican-American culture fa-
vorably, and she has in fact combined the best from each to form a
richer culture.

258

These illustrated types are "ideal," since in reality, most Mexican
Americans do not fit any of these identities perfectly. However, Paul,
Roberto, and Rosa are representative of our largest ethnic minority in
the Southwest as they deal with the realities of a subordinate social group.

BIBLIOGRAPHY

DANIELS, ROGER and HARRY H. L. KITANO (1970). *American Racism.* Englewood Cliffs, N.J.: Prentice-Hall, Inc.

DIAZ, BERNAL (1963). *The Conquest of New Spain.* Trans. J. M. Cohen.
Baltimore: Penguin Books.

GREBLER, LEO (1966). "The Naturalization of Mexican Immigrants in the
United States." *International Migration Review,* 1: 17–32.

———, JOAN MOORE and RALPH GUZMAN (1970). *The Mexican American
People.* New York: The Free Press.

HERNANDEZ, DELUVINA (1970). "La Raza Satellite System." *Aztlan* 1 (1):
13–34. Los Angeles: University of California, Chicano Cultural Center.

KAGAN, S. and M. C. MADSEN (1971). "Mexican American and Anglo American Children of Two Different Ages Under Four Instructional Sets."
Developmental Psychology.

KITANO, HARRY H. L. (1969). "Japanese American Mental Illness." In
Plog and Edgerton, eds., *Changing Perspectives of Mental Illness.*
New York: Holt, Rinehart & Winston, Inc.

KLUCKHOHN, FLORENCE and FRED L. STRODTBECK (1961). *Variations in Value
Orientations.* Evanston, Ill.: Row, Peterson and Co.

McCURDY, JACK (1971). "L. A. Labelled as Bad as Texas in Mexican-
American Schooling." Los Angeles *Times* (December 8).

McWILLIAMS, CAREY (1933). "Getting Rid of the Mexicans." *American
Mercury.*

MITTELBACK, FRANK G. and GRACE MARSHALL (1966). *The Burden of
Poverty.* Advance Report 5. Los Angeles: University of California,
Mexican American Study Project.

MOORE, JOAN (1970). *Mexican Americans.* Englewood Cliffs, N.J.: Prentice-
Hall, Inc.

RAMIREZ, MANUEL II (1970). "Identity Crises in the Barrios." *Music Educators Journal,* 5(57): 69–70.

——— and CLARK TAYLOR, JR. (1971). "Mexican American Cultural Membership and Adjustment to School." *Developmental Psychology,* 4(2):
141–48.

TIRADO, MIGUEL DAVID (1970). "Mexican American Political Organization."
Aztlan, 1(1): 53–78. Los Angeles: University of California, Chicano
Cultural Center.

THE
PUERTO
RICANS 13

The Puerto Ricans are unusual in that their migration is still in progress, therefore, many of the observations about them are tentative because of the scarcity of data. The majority of Puerto Ricans reside in New York, which has been the host to several generations of immigrants— Irish, Italians, and the Jews, to name but a few. The Puerto Ricans are entering the city when symptoms of social disorganization are especially prominent. Large cities have always been plagued by outbreaks of violence and disorder, and residents have constantly feared for their personal safety, but such anxieties appear to have reached a zenith in present-day New York. Under such conditions, majority-group members find it easy to blame their problems on groups such as the newly arrived Puerto Ricans.

BACKGROUND

Puerto Rico was ruled by Spain for over four hundred years. The Spanish-American War and the Treaty of Paris in 1898 ceded the islands to the United States, and formal interaction between the two countries is   **261** acknowledged from that year. The significant migration of Puerto Ricans to the United States, however, did not take place for several decades. World War I and the need for labor provided the impetus for a small migration; and by 1930, approximately 53,000 Puerto Ricans were residing on the mainland. But the depression years and World War II brought a virtual halt to immigration.

The great migration came after World War II. There were several reasons for this: first, Puerto Ricans were U.S. citizens and were therefore under no quota restrictions; second, there was unemployment at home and employment on the mainland; third, there was cheap transportation; and finally, many had friends and relatives living in New York and elsewhere on the East Coast.

In 1960, the U.S. Census reported almost 900,000 Puerto Ricans living in the United States, and by 1971, the *New York Times Almanac* (1972) reported 1.8 million Puerto Ricans in the United States. Of that number, approximately one million were residents of New York City.

The Puerto Rican immigration pattern is unusual because of its departure rate. Although figures for net migration are difficult to ascertain, in 1969 the Puerto Rican Planning Board reported 2,105,217 departures, and 2,112,264 arrivals. There is of course no way of identifying how many Puerto Ricans were coming to the mainland for the first time, how many were tourists, or how many planned to stay permanently. However, migration back to the island has been heavy; and some even refer to the Puerto Ricans as "commuters."

Contract Laborers

Many of the early Puerto Rican immigrants came to the United States as contract laborers. Such an arrangement was typical for nonwhites; their labor was desired but not their permanent residence. The farm labor contracts in the 1940s proved to be particularly attractive because they enabled the laborer to find more than seasonal work—he could harvest in the United States through the summer and fall, then return to Puerto Rico in time to work on the sugar-cane plantations. However, migrant labor conditions were generally far from ideal, and the Puerto Rican government had to supervise constantly in order to ensure the fulfillment of the contracts. However, by this means large numbers of Puerto Ricans were exposed to the American system, and much of the groundwork was laid for the subsequent large migration. Many Puerto Rican communities arose from groups of early contract laborers who remained on the mainland.

In common with some of the Asian ethnic groups on the West Coast, Puerto Ricans were unwelcome on any permanent basis. Small, rural Southern towns were inhospitable to Puerto Ricans since these communities were largely unprepared to deal with people who spoke a foreign language and whose culture was alien. Tensions mounted, especially in schools, employment, recreation, and housing.

The number of Puerto Ricans working as migrant laborers is difficult to estimate. However, the major stream of Puerto Rican migration has flowed into New York City and other urban areas.

New York City

The rise of ·the Puerto Rican population in New York City has been dramatic. The 1920 Census reported 7,364 persons; the 1940 figures were 61,463; in 1960, there were 612,574 and by 1971, it was at 1,000,000. The heaviest concentration of Puerto Ricans is now in the South Bronx, but the East Harlem community is considered to be the original barrio.

The Puerto Ricans have been a very mobile people. They have spread out rapidly, not being content to stay long in one place, in their search for better housing. One consequence of their housing patterns (which is also due to overcrowded conditions in New York) has been the lack of a tightly knit, strong, physically contiguous ethnic community. They have not developed "Little Italies," or Chinatowns. The self-contained ethnic enclaves (despite many of their handicaps) were often very functional; the "culture" could be maintained while the groups became familiar with the new country. Friends and relatives could move in; ethnic blocs could wield a degree of political power; and a consensus of norms and a high degree of social cohesion served to control deviant behavior. The quick integration of the Puerto Rican (aided by the nondiscriminatory policies of the New York City Housing Authority) will probably hasten the acculturation of the group, but there may also be many serious social problems.

COLOR AND VISIBILITY

There are many contradictory findings concerning color prejudice in Puerto Rico, as there are in most Latin American countries. Some claim that Puerto Ricans are completely integrated and color blind; others claim that they are highly, but subtly stratified. Color does not seem to be as important an indicator of social status as social class, but there is a correlation between darker skin color and low status. However, color is less a sign of pariah status among Puerto Ricans than among Americans.

There is a high degree of color integration in Puerto Rico. They did not develop the two-category, black-white structure as found in the United States; rather, the differentiations of color were spread over a wider spectrum. For example, words such as *pardo, moreno, mulatto,* and *trigueño* classify a range of colors other than black and white. Terms such as *indio* and *grifo* denote other identifying characteristics. (The U.S. 263

practices of segregation and antimiscegenation laws, were not a part of the Puerto Rican experience.)

However, social class plays an important part in the Puerto Rican stratification system. Although whiteness may be considered desirable, an individual's status is more clearly demarcated by his class position. Fitzpatrick cites a saying that provides some insight concerning color and class: "In the United States, a man's color determines what class he belongs to; in Puerto Rico, a man's class determines what his color is." Therefore, living in a barrio is an indication of one's status, whether black, *trigueño,* or white, as is occupation, income, and education. Color is viewed within the context of other role signs and is not the sole criterion.

Fitzpatrick mentions a number of cultural and historical factors in Puerto Rico that have contributed to their more tolerant racial attitudes.

1. The long Spanish experience with people of darker skin color (e.g. Moors), including intermarriage.
2. Different experiences under slavery. In the wars of the Christians against the Moors and Saracens, captured whites also became slaves. Therefore there were attempts to protect slaves who were white and such attitudes were carried over to the Negroes.
3. Upper-class men in the Spanish colonies baptized and recognized their illegitimate children by colored women.
4. The practice of *compadrazgo,* in which outstanding white members of a community would frequently be the godparents of colored children at baptism. The "padrino" or "compadre" could become a significant person in a child's life, and although the real father might be obscure, the godparents would be well known.
5. The concept of a Puerto Rican community whereby all, whether rich or poor, white or colored, shared a sense of communal identity. Therefore all persons were conscious of having a place, especially during community events such as fiestas, religious processions, and public events.

As a consequence, color was not so strong a barrier, and upward mobility under this more open system was a theoretical possibility. But Puerto Rico has advanced very rapidly in education, industry, government services, and the like, and a middle class has formed. Upward social and economic mobility complicates the role of color and class, and color prejudice is growing. For example, Fitzpatrick (1971: 105) mentions that societies and clubs are now not as open to people of color. The Puerto Rican quickly learns that color is an important role sign in the United States. He sees that the two-category system has abolished the intermediate categories, and that social acceptance and economic advantages are easier to obtain if one is white.

Perhaps the most difficult position is that of the *trigueños* of intermediate color. In one study (Padilla, 1958) they showed the least evidence of assimilation into the New York community. They were not accepted as white; many did not want to be classified as Negroes and were therefore caught in a marginal position. Many responded by retaining a strong Puerto Rican identity. Another study (Berle: 1959) of twenty young Puerto Rican drug addicts showed that nineteen of them were the darkest members of their families.

Puerto Ricans are also visible on levels other than color. The Spanish language and their preference for more colorful clothing styles make them conspicuous as a group.

THE PROBLEM OF IDENTITY

A major Puerto Rican problem is identity. Historically, they were a part of the Spanish empire with Latin traditions for many years; then suddenly they became a part of the United States. Currently, several different identifications have surfaced. For example, one group advocates complete autonomy and independence because they fear that they will lose their culture, language, and sense of independence if they maintain close relations with the United States. The advocates of statehood feel that only by becoming an integral part of the United States can Puerto Ricans achieve a true identity. Statehood would not necessarily mean the destruction of their culture; rather, the gains through political and economic stability would give them more freedom in shaping and identity. Then there are those who seek to maintain Puerto Rico as a "free associated state." They cite the current situation whereby Puerto Ricans can maintain their own culture and identity, while still benefiting from close ties with the United States.

Puerto Ricans were able to express their preferences in the 1967 elections. The advocate for the free associated state won; he was followed by the advocate for statehood, while independence candidate ran a poor third. But the intensity of the conflict represented "the anxiety and uncertainty of a people in danger of losing themselves, and seeking to discover the political and social institutions which will enable them to preserve a genuine sense of identity in the presence of rapid changes with which they seek to cope. Thus before any question of large-scale migration arose, the Puerto Ricans had been facing a crisis of national and cultural identity" (Fitzpatrick, 1971: 46).

INTEGRATION

It is difficult to find consistent evidence on the extent of Puerto Rican intermingling in New York City. They have brought their more relaxed racial attitudes with them, and Puerto Rican gatherings present a wider range of color mixtures. But as they advance to middle-class status, they may become much more sensitive to American definitions of race.

The relations between Puerto Ricans and Negroes have been

strained. They are both involved in similar struggles for power and
control and are sometimes pitted against each other. But among the more
militant young there is some degree of cooperation.

THE
PUERTO
RICANS

There is evidence that the outmarriage rate of Puerto Ricans (7.8
percent in 1959) is higher than the general rates of such marriages in the
United States. Fitzpatrick (1971: 112) also noted that Puerto Ricans of
different "color" were intermarrying at a high rate (26 percent) in New
York City, but that marriage patterns in other areas would probably be
different.

ROLE OF THE CHURCH AND FAMILY

The Puerto Ricans come from a predominant Roman Catholic country.
However, Church membership was somewhat different from the United
States model of organized membership and a consistent Church affiliation.
Rather, they had a much more personalized spiritual relationship, and this
often took place outside the organized Church structure. Adherence to
Roman Catholic practices was not so strict that native cult practices,
spiritism, and other religious variations could not flourish. The Protestant
religion was introduced by the United States, and by 1970, roughly 20
percent of the island's inhabitants were of that faith. Church influence
is diffused in Puerto Rican life on the mainland. There are of course
many parochial schools, but partly because of the distribution of the
Puerto Ricans, it is difficult to assess the specific role of religion in their
lives.

The family structure in Puerto Rico is described by Fitzpatrick
(1971: 83) as falling into the following fourfold typology:

1. An extended family system. These families have strong bonds, and
   grandparents, parents, and children may often live together in the same
   household. It may include consensual unions as well as regular marriages.[1]
2. The nuclear family. The rise of the middle class has increased the
   number of families following the United States pattern of an independent unit of father, mother, and children.
3. Father, mother, their children, and children of another union or unions
   of husband and wife. This is not an uncommon pattern in Puerto Rico
   with children of different names residing in the same household.
4. The mother-based family, with children of one or more men, but with no
   permanent male in the home.

All four typologies are present in the United States. The greatest
white animosity is directed toward the Type 4 family unit, often found in

---

[1] Consensual unions have been recognized in Puerto Rico, although their number
is declining.

welfare families. Pragmatic politicians are especially adept at laying the blame for much of society's ills on "those welfare chiselers," who if one were to believe the claims, are the main contributors to the financial and moral crises of our time. Because certain ethnic groups are stereotyped in this fashion, prejudice and discrimination against them are strengthened.

VALUES

PERSONALISM

A number of values have been hypothesized to explain Puerto Rican behavior in a broad context. The most important is personalism, which is described as "a form of individualism which focuses on the inner importance of a person." The culture values "those inner qualities which constitute the uniqueness of the person and his goodness or worth in himself" (Fitzpatrick, 1971: 90). This value derives its strength from the relatively rigid class structure in which a man is respected if he knows his position and behaves with dignity and sensitivity. He takes his family obligations seriously.

Puerto Ricans have developed a strong sense of the hierarchical class structure. Lower and upper classes were taken for granted; therefore a person's personal worth was distinct from his position in the social class structure. The idea of upward mobility was not a common one on the Islands, rather an acceptance of playing a designated role with dignity was valued highly.

Like other ethnic groups, Puerto Ricans have their own ideas of what constitutes a joke or is likely to cause embarrassment. Behavior of the informal, offhand American manner may bring a different reaction from a Puerto Rican group. The behavior styles of various groups are an important aspect, especially those of older generations.

The Puerto Rican values of personalism conflict with American values. In the Latin system, the individual is to be trusted above all; life is a network of personal relationships, and a man's word, honor, and style are to be reckoned with and respected. In contrast, the American style of individualism emphasizes the ability to compete aggressively for social and economic gain. Americans have a high regard for systems, organizations, legal regulations, and efficiency; and they become uneasy when the system fails. It is said, however, that Latin Americans become uneasy when the system works too well—they feel that impersonal elements have taken precedence over personal relationships.

The *padrino* system is another Puerto Rican structure which is related to personalism and reflects a rigid class structure. It involves "a person, strategically placed in a higher position of the social structure, who has a personal relationship with the poorer person in which he provides employment, assistance at times of need, and acts as an advocate if the poor person becomes involved in trouble" (Fitzpatrick, 1971: 91). The *padrino* serves as an "ombudsman" who helps the less knowledgeable and unsophisticated in dealing with more powerful and influential individuals and institutions. Of course, these relationships are open to exploitation. Although the role of the *padrinos* has diminished in Puerto Rico, they are still sought out, especially in business affairs.

MACHISMO

Machismo is another aspect of personalism; it connotes masculinity and personal daring "by which one faces challenge, danger, and threat with calmness and self-possession; this sometimes takes the form of bravado" (Fitzpatrick, 1971: 91). Associated attributes and qualities include personal magnetism, sexual prowess, and power over women, including the jealous protection of wife or sweetheart.

MATERIALISM

The Latin feels that most Americans are grossly materialistic. Although it is highly debatable as to which culture places a greater value on the acquisition of material things, the Latin emphasizes that his fundamental concerns have nothing to do with worldly things or their tangible features. "He has a sense of spirit and soul as much more important than the body, and as being intimately related to his value as a person; he tends to think in terms of transcendent qualities, such as justice, loyalty, or love, rather than in terms of practical arrangements which spell out justice or loyalty in the concrete" (Fitzpatrick, 1971: 91–92). He is more willing to sacrifice material satisfactions for ultimate or spiritual goals and does not emphasize mastering and subjecting the physical universe through continuous technological advancements.

FATALISM

The fatalistic attitude is best summed up by the phrase, *"Que, será, será"* ("Whatever will be, will be"). There is a strong sense that certain events are inevitable and are dictated by God. This modifies the impact of failure or success and the attendant sense of guilt or satisfaction because "God willed it."

Change of Values

The values of the Puerto Rican, as described above, are not so different from those of many other immigrant groups, and they will probably handle their value conflicts in the same manner. These conflicts will be resolved or perpetuated by:

1. the cohesion and strength of the ethnic family and community system in order to reinforce their way of life;

2. the functional or dysfunctional actions of the values themselves, as well as their similarity and complementarity with those of the majority culture;
3. the potential for symbiotic interaction; and
4. the strength of the competing socializing institutions in the United States.

It is anticipated that the heaviest burden of the conflict will be felt by the second-generation child—that is, the individual who is born of Puerto Rican immigrant parents in the United States. The stress, tension, and disorganization faced by Puerto Ricans are evident from their more visible social problems.

Social Problems

EDUCATION AND THE SCHOOL SYSTEM

The Puerto Rican Study, 1953–57 (Board of Education, 1958) pointed out some of the difficulties faced by Puerto Rican students in New York City. Special problems included the language handicap and the tenuous relationship between the school system and Puerto Rican parents. Subsequent studies have shown that these problems have grown progressively worse. Very few survive the competition to enter colleges and universities, although the open admissions policy in New York may increase Puerto Rican attendance in the city college and university system. The route to "success" by way of education, used by many other immigrant groups, remains an expectation, rather than a reality for most Puerto Ricans.

One fundamental issue, difficult to resolve, centers around cultural pluralism in education. Bilingualism and English as a second language are unresolved issues, and the debate over the validity of various models continues. There are also the larger issues of the school strikes of 1968–69 and the decentralization controversy.

WELFARE

A special problem for the Puerto Ricans has been their relatively high numbers on public welfare. For example, one study estimated that as many as 35 percent of Puerto Rican families were receiving Aid to Families with Dependent Children (AFDC) benefits. Without going into the accuracy of these figures, it is of critical importance to understand that dependence on public welfare will affect Puerto Rican adaptation to the United States. Although the goals of AFDC and other welfare programs are appealing, and the planners no doubt had the best intentions, the actual programs have become an embarrassment to the American public. It would be difficult to conceive of a worse institutionalized alternative to American life, considering the current American attitudes towards welfare recipients. The degradation of the recipients is a result of both inadequate resources and an unpopular program.

MENTAL ILLNESS

Rogler and Hollingshead (1965) provided systematic data on mental illness in Puerto Rico and identified several contradictory strains that contributed to the problem. Girls were carefully protected from sexual experience, while boys were allowed great freedom; the housewife was expected to be submissive, while the husband had to embody all aspects of *machismo;* there was a great discrepancy between expected and achieved standards of living; and poverty exerted a severe pressure on everyone's life.

Rates of mental illness are higher for the Puerto Rican than for the general population. For example, Malzberg (1956) noted that the rate of first admissions for schizophrenia for Puerto Rican males in New York State was 122 per 100,000 as compared to the general population rate of 36.6 per 100,000. He could find no convincing reason behind this differential, which is apparently related to such diverse variables as the experience of migration, language difficulties, occupational problems, and segregation into areas that have a high incidence of mental illness. A major problem, of course, is that the poor have little access to health services because of high cost and superstition.

The Midtown Manhattan Study (Langner, 1963) also noted a high incidence of mental illness among Puerto Ricans, mostly because of the shortage of Spanish-speaking professionals, the lack of communication and understanding, and other cultural disparities.

In spite of certain biases in the statistics on mental illness, the available evidence indicates that the stress and tension of migration and urban living have exacted a high toll in mental illness on Puerto Ricans. The question is now whether this is a preliminary adaptive stage for any newly arrived immigrant group, and whether it is followed by another stage.

There is also evidence of high drug use in certain Census tracts in New York City. There is also high poverty in these areas and a high proportion of Negroes and Puerto Ricans. The relationships between poverty, drug use, and ethnicity should be targets for future research.

It is possible to make a few summarizing statements concerning Puerto Ricans:

1. The early immigrant model of ethnic communities will probably not be achieved. Urban redevelopment and public housing have forced a pattern of integration. Religious "parish clusters" have also been broken up for the same reasons.
2. The Puerto Rican migration is basically by family, and there is much going and coming between the island and the mainland.
3. Poverty (and its associated problems) is the basic difficulty. Poverty is

exacerbated by culture conflicts, racism, generational conflict, and problems of identity.

4. As with all other ethnic groups, militancy and ethnic awareness has developed especially among the younger generations.

Fitzpatrick (1971: 70–71) says of the Puerto Ricans in New York City:

. . . Containing probably a million people in 1970, it constitutes the largest Puerto Rican city in the world, about one-third larger than the city of San Juan; its population is about 40 percent of the size of the entire population of Puerto Rico. It is a population mainly of poor working people, the backbone of the labor force for hotels, restaurants, hospitals, the garment industry, small factories, and shops, without whom the economy of the city would collapse. It is youthful, now about one-fourth of the entire public school population of the city. . . .

All this adds up to a struggling, suffering, poor, but vital segment of the city. It is a community without a visible, powerful leader, and one which has not been able to make a unified impact on the city proportionate to its representation in the population. The community is continually losing experienced persons to the Island in return migration, and is replenishing its poorest ranks with newcomers from the Island. It stands at an uncertain moment in its struggle for stability, identity, and strength.

BIBLIOGRAPHY

BERLE, BEATRICE (1959) *Eighty Puerto Rican Families in New York City*. New York: Columbia University Press.

BOARD OF EDUCATION (1958). *The Puerto Rican Study, 1953–57*. New York.

CHEIN, ISADORE (1964). *The Road to H*. New York: Basic Books, Inc.

ELMAN, RICHARD (1966). *The Poorhouse State*. New York: Pantheon Books.

FITZPATRICK, JOSEPH P. (1971). *Puerto Rican Americans*. Englewood Cliffs, N.J.: Prentice-Hall, Inc.

LANGNER, THOMAS S. and MICHAEL T. STANLEY (1963). *The Midtown Manhattan Study*. New York: The Free Press.

MALZBURG, BENJAMIN (1956). "Mental Illness Among Puerto Ricans in New York City, 1949–51." *Journal of Nervous and Mental Disease*, 123: 457–65.

New York Times Almanac (1972). New York. P. 236.

PADILLA, ELENA (1958). *Up From Puerto Rico*. New York: Columbia University Press.

PODELL, LAWRENCE (1968). *Families on Welfare in New York City*. New York: City University, Center for the Study of Urban Problems, Bernard Baruch College.

ROGLER, LLOYD H. and AUGUST B. HOLLINGSHEAD (1965). *Trapped: Families and Schizophrenia*. New York: John Wiley & Sons, Inc.

SUMMARY
AND
CONCLUSIONS 14

It is easy to criticize America's race relations because the discrepancies between ideals, as embodied in our slogans of justice and equality, and reality, as demonstrated by our racial boundaries and inequities, are plainly visible. The search for solutions to social problems has never been an easy one.

One problem is that of conflicting goals: there can be no evaluation of success in race relations unless there is a clear definition of terms. We have an overabundance of goals, with each definer expressing the experiences, perspectives, ideologies, and beliefs from his own position. Therefore, successful race relations in our country could mean any of the following: "they should become like us"; "let every race do their own thing"; "there should be a revolutionary change"; "we want what they have, nothing more"; "when we get on top we'll show them how things should be"; "when they can prove that they can act civilized, then we'll be glad to welcome them"; and a number of other variations.

Our current issues in race relations are different from those of a previous era when the goal of forming a "melting pot" was reasonably clear but the access to the goal was blocked. The barriers against persons who belonged to a racial minority—i.e., those not white, Anglo-Saxon, and Protestant—were so formidable that goal achievement was not possible. **273**

When we talk about present-day goals and the means for achieving them, at least three major points of view should be considered. One
perception is that of the dominant, white majority. Although there are
many viewpoints within this body, majority-group values and majority-
group culture, long equated with being American, have been primary in
shaping the country's race relations. After the dominant group conquered,
overwhelmed, outfought, and outdealt the natives for this land, they
forced some nonwhites to join them as slaves and invited others to work
as cheap labor. For these people of color, almost impassable barriers
against any degree of upward mobility were erected, and the means of
becoming like the dominant group were denied. The white majority
holds the power in our society, therefore it is imperative that their
definitions of success and their expectations in regard to race relations be
considered one major input.

The second perception is that of the dominated ethnics, and here
too there are varied opinions. They are the victims of racism, and
they lack the resources and the power of the majority group. Their goals,
their expectations, and their solutions have been too long ignored. They
have suffered under prejudice, discrimination, and segregation; they
have felt the effects of incarceration, concentration camps, and genocide,
and most are no longer content to remain victims of the social system.
Unless the majority group desires to erect new barriers, or use its power
to eliminate the minorities, there is no alternative but to begin discussions with ethnics about goals and means.

The third perspective, which draws from both the dominant and
dominated groups, is that of scholars and professionals who are knowledgeable about race and race relations. Being a small group with inadequate resources and all too limited information and techniques to
cope with the racial afflictions in our society, they are generally powerless, but they are all we have. However, the field is becoming a legitimate
area for scholarly research; a body of data and research studies is developing quickly. Major tasks of this group include creating theories and
models and conducting empirical studies in order to better understand
the phenomena involved and to ameliorate some of the deleterious effects
of intergroup conflict.

But for the present, it may be too much to ask that scholars in this
field divorce themselves from long-held value positions. Social scientists
have been (and will continue to be) used for political purposes; many of
the most racist pronouncements in the past were given legitimacy by the
theories of leading scientists. But an open discussion of the issues requires
receptivity to various ideas and perceptions.

The task is complicated by the interdisciplinary nature of the problem, for as Van den Berghe (1967) emphasizes, race and racism are
empirical data that can be used by all the behavioral sciences. To the
physical anthropologist, race, in the genetic sense, may be a case of
subspeciation in *homo sapiens;* to the social psychologist, it may be a

special instance of prejudice; to the political scientist, a special kind of political ideology; to the sociologist, a form of stratification; to the historian, a byproduct of slavery and colonial expansion; and to the economist, a nonrational factor influencing economic behavior.

Up to the present, the powerful majority group's perceptions, goals, means, and solutions have defined the issues. But the conflict and strife of the past decade indicates that these solutions have not worked too well, and that it is time to incorporate other perspectives.

ETHNIC-GROUP SIMILARITIES AND DIFFERENCES: THEIR PERSPECTIVES

As we have shown, there are many ethnic-group similarities. Many came here with "old world" values and corresponding family structures and life styles. Most were treated alike by the dominant majority. Group size, color, cohesion, and national background are some important differences. Some factors, such as personality and values, are so varied within an ethnic group that intergroup comparisons are virtually meaningless.

But certain variables help reveal the differential reaction of minorities to their place in the American system. These include: (1) initial contact, (2) resources and power of the minorities, (3) unique factors, and (4) attitudes of the majority.

Initial Contact

Initial contact provides the baseline for experiences and for perceptions that groups hold about each other. Three different patterns emerge: forced immigration (the Negro slaves); voluntary immigration (the Asian groups, Puerto Ricans, more recent Mexican arrivals); and groups overwhelmed and conquered (the Indians and the early Mexicans).

Voluntary immigrants have several options that are unavailable to other groups. They may return to the old country whether they are "successful" (financially or socially) or not. Because there is a difference in motivation to "become American," the voluntary immigrant would hold the most adaptable orientation. Other things being equal, voluntary immigrants make an easier adjustment to the American culture than those whose initial contacts were of a different order. Those who were overwhelmed and conquered have the most difficult time in becoming "American."

Resources and Power of the Minorities

Minorities have had, and will continue to have, differential resources and power as they attempt to adapt to the American system. Blacks and Chicanos have the power of numbers, but the Chinese and Japanese have more cohesive units, while still other groups may be more concentrated for effective political participation.

Probably because of their cultural values, the Chinese and Japanese have used an educational elitist strategy (e.g., college education, professional degrees). Some groups have used politics, entertainment, or athletics as primary means of upward mobility. The problem with elitist approaches is that they do little for the large numbers who do not possess these special abilities and qualities.

There are a number of other factors in ethnic-group cohesion. Some ethnic groups (e.g. Chinese and Japanese) have developed a parallel "opportunity structure" and are less dependent on the dominant group for economic support, whereas others have had to deal with unemployment and financial need through government programs.

Color is another variable that affects ethnic-group cohesion. Groups with a wide range of color (e.g. very dark to very light) will tend to adopt a color stratification system within their own group which tends to be divisive, whereas groups with a higher degree of color homogeneity will tend to be less divided.

The similarity or congruence of the ethnic culture with that of the dominant culture can also aid group cohesion. Those subcultures (i.e., Chinese, Japanese) whose values are congruent with those of the dominant group will tend to retain their ethnic culture. Factors such as geographic and cultural isolation will not affect this adaptation. Conversely, those subcultures that are at variance with the American system (e.g., Mexican Americans and Indians) may find it difficult to retain their own ways comfortably when forced to interact with the dominant group. "Culture conflict" will be one hypothesized result. Furthermore, geographic and cultural isolation may exacerbate the culture conflict since the differences will be maintained.

Many of the generalizations concerning power cut across ethnic lines. Much minority-group adaptation can be attributed to coping from weaker power positions, and their adaptation is often independent of their culture. The same holds true for the majority group, whose behavior may be due more to their dominant position and not their culture.

For example, during the Revolutionary War, Americans used guerilla tactics. Our heroes, with names such as "Swamp Fox," employed a strategy of retreat and avoided direct conflict. The British generals probably felt that this realistic adaptation to superior forces was tricky and sly and that Americans never stood up and fought in the open like "real men." But our technological advances have made us the most powerful nation, and it is we who now question the masculinity of foes who prefer to hit and run, rather than facing us like "real men."

Similarly, much minority-group adaptation has been a matter of survival in a powerless position. All of our ethnic groups have developed their own etiquette for dealing with the dominant group. Either because

of incredible naivete or the arrogance that often accompanies power, the
dominant group has been blind to the feelings that lie behind the
etiquette. Only when violence erupts, such as at Watts, is there some
awareness that everything is not quite right.

Yet, powerless groups learn that they would be risking mass suicide
if they consistently attempted to meet issues head-on with the group in
power. Young militants have learned this lesson the hard way. The
majority group controls the courts, the law-enforcement system, the
political and economic system, and overall resources, and its power
remains so disproportionate that the probabilities of effecting any
significant change through a direct challenge is totally unrealistic. The
system can be disrupted, but only temporarily.

Unique Factors

By unique factors, we refer to relatively idiosyncratic conditions that
affect ethnic groups. For example, both the Mexican and Puerto Rican
groups are very close to their mother countries. Therefore, there is a
constant migration in and out of the country that significantly affects
ethnic cohesion and resources. The wartime evacuation of the Japanese
(1942–45) was another unique event. One effect of this incident was to
break down old community and family structures and hasten acculturation.

Attitudes of the Majority

In spite of the uniqueness of each ethnic group, the overriding factor in
a group's ability to cope has been, and will continue to be, their reception by the majority group. In one sense all nonwhites were considered
to be pariahs and, therefore, unacceptable except under certain conditions. But there were gradations of acceptability based on variables such
as time, place, and circumstances, as well as power threat and cultural
styles.

These variables have led to the development of a variety of ever-
changing ethnic subcultures. If we combine all of the variables: initial
contact, resources, power, unique experiences, and the attitudes of the
majority, we may be able to arrive at certain predictions for each of the
minority groups. The predictions would be more valuable if they did
not include moralistic concepts and tried instead to clarify why different
coping strategies were employed by various groups. There are no "good"
or "bad" minorities; each was shaped by its own perceptions and resources, and all have attempted to become part of the American system
in the ways felt to be most appropriate.

At present the ethnic groups who have adapted in the United States
with the least amount of stress should be those that: came voluntarily,

have cultures congruent with the host system, have resources and power permitting a degree of independence, experienced unique factors fostering cohesion, and were more accepted by the group in power. Minority-group goals are closely related to their current position, their adaptive styles, and their success in realizing past goals.

ORDERS OF PLURALISM: TYPES OF STRUCTURES

The development of pluralistic systems in America is not difficult to trace. The country is composed of groups with obvious physical differences, dissimilarities in habits and life styles, and variations in language and nationality. Social hostility, discrimination, prejudice, and economic necessity tended to shape segregated living patterns with various degrees of isolation and separation. Differential opportunities restricted the mobility of selected populations; therefore, a variety of pluralistic structures, based on variables such as nationality, ethnicity, religion, culture, and race, developed.

Various forms of pluralism can be ranked according to characteristics such as rigidity, voluntarism, and permanence. From this perspective racial pluralism is the most rigid, involuntary, and permanent. Other forms of pluralism are much less so; for example, cultural pluralism and nationality groupings can be temporary (e.g., participating in the yearly ethnic festival) and voluntary. Although there are periodic efforts to revive ethnic identity among some European groups, most have acculturated and intermarried to the point where their nationality and ethnic differences have virtually disappeared.

Racial pluralism is the most extreme since it is generally reinforced by the majority group in power, which elects to maintain social and psychological distance. The institutions that maintain segregation are among the most powerful; discriminatory laws, although changing, and lack of opportunity combine to force people of color to attend separate and unequal schools (the moves toward school desegregation are among the most fiercely resisted). In the past, there were attempts to maintain total structural differentiation based on race: schools for blacks, Asians, Indians, and Chicanos, separate eating and recreational facilities, and specified low-status occupational roles. Current housing segregation has encouraged this historical tradition. The general effect has been racial pluralism of a restrictive nature that has kept high proportions of minority individuals separated and occupying lower-class positions.

However, even though separated, most ethnics are exposed to the society and learn how to be "American." Although there are qualitative differences in school systems, the language, the curriculum, the goals, and the expectations are typically "American" to the extent that racial **278** pluralism has not carried over too deeply into the cultural area of minority groups. Therefore, most ethnic groups, although structurally separated, are American by culture; but because so many are caught in lower-class positions, their pervading life styles are heavily influenced by lower-class perspectives.

Factors such as cultural drift, stereotypical interaction, differential goals, experiences, opportunities, and individual differences have developed other kinds of pluralism. The term "bicultural" is one such variation. It is a partial integration of the ethnic and the dominant culture that is neither fully one nor the other. It may also include individuals whose parents are of different races, or the "marginal man" as described by Park.

The kinds of pluralism are important in race relations because they are related to racial conflict. The rigidity of our racial stratification system may be reshaping a racial pluralism that is approaching a high level of separatism despite the openness of some of the other orders. As racial differentiation continues to signify pariah status, some groups may opt to retain a "non-English" language, and to develop values and styles of life that are different from the group in power. Such a development can lead to heightened intergroup conflict.

FOUR LEVELS OF PLURALISM

The kinds and forms of pluralism occur on different levels. Van den Berghe (1967) analyzes four main levels of pluralistic societies: groups, institutions, values, and individuals. We will amplify each of these and hypothesize how they affect racist practices.

Groups

The differences in size and the rigidity of boundaries between diverse ethnic and racial groups are important factors leading to intergroup conflict. In the United States with its many diverse ethnic, religious, nationality, and racial groups, there is a high degree of group pluralism and a high potential for intergroup conflict which is reinforced by racial boundaries and class stratifications.

Institutions

A country with a racially segregated school system, a separate economic system, and various sets of legal, political, and social institutions for its groups ranks high in institutional pluralism. South Africa is an example of such a society: the United States appears less pluralistic in this respect, especially since there has been a trend towards the desegregation of facilities, including those of the public school system. There is still a

279

high degree of separation in our religions and in our social and fraternal organizations, but many of our institutions reflect a social class rather than a strict racial stratification.

However, as we have emphasized, racial pluralism may be reshaping the trend. Appeals are being made for black, red, brown, and yellow power, and it is our hypothesis that separate institutions representing these racial diversities may lead to higher interracial conflict. Whether these potential conflicts are healthy or unhealthy for the culture is a question of values.

But ethnic pluralism rests on a precarious base. Ethnic structures, rather than being a set of parallel but generally equal structures that lead to some type of accommodation, instead contain a high proportion of the very poor. The welfare system, one example of an institution that tends to perpetuate an inequality, hinders the development of a viable ethnic social system. It is difficult to maintain an independent pluralistic structure when the major economic controls and power sources lie outside the group, or when a high proportion of the population is poor and disorganized. Nevertheless, the current call for a pluralistic society on the part of ethnics is of a different level because it is a *voluntary* effort, whereas in previous eras it was *forced* upon them by majority-group power.

Values, Goals, and Life Styles

Cultural pluralism is generally characterized by the coexistence of several value systems, differential goals, and a variety of life styles. Shared values lead to social integration, and in culturally pluralistic societies such consensus is often difficult to obtain. It is our judgment that in the past, the United States, despite its diverse ethnic and other groups, was characterized by remarkably homogeneous goals, values, and life styles. Public schools, the widespread mass communication network, and the effectiveness of advertising have led to relatively high consensus in values.

Nevertheless, our racial stratification system has developed subcultures with their own values, goals, and life styles. But, our analysis of various ethnic groups indicates that what is often labelled "cultural pluralism" may be the culture of survival, the culture of poverty, and the culture of a lower-class life style. These are natural consequences of the white-nonwhite stratification system that was extremely effective in restricting the educational, occupational, and social mobility of the ethnics. Generally as jobs become steadier and incomes rise, minority-group values and life styles show a corresponding change. Majority-group observers may comment on the "success" of those who have become more like them, while members of ethnic organizations may call these same individuals "Uncle Tom's."

Even though there may be institutions and organizations that shape be-havior and a legal system that enforces and provides sanctions, the individual may still move back and forth through structural and cultural space. The current emphasis on everyone "doing their own thing" reflects an individualistic approach that can lead to high conflict. In a more rigidly stratified system, which allowed for little individuality (e.g., feudal Japan), individual perceptions, needs, and goals had a lower priority than group expectations. But the individual emphasis as opposed to a group emphasis can work in multiple directions. The individual who feels that it is his "right" to discriminate can remain a major stumbling block to racial harmony, especially since he will find group support for his position.

But individualism may also provide one "solution" to our racial problems. The relative openness of certain institutions, especially in edu-cational fields, and the chance for upward mobility are developing a "melting pot" at a surprising time. A study by Manning and Kitano (1973) on Japanese-American interracial marriage in areas as diverse as Honolulu, Los Angeles, San Francisco, and Fresno shows a high rate of approximately 50 percent. In view of the low rates of interracial marriage for Japanese in the past, this study indicates that one of the most rigid strictures in race relations has begun to erode. The change is hypothesized as one stemming primarily from an individual orientation.

A brief review of the Japanese will serve to illustrate this change. The Issei, or immigrant first generation, came from a culture that empha-sized group solidarity and did not allow much freedom in marital choice. A language barrier, few opportunities to interact with majority-group females, discrimination, prejudice, and a high desire for in-group marriage limited interracial unions. Estimates of interracial marriage for this group are below 10 percent (Manning and Kitano, 1973).

The second-generation Nisei were highly acculturated but lived in a structurally pluralistic system. Their primary friends were fellow Nisei, and social interaction was generally limited to their own ethnic group. There was rapid mobility for some through higher education and en-trance into the professions, but this was still the era of rampant dis-crimination (antimiscegenation laws); and in-group social pressure encouraged marriages to other Japanese. The group orientation remained strong, and estimates of interracial marriage for the Nisei were around 20 percent (Manning and Kitano, 1973).

The third-generation Sansei are much more individualistic and are less tied to ethnicity or to the Japanese culture. The American expecta-tion of freedom of choice is their current model. Even though 98 percent of their Nisei parents prefer that they marry other Japanese (Kitano,

1969), the Sansei are deciding for themselves. Many come from families of high status, most are in college (Chapter Ten), and few ethnic institutions control their social interaction. Conversely, the attitudes held by members of the dominant culture have also changed; race prejudice and discrimination have diminished, and there are better occupational and social opportunities for the Sansei. A social-class bias has become more common; and Nisei parents now ask their Sansei children "What does he do?" rather than "Is he Japanese?". Issues of love and happiness are taking precedence over duty and obligation; individual needs and perceptions are of primary importance, and one out of every two Sansei are marrying out of the group. Our preliminary analysis indicates that, especially for the woman, marital choice means a degree of upward mobility (Manning and Kitano, 1973). The majority of Sansei marriages are with Caucasians.

We hypothesize that the rates of intermarriage for other ethnic groups may be even higher than for the Sansei, since the Japanese have been one of the most exclusive groups. For example, Adams recognized "that they [the Japanese] marry within their own group in higher proportion than any other of the peoples in Hawaii" (1937: 160).

THE MELTING POT

It is ironic that at a time when ethnic awareness and solidarity are being promoted, other forces are pushing toward consolidation—the melting pot. The "melting" is gradually occurring because the organizations and institutions most concerned with racial separateness have changed. For example, our marital customs have stressed free individual choice; our educational institutions have opened up, albeit slowly; and hiring practices absorb many more minorities, although not quickly enough.

It is difficult to appreciate the relative openness of American society unless one has spent some time abroad. Most other countries do not automatically grant citizenship to "foreigners," and their educational institutions remain either primarily for the wealthy, for those from proper family backgrounds, or for the few who can pass a number of examinations. Rather than weakening it, marriage generally strengthens the existing stratification scheme.

Although Japanese society is rapidly changing, its marital customs uphold the conservative links with the past, and the possibilities of interracial (or in this case, interclass) marriage are few. There is no one single institution that shapes marital practices—it is supported on all levels; but a description of the *ie* (pronounced "ee-eh"), or household unit, provides an insight into the conservative nature of Japan's social structure (Nakane, 1965, 1972). As Kitano and Manning (1973) say:

282

The *ie* is a community and social system that controls and manages individuals comprising the unit. Even today, marriages in Japan are often between *ie*'s rather than between individuals. Since the *ie* provides the socialization, a person marrying into an *ie* is reasonably certain of the type of "product" from that *ie*. A good *ie* will teach a certain style of life, values, and roles so that it almost acts as a "certification" or finishing school.

Marriages are therefore arranged between *ie*'s, and variables such as education, occupation, past health, and other background information are closely checked before proper introductions are made. "Good marriages" bring together people of like backgrounds; and although the Western styles of love, romance, and individual choice have been introduced, those who prefer to remain in Japan and launch a successful career will probably be married the Japanese way. Family name and background remain more important than newly acquired wealth or unusual achievement. Under such a system, marrying out of the group or one's social class would be considered a deviant act.

Although there is no standard American model of marriage (just as there is no standard Japanese practice), in the United States there is less emphasis on family name, family background, and parental wishes; looks, personality, ability, and potential are given a higher priority. Therefore, as ethnics achieve a degree of upward mobility, they become more attractive and may be more attracted to others of a similar disposition. Although interracial marriage used to be prohibited by law (sixteen states still retain antimiscegenation statutes that are constitutionally illegal), it can be argued that, racist as it was, the attitude behind this law was also heavily class oriented, since most ethnics were in the lower classes.

The major reason for the delay in achieving a true melting pot of races, then, has been the barriers of racial prejudice, discrimination, and segregation. The major effect has been the restricted mobility of non-whites so that significant proportions have occupied the lower positions in our social structure.

However, as ethnics rise in status, mutual acceptability has also risen, and with it, more intimate degrees of social interaction. The answer to the classic racist question, "Do you want your daughter to marry one?" has changed from an outright "No" to "Well, if he's wealthy" (or handsome, or intelligent, or a professional, or if it's love).

RACIAL PROBLEMS AND SOCIAL CLASS

It is difficult to argue against the hypothesis that our racial problems are basically tied to social class. At one stage the high correlation between the two variables made the difference difficult to detect because the great majority of ethnics were also in the lower classes, and even now the 283 proportions are unequal. It may be most accurate to describe America's racial problem as that of disadvantaged social classes compounded by the factor of race.

Previous studies of miscegenation (e.g., whites with Indians and blacks) indicate very little change in the attitudes toward these pariah groups, probably because most of these marriages were between power-less groups, such as the marginals and the lower classes. However, as miscegenation begins to occur in the higher social strata, it may begin to affect racial attitudes.

The problem would be primarily racial if *all* avenues of mobility were closed on the basis of race alone (it remains a matter of degree—some ethnic groups such as the Asians currently have a higher rate of mobility). But the barriers are like sieves or filters that permit upward mobility only for some. It is among those who have been upwardly mobile—the better educated, more acculturated, and more affluent—that interracial marriage and equal-status contacts have occurred more fre-quently.

The problem of upward mobility is not strictly a racial one. If the racial stratification system worked "perfectly," all whites would be at the top and all colored minorities would remain at the bottom. Although many barriers are racial, there are other barriers that make mobility difficult for those individuals and groups of any color less motivated to compete in the system. As we have indicated (Chapter 8, p. 181), although 4.3 million blacks were receiving public assistance, so were 6.5 million whites. But racial pluralism has been one strong factor in minimizing any significant alliance among groups caught in a residual position.

Sometimes there is the temptation to romanticize poverty and equate it with purity. It is a fantasy that only those who are not poor can afford. There is a vast difference between the voluntary poor and the involuntary poor; the latter are caught in a web of poverty, alienation, hopelessness, and suffering from which there is little escape. Exhortations to work hard or threats to cut off welfare are poor substitutes for pro-viding better opportunities in a more open society.

For the ethnics, as well as for members of the underclass, the highest priority should be given to maximizing the means for achieving economic independence so that they may create their own goals. Steady incomes, better education, and decent housing have transformed some of our former pariah groups into "model minorities," and similar predictions may be made for other groups. It does not mean that life will then become problem free, for all positions in a social structure have their advantages and disadvantages. But for the minorities, the achievement of some degree of control over their daily lives is a dream that has eluded them for so long that any further delay will be critical in their own lives, and may even prove fatal to the entire society.

ADAMS, ROMANZO (1937). *Interracial Marriage in Hawaii.* New York: The Macmillan Company.

KITANO, HARRY H. L. and AKEMI K. MANNING (1973). "The Japanese American Family." In Habenstein and Mindel, eds., *American Minority Family Life Styles.* (In press.)

MANNING, AKEMI K. and HARRY H. L. KITANO (1973). "Interracial Marriage: A Picture of the Japanese." *Journal of Social Issues* (in press).

NAKANE, CHIE (1972). *Japanese Society.* Berkeley and Los Angeles: University of California Press.

———— (1965). "Towards a Theory of Japanese Social Structure." *The Economic Weekly.*

PARK, ROBERT E. (1950). *Race and Culture.* New York: The Free Press.

VAN DEN BERGHE, P. (1967). *Race and Racism.* New York: John Wiley & Sons, Inc.

INDEX